KICK-ASS 2. Contains material originally published in magazine form as KICK-ASS 2 #1-7. First printing 2013. ISBN# 978-0-7851-5246-0. Published by MARVEL WORLDWIDE, INC., a subsidiary of MARVEL ENTERTAINMENT, LLC. OFFICE OF PUBLICATION: 135 West 50th Street, New York, NY 10020. Copyright © 2010, 2011, 2012, and 2013 Millarworld, Limited and John S. Romita. All rights reserved. "Kick-Ass," "Kick-Ass 2," the Kick-Ass logo, and all characters and content herein and the likenesses thereof are trademarks of Millarworld, Limited and John S. Romita. The events and characters presented are intended as fiction. Any similarity to real events or to persons living or dead is purely coincidental. This work may not be reproduced, except in small amounts for journalistic or review purposes, without permission of the authors. ICON and the Icon logo are trademarks of Marvel Characters, Inc. "Millarworld" and the Millarworld logo are trademarks of Millarworld, Limited. **Printed in the U.S.A.** ALAN FINE, EVP - Office of the President, Marvel Worldwide, Inc. and EVP & CMO Marvel Characters B.V.; DAN BUCKLEY, Publisher & President - Print, Animation & Digital Divisions; JOE QUESADA, Chief Creative Officer, TOM BREVOORT, SVP of Publishing; DAVID BOGART, SVP of Operations & Procurement, Publishing; RUWAN JAYATILLEKE, SVP & Associate Publisher, Publishing; C.B. CEBULSKI, SVP of Creator & Content Development; DAVID GABRIEL, SVP of Print & Digital Publishing Sales; JIM O'KEEFE, VP of Operations & Logistics; DAN CARR, Executive Director of Publishing Technology; SUSAN CRESPI, Editorial Operations Manager; ALEX MORALES, Publishing Operations Manager; STAN LEE, Chairman Emeritus. For information regarding advertising in Marvel Comics or on Marvel.com, please contact Niza Disla, Director of Marvel Partnerships, at ndisla@marvel.com. For Marvel subscription inquiries, please call 800-217-9158. Manufactured between 2/6/2013 and 3/1/2013 by R.R. DONNELLEY, INC., SALEM, VA, USA.

10 9 8 7 6 5 4 3 2 1

KICK-ASS 2

Writer & Co-Creator
MARK MILLAR

Penciler & Co-Creator
JOHN ROMITA JR.

Inker & Tones
TOM PALMER

Colorist (Issues #1-5 & #7)
DEAN WHITE
with **MICHAEL KELLEHER**

Colorist (Issue #6)
DAN BROWN

Letterer
CHRIS ELIOPOULOS
with **CLAYTON COWLES**

Editor
AUBREY SITTERSON
with **JOHN BARBER AND CORY LEVINE**

Collection Editor: **AUBREY SITTERSON**
Book Designer: **SPRING HOTELING**
SVP of Print & Digital Publishing Sales: **DAVID GABRIEL**
SVP of Operations & Procurement, Publishing: **DAVID BOGART**

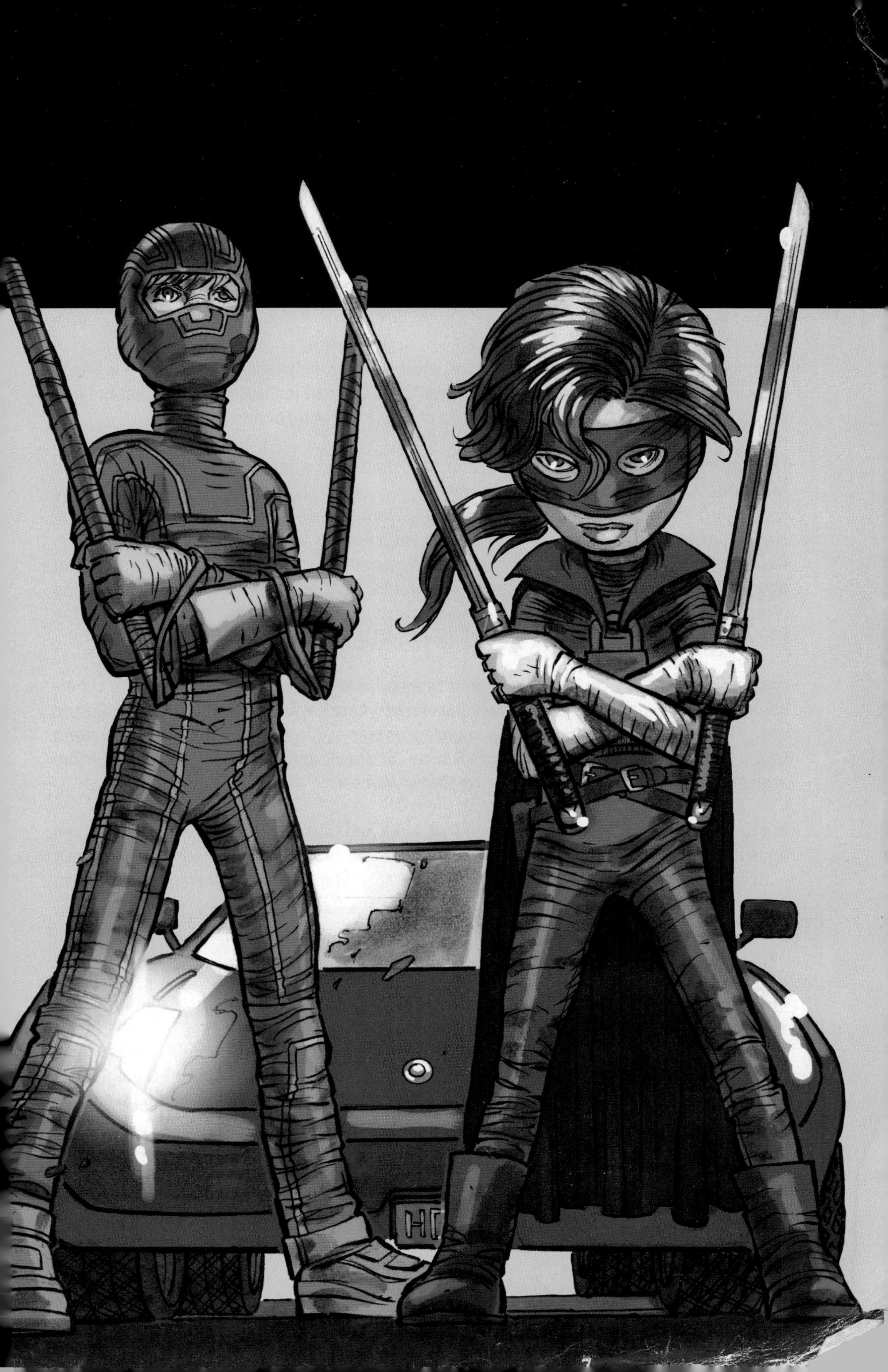

Hey fucker.

Let's face facts, you're one of these fucking fetishistic "fanboy" jerkoffs who secretly wishes that *he* could be Dave Lizewski, beating the shit out of muggers, gangbangers and mob heavies with those akimbo batons as a comely, prepubescent Hit Girl slashes and burns by your side.

It's cool. <u>Me too</u>. I mean good money says most of us already have our dicks in our hands and we're not even out of the intro... but just pace yourself pal and don't pop that nut just yet 'cuz what follows in these pages is one great white *whale* of a wank.

I suppose some basic backstory is in order. Mark and I met where folks not living in an igloo in Bumfuck, Antarctica tend to meet nowadays... online. Twitter to be precise. Someone reposted (I fucking flat-out refuse to use the word *'Retweet'* for fear that my balls will spontaneously detonate) a Millar passage mentioning his love of *The A-Team* as well as the fact that he had named a character in *Nemesis* "Carnahan" after yours truly. What Mark didn't know, was that I, along with my brother Matt, had been charged with adapting *Nemesis* for Fox but it had all gone sideways under the stewardship of this conniving shithead who singlehandedly torpedoed the project... for the time being.

I reached out to Mark on Twitter and he responded, a fast friendship formed and its cyber-content was reprinted on websites vast and varied where it was poured over and scrutinized at an almost forensic fucking level. <u>The consensus was excitement</u>. It seemed totally natural that two like-minded lads with a mutual taste for shock and awe should team up for the grand guignol-like assault on good taste that is *Nemesis*.

But the bond goes quite a bit deeper than that. Mark and I are of both shared ethnic stock and ancestral discord. We're displaced modern day Celts from a long bloodline chock-a-block with bludgeonings and beheadings. Our forefathers fought Viking invaders on forgotten shores, losing their women, their land and finally, <u>their minds</u>.

They were *The Fraternity Of The Fucked*... and we are their proud descendants.

In keeping that spirit alive and ablaze with wanton bloodlust, my Scottish chum (despite the arrival of another Millar heir and him being dry as a 90-year-old nun's snatch in honor of Lent) has nevertheless managed to purge his most putrid cranial pools; the brackish backwaters of the brain where traditional narratives get gang-raped by roid-raging, beer-bellied, gore-soaked gargantuans... to give you sonsabitches yet *another* magnum opus.

In *Kick-Ass 2*, Millar and creative cohort John Romita, Jr. have hotwired the elevator of their frayed mental state to plunge you, fair reader, deeper down into the dripping sub-basement of his perfectly *pitch-black* psychosis. There are no headlamps to light the way down here my lovelies... only the stink of sulfur and suppressed rage. Their off-brand of storytelling is *exactly* the type of perversely, unprintable shit that A.) <u>I love</u> and B.) Affords a battalion's worth of shrinks beachfront homes and Bel Air addresses.

In short, it's a shit-ton of fun.

What you're about to embark on is a true tour de force and the *Kick-Ass* team is in full command of their craft; master illusionists who have perfected the legerdemain of the lewd and vicious, the loathsome and the vile. Blending humor, emotion, sorrow, pain and regret while supercharging the stakes and never forsaking the spirit of what *Kick-Ass* ultimately is: A kid with a ridiculously outsized dream, who dared to make it a reality... and did.

Gone is the rank teenage ennui of the original and in its place a superheroic dystopia. Dave Lizewski has come to terms with what being a famous public figure is. Larger than life is harder than hell when you're still in high school but growing pains, like a brand new patch of pubes, is par for the course and Dave's willingness to throw himself headlong into shitstorm after shitstorm reconfirms his unbreakable conviction to the ethos of his alter ego, *Kick-Ass*.

Pushing him ruthlessly along in his journey is the former Red Mist, now rechristened "The Motherfucker." Chris Genovese is no more. The soul-patched nihilist that now inhabits his form thinks nothing of laying waste to an entire suburb for shits and grins or assassinating a sidewalk full of school kids for sport. This "Motherfucker" is the sneering embodiment of society's mindless, amoral masochism.

Rounding out the trifecta is that sweet, chocolate-covered little claymore mine formerly known as "Hit-Girl." Ironically, it's young Mindy McCready that provides the most unlikely moral core for our story. Resigned to a quiet life in relative seclusion with her adopted parents, she reluctantly returns to the mask only when all seems lost to once again embrace her god-given gifts as a taker of unholy souls, a death machine in overdrive, a living, breathing, paean to pain.

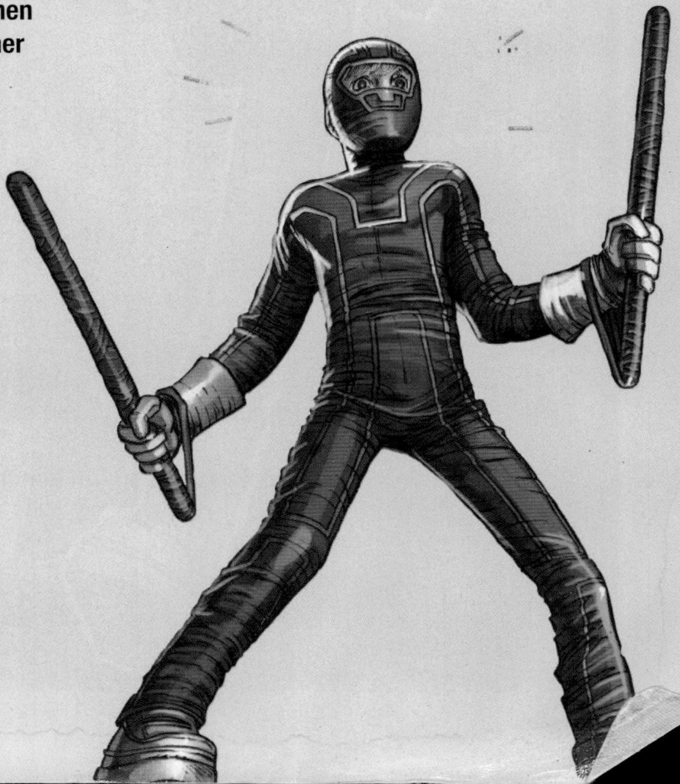

So, with appetites whetted and palms slicked, sit back and have at it kids. What follows is a nightmarish, nuclear meltdown of a mindfuck, lovingly cooked up in the shared mental meth lab of Mark Millar and John Romita, Jr.

Enjoy... *cocksuckers!*

Joe Carnahan
Los Angeles,
March 2012

ONE

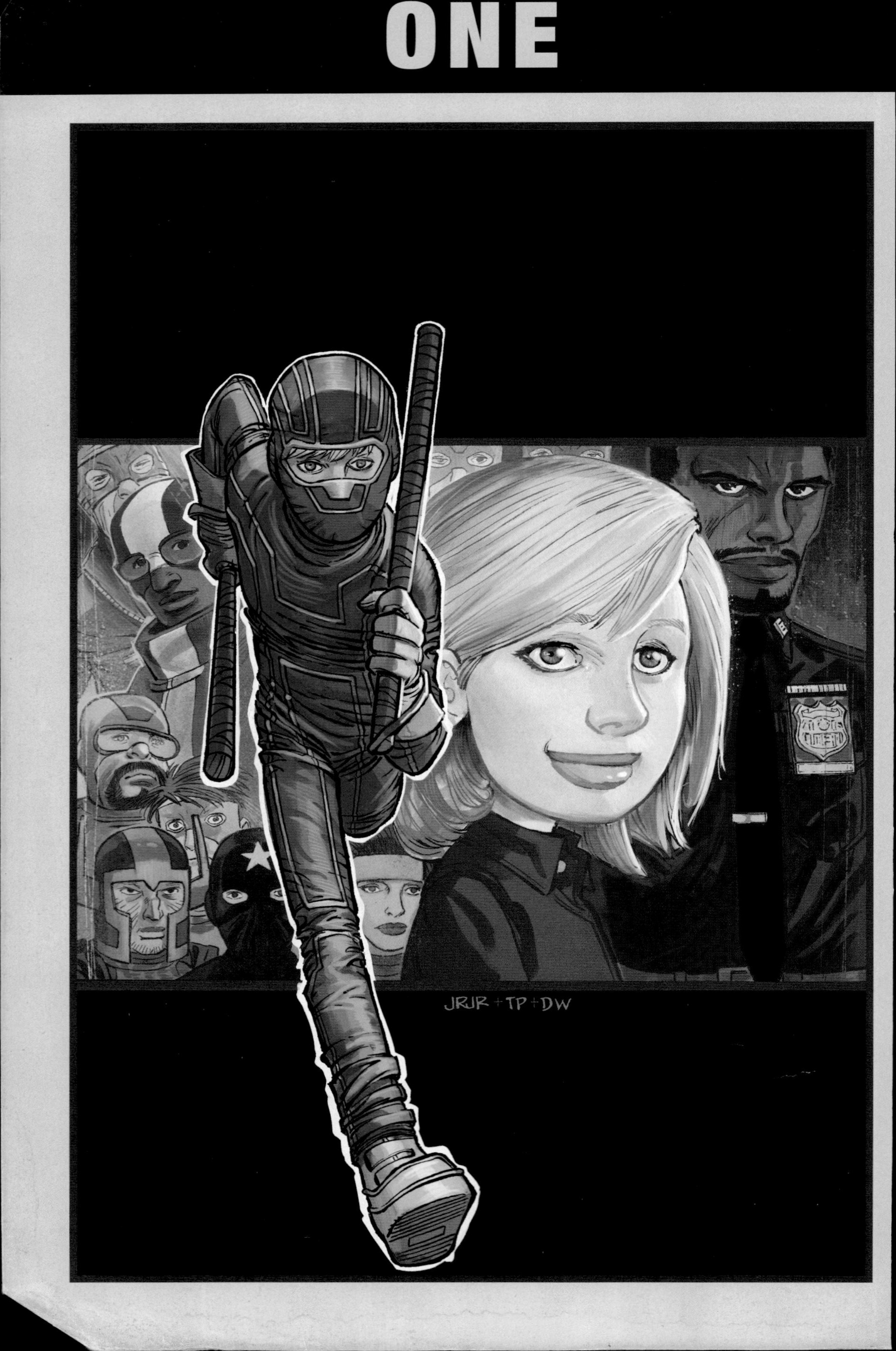
JRJR + TP + DW

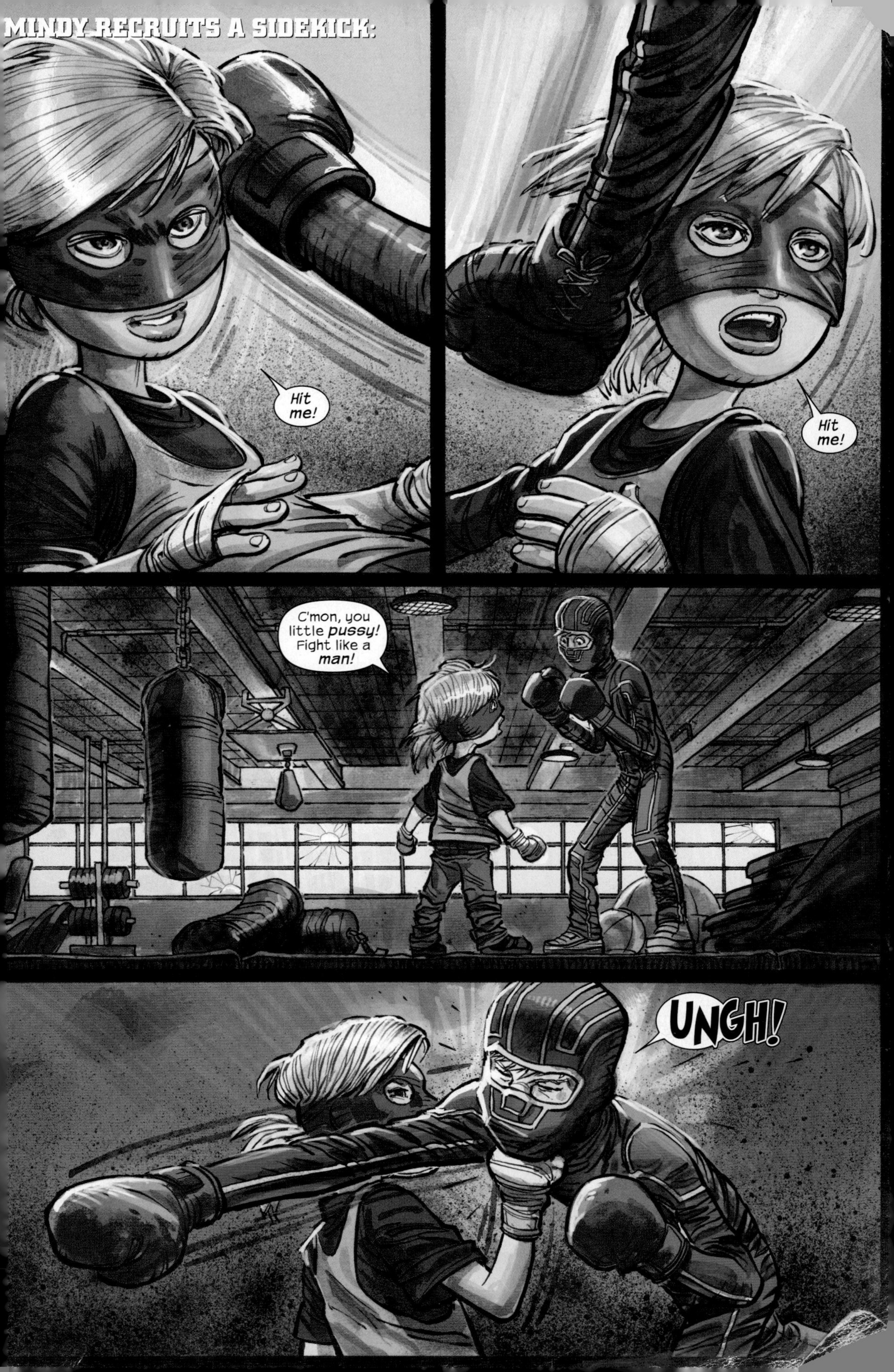
MINDY RECRUITS A SIDEKICK:
Hit me!
Hit me!
C'mon, you little *pussy!* Fight like a *man!*
UNGH!

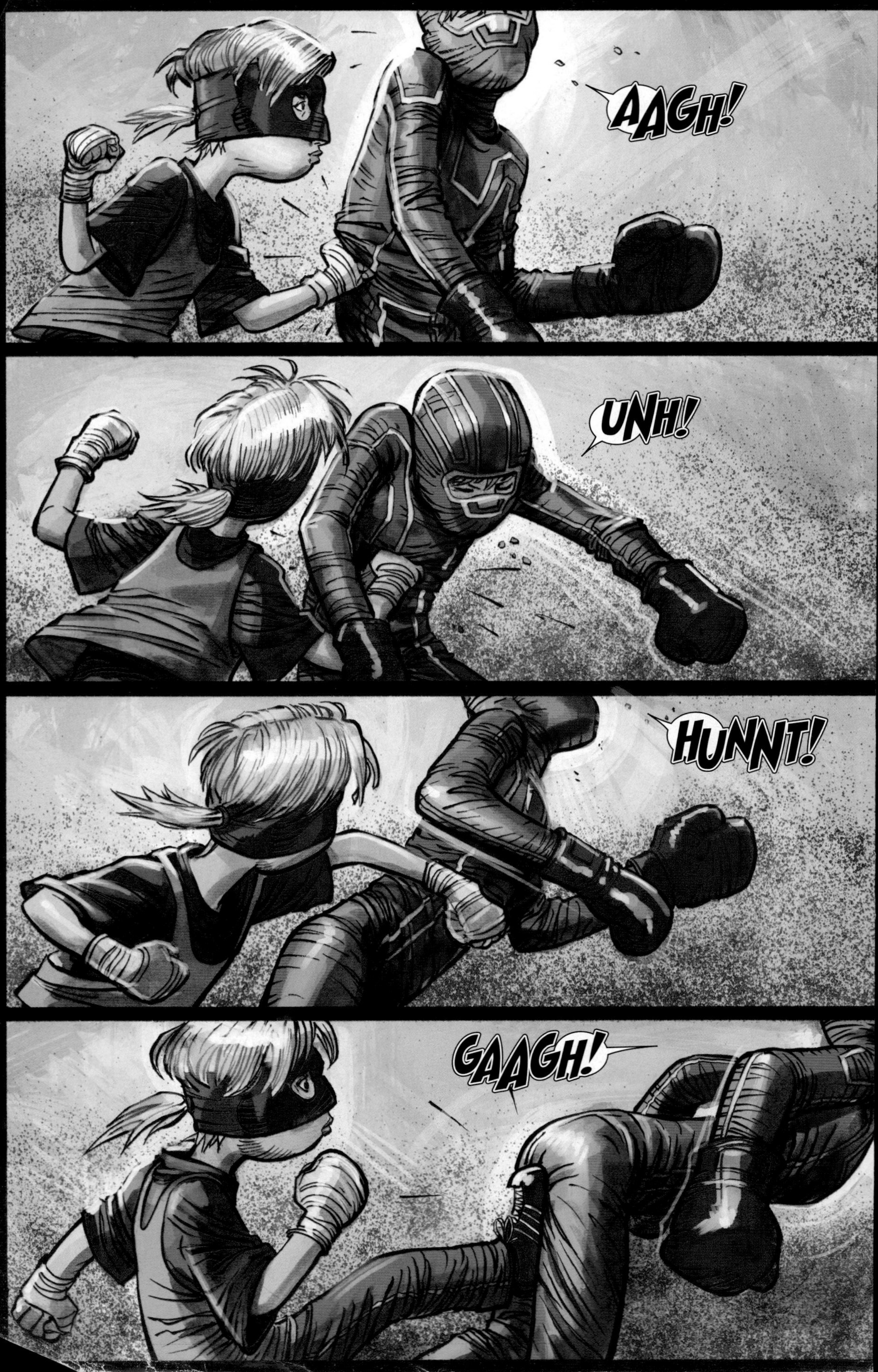
AAGH!
UNH!
HUNNT!
GAAGH!

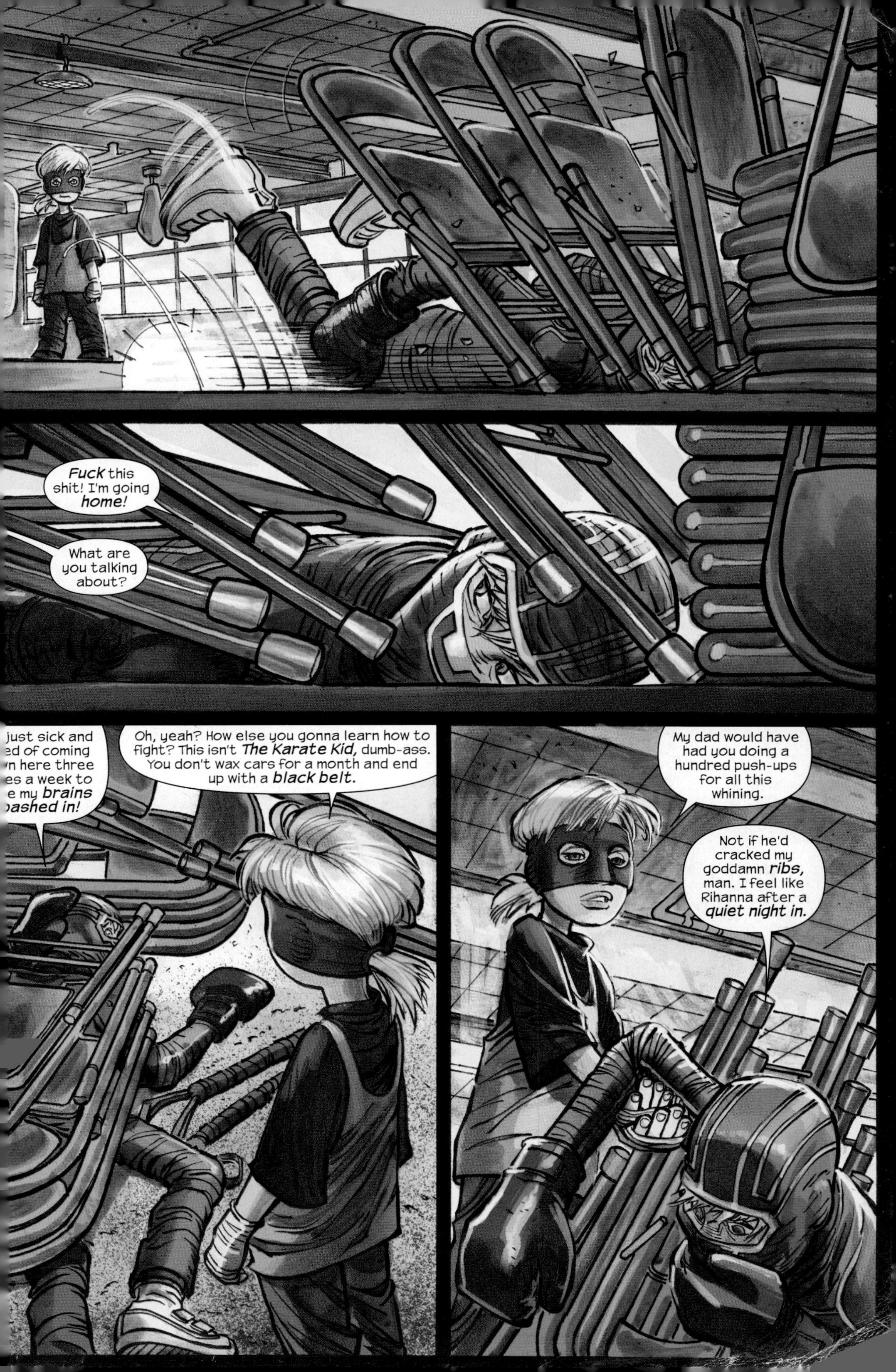
Fuck this shit! I'm going home!
What are you talking about?
just sick and ed of coming n here three es a week to e my brains bashed in!
Oh, yeah? How else you gonna learn how to fight? This isn't The Karate Kid, dumb-ass. You don't wax cars for a month and end up with a black belt.
My dad would have had you doing a hundred push-ups for all this whining.
Not if he'd cracked my goddamn ribs, man. I feel like Rihanna after a quiet night in.

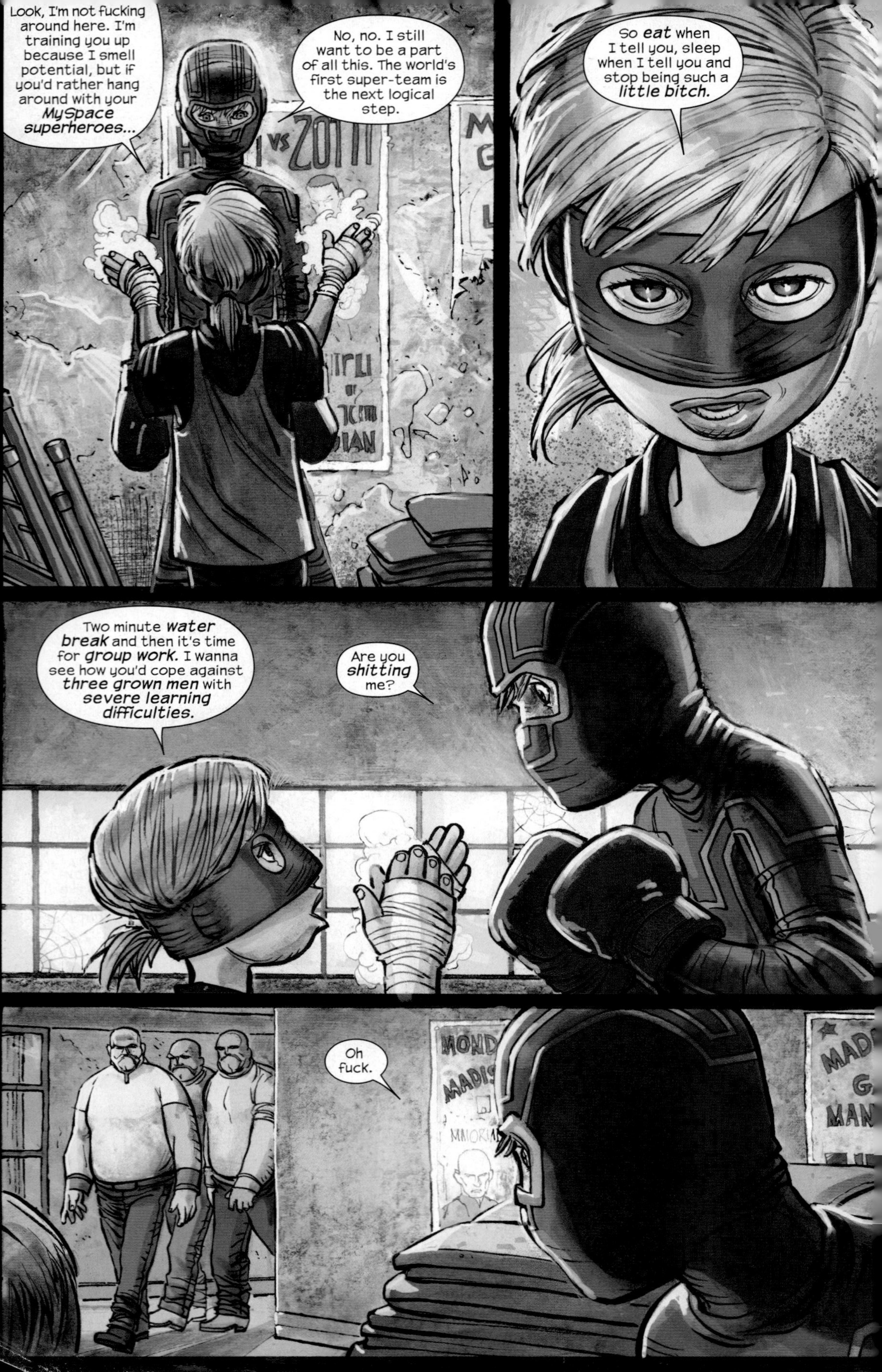
Look, I'm not fucking around here. I'm training you up because I smell potential, but if you'd rather hang around with your MySpace superheroes...
No, no. I still want to be a part of all this. The world's first super-team is the next logical step.
So eat when I tell you, sleep when I tell you and stop being such a little bitch.
Two minute water break and then it's time for group work. I wanna see how you'd cope against three grown men with severe learning difficulties.
Are you shitting me?
Oh fuck.

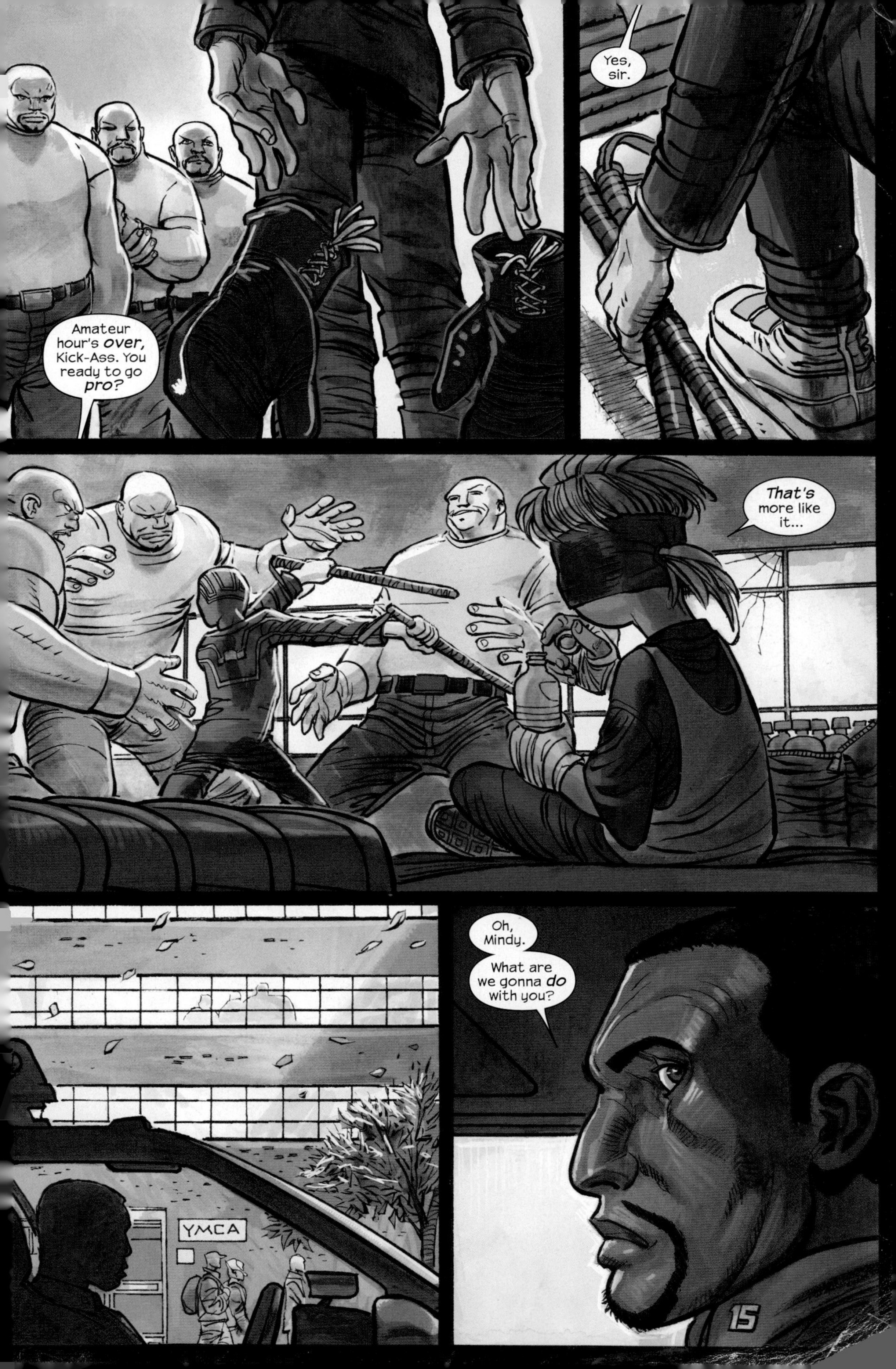
Amateur hour's **over,** Kick-Ass. You ready to go ***pro?***
Yes, sir.
That's more like it...
YMCA
Oh, Mindy.
What are we gonna ***do*** with you?

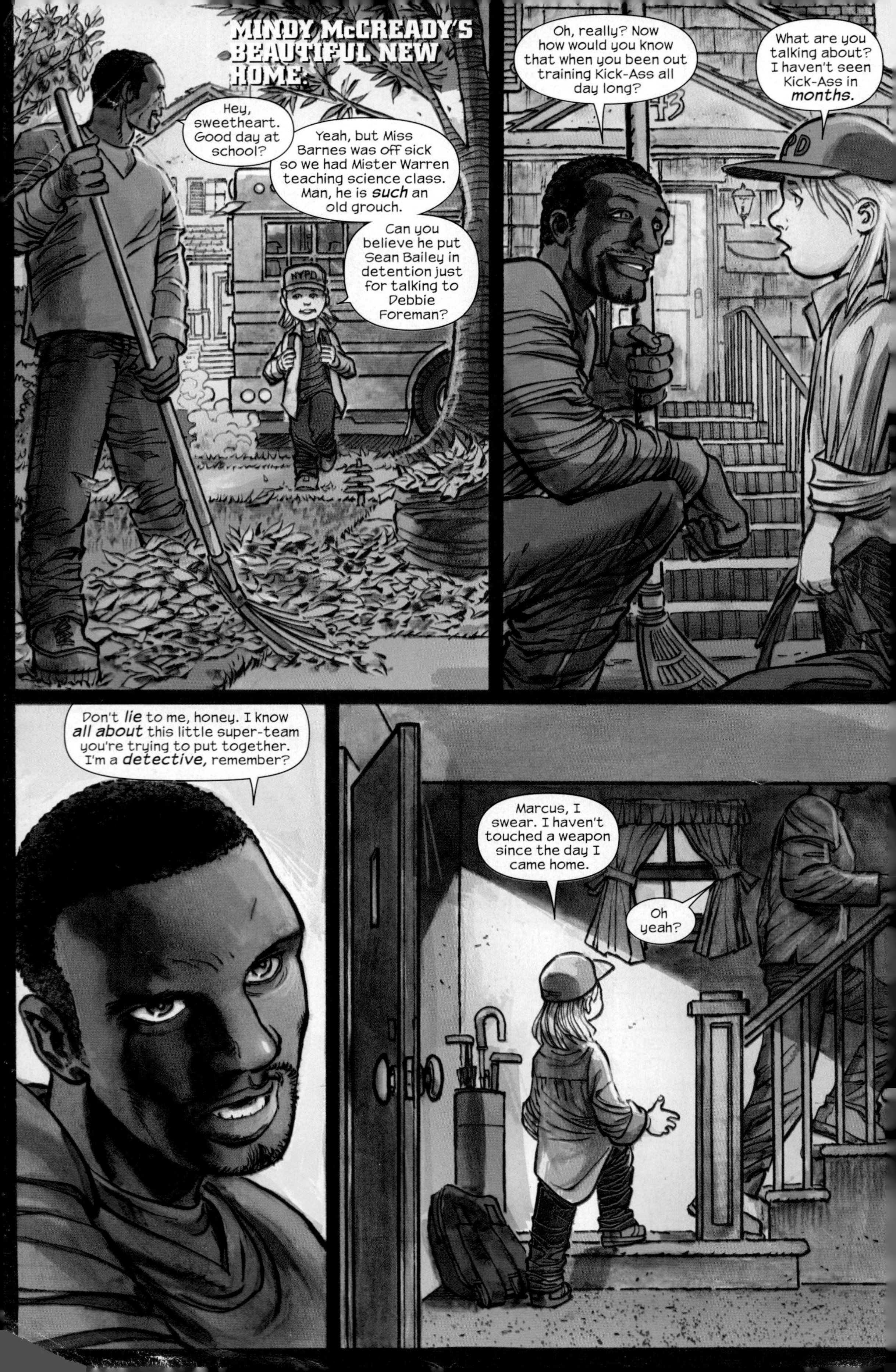
MINDY McCREADY'S BEAUTIFUL NEW HOME:
Hey, sweetheart. Good day at school?
Yeah, but Miss Barnes was off sick so we had Mister Warren teaching science class. Man, he is *such* an old grouch.
Can you believe he put Sean Bailey in detention just for talking to Debbie Foreman?
NYPD
Oh, really? Now how would you know that when you been out training Kick-Ass all day long?
What are you talking about? I haven't seen Kick-Ass in *months.*
Don't *lie* to me, honey. I know *all about* this little super-team you're trying to put together. I'm a *detective,* remember?
Marcus, I swear. I haven't touched a weapon since the day I came home.
Oh yeah?

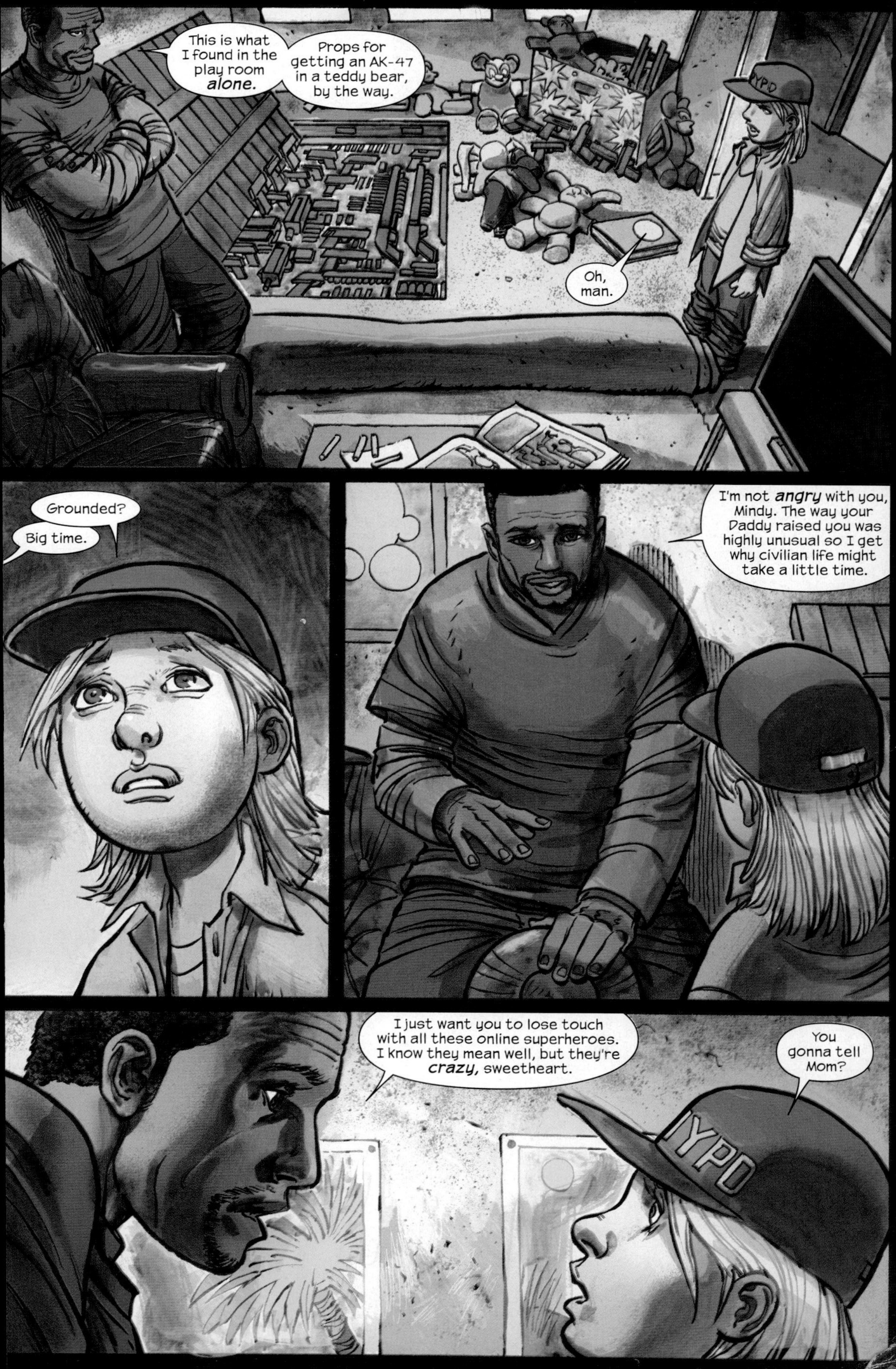
This is what I found in the play room *alone.*
Props for getting an AK-47 in a teddy bear, by the way.
Oh, man.
Grounded?
Big time.
I'm not *angry* with you, Mindy. The way your Daddy raised you was highly unusual so I get why civilian life might take a little time.
I just want you to lose touch with all these online superheroes. I know they mean well, but they're *crazy,* sweetheart.
You gonna tell Mom?

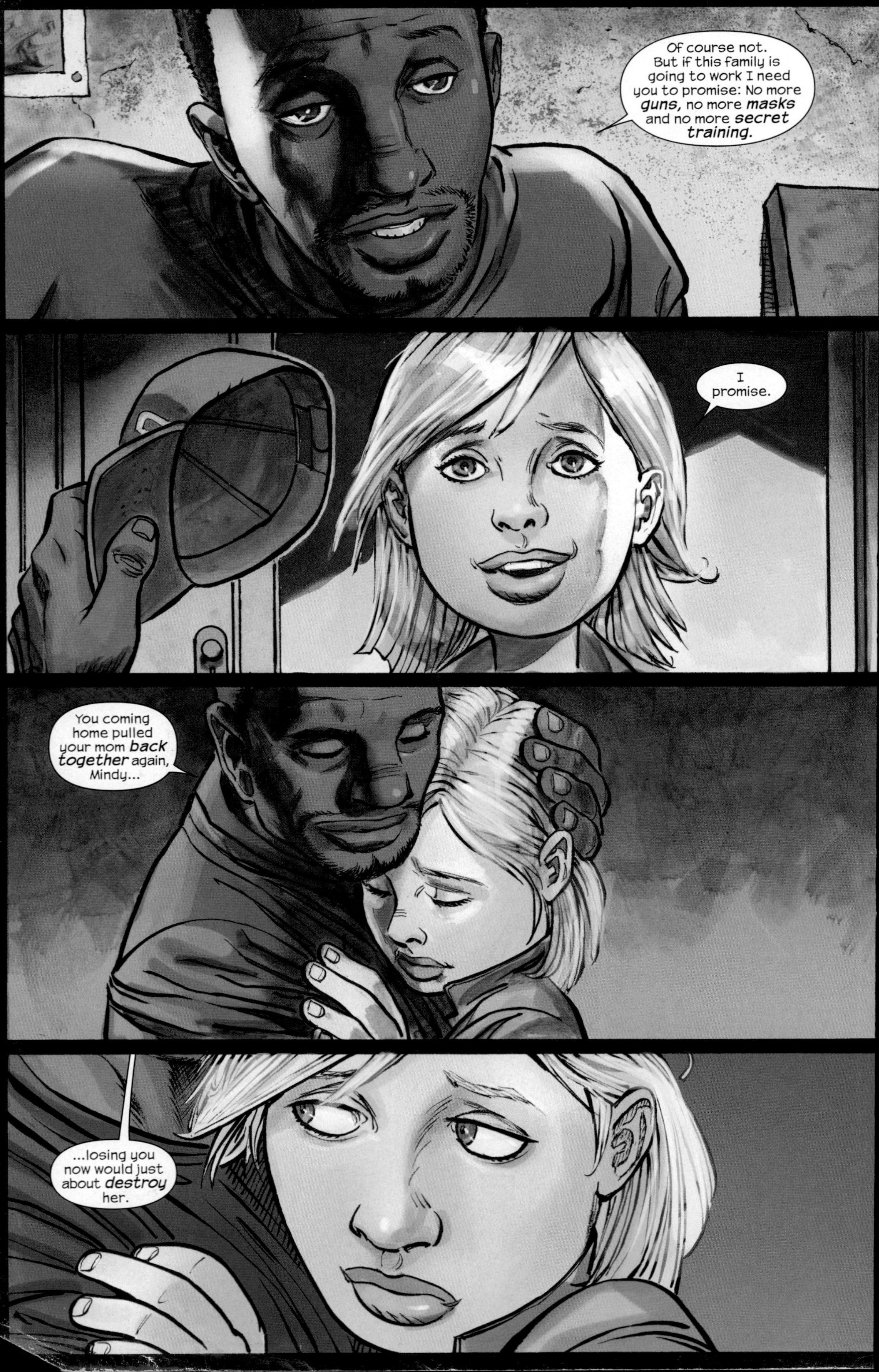

Of course not. But if this family is going to work I need you to promise: No more *guns,* no more *masks* and no more *secret training.*
I promise.
You coming home pulled your mom *back together* again, Mindy...
...losing you now would just about *destroy* her.

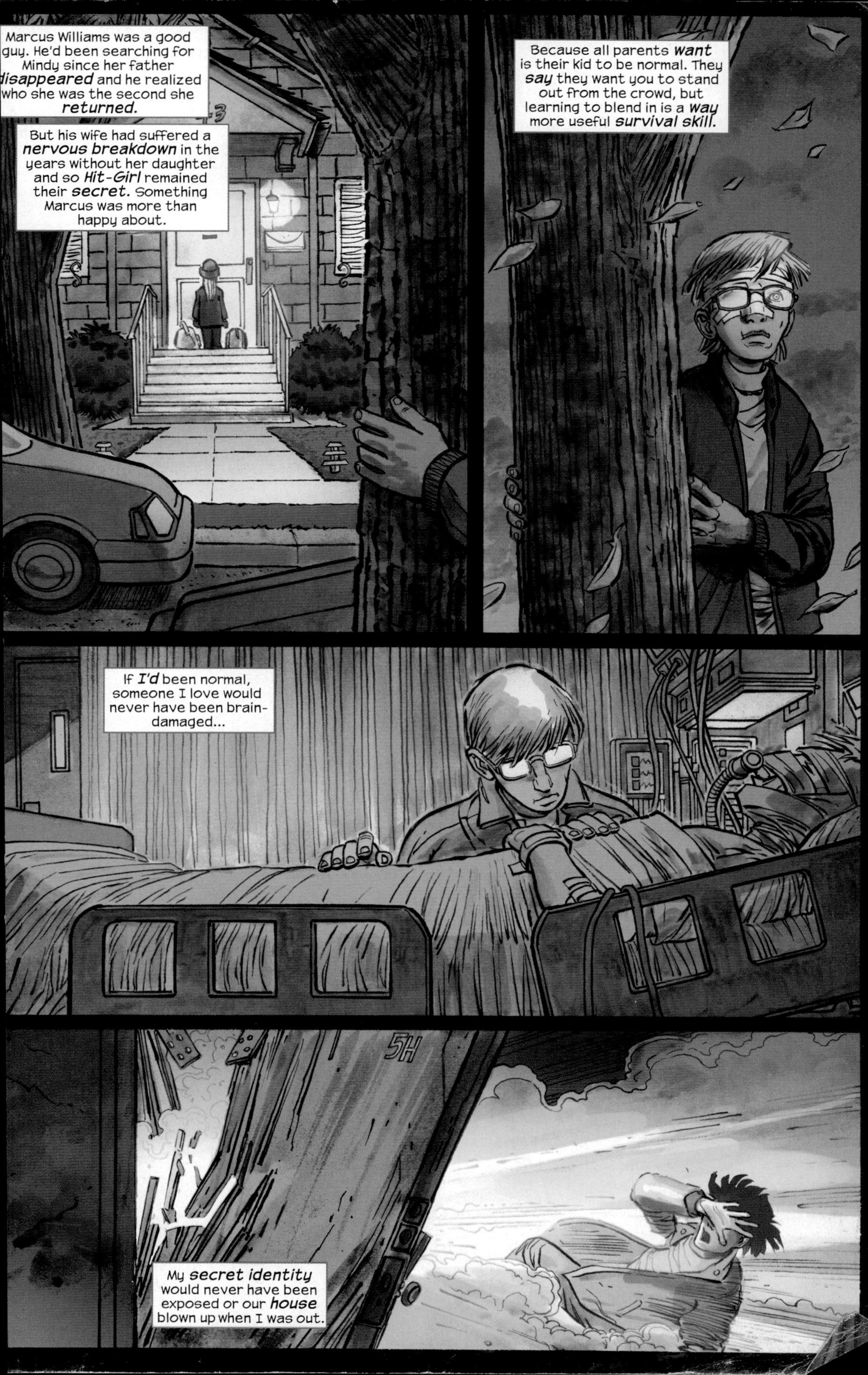

Marcus Williams was a good guy. He'd been searching for Mindy since her father disappeared and he realized who she was the second she returned.
But his wife had suffered a nervous breakdown in the years without her daughter and so Hit-Girl remained their secret. Something Marcus was more than happy about.
Because all parents want is their kid to be normal. They say they want you to stand out from the crowd, but learning to blend in is a way more useful survival skill.
If I'd been normal, someone I love would never have been brain-damaged...
5H
My secret identity would never have been exposed or our house blown up when I was out.

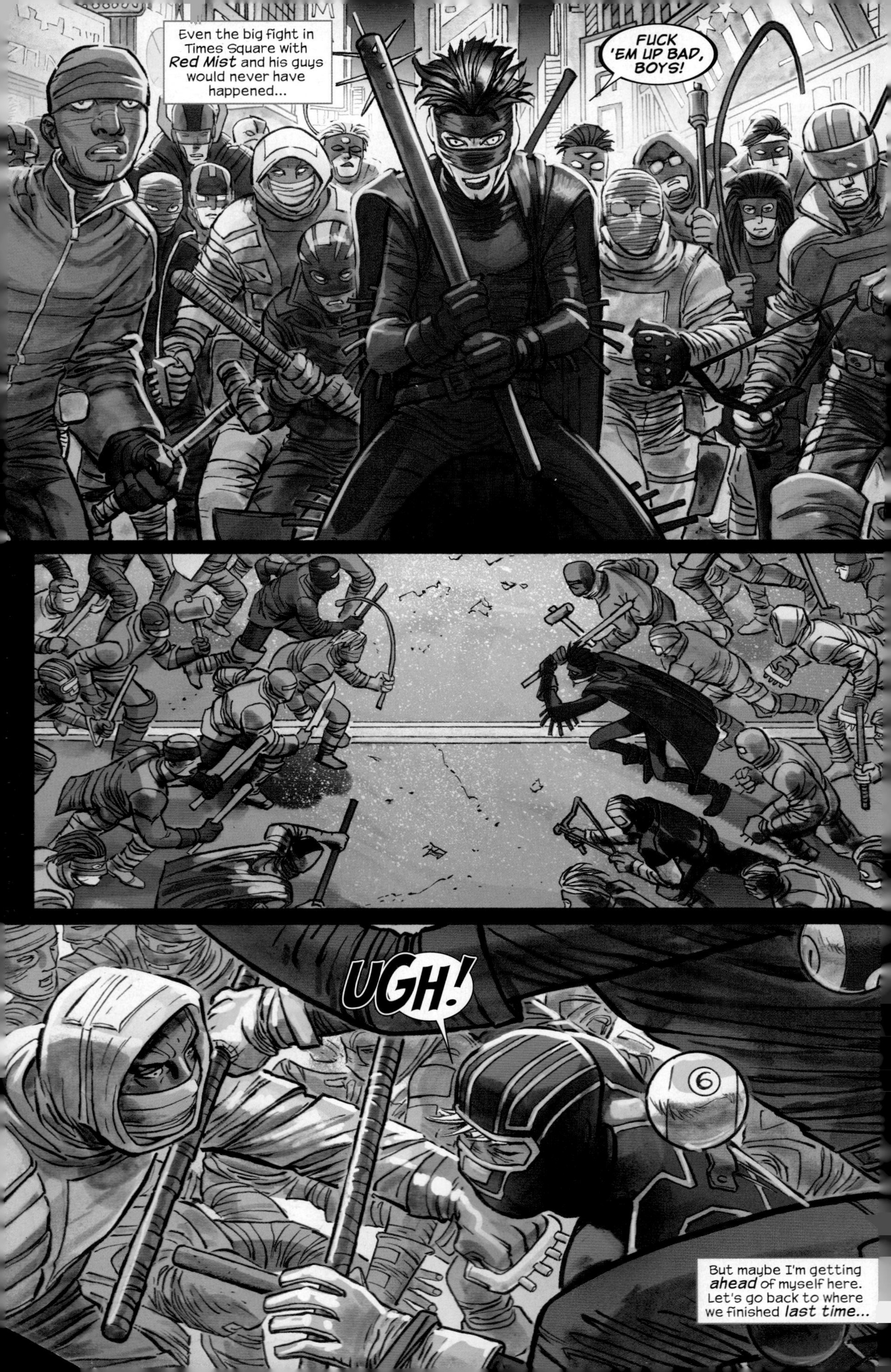
Even the big fight in Times Square with Red Mist and his guys would never have happened...
FUCK 'EM UP BAD, BOYS!
UGH!
But maybe I'm getting ahead of myself here. Let's go back to where we finished last time...

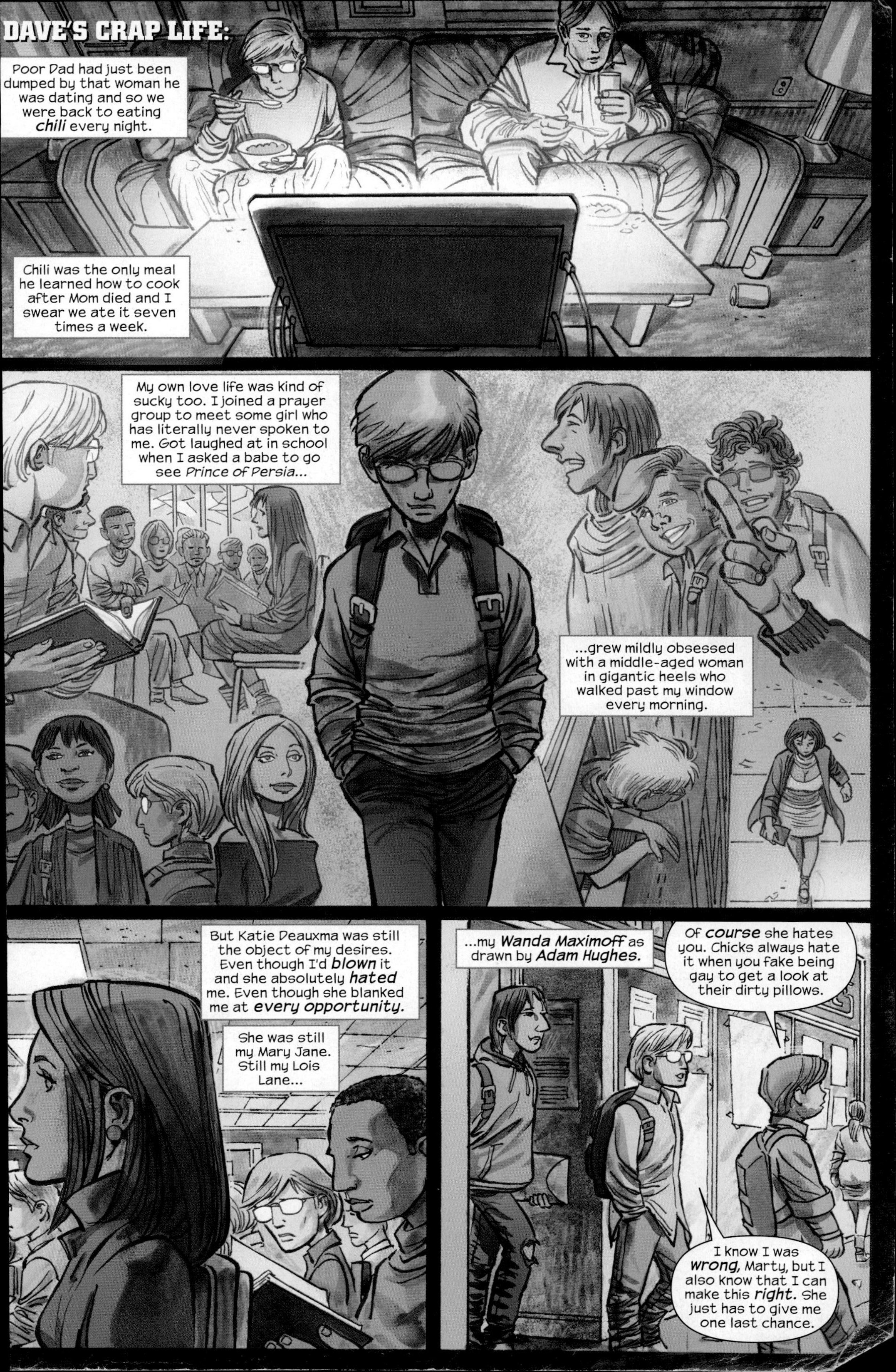
DAVE'S CRAP LIFE:
Poor Dad had just been dumped by that woman he was dating and so we were back to eating *chili* every night.
Chili was the only meal he learned how to cook after Mom died and I swear we ate it seven times a week.
My own love life was kind of sucky too. I joined a prayer group to meet some girl who has literally never spoken to me. Got laughed at in school when I asked a babe to go see *Prince of Persia*...
...grew mildly obsessed with a middle-aged woman in gigantic heels who walked past my window every morning.
But Katie Deauxma was still the object of my desires. Even though I'd *blown* it and she absolutely *hated* me. Even though she blanked me at *every opportunity.*
She was still my Mary Jane. Still my Lois Lane...
...my *Wanda Maximoff* as drawn by *Adam Hughes.*
Of *course* she hates you. Chicks always hate it when you fake being gay to get a look at their dirty pillows.
I know I was *wrong,* Marty, but I also know that I can make this *right.* She just has to give me one last chance.

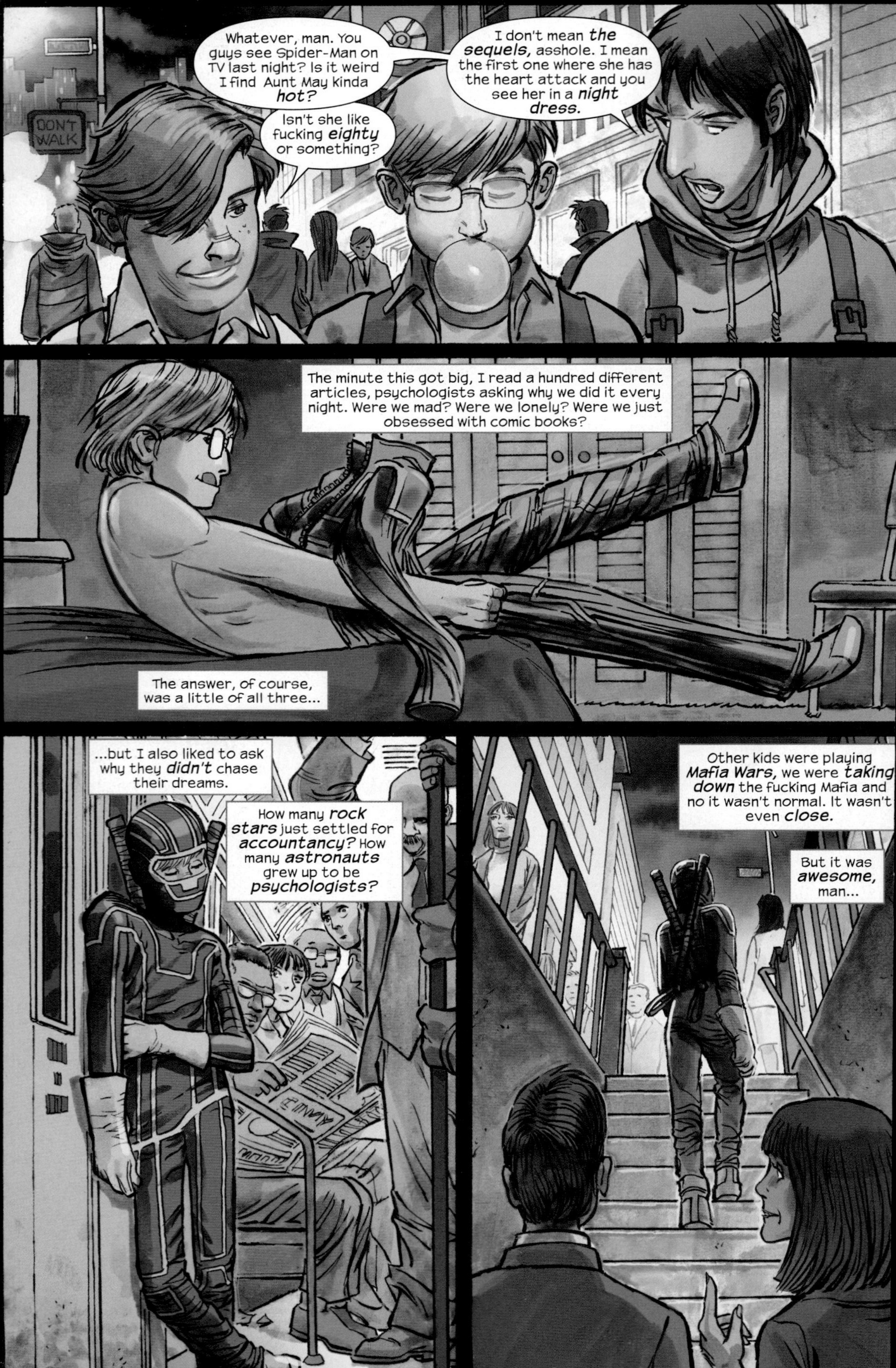

DON'T WALK
Whatever, man. You guys see Spider-Man on TV last night? Is it weird I find Aunt May kinda hot?
Isn't she like fucking eighty or something?
I don't mean the sequels, asshole. I mean the first one where she has the heart attack and you see her in a night dress.
The minute this got big, I read a hundred different articles, psychologists asking why we did it every night. Were we mad? Were we lonely? Were we just obsessed with comic books?
The answer, of course, was a little of all three...
...but I also liked to ask why they didn't chase their dreams.
How many rock stars just settled for accountancy? How many astronauts grew up to be psychologists?
Other kids were playing Mafia Wars, we were taking down the fucking Mafia and no it wasn't normal. It wasn't even close.
But it was awesome, man...

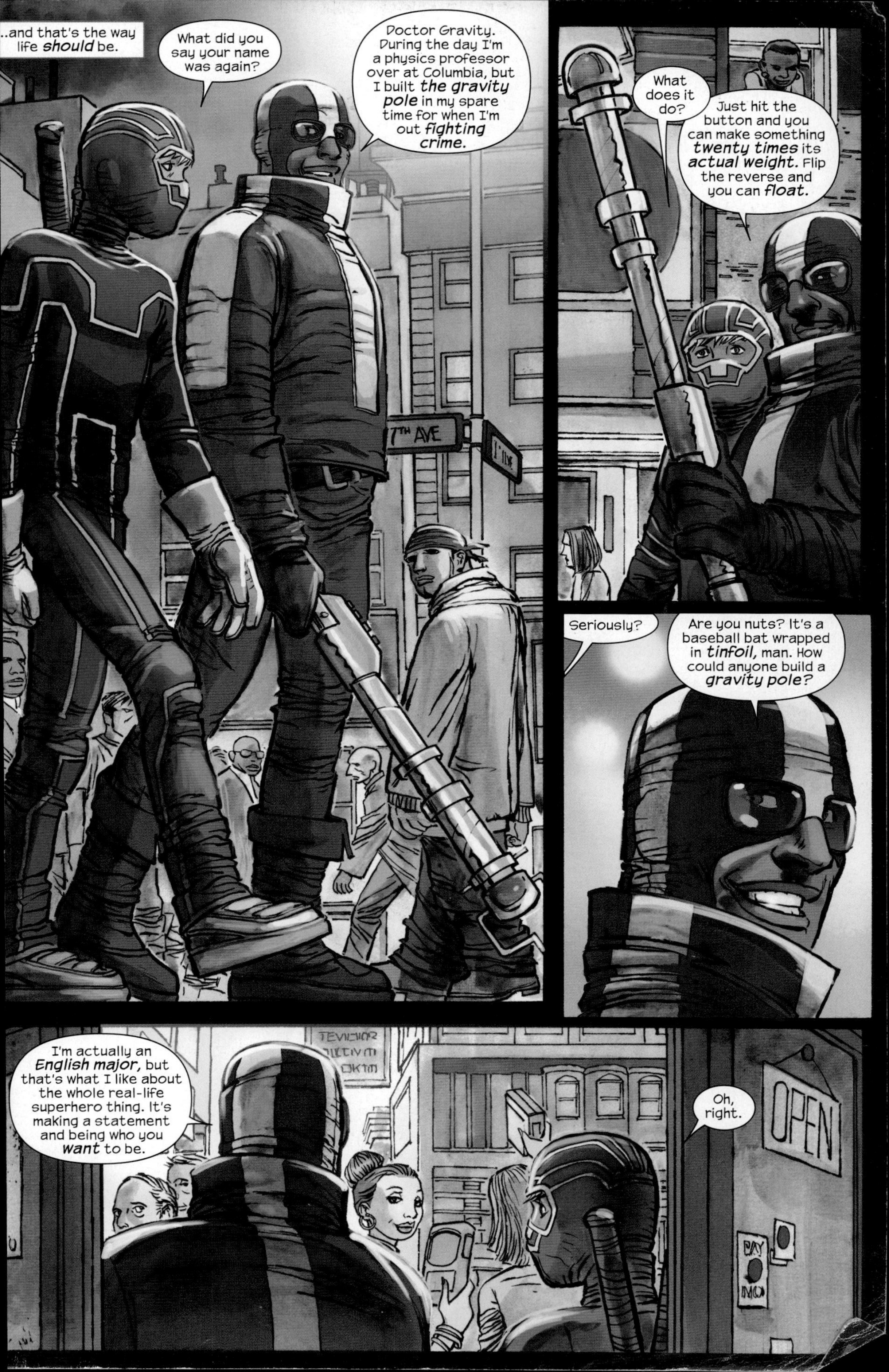
...and that's the way life *should* be.
What did you say your name was again?
Doctor Gravity. During the day I'm a physics professor over at Columbia, but I built ***the gravity pole*** in my spare time for when I'm out ***fighting crime.***
7TH AVE
What does it do?
Just hit the button and you can make something ***twenty times*** its ***actual weight.*** Flip the reverse and you can ***float.***
Seriously?
Are you nuts? It's a baseball bat wrapped in ***tinfoil,*** man. How could anyone build a ***gravity pole?***
I'm actually an ***English major,*** but that's what I like about the whole real-life superhero thing. It's making a statement and being who you ***want*** to be.
Oh, right.
OPEN

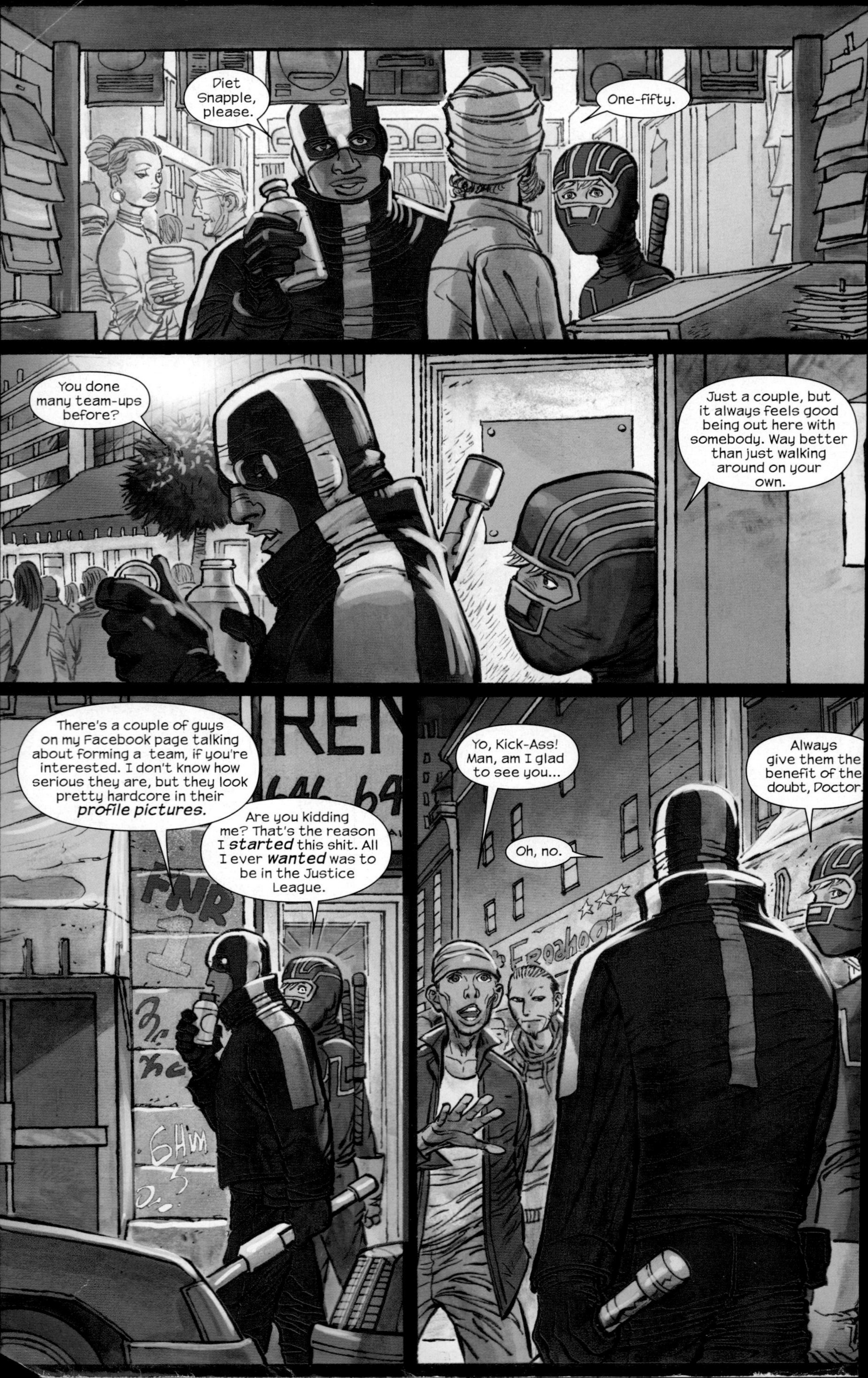
Diet Snapple, please.
One-fifty.
You done many team-ups before?
Just a couple, but it always feels good being out here with somebody. Way better than just walking around on your own.
There's a couple of guys on my Facebook page talking about forming a team, if you're interested. I don't know how serious they are, but they look pretty hardcore in their profile pictures.
Are you kidding me? That's the reason I started this shit. All I ever wanted was to be in the Justice League.
Yo, Kick-Ass! Man, am I glad to see you...
Oh, no.
Always give them the benefit of the doubt, Doctor.

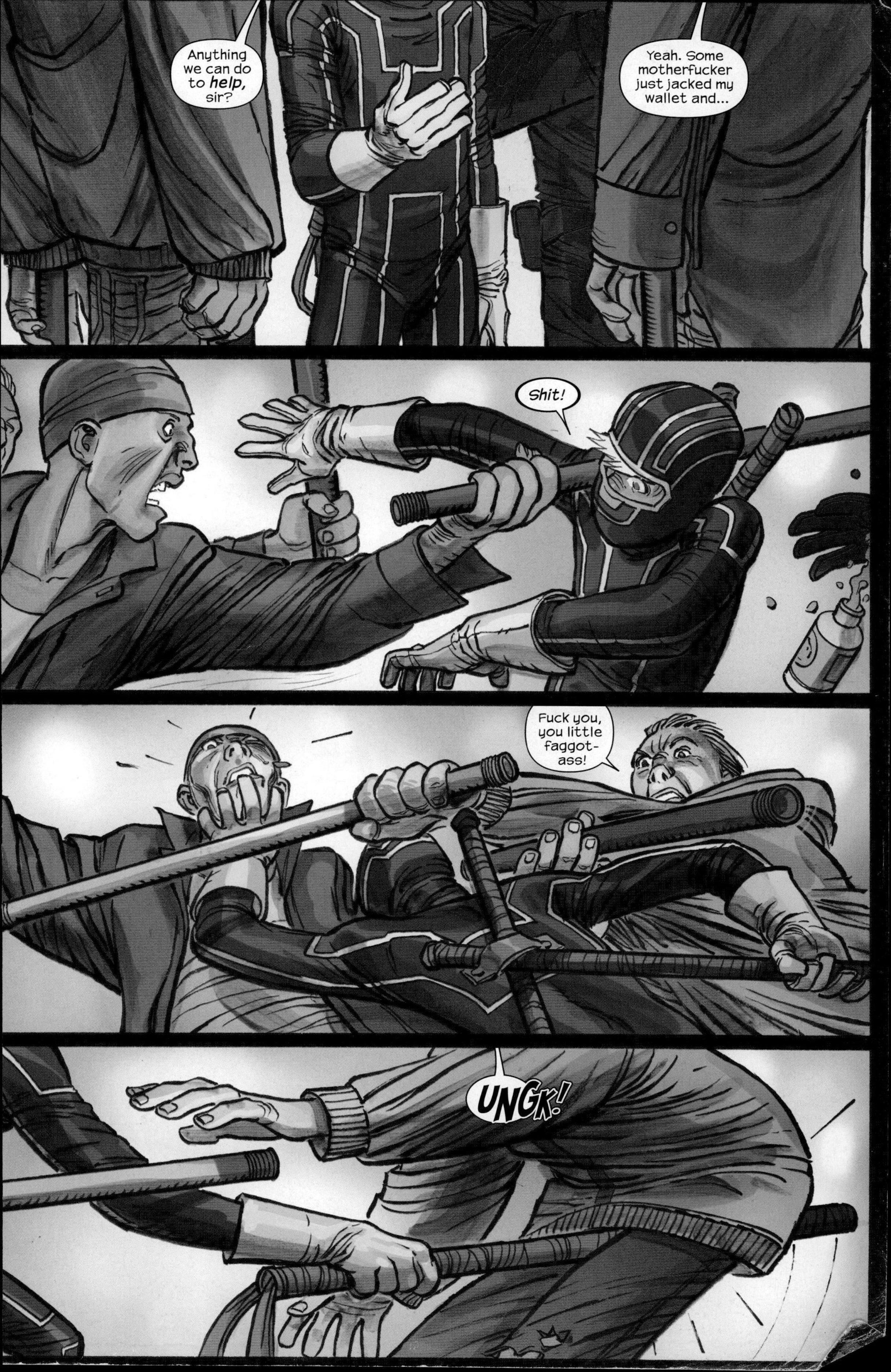
Anything we can do to help, sir?
Yeah. Some motherfucker just jacked my wallet and...
Shit!
Fuck you, you little faggot-ass!
UNGK!

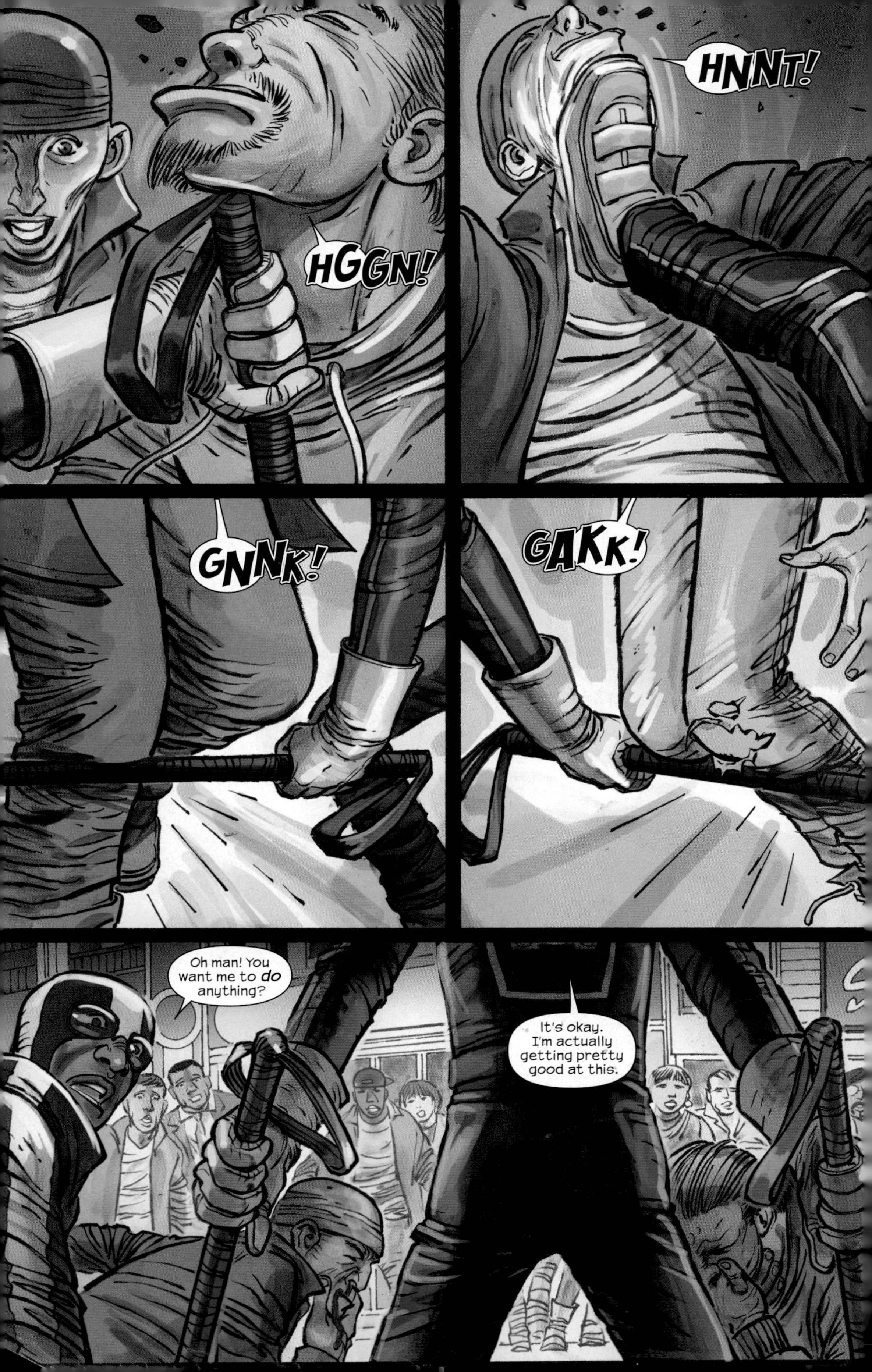
HGGN!
HNNT!
GNNK!
GAKK!
Oh man! You want me to do anything?
It's okay. I'm actually getting pretty good at this.

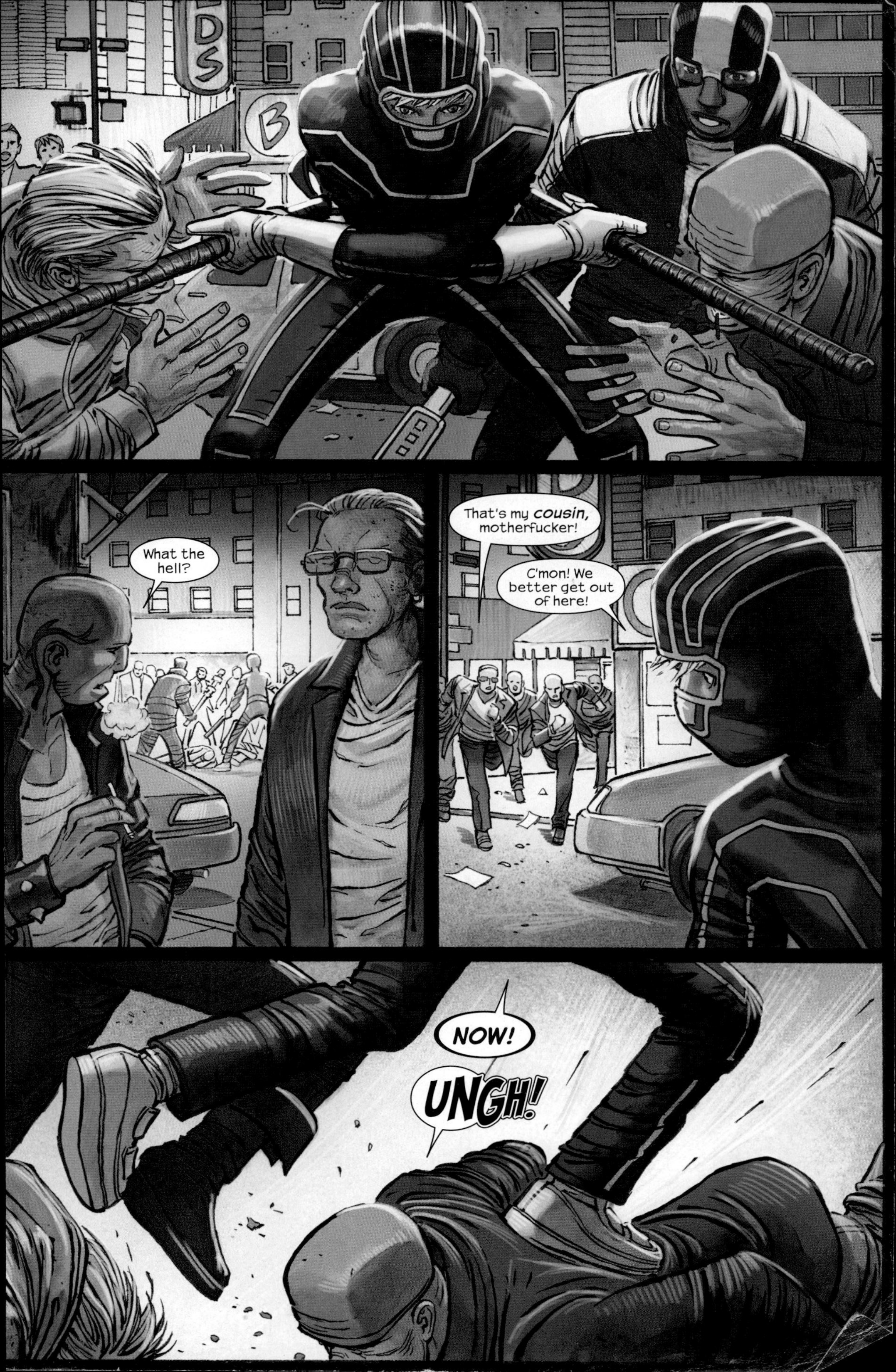
What the hell?
That's my *cousin,* motherfucker!
C'mon! We better get out of here!
NOW!
UNGH!

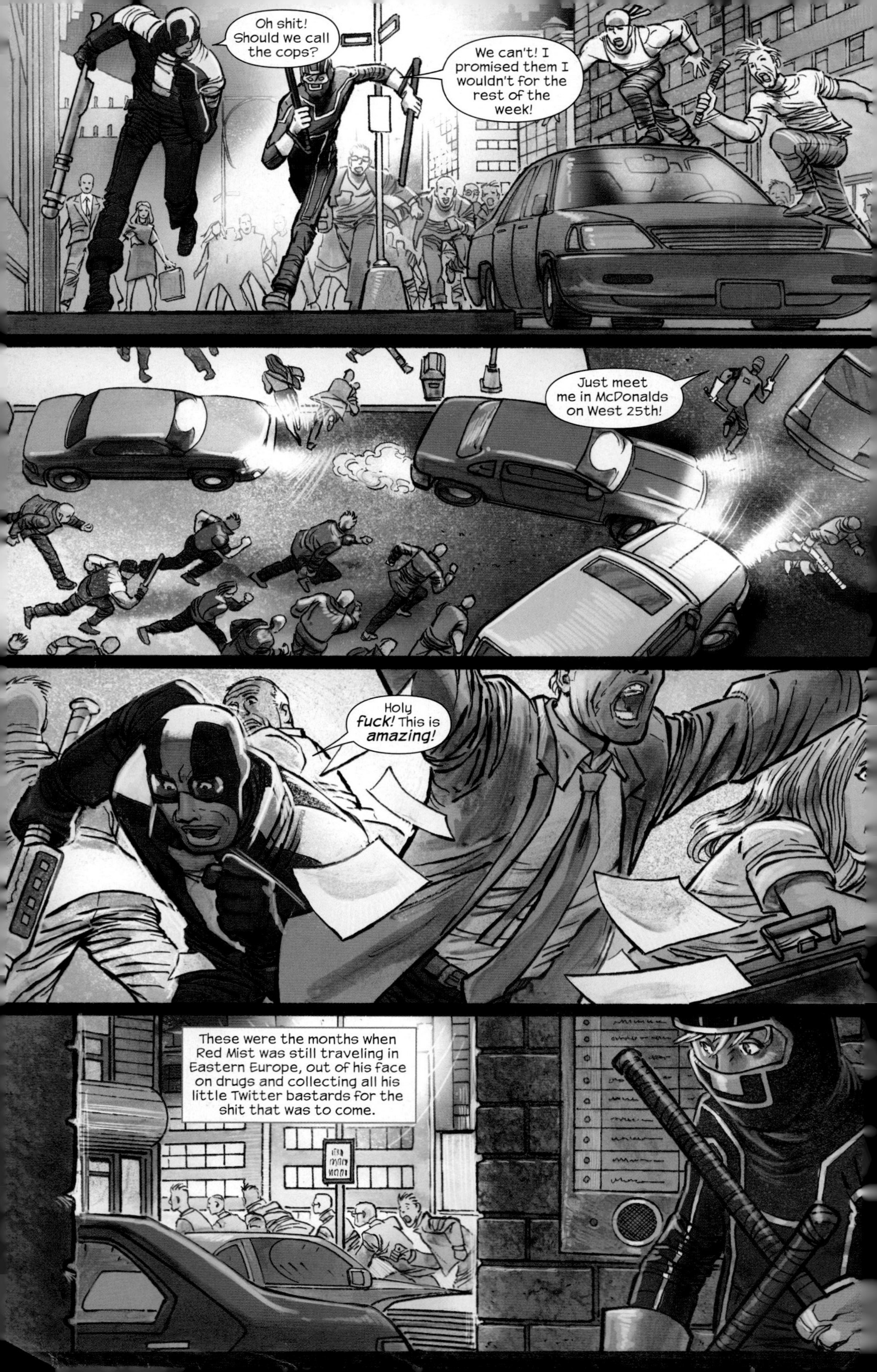
Oh shit! Should we call the cops?
We can't! I promised them I wouldn't for the rest of the week!
Just meet me in McDonalds on West 25th!
Holy *fuck!* This is *amazing!*
These were the months when Red Mist was still traveling in Eastern Europe, out of his face on drugs and collecting all his little Twitter bastards for the shit that was to come.

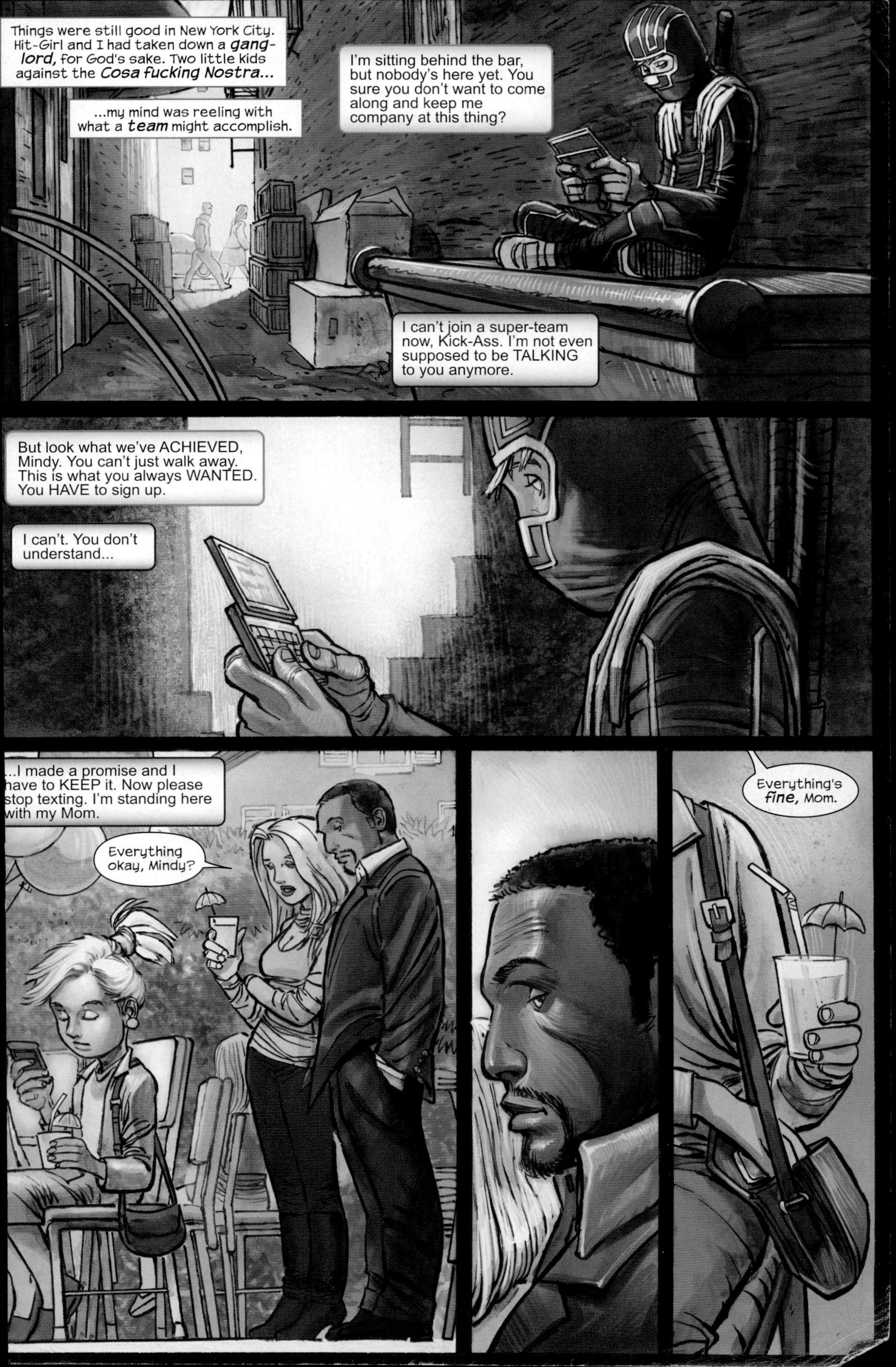
Things were still good in New York City. Hit-Girl and I had taken down a *gang-lord,* for God's sake. Two little kids against the *Cosa fucking Nostra...*
...my mind was reeling with what a *team* might accomplish.
I'm sitting behind the bar, but nobody's here yet. You sure you don't want to come along and keep me company at this thing?
I can't join a super-team now, Kick-Ass. I'm not even supposed to be TALKING to you anymore.
But look what we've ACHIEVED, Mindy. You can't just walk away. This is what you always WANTED. You HAVE to sign up.
I can't. You don't understand...
...I made a promise and I have to KEEP it. Now please stop texting. I'm standing here with my Mom.
Everything okay, Mindy?
Everything's *fine,* Mom.

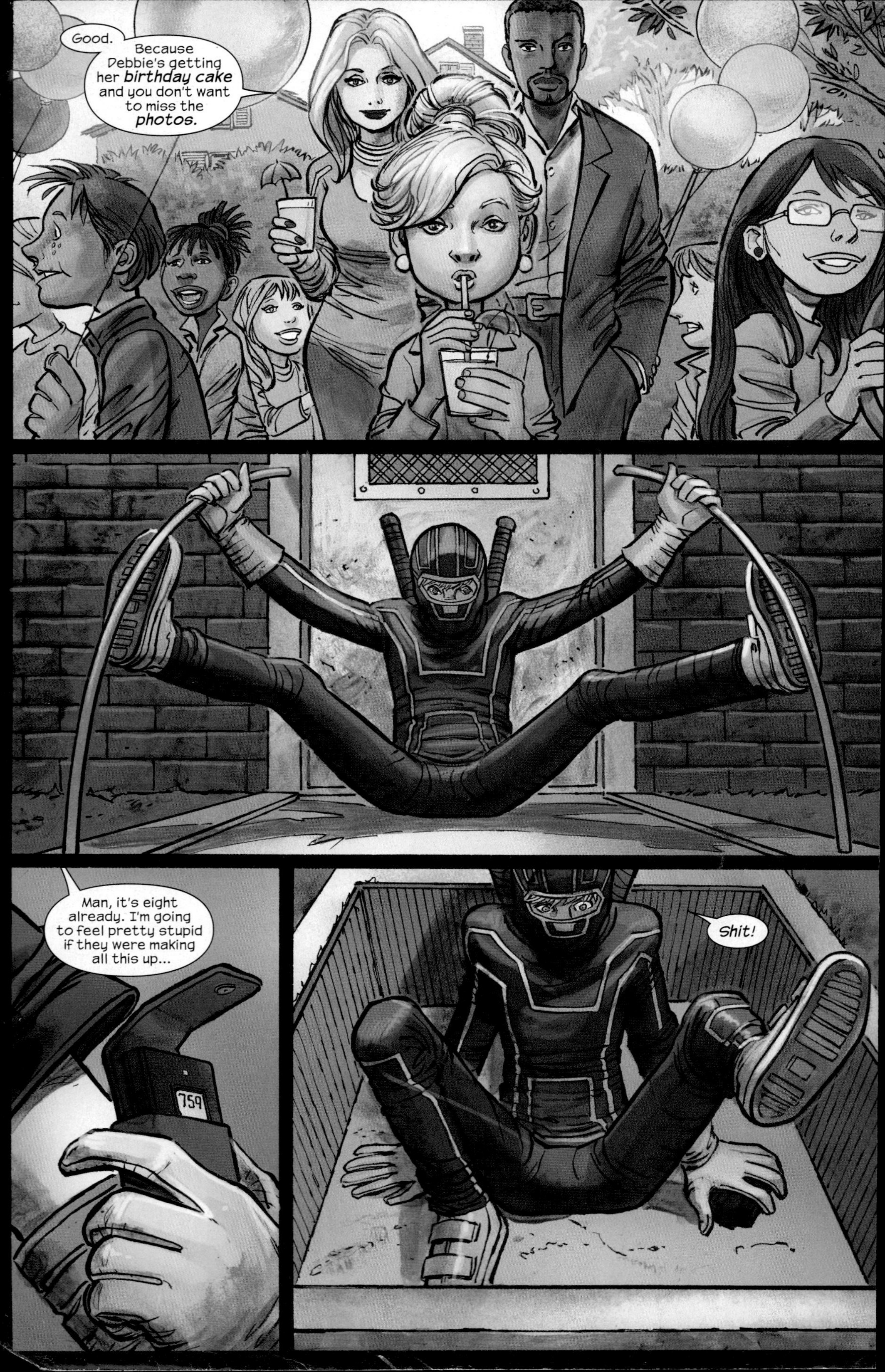
Good.
Because Debbie's getting her birthday cake and you don't want to miss the photos.
Man, it's eight already. I'm going to feel pretty stupid if they were making all this up...
759
Shit!

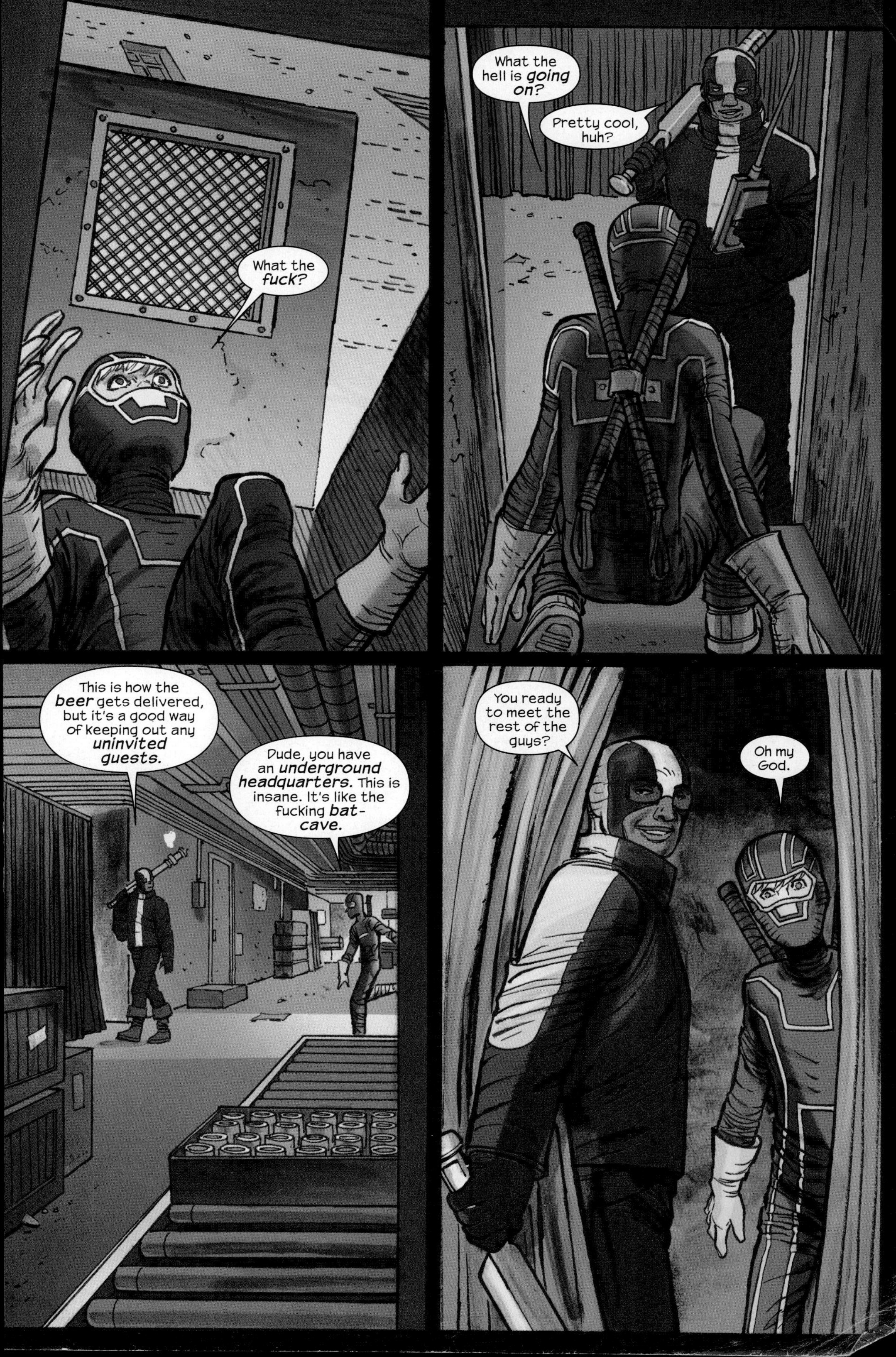
What the fuck?
What the hell is going on?
Pretty cool, huh?
This is how the beer gets delivered, but it's a good way of keeping out any uninvited guests.
Dude, you have an underground headquarters. This is insane. It's like the fucking bat-cave.
You ready to meet the rest of the guys?
Oh my God.

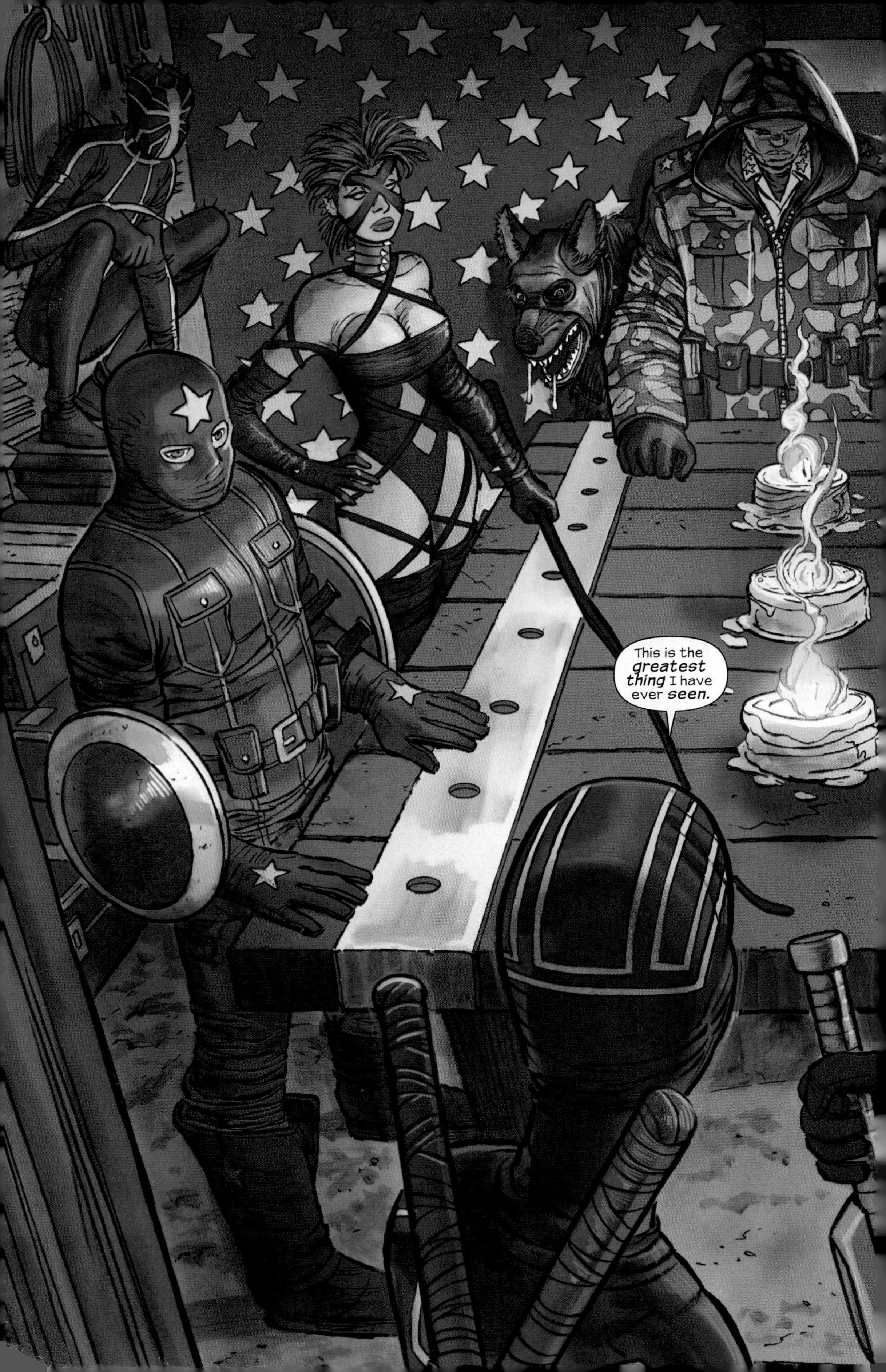
This is the greatest thing I have ever seen.

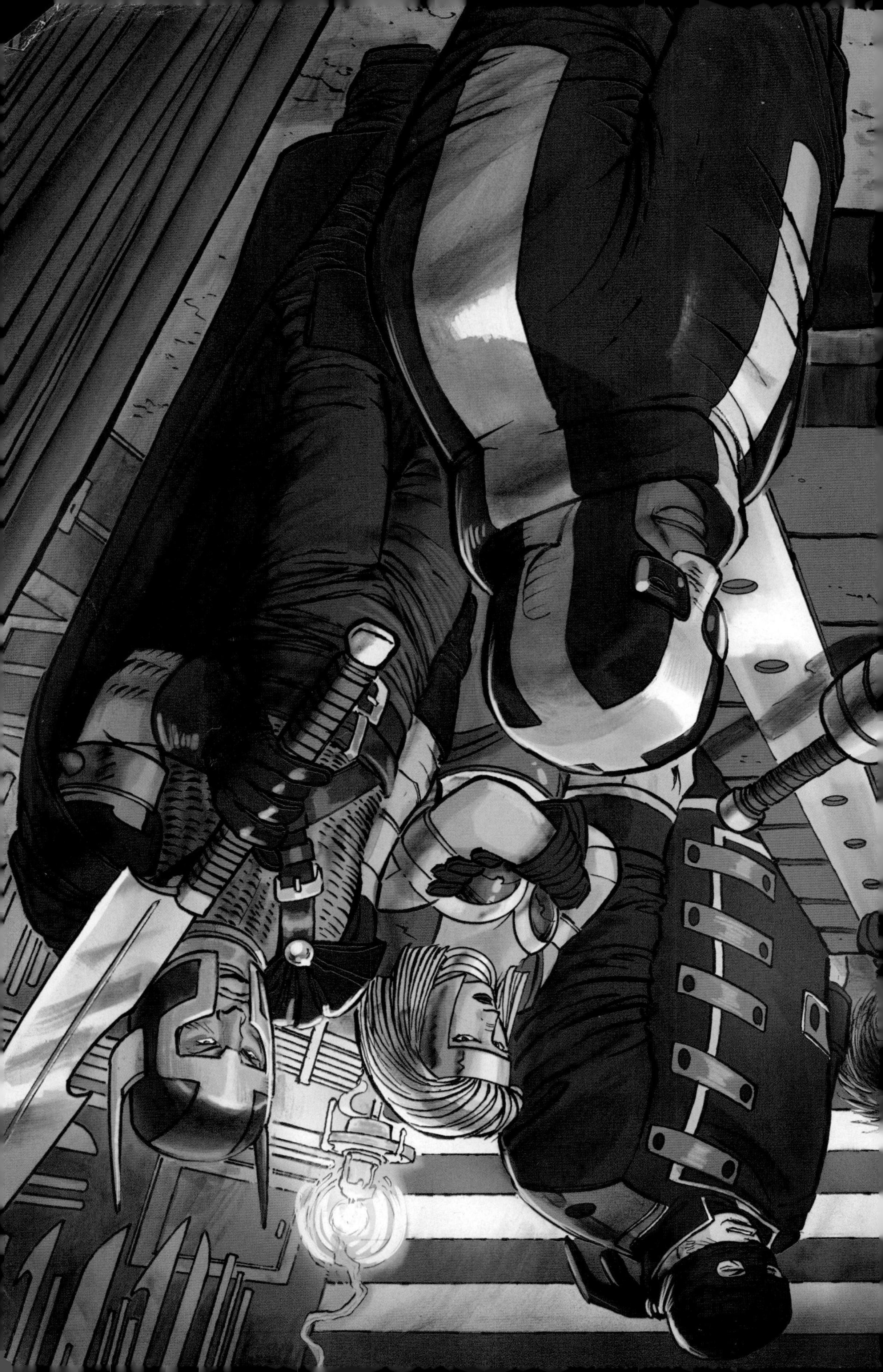

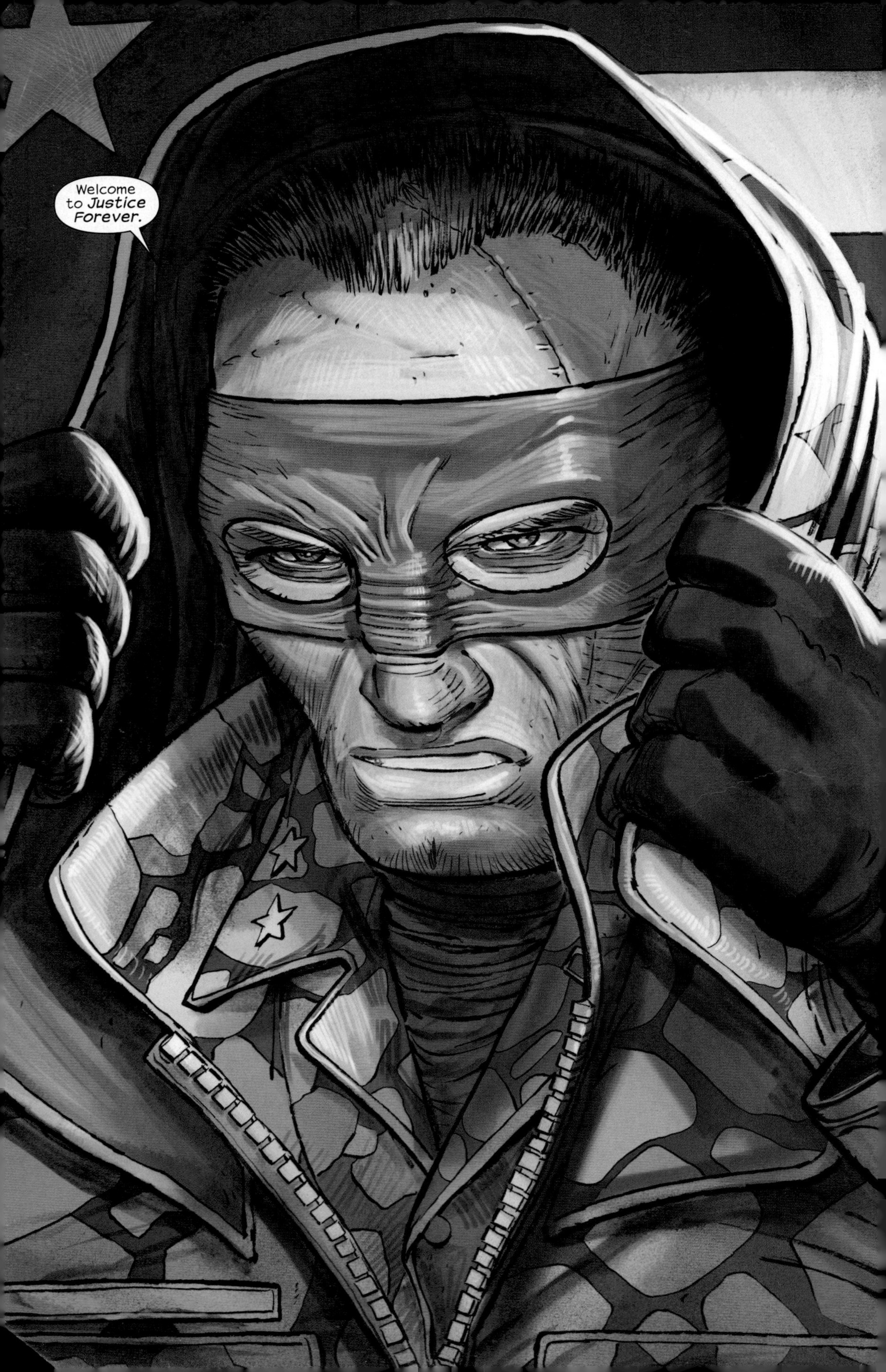
Welcome to *Justice Forever.*

TWO

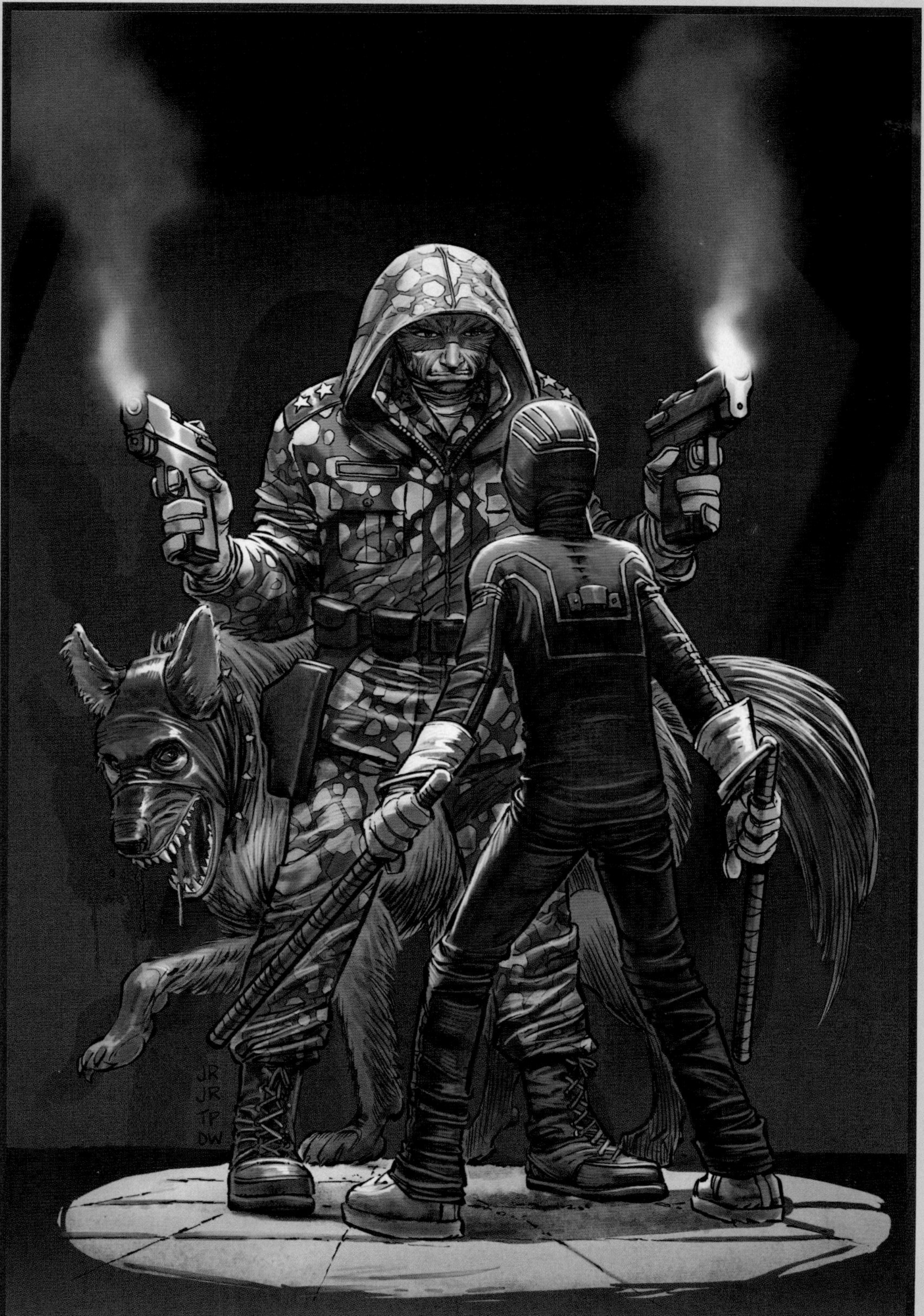
JR
JR
TP
DW

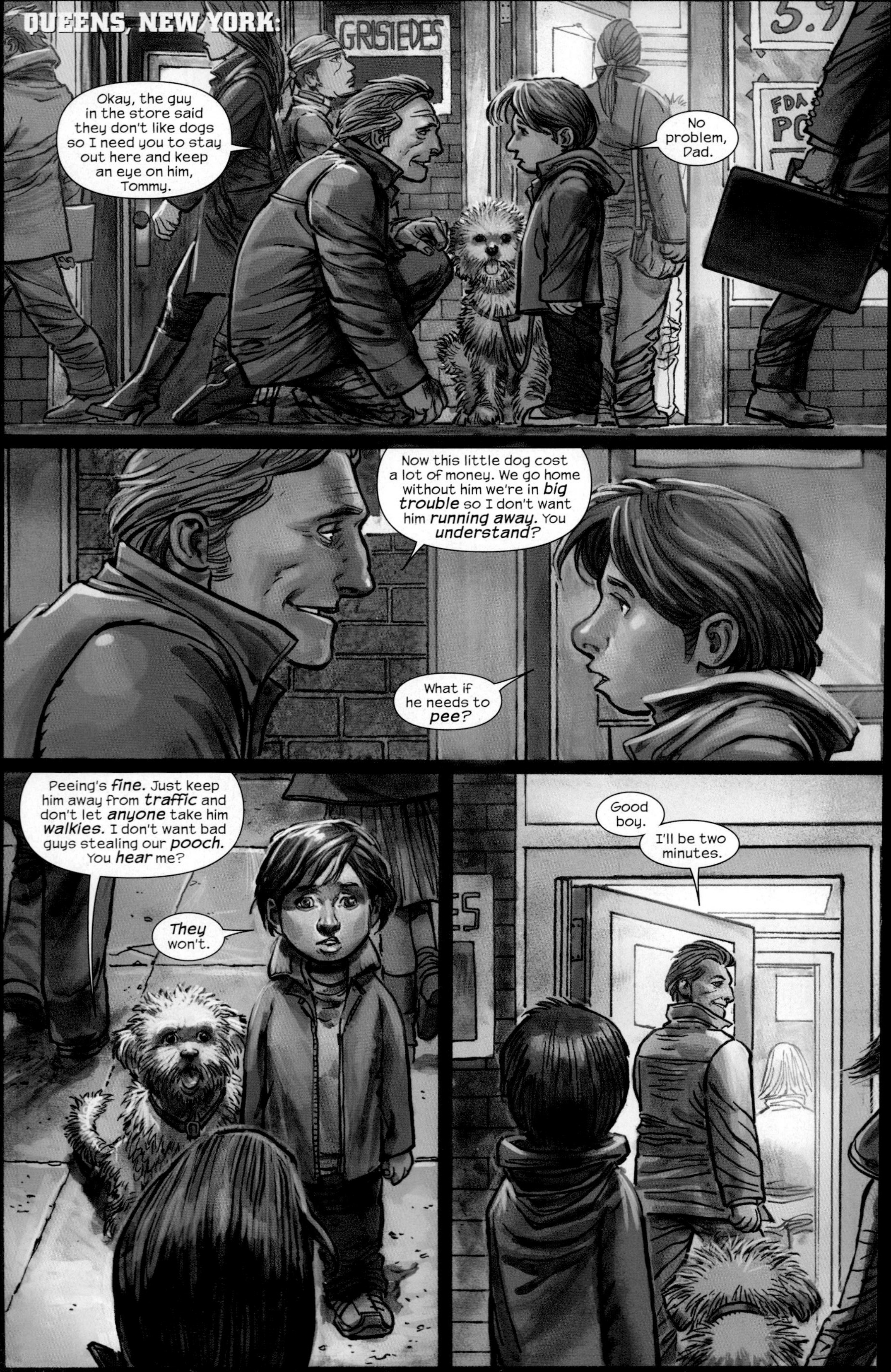
QUEENS, NEW YORK:
GRISTEDES
Okay, the guy in the store said they don't like dogs so I need you to stay out here and keep an eye on him, Tommy.
No problem, Dad.
Now this little dog cost a lot of money. We go home without him we're in *big trouble* so I don't want him *running away.* You *understand?*
What if he needs to *pee?*
Peeing's *fine.* Just keep him away from *traffic* and don't let *anyone* take him *walkies.* I don't want bad guys stealing our *pooch.* You *hear* me?
They won't.
Good boy.
I'll be two minutes.

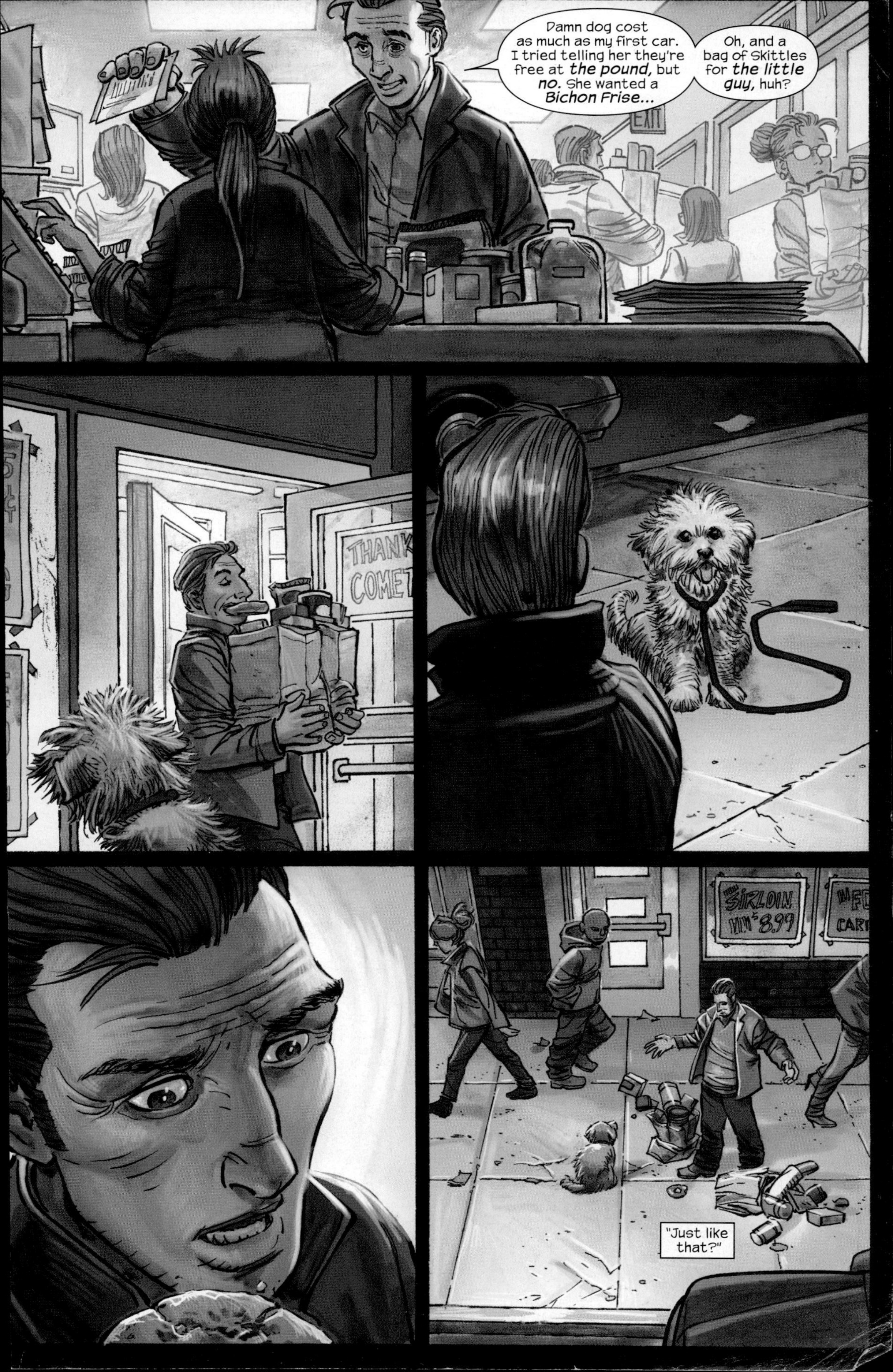
Damn dog cost as much as my first car. I tried telling her they're free at *the pound,* but *no.* She wanted a *Bichon Frise...*
Oh, and a bag of Skittles for *the little guy,* huh?
THANK
COME T
SIRLOIN
$8.99
"Just like that?"

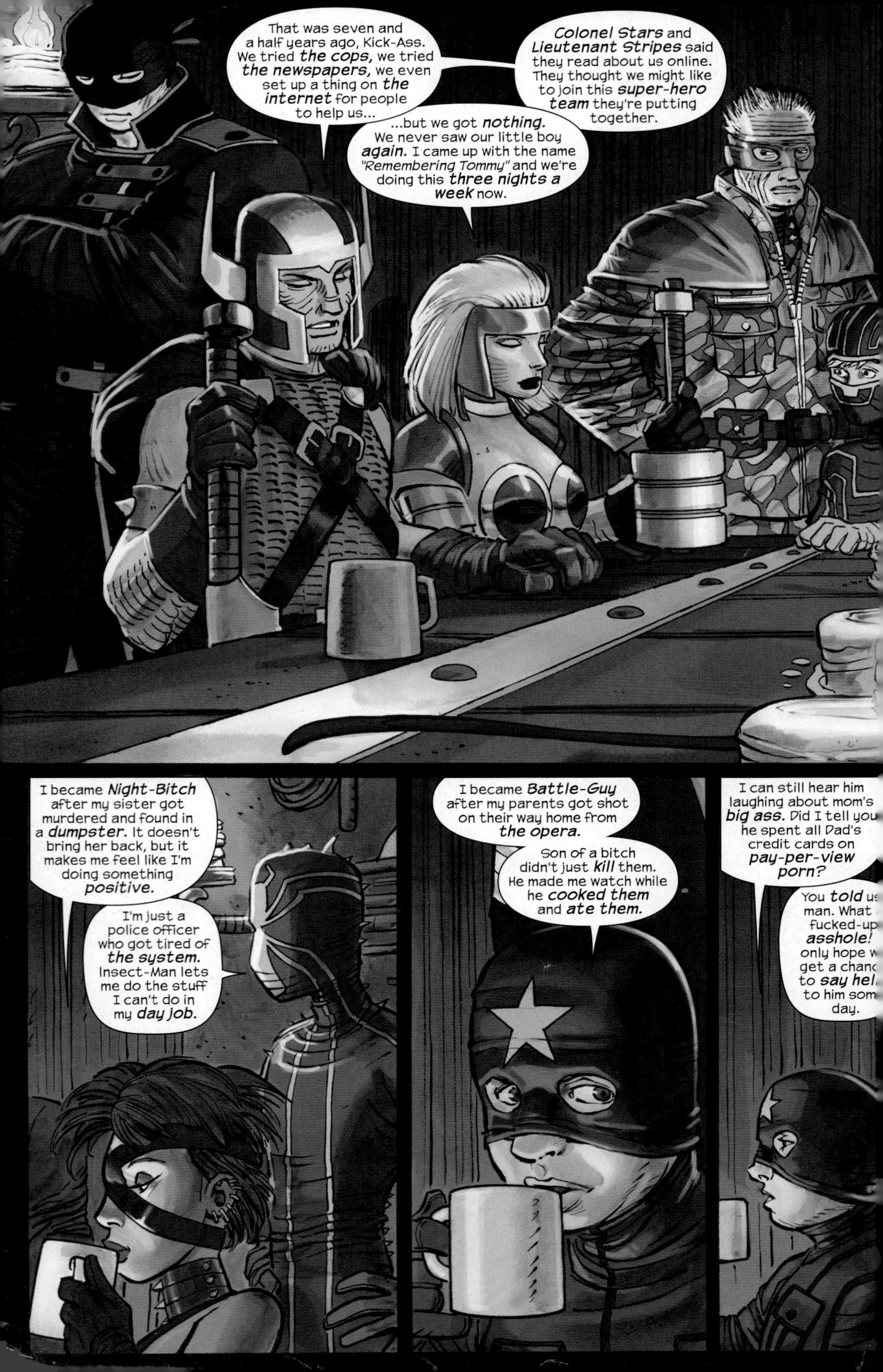
That was seven and a half years ago, Kick-Ass. We tried the cops, we tried the newspapers, we even set up a thing on the internet for people to help us...
...but we got nothing. We never saw our little boy again. I came up with the name "Remembering Tommy" and we're doing this three nights a week now.
Colonel Stars and Lieutenant Stripes said they read about us online. They thought we might like to join this super-hero team they're putting together.
I became Night-Bitch after my sister got murdered and found in a dumpster. It doesn't bring her back, but it makes me feel like I'm doing something positive.
I'm just a police officer who got tired of the system. Insect-Man lets me do the stuff I can't do in my day job.
I became Battle-Guy after my parents got shot on their way home from the opera.
Son of a bitch didn't just kill them. He made me watch while he cooked them and ate them.
I can still hear him laughing about mom's big ass. Did I tell you he spent all Dad's credit cards on pay-per-view porn?
You told u man. What fucked-up asshole! only hope w get a chanc to say hel to him som day.

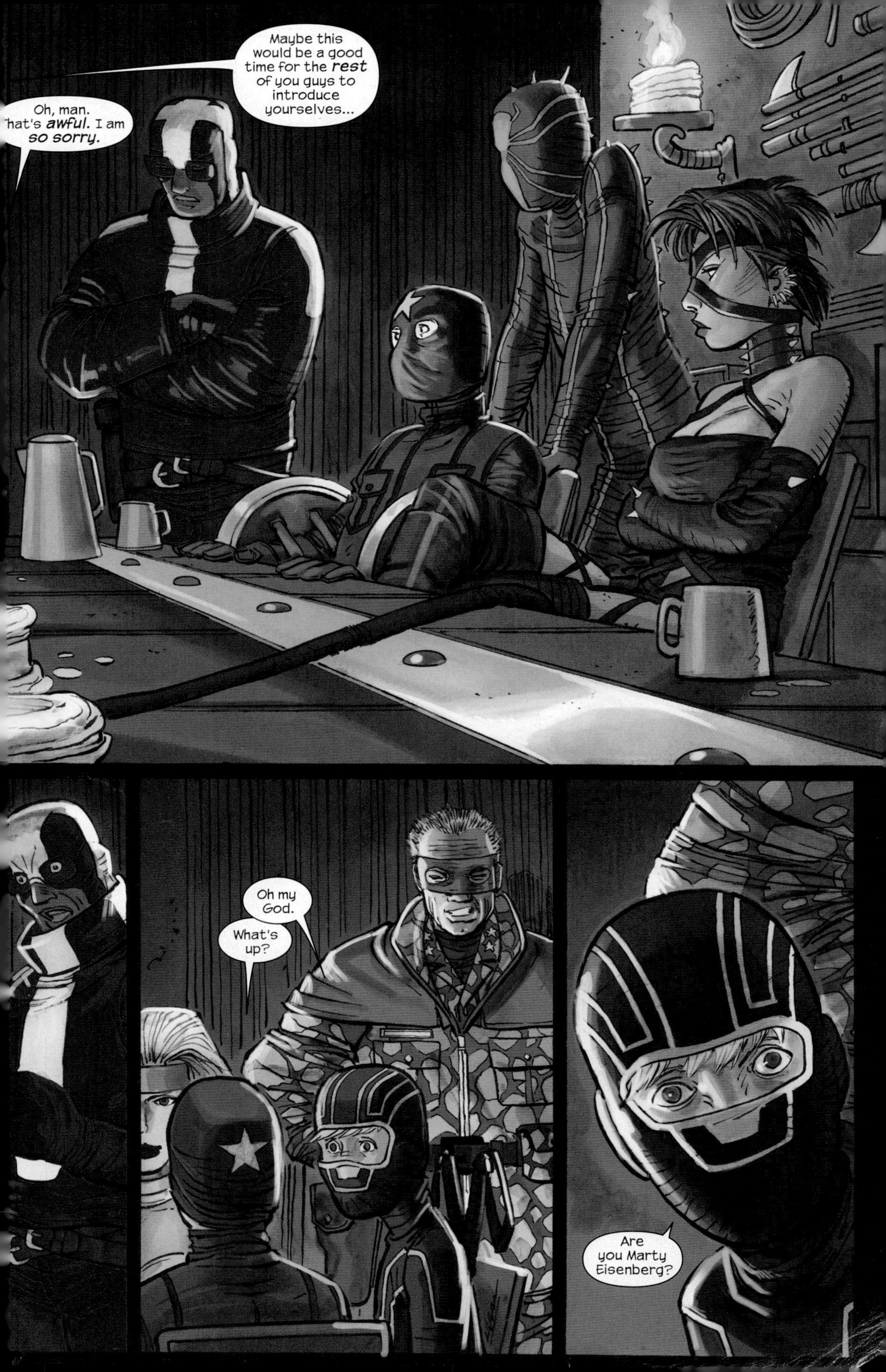
Oh, man. hat's awful. I am so sorry.
Maybe this would be a good time for the rest of you guys to introduce yourselves...
Oh my God.
What's up?
Are you Marty Eisenberg?

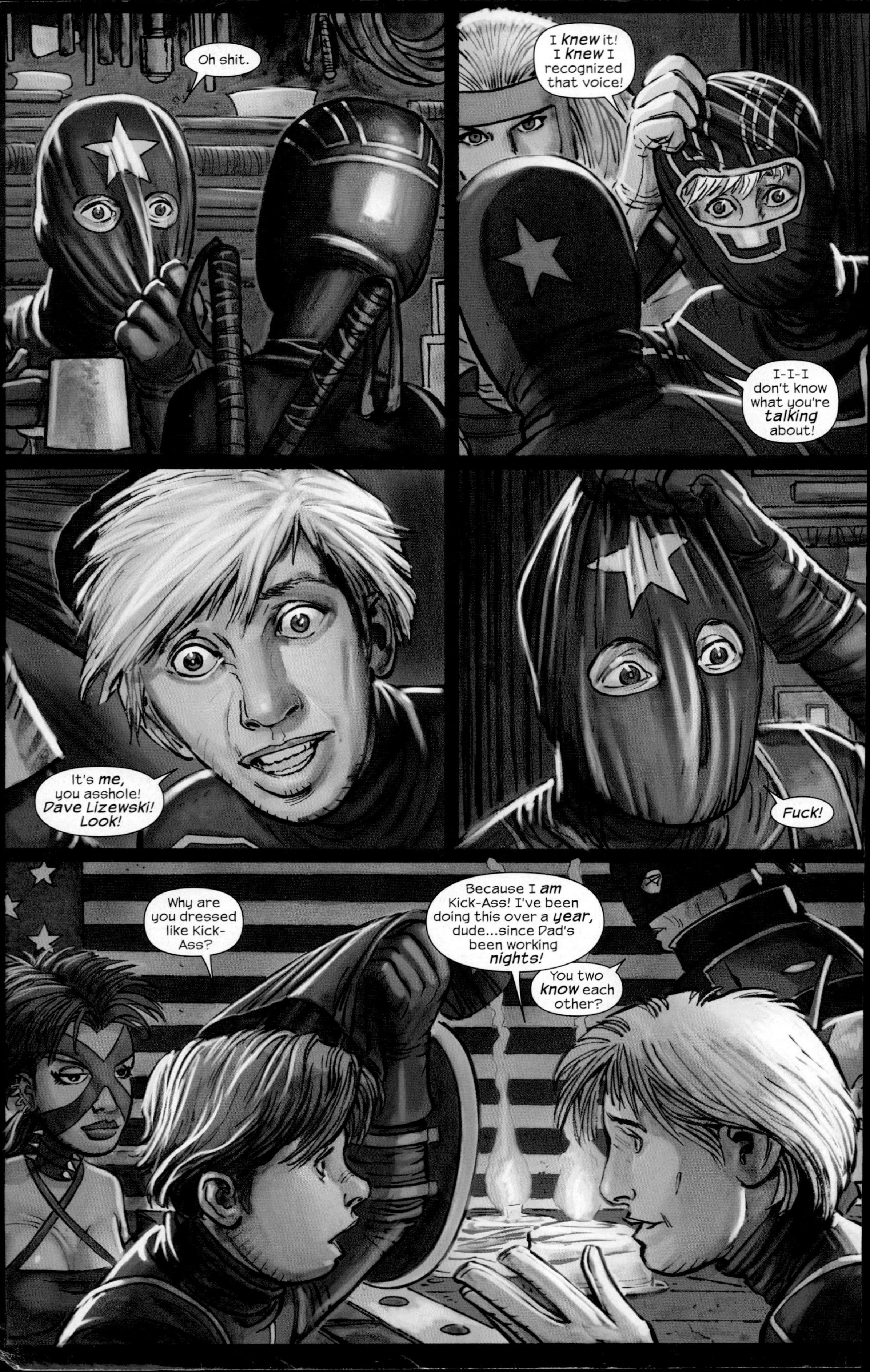

Oh shit.
I *knew* it! I *knew* I recognized that voice!
I-I-I don't know what you're *talking* about!
It's *me,* you asshole! *Dave Lizewski! Look!*
Fuck!
Why are you dressed like Kick-Ass?
Because I *am* Kick-Ass! I've been doing this over a *year,* dude...since Dad's been working *nights!*
You two *know* each other?

Are you crazy? We've been friends since we were *five!* What's all this bullshit about your *parents* getting killed? I saw your Mom at the *grocery store* this morning!
What?
Thanks a *lot,* Dave.
Is this true?
Oh, Jesus. How do I say this without coming off like a *total retard?*
When I found you guys online you were swapping all these *awesome stories.* I mean, you and the Lieutenant are a couple of *ex-Mafia guys,* for God's sake...
I didn't think you'd let me *join* unless I was cool too.
Don't be *ridiculous.* You signed up for this team to look after *the neighborhood,* Battle-Guy. That's the only thing that matters here.
We protect the people when the system *fails.* Catch the guys the cops let *get away.*
That's what all the *computers* are for: To track down *miscarriages of justice.* That's what all these *clippings* are on the wall: Punks we need to *pay a little visit.*

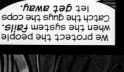

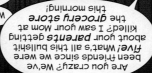

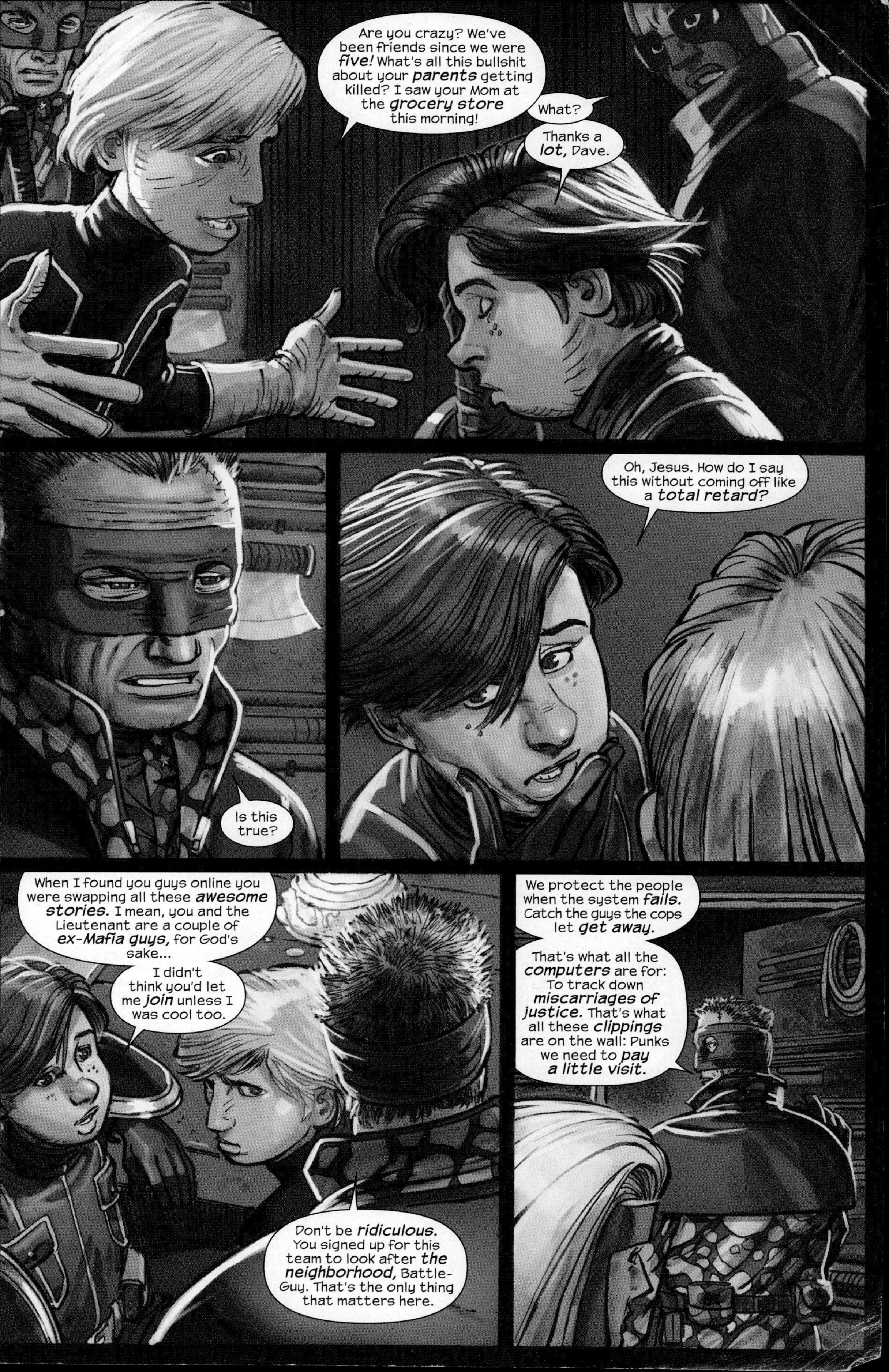

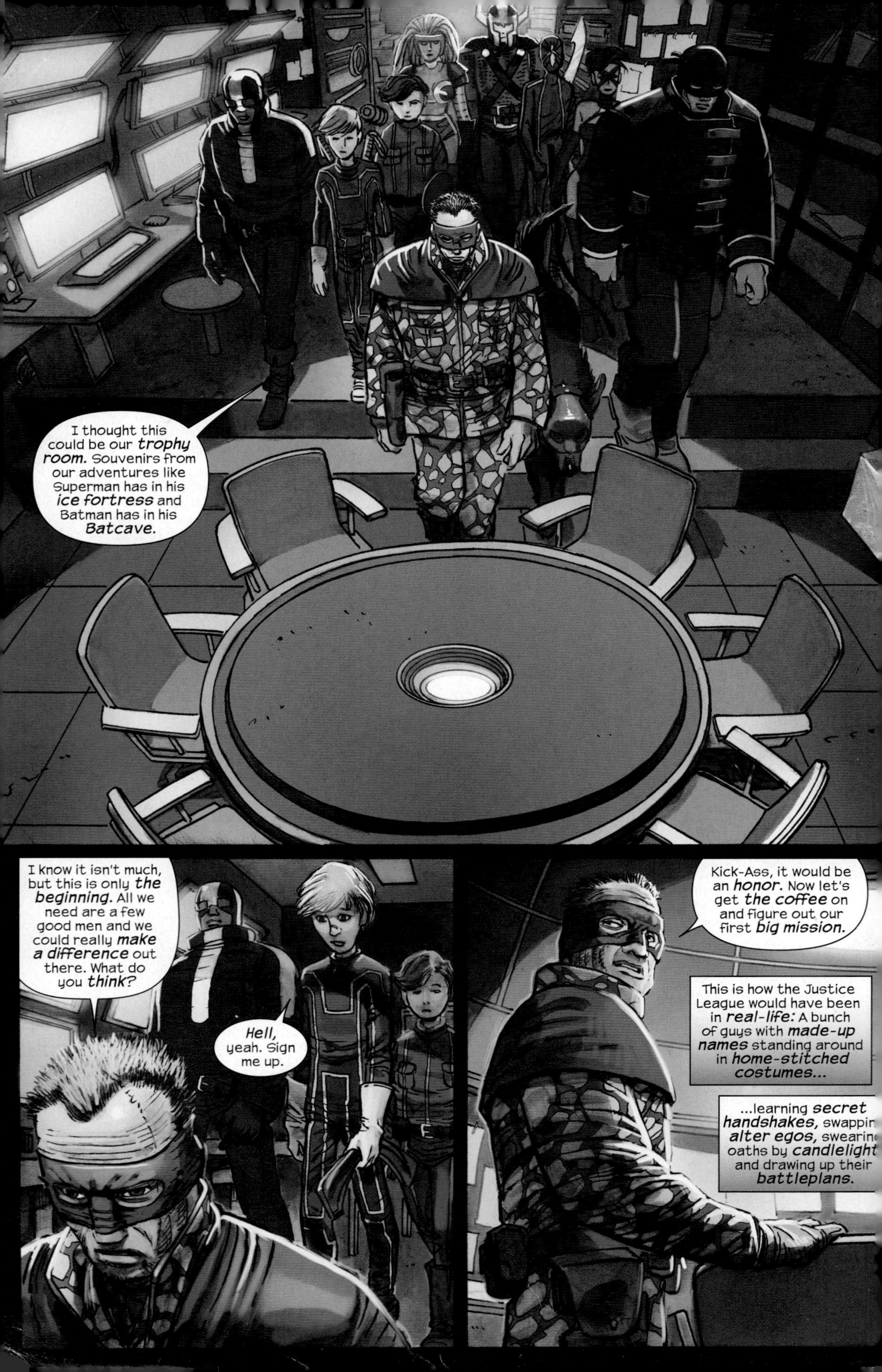
I thought this could be our trophy room. Souvenirs from our adventures like Superman has in his ice fortress and Batman has in his Batcave.
I know it isn't much, but this is only the beginning. All we need are a few good men and we could really make a difference out there. What do you think?
Hell, yeah. Sign me up.
Kick-Ass, it would be an honor. Now let's get the coffee on and figure out our first big mission.
This is how the Justice League would have been in real-life: A bunch of guys with made-up names standing around in home-stitched costumes...
...learning secret handshakes, swappin alter egos, swearin oaths by candlelight and drawing up their battleplans.

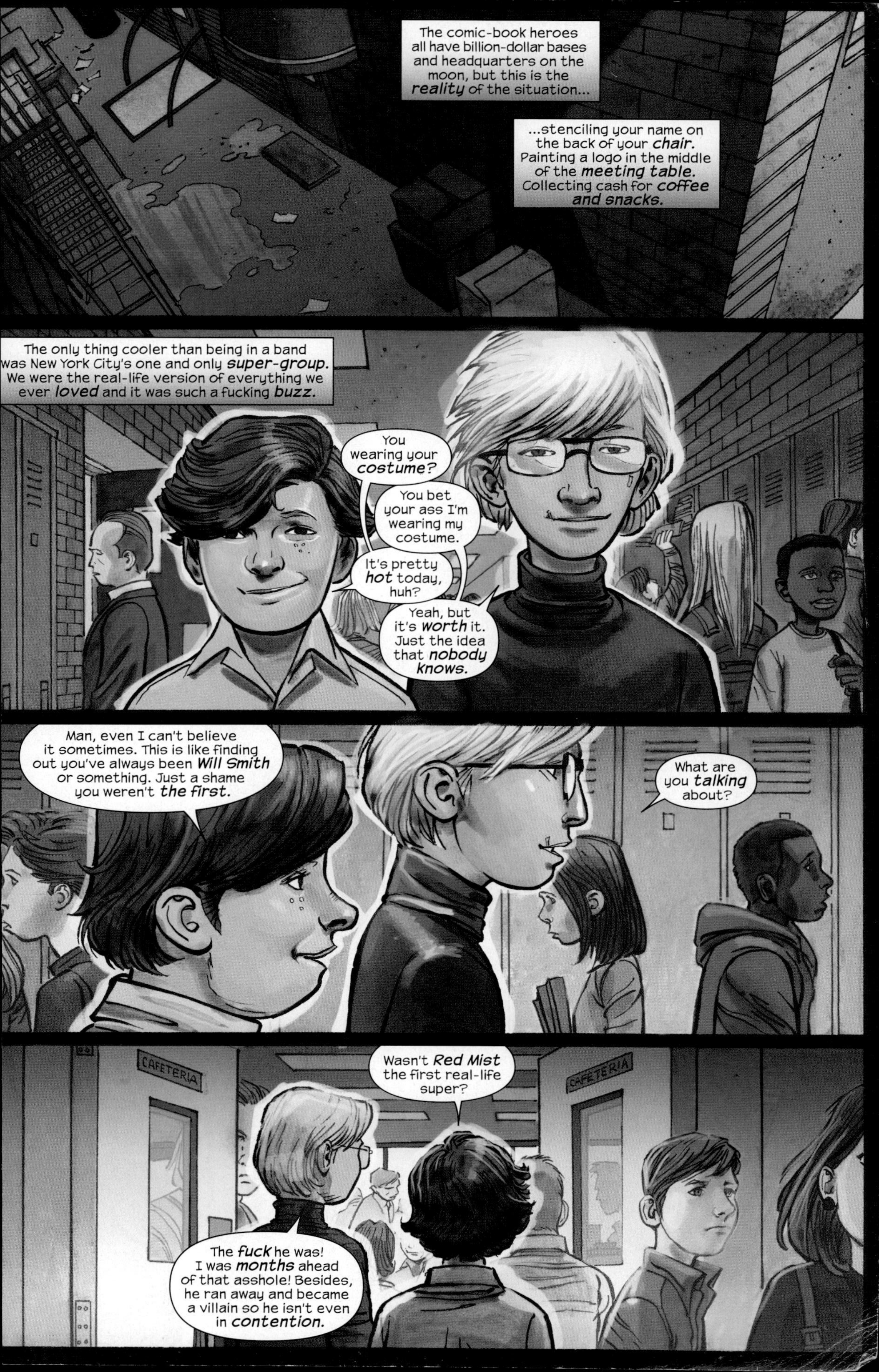
The comic-book heroes all have billion-dollar bases and headquarters on the moon, but this is the *reality* of the situation...
...stenciling your name on the back of your *chair*. Painting a logo in the middle of the *meeting table*. Collecting cash for *coffee and snacks*.
The only thing cooler than being in a band was New York City's one and only *super-group*. We were the real-life version of everything we ever *loved* and it was such a fucking *buzz*.
You wearing your *costume?*
You bet your ass I'm wearing my costume.
It's pretty *hot* today, huh?
Yeah, but it's *worth* it. Just the idea that *nobody knows.*
Man, even I can't believe it sometimes. This is like finding out you've always been *Will Smith* or something. Just a shame you weren't *the first.*
What are you *talking* about?
CAFETERIA
CAFETERIA
Wasn't *Red Mist* the first real-life super?
The *fuck* he was! I was *months* ahead of that asshole! Besides, he ran away and became a villain so he isn't even in *contention.*

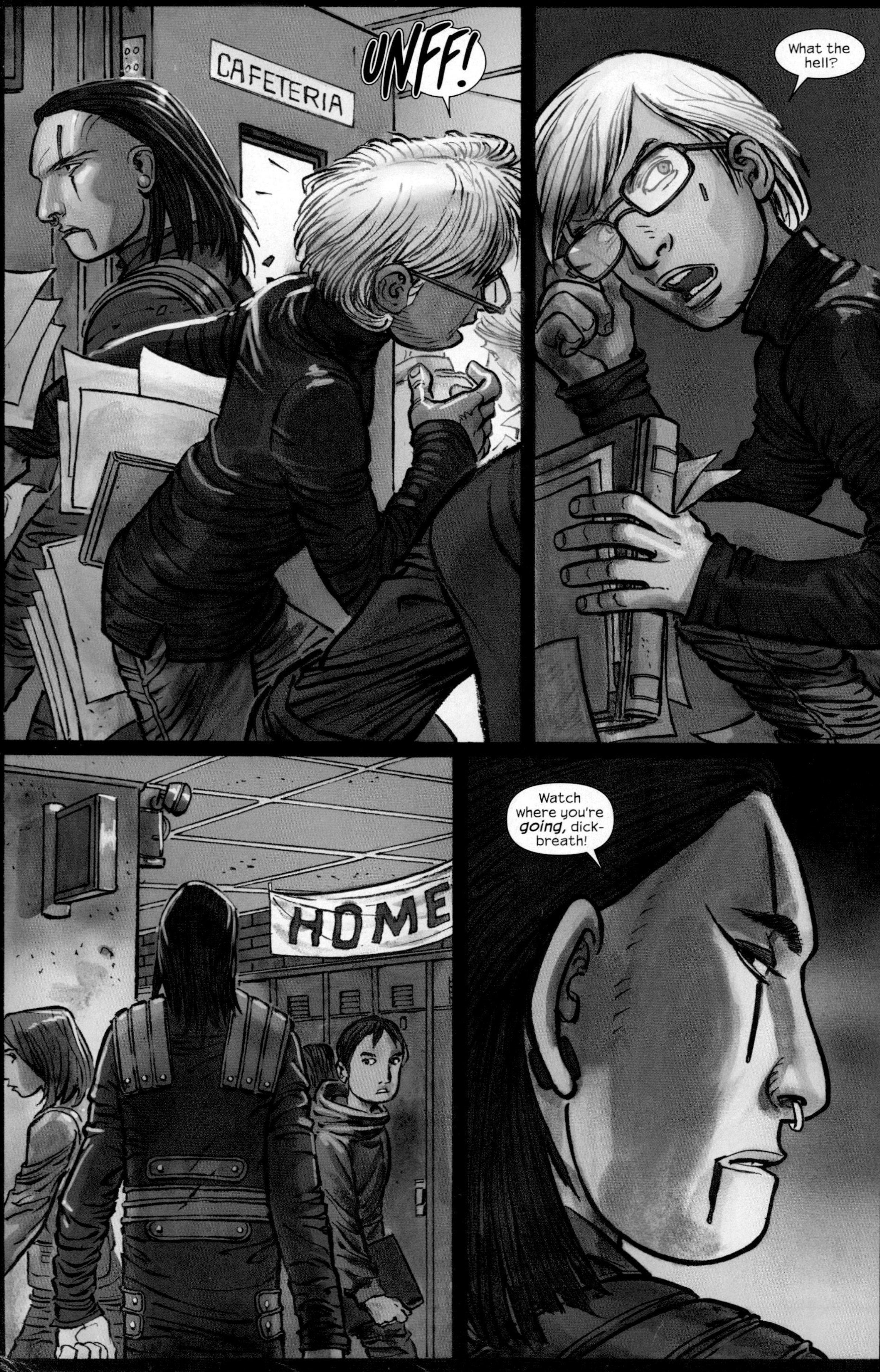
CAFETERIA
UNFF!
What the hell?
HOME
Watch where you're *going,* dick-breath!

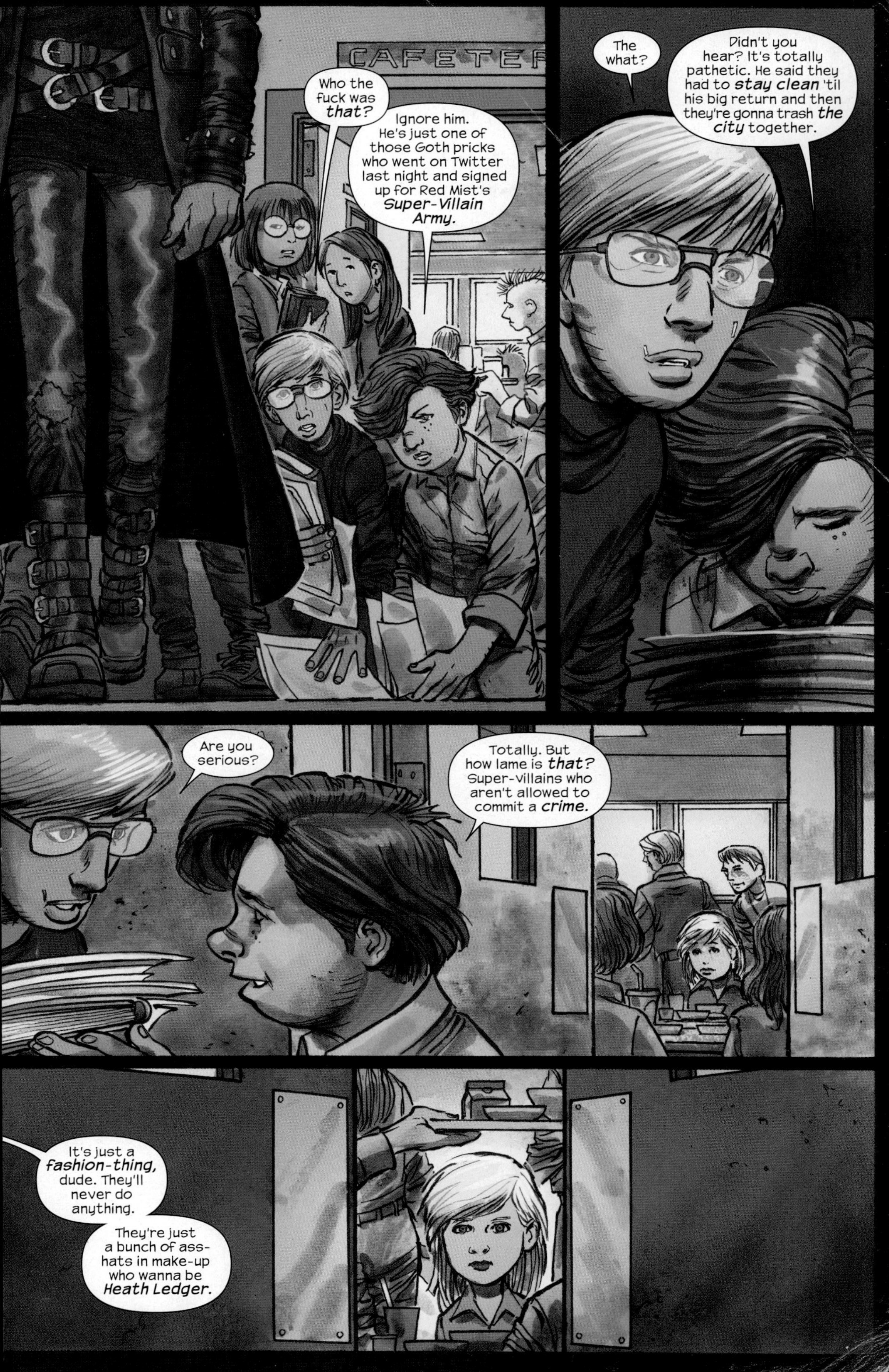
CAFETER
Who the fuck was *that?*
Ignore him. He's just one of those Goth pricks who went on Twitter last night and signed up for Red Mist's *Super-Villain Army.*
The what?
Didn't you hear? It's totally pathetic. He said they had to *stay clean* 'til his big return and then they're gonna trash *the city* together.
Are you serious?
Totally. But how lame is *that?* Super-villains who aren't allowed to commit a *crime.*
It's just a *fashion-thing,* dude. They'll never do anything.
They're just a bunch of ass-hats in make-up who wanna be *Heath Ledger.*

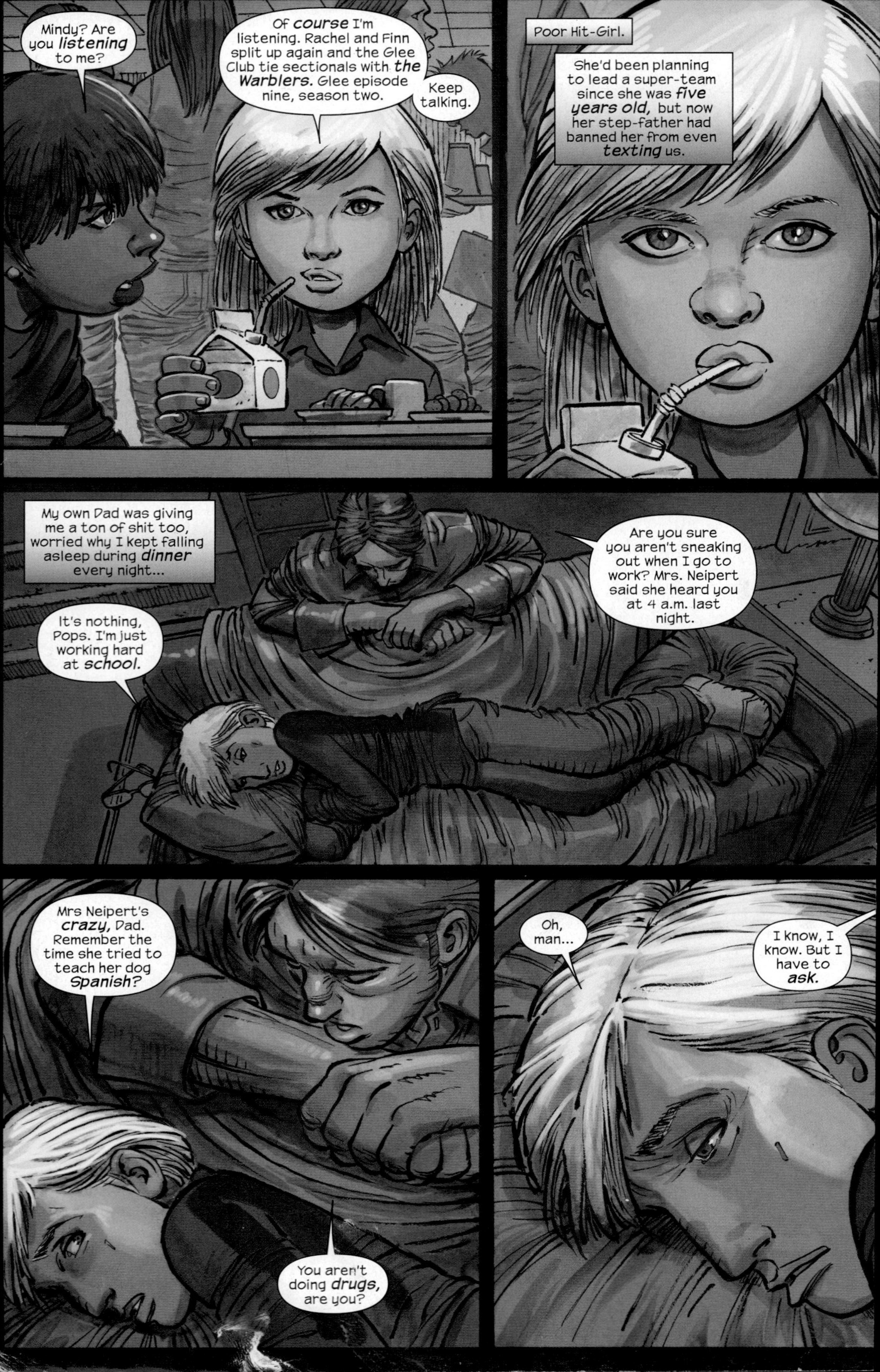
Mindy? Are you listening to me?
Of course I'm listening. Rachel and Finn split up again and the Glee Club tie sectionals with the Warblers. Glee episode nine, season two.
Keep talking.
Poor Hit-Girl.
She'd been planning to lead a super-team since she was five years old, but now her step-father had banned her from even texting us.
My own Dad was giving me a ton of shit too, worried why I kept falling asleep during dinner every night...
Are you sure you aren't sneaking out when I go to work? Mrs. Neipert said she heard you at 4 a.m. last night.
It's nothing, Pops. I'm just working hard at school.
Mrs Neipert's crazy, Dad. Remember the time she tried to teach her dog Spanish?
You aren't doing drugs, are you?
Oh, man...
I know, I know. But I have to ask.

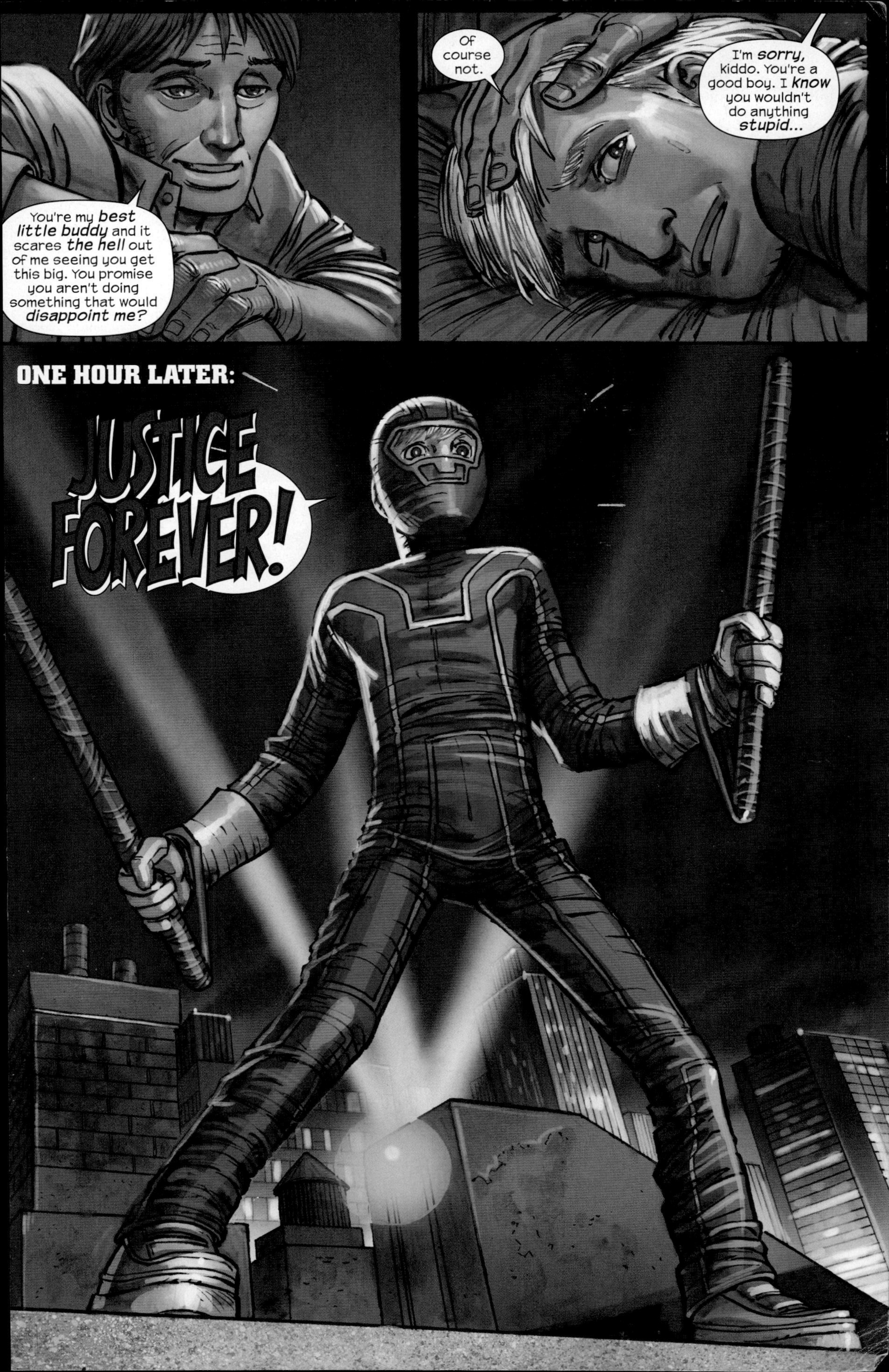
You're my best little buddy and it scares the hell out of me seeing you get this big. You promise you aren't doing something that would disappoint me?
Of course not.
I'm sorry, kiddo. You're a good boy. I know you wouldn't do anything stupid...
ONE HOUR LATER:
JUSTICE FOREVER!

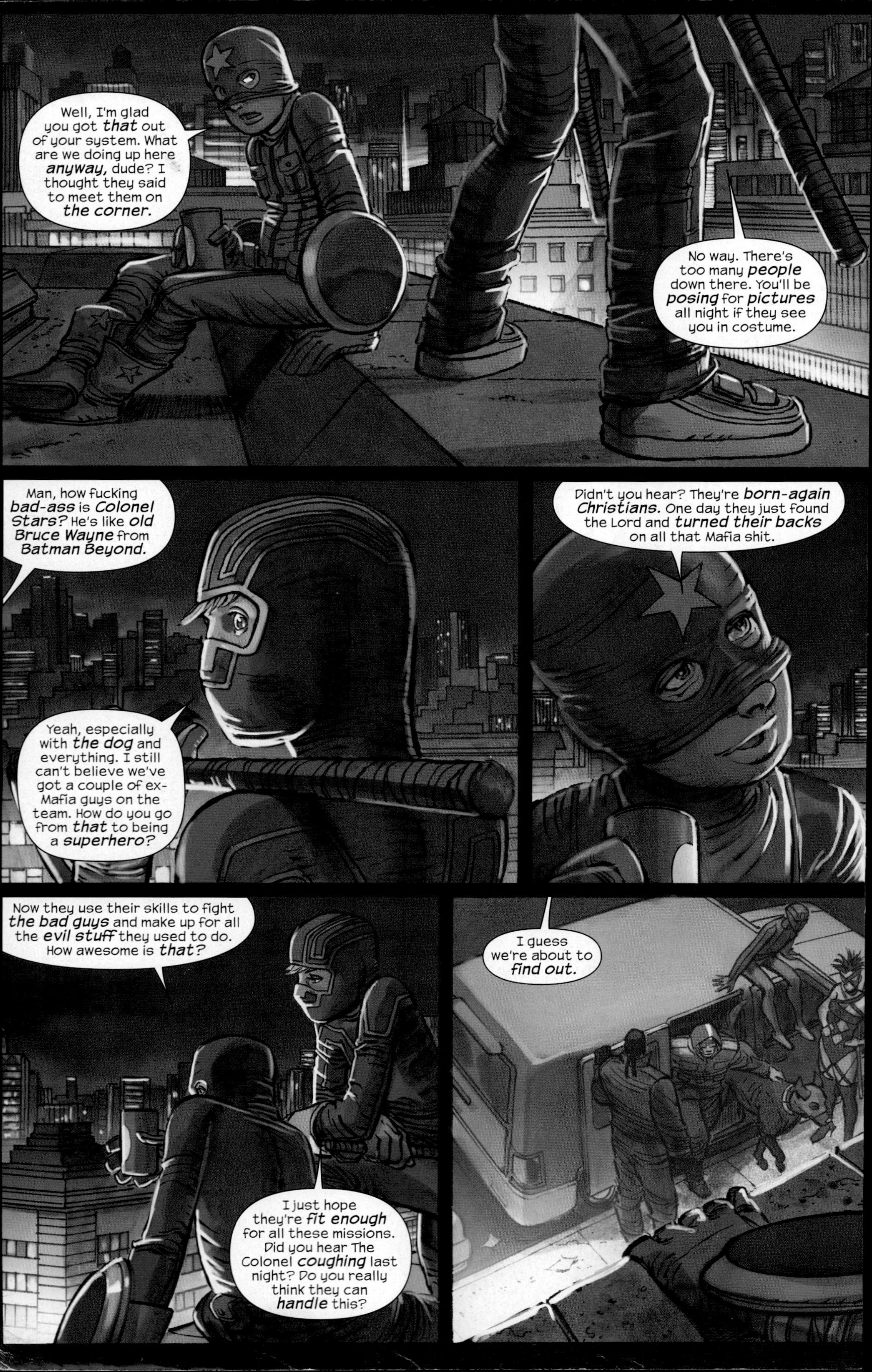
Well, I'm glad you got that out of your system. What are we doing up here anyway, dude? I thought they said to meet them on the corner.
No way. There's too many people down there. You'll be posing for pictures all night if they see you in costume.
Man, how fucking bad-ass is Colonel Stars? He's like old Bruce Wayne from Batman Beyond.
Yeah, especially with the dog and everything. I still can't believe we've got a couple of ex-Mafia guys on the team. How do you go from that to being a superhero?
Didn't you hear? They're born-again Christians. One day they just found the Lord and turned their backs on all that Mafia shit.
Now they use their skills to fight the bad guys and make up for all the evil stuff they used to do. How awesome is that?
I just hope they're fit enough for all these missions. Did you hear The Colonel coughing last night? Do you really think they can handle this?
I guess we're about to find out.

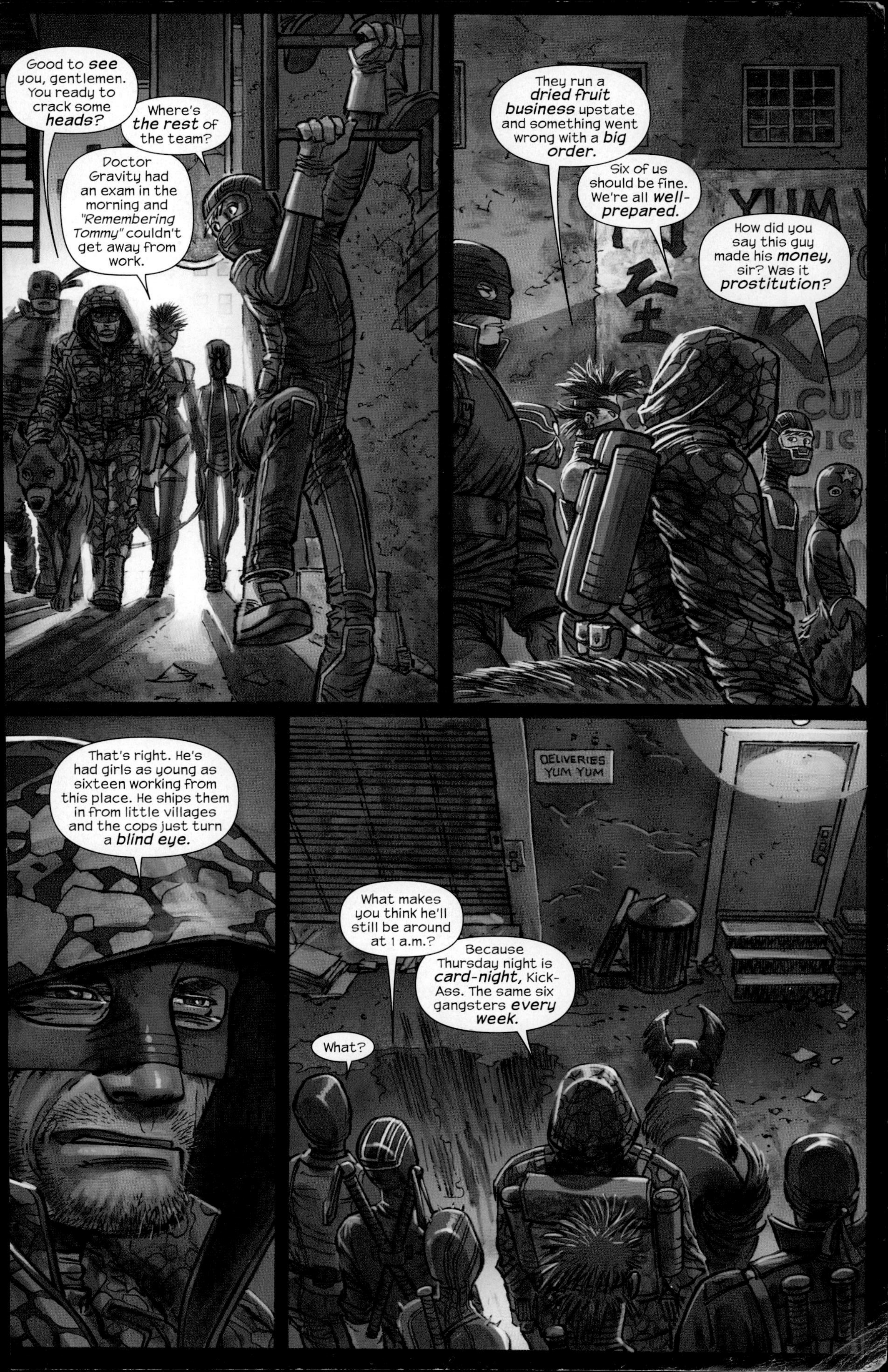
Good to **see** you, gentlemen. You ready to crack some **heads?**
Where's **the rest** of the team?
Doctor Gravity had an exam in the morning and *"Remembering Tommy"* couldn't get away from work.
They run a **dried fruit business** upstate and something went wrong with a **big order.**
Six of us should be fine. We're all **well-prepared.**
YUM
CUI
How did you say this guy made his **money,** sir? Was it **prostitution?**
That's right. He's had girls as young as sixteen working from this place. He ships them in from little villages and the cops just turn a **blind eye.**
DELIVERIES YUM YUM
What makes you think he'll still be around at 1 a.m.?
Because Thursday night is **card-night,** Kick-Ass. The same six gangsters **every week.**
What?

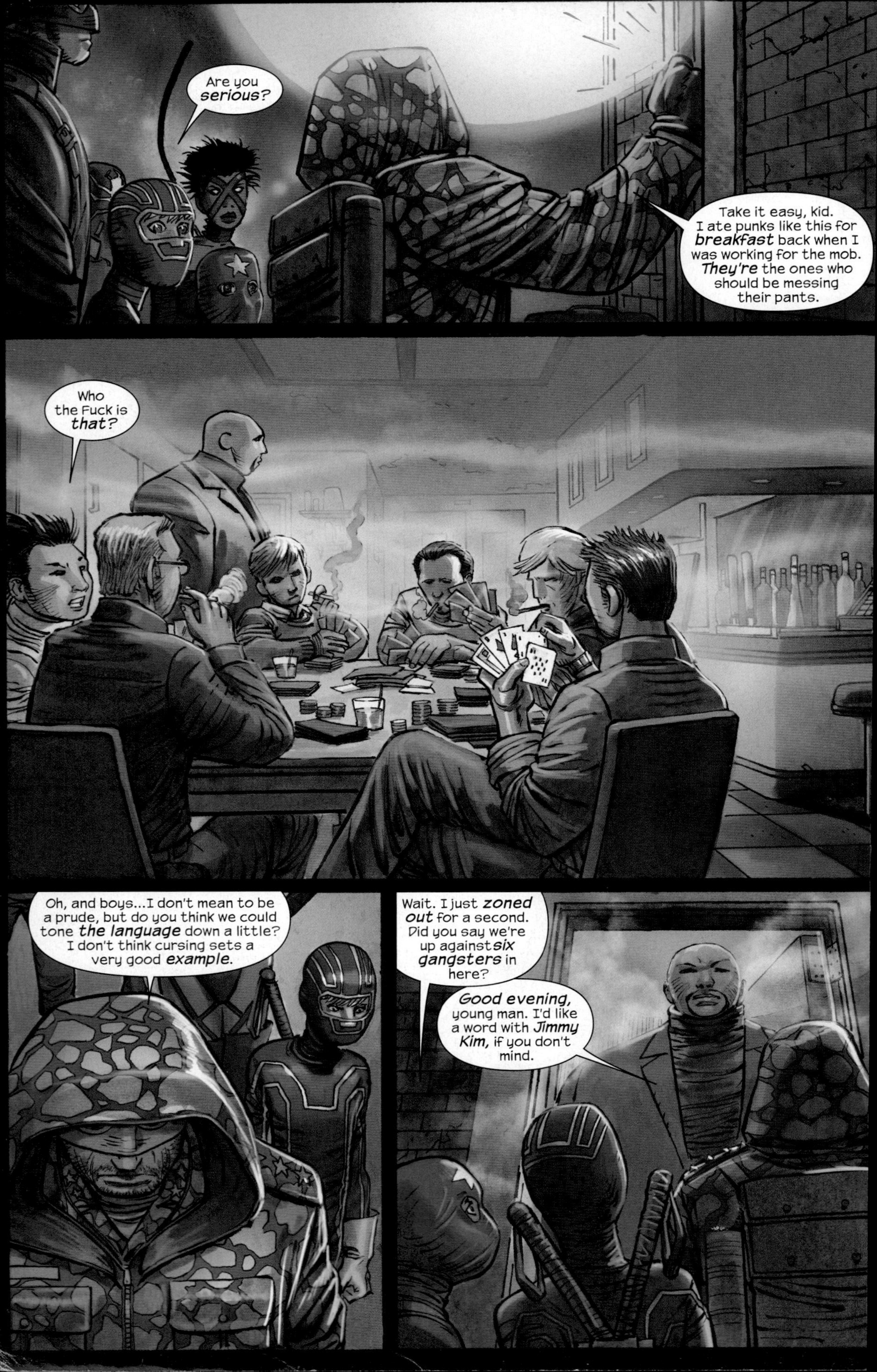

Are you serious?
Take it easy, kid. I ate punks like this for breakfast back when I was working for the mob. They're the ones who should be messing their pants.
Who the Fuck is that?
Oh, and boys...I don't mean to be a prude, but do you think we could tone the language down a little? I don't think cursing sets a very good example.
Wait. I just zoned out for a second. Did you say we're up against six gangsters in here?
Good evening, young man. I'd like a word with Jimmy Kim, if you don't mind.

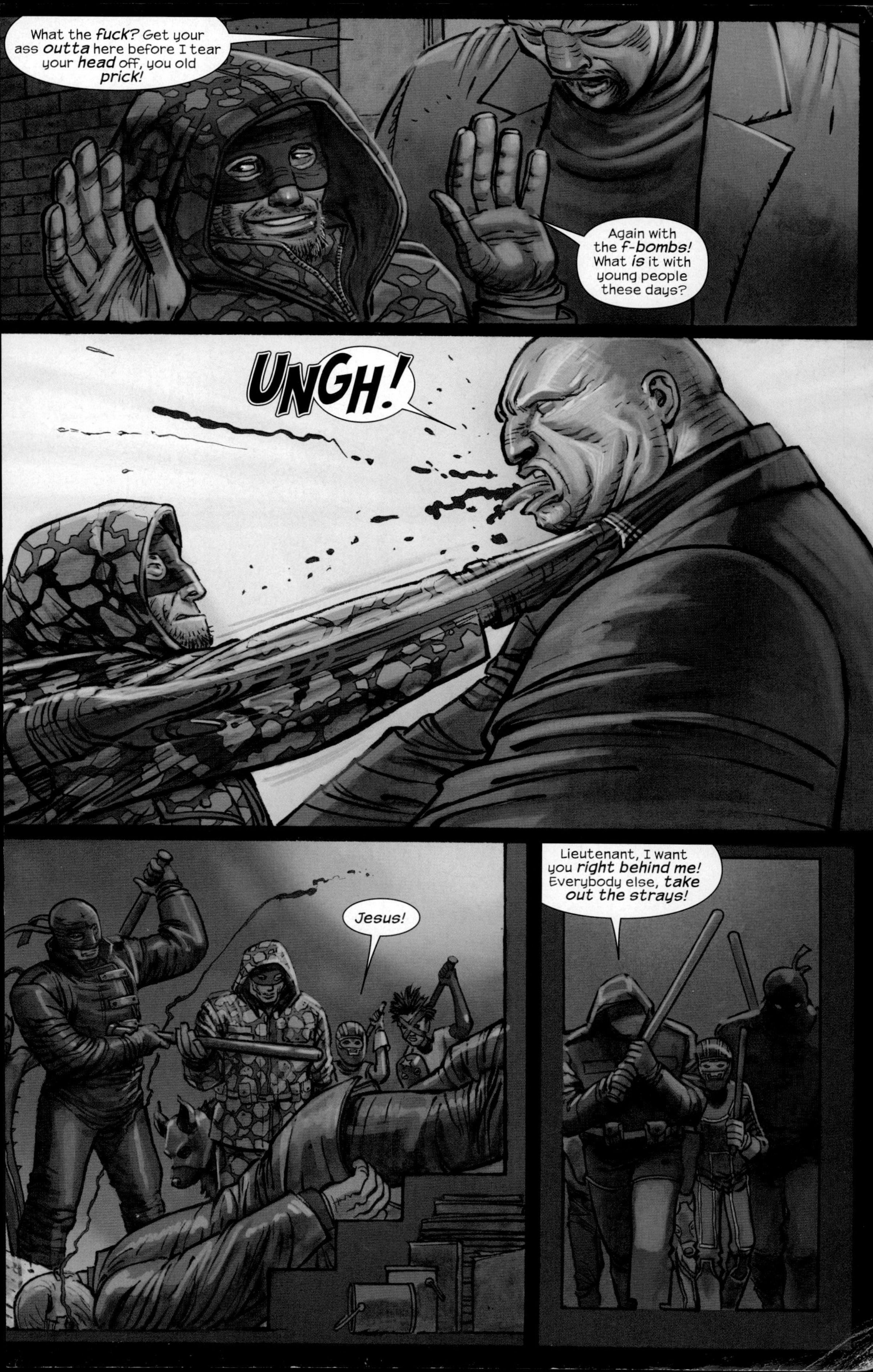
What the *fuck?* Get your ass *outta* here before I tear your *head* off, you old *prick!*
Again with the *f-bombs!* What *is* it with young people these days?
UNGH!
Jesus!
Lieutenant, I want you *right behind me!* Everybody else, *take out the strays!*

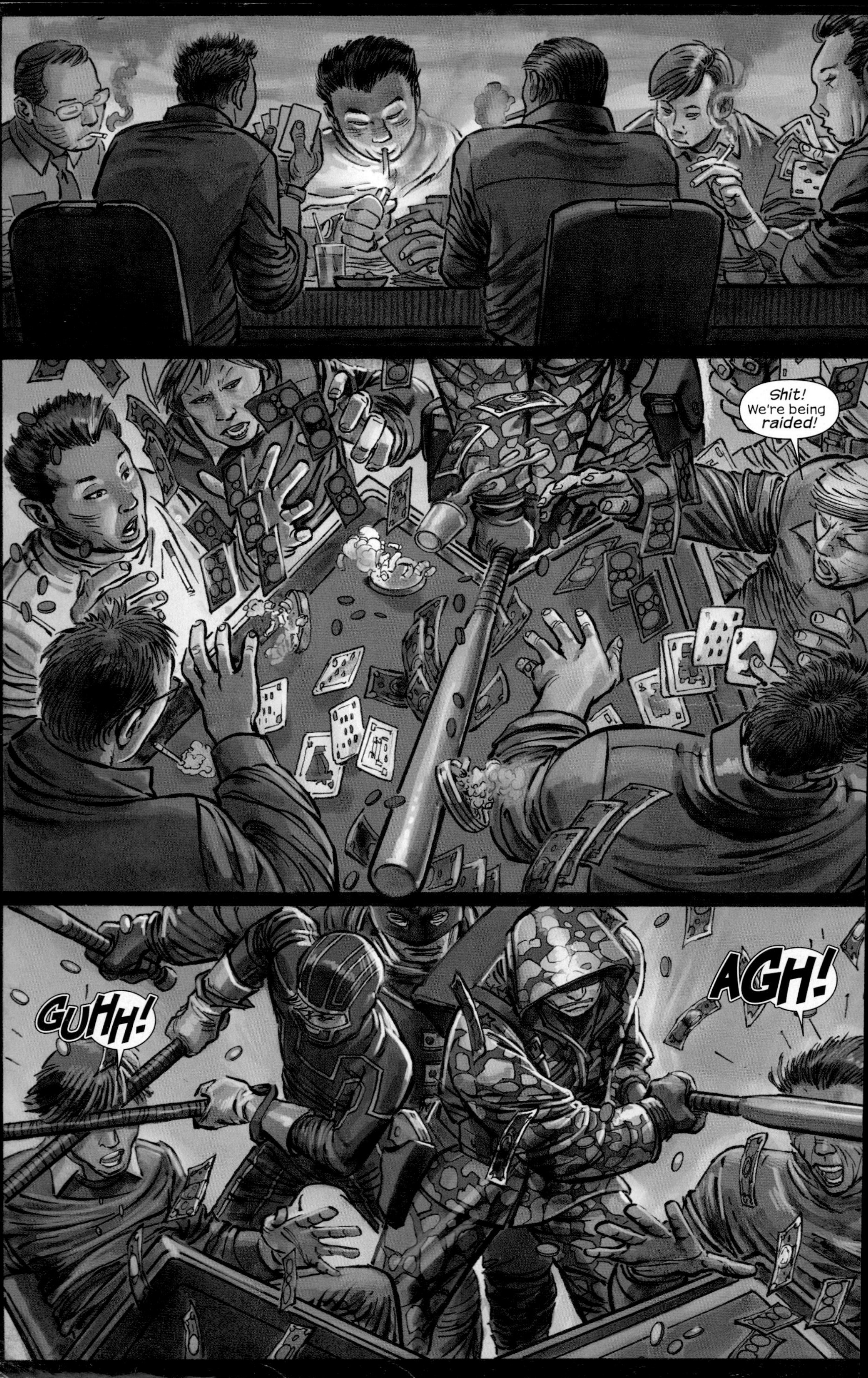
Shit! We're being raided!
GUHH!
AGH!

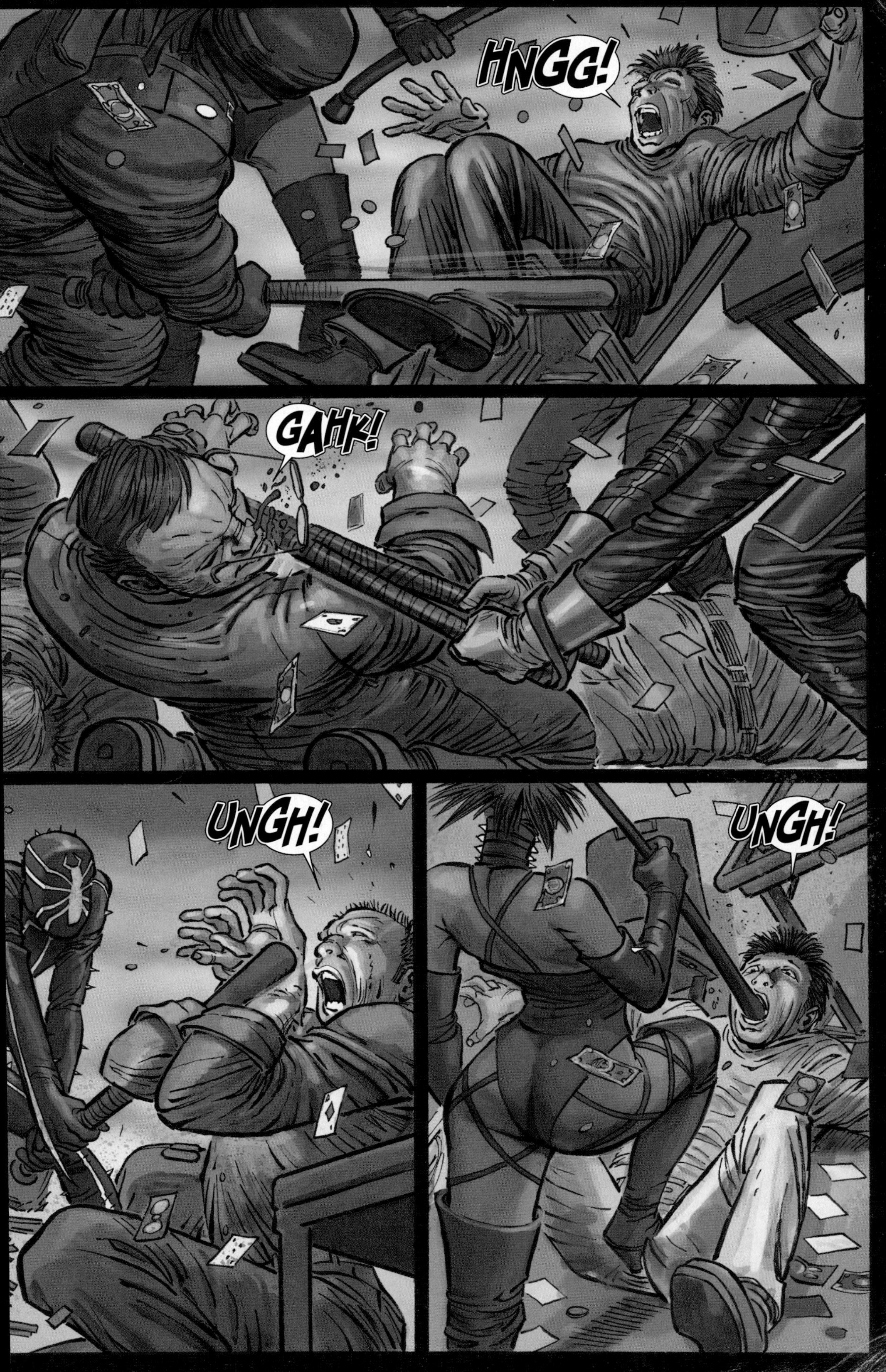
HNGG!
GAHK!
UNGH!
UNGH!

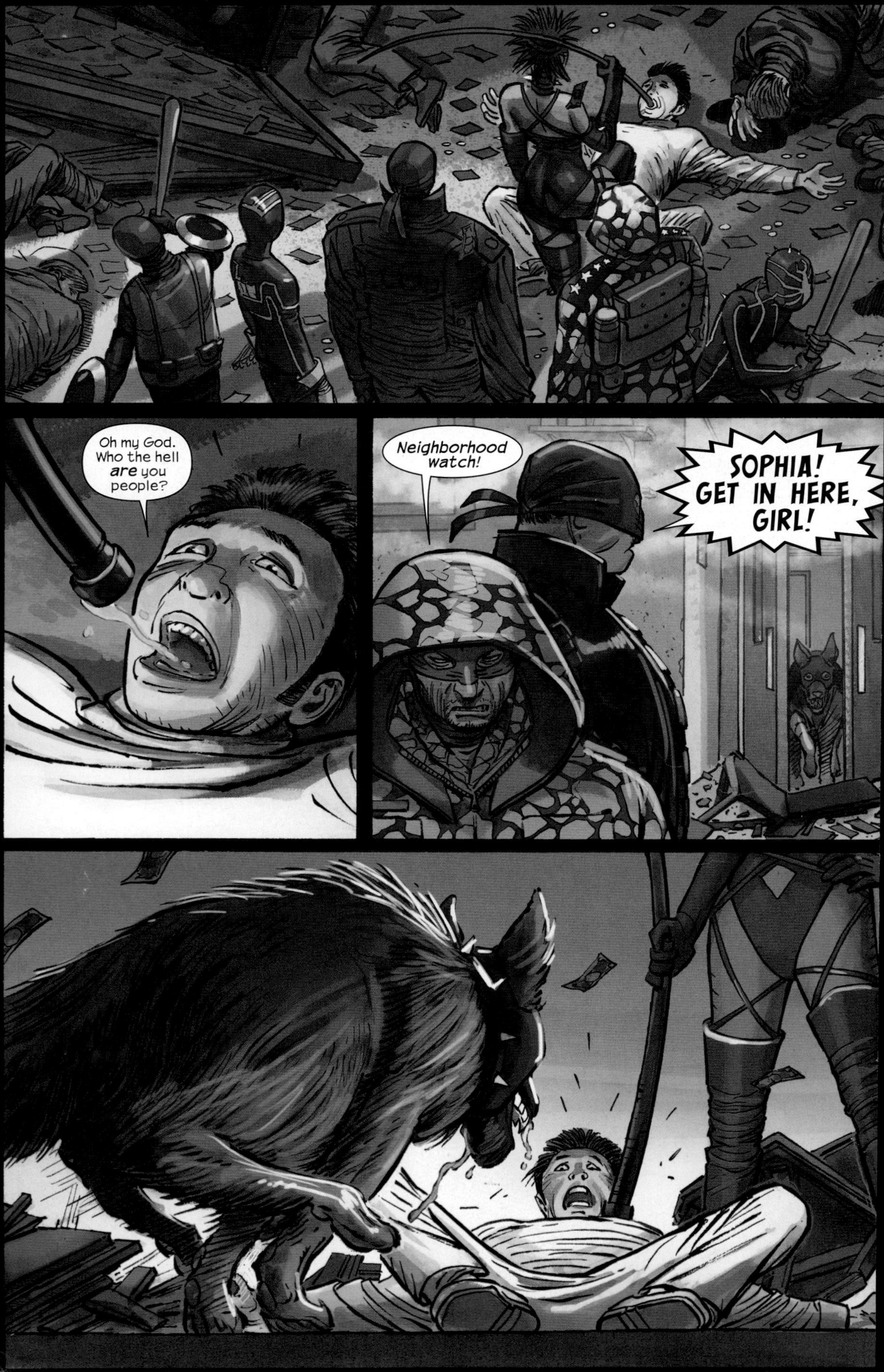
Oh my God. Who the hell *are* you people?
Neighborhood watch!
SOPHIA! GET IN HERE, GIRL!

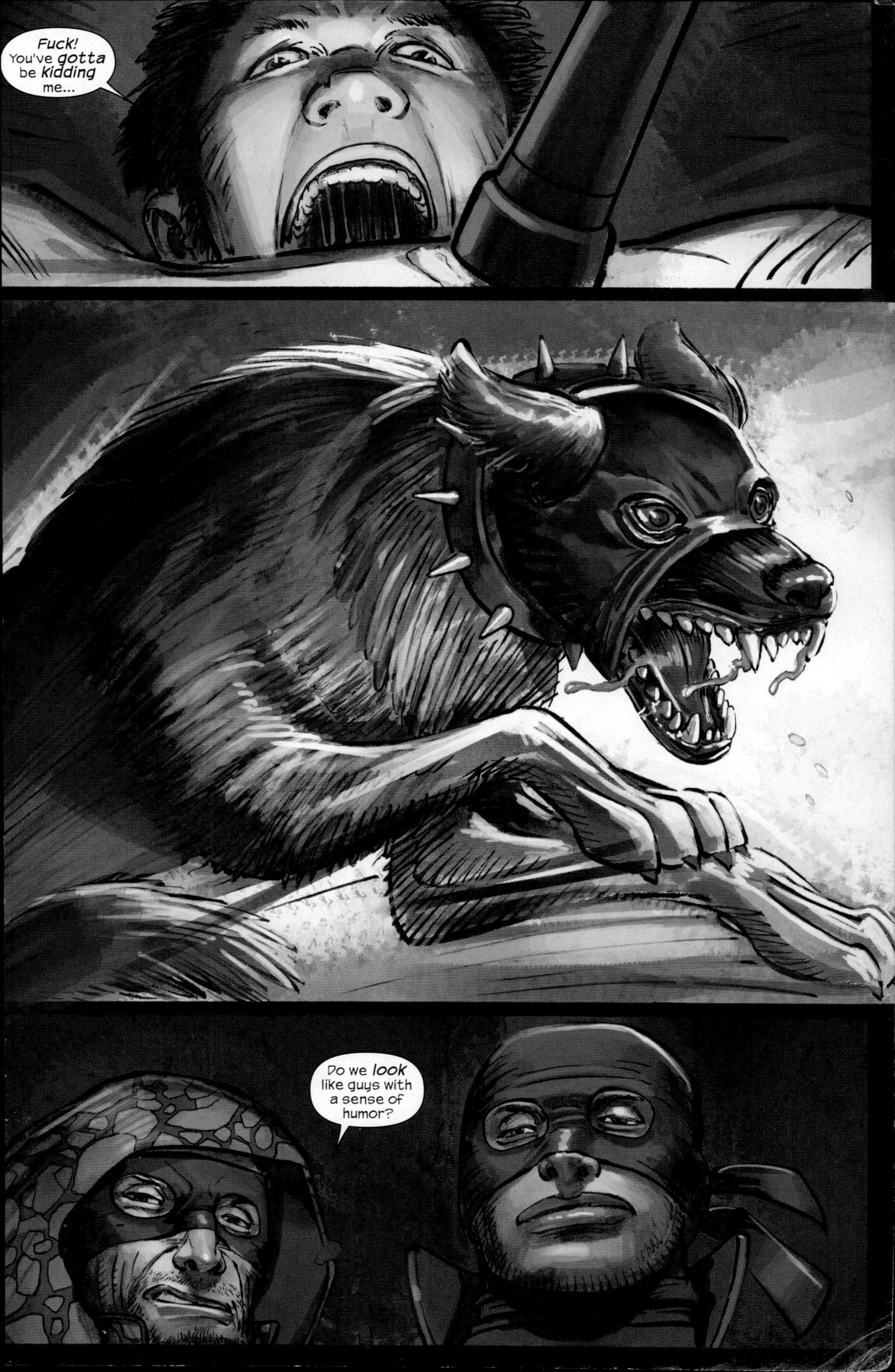
Fuck! You've *gotta* be *kidding* me...
Do we *look* like guys with a sense of humor?

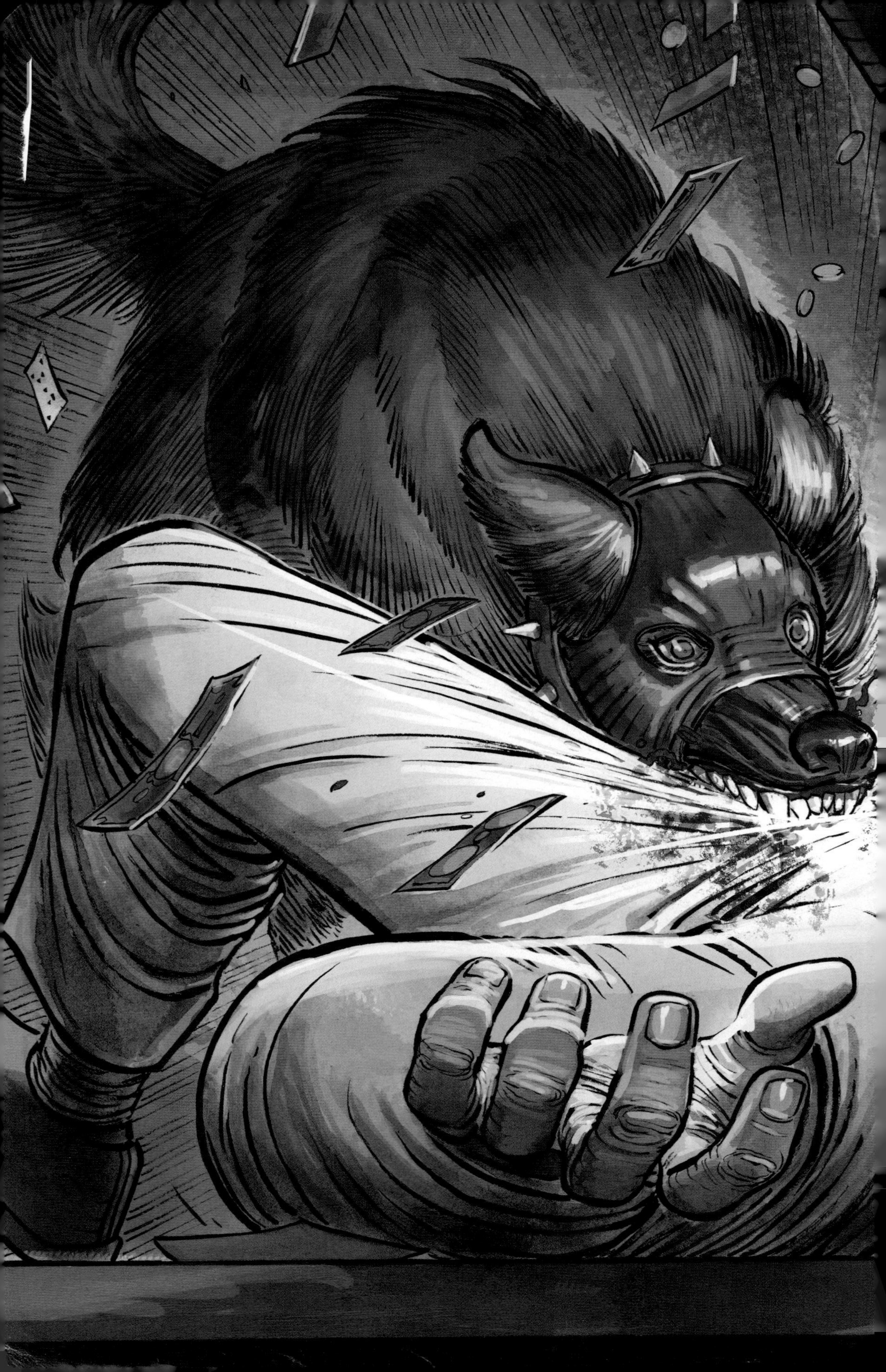

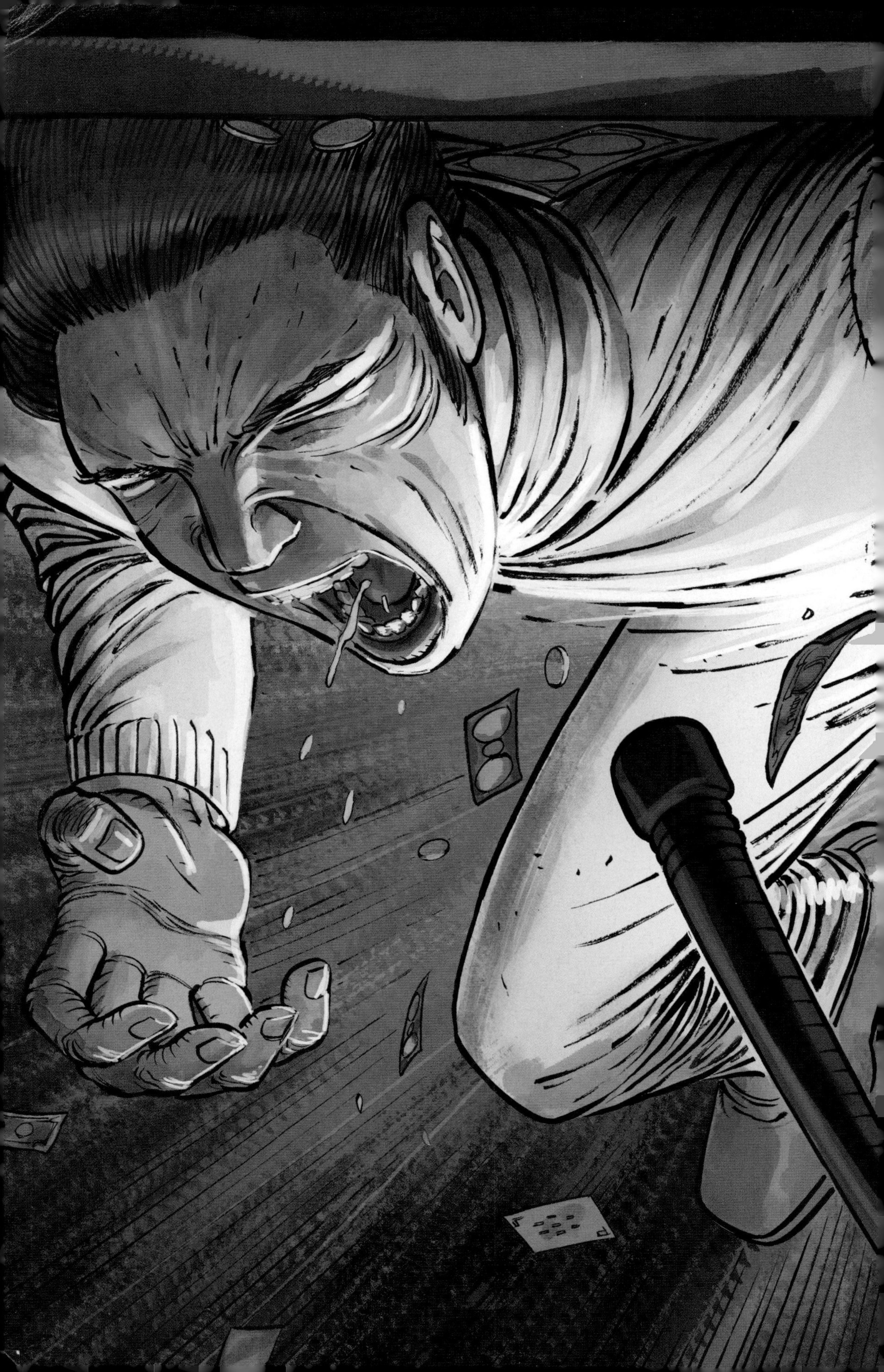

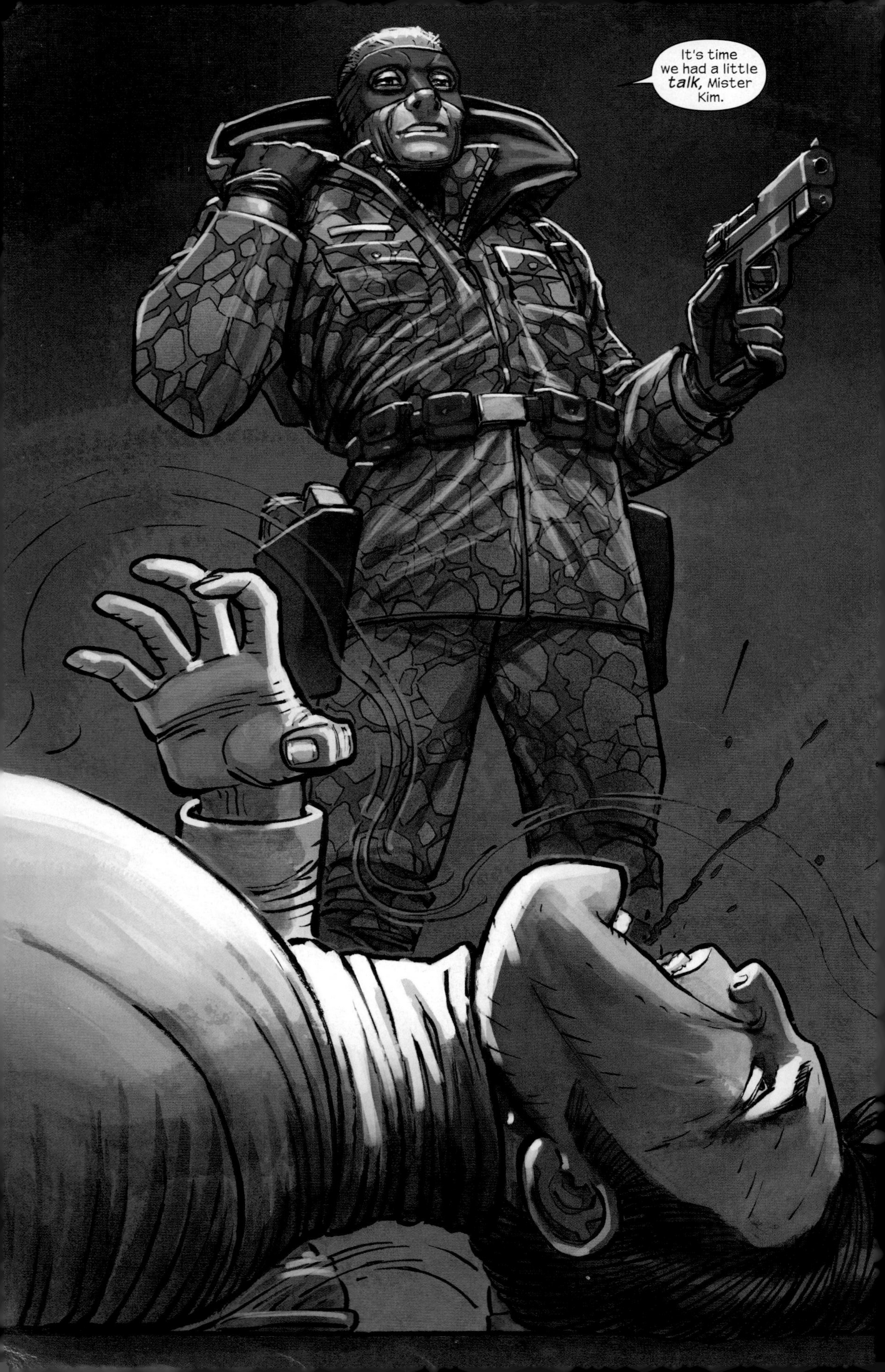
It's time we had a little *talk,* Mister Kim.

THREE

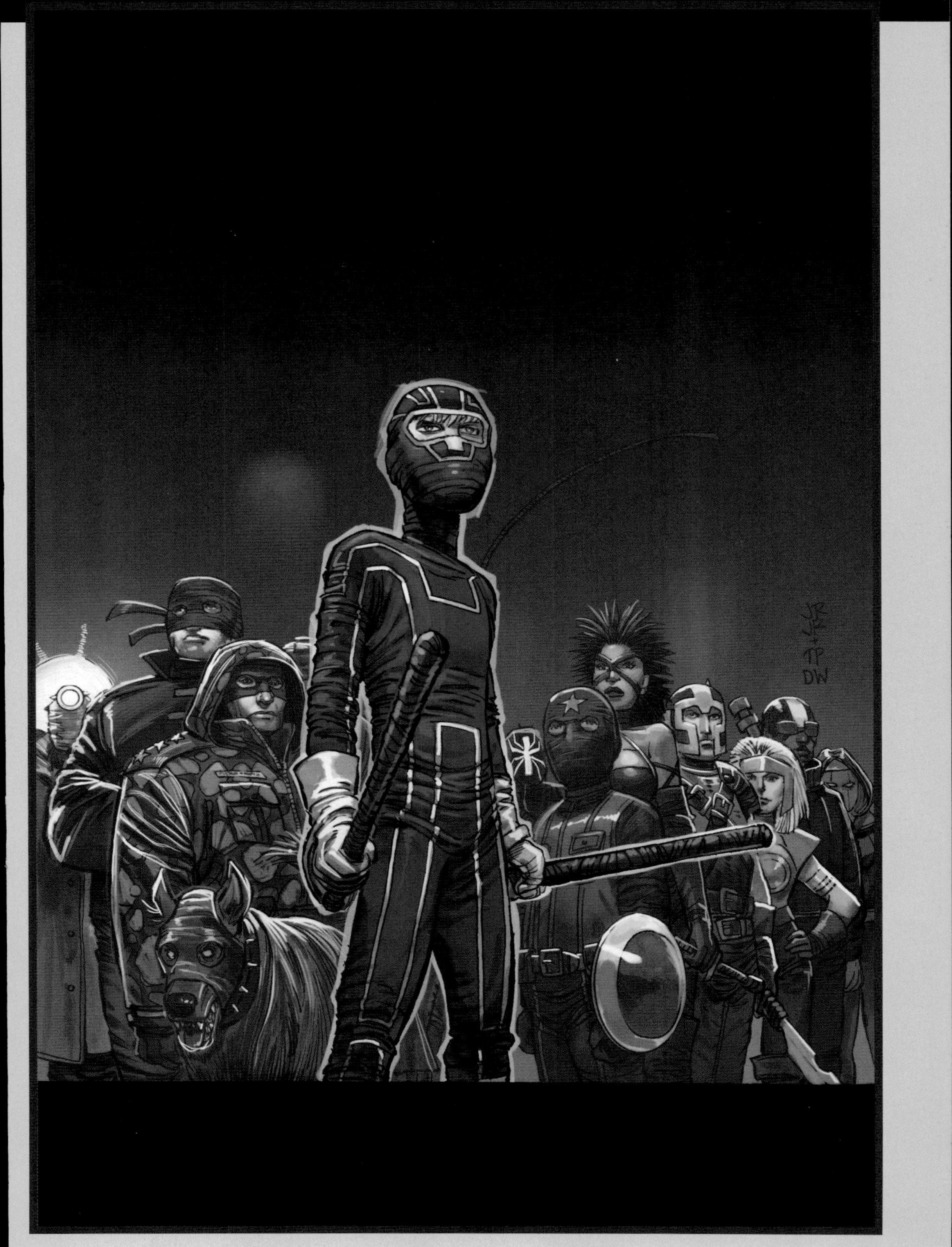

JR
JR
+
TP
DW

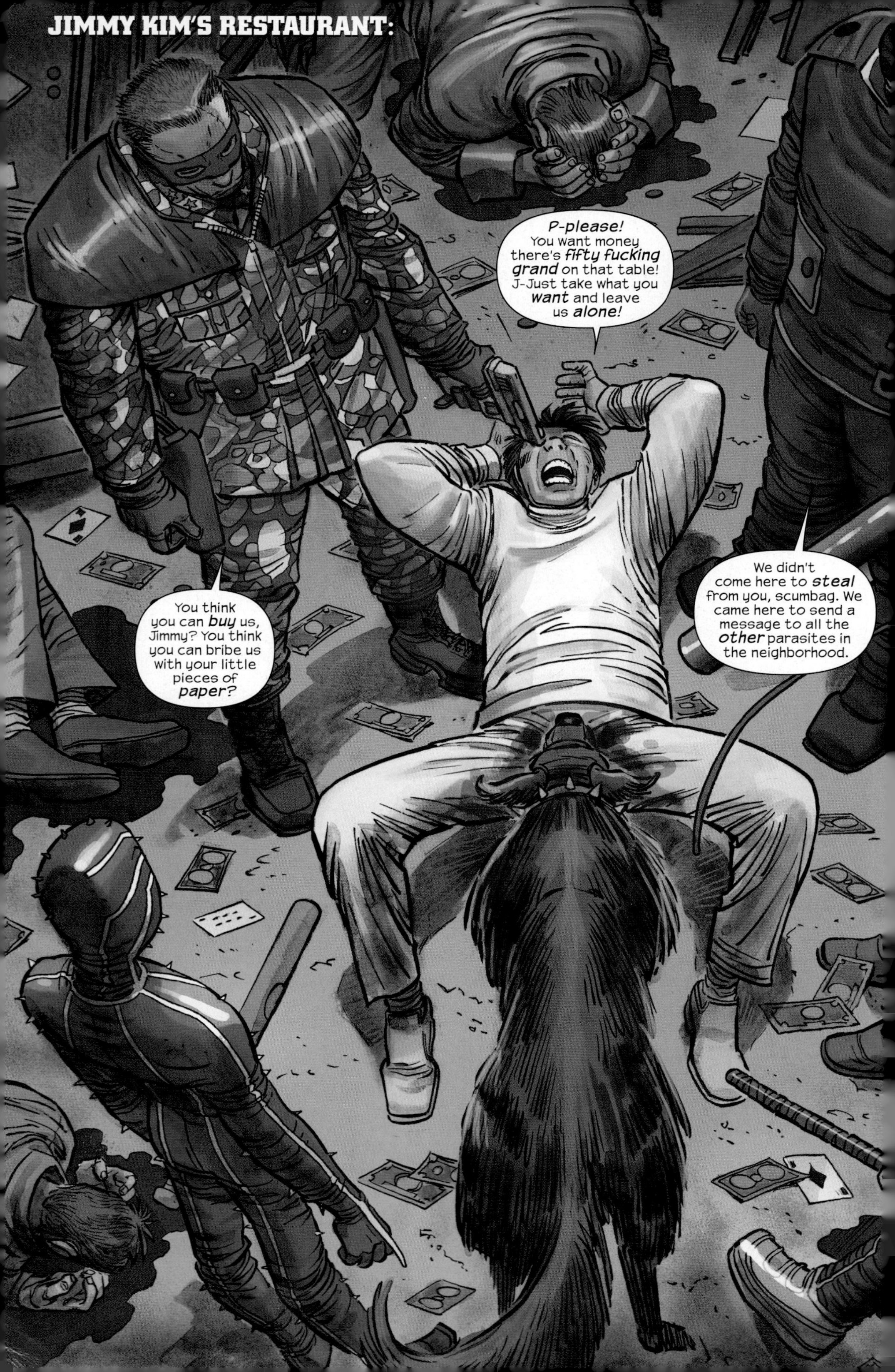
JIMMY KIM'S RESTAURANT:
P-please! You want money there's fifty fucking grand on that table! J-Just take what you want and leave us alone!
You think you can buy us, Jimmy? You think you can bribe us with your little pieces of paper?
We didn't come here to steal from you, scumbag. We came here to send a message to all the other parasites in the neighborhood.

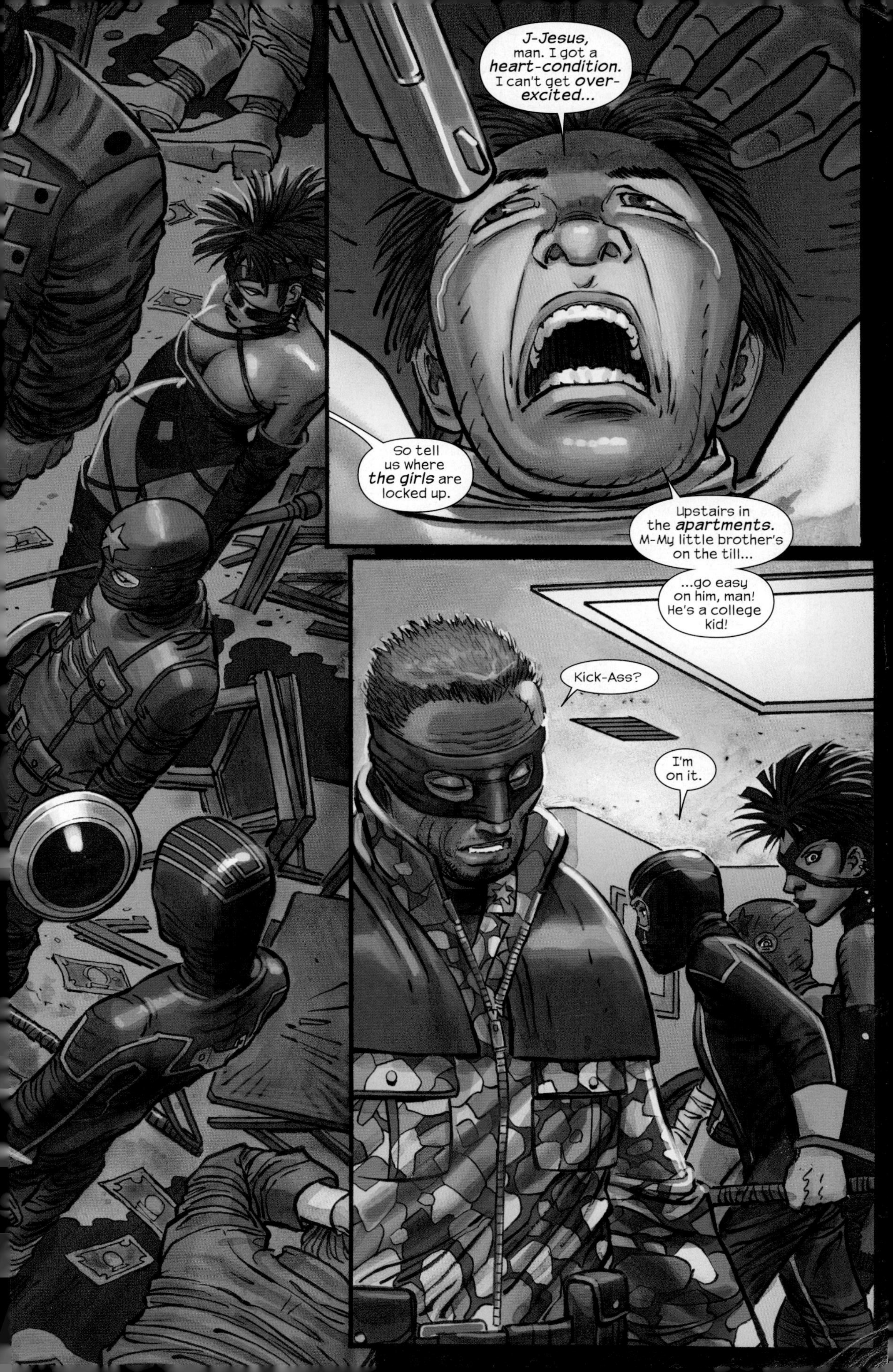
J-Jesus, man. I got a heart-condition. I can't get over-excited...
So tell us where the girls are locked up.
Upstairs in the apartments. M-My little brother's on the till...
...go easy on him, man! He's a college kid!
Kick-Ass?
I'm on it.

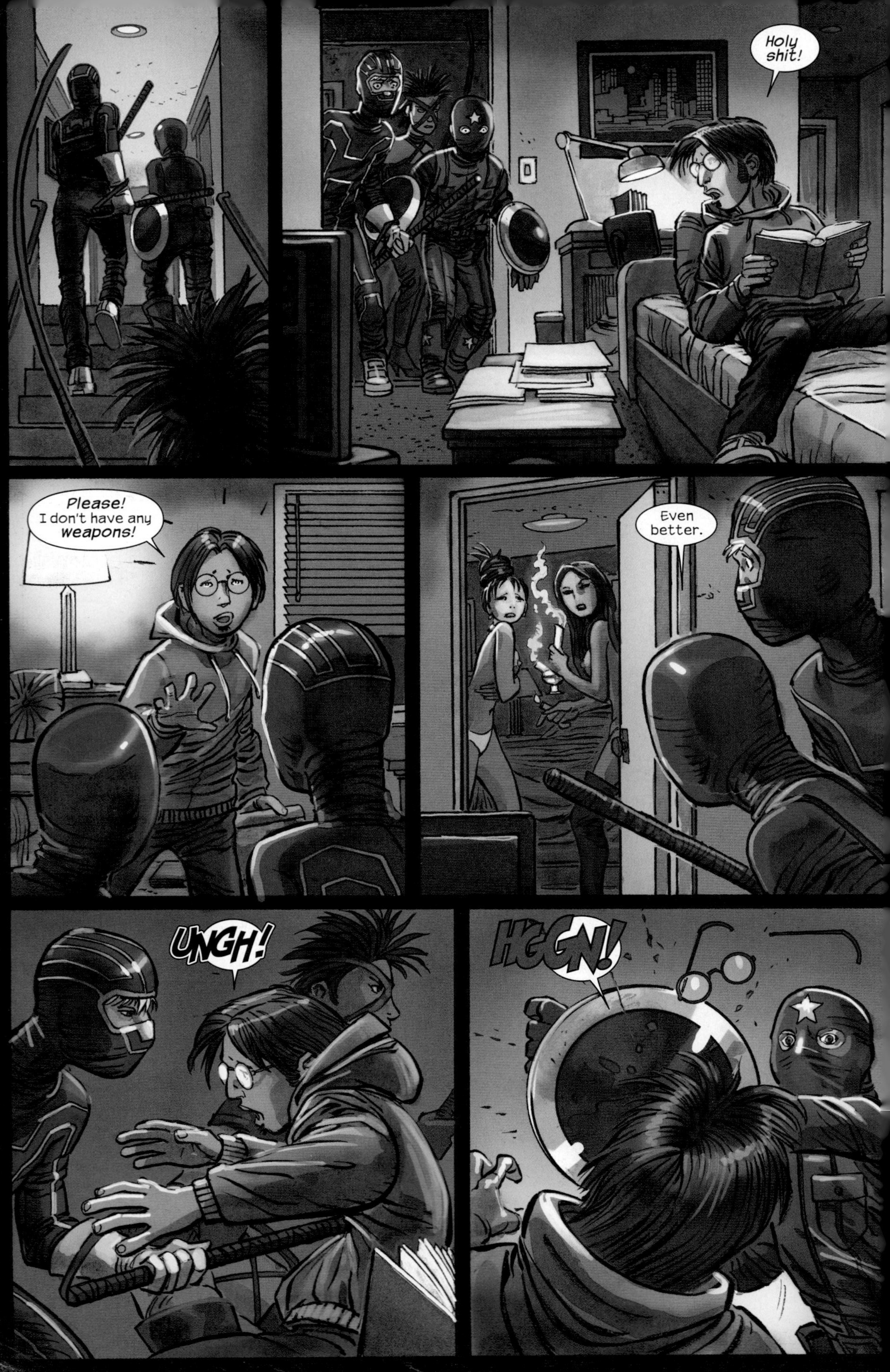
Holy shit!
Please! I don't have any weapons!
Even better.
UNGH!
HGGN!

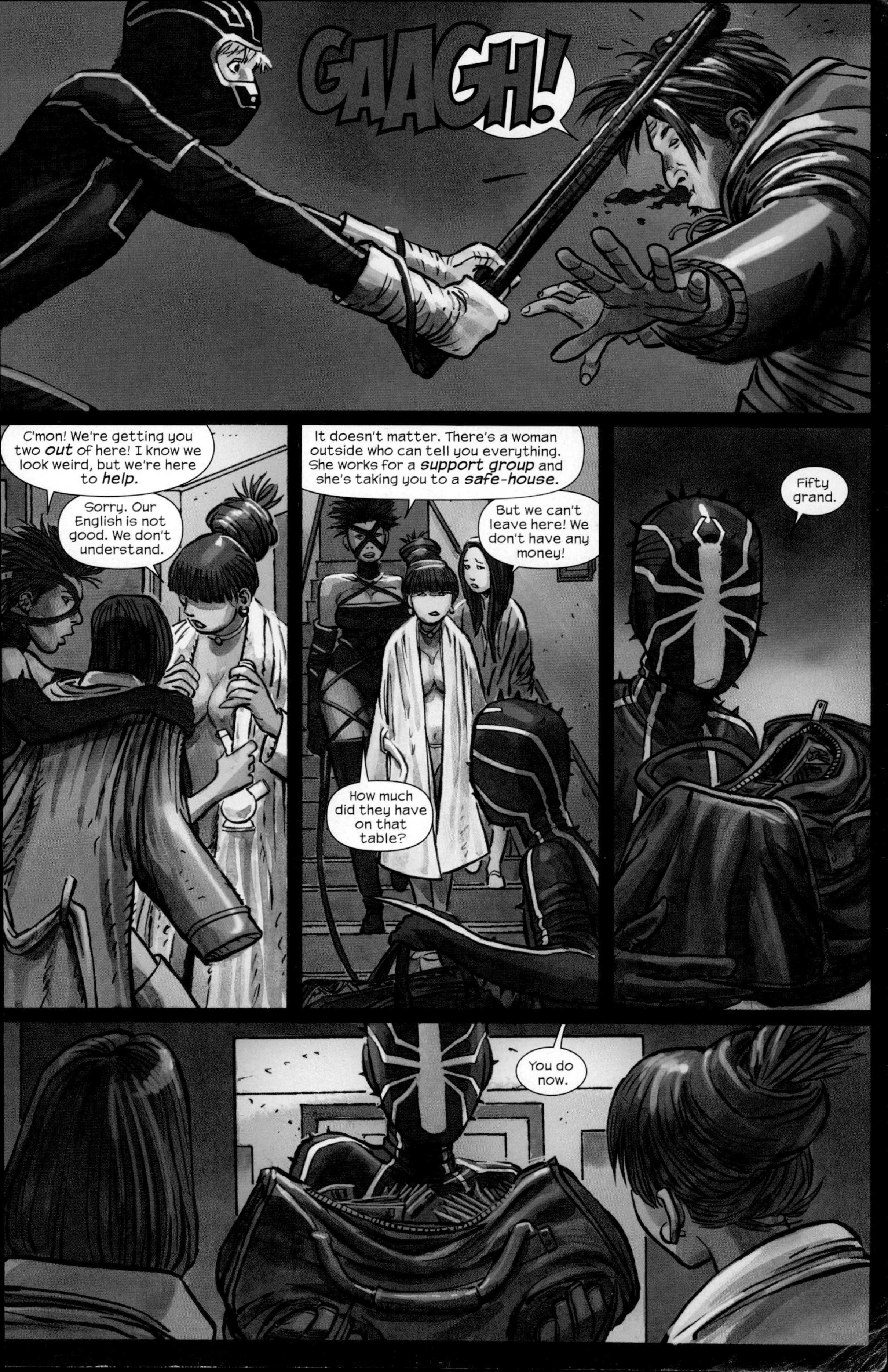
GAAGH!
C'mon! We're getting you two *out* of here! I know we look weird, but we're here to *help.*
Sorry. Our English is not good. We don't understand.
It doesn't matter. There's a woman outside who can tell you everything. She works for a *support group* and she's taking you to a *safe-house.*
But we can't leave here! We don't have any money!
How much did they have on that table?
Fifty grand.
You do now.

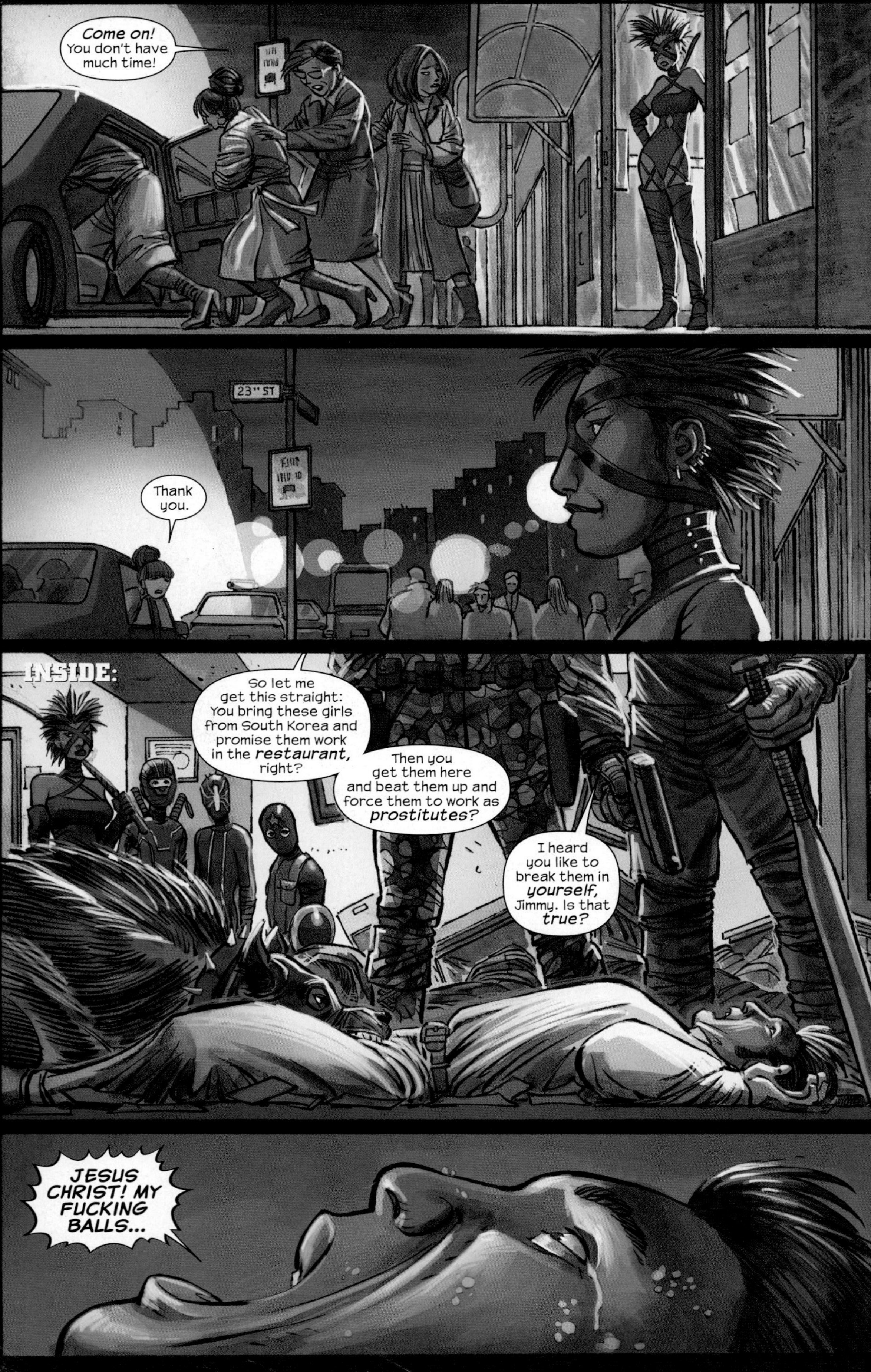
Come on! You don't have much time!
Thank you.
INSIDE:
So let me get this straight: You bring these girls from South Korea and promise them work in the restaurant, right?
Then you get them here and beat them up and force them to work as prostitutes?
I heard you like to break them in yourself, Jimmy. Is that true?
JESUS CHRIST! MY FUCKING BALLS...

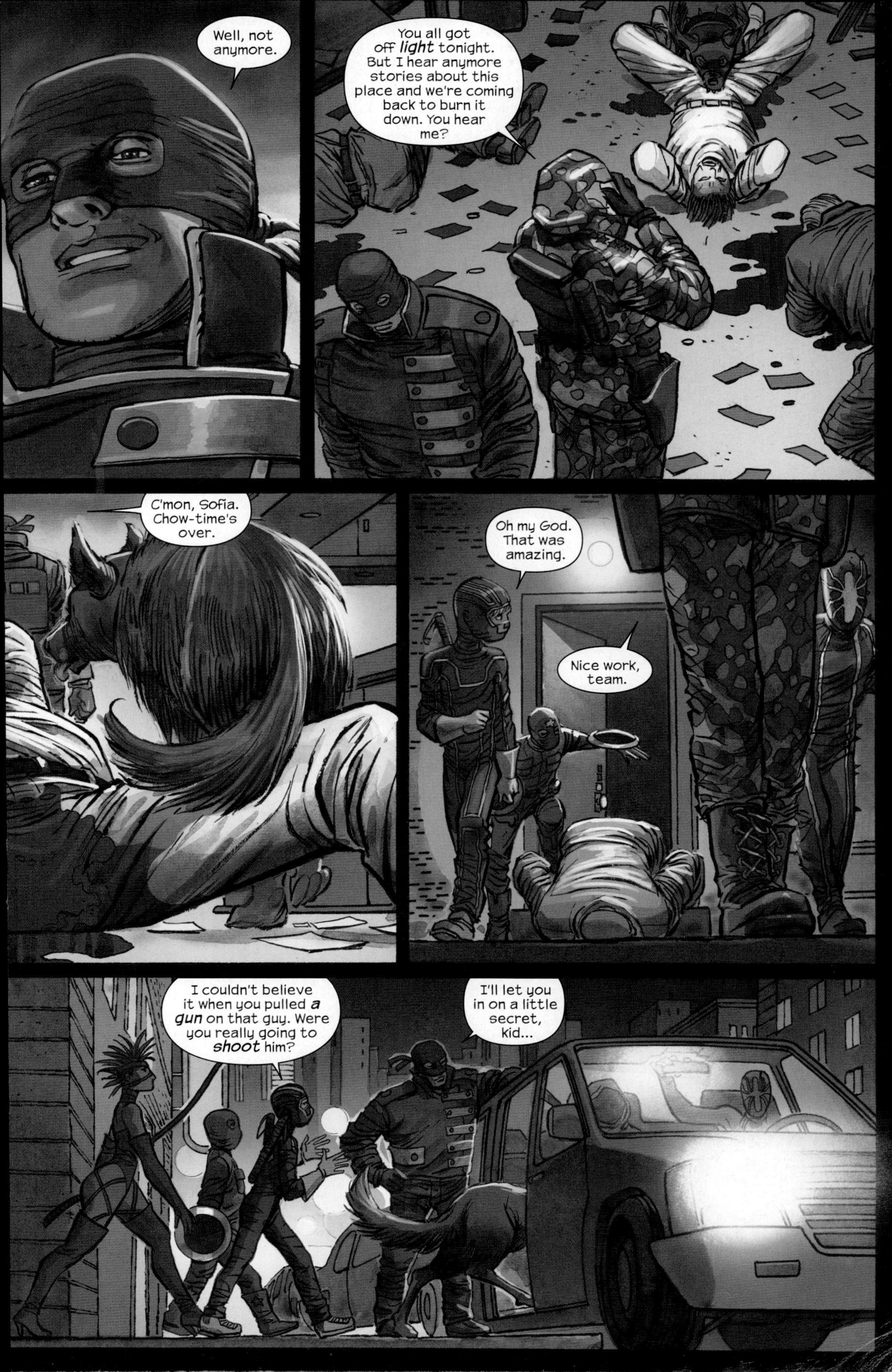
Well, not anymore.
You all got off *light* tonight. But I hear anymore stories about this place and we're coming back to burn it down. You hear me?
C'mon, Sofia. Chow-time's over.
Oh my God. That was amazing.
Nice work, team.
I couldn't believe it when you pulled *a gun* on that guy. Were you really going to *shoot* him?
I'll let you in on a little secret, kid...

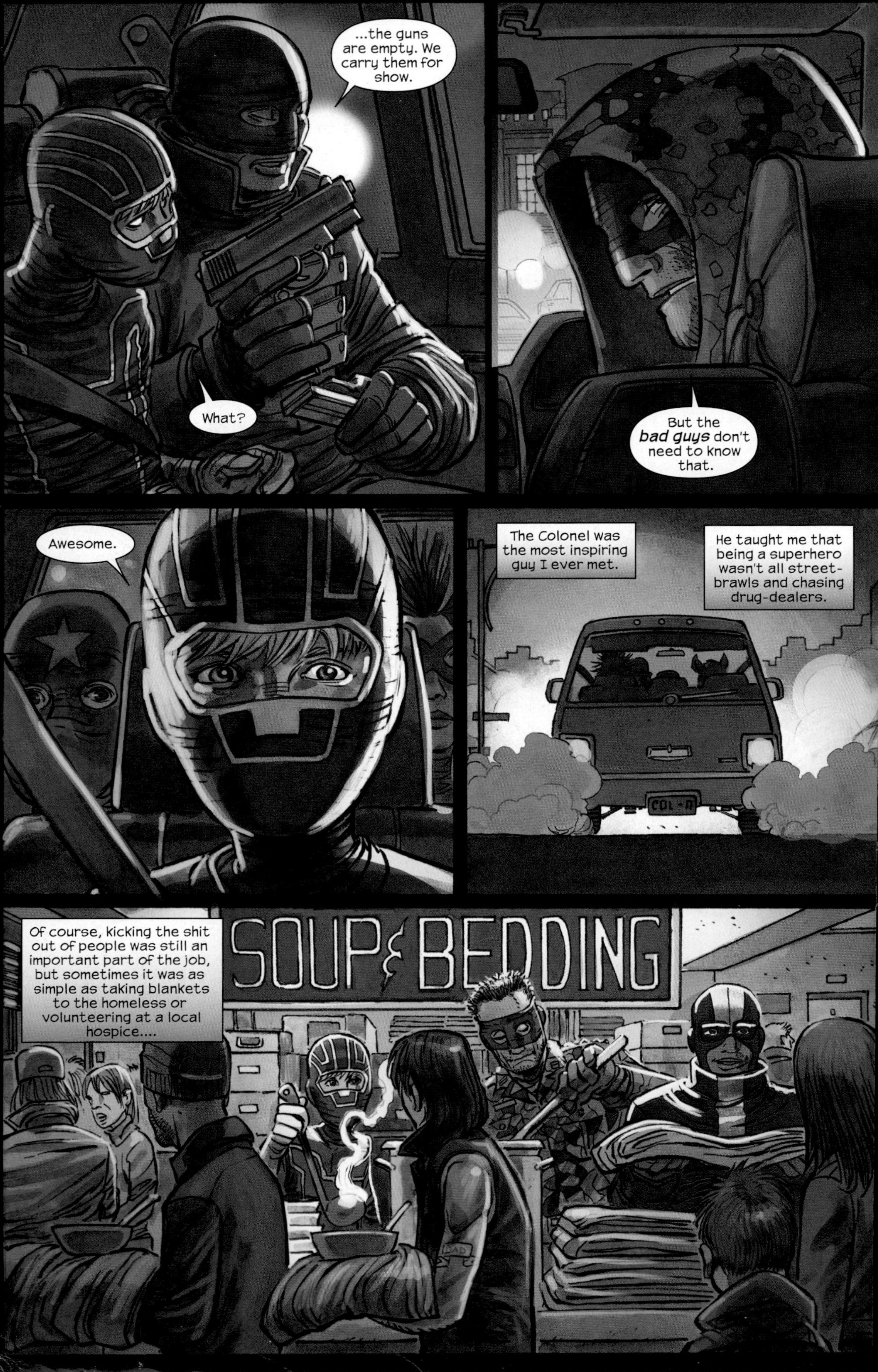
...the guns are empty. We carry them for show.
What?
But the *bad guys* don't need to know that.
Awesome.
The Colonel was the most inspiring guy I ever met.
He taught me that being a superhero wasn't all street-brawls and chasing drug-dealers.
COL-A
Of course, kicking the shit out of people was still an important part of the job, but sometimes it was as simple as taking blankets to the homeless or volunteering at a local hospice....
SOUP & BEDDING
DAD

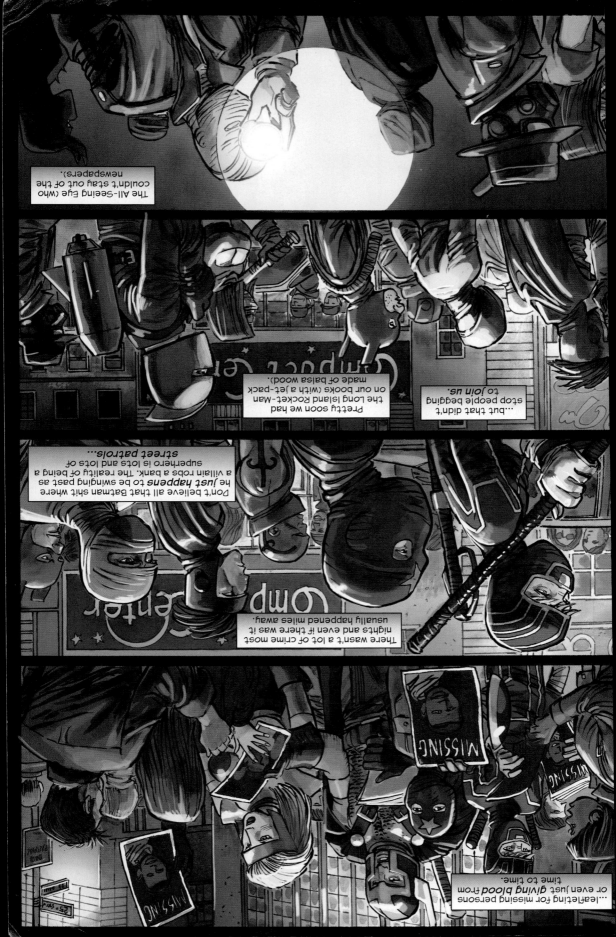

The All-Seeing Eye (who couldn't stay out of the newspapers).

Pretty soon we had the Long Island Rocket-Man on our books (with a jet-pack made of balsa wood).

...but that didn't stop people begging to join us.

Don't believe all that Batman shit where he *just happens* to be swinging past as a villain robs a bank. The reality of being a superhero is lots and lots of *street patrols...*

There wasn't a lot of crime most nights and even if there was it usually happened miles away.

...leafleting for missing persons or even just *giving blood* from time to time.

MISSING

MISSIN

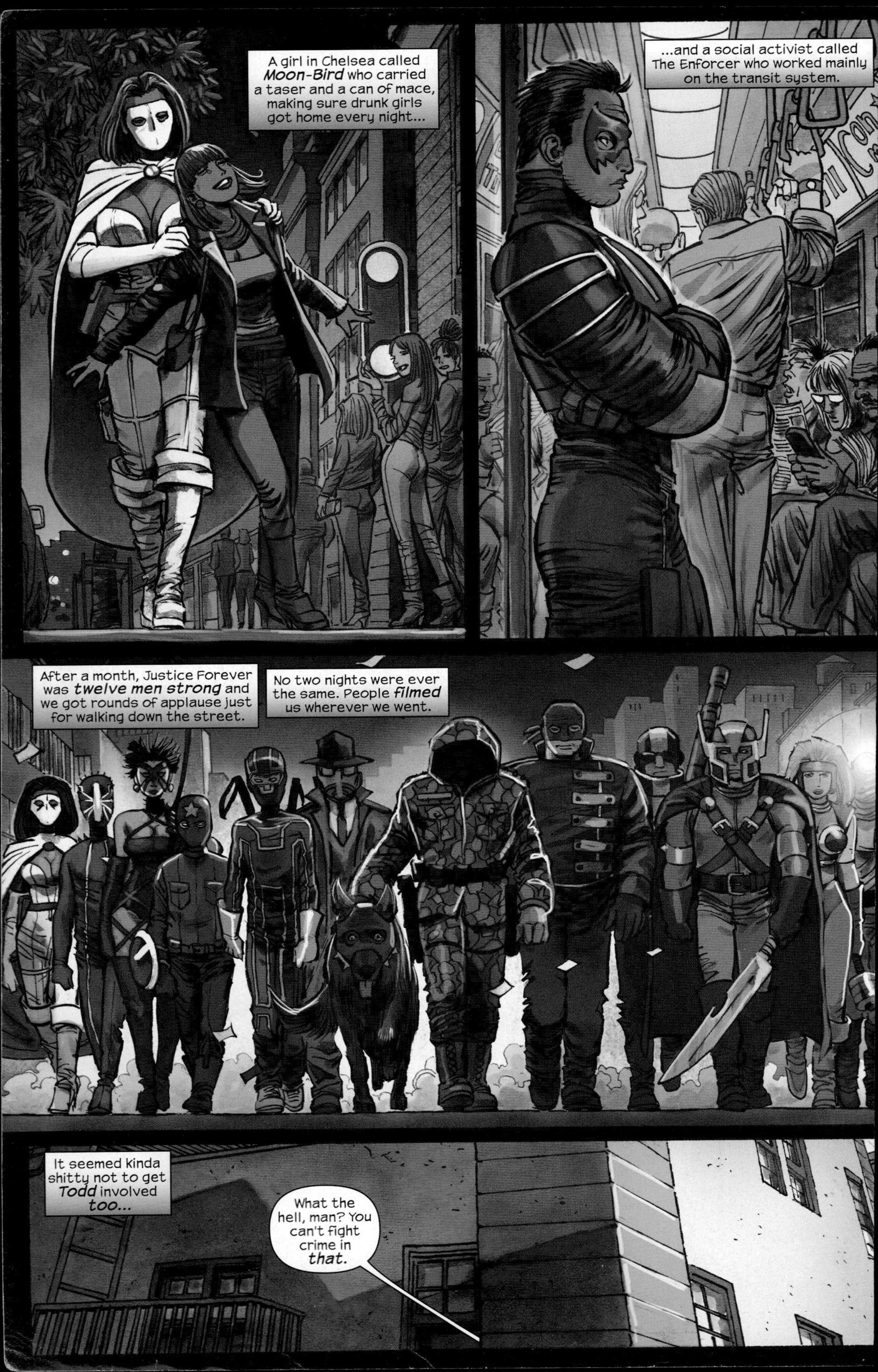
A girl in Chelsea called *Moon-Bird* who carried a taser and a can of mace, making sure drunk girls got home every night...
...and a social activist called The Enforcer who worked mainly on the transit system.
After a month, Justice Forever was *twelve men strong* and we got rounds of applause just for walking down the street.
No two nights were ever the same. People *filmed* us wherever we went.
It seemed kinda shitty not to get *Todd* involved *too...*
What the hell, man? You can't fight crime in *that.*

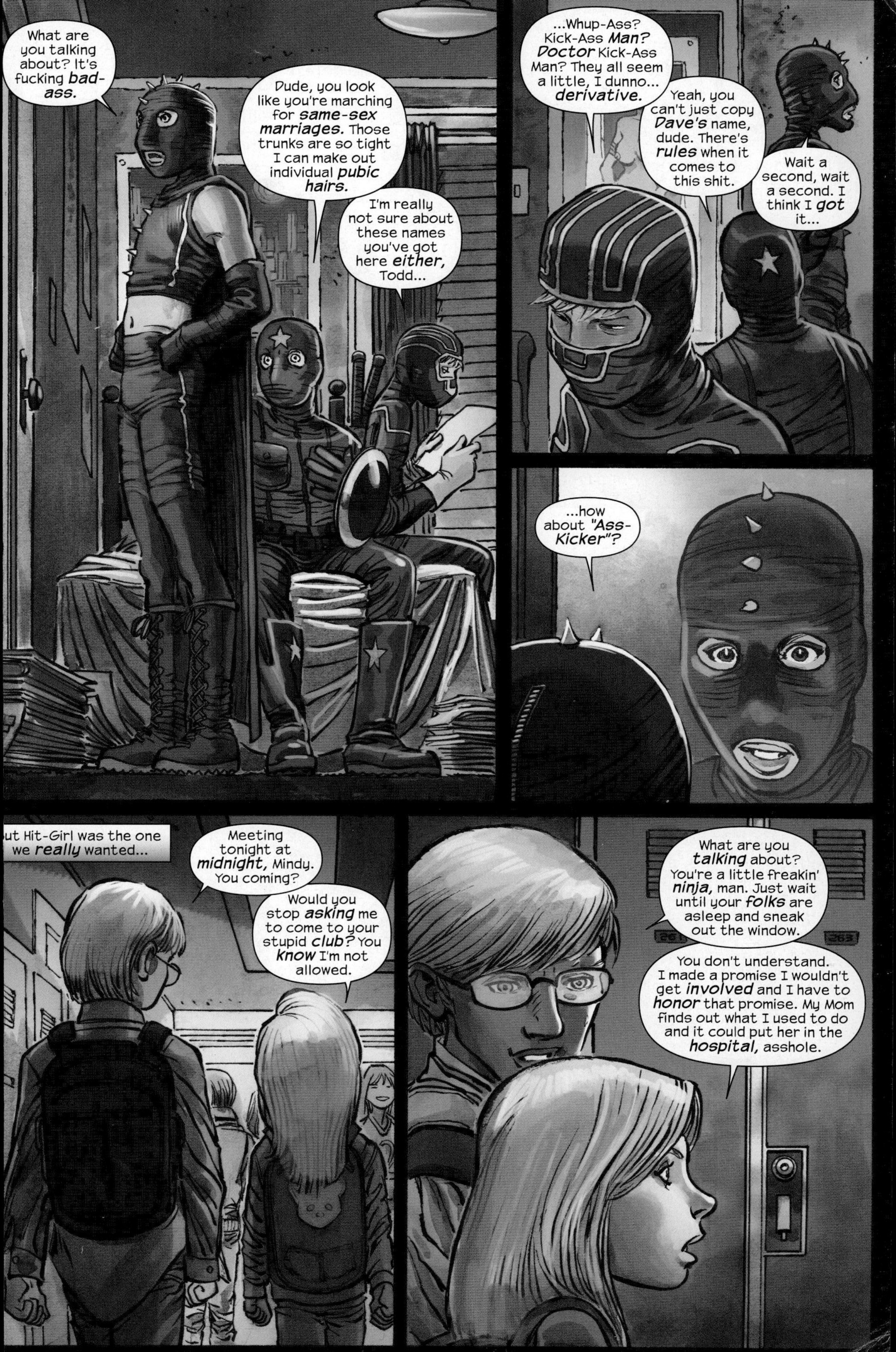
What are you talking about? It's fucking bad-ass.
Dude, you look like you're marching for same-sex marriages. Those trunks are so tight I can make out individual pubic hairs.
I'm really not sure about these names you've got here either, Todd...
...Whup-Ass? Kick-Ass Man? Doctor Kick-Ass Man? They all seem a little, I dunno... derivative.
Yeah, you can't just copy Dave's name, dude. There's rules when it comes to this shit.
Wait a second, wait a second. I think I got it...
...how about "Ass-Kicker"?
ut Hit-Girl was the one we really wanted...
Meeting tonight at midnight, Mindy. You coming?
Would you stop asking me to come to your stupid club? You know I'm not allowed.
What are you talking about? You're a little freakin' ninja, man. Just wait until your folks are asleep and sneak out the window.
You don't understand. I made a promise I wouldn't get involved and I have to honor that promise. My Mom finds out what I used to do and it could put her in the hospital, asshole.

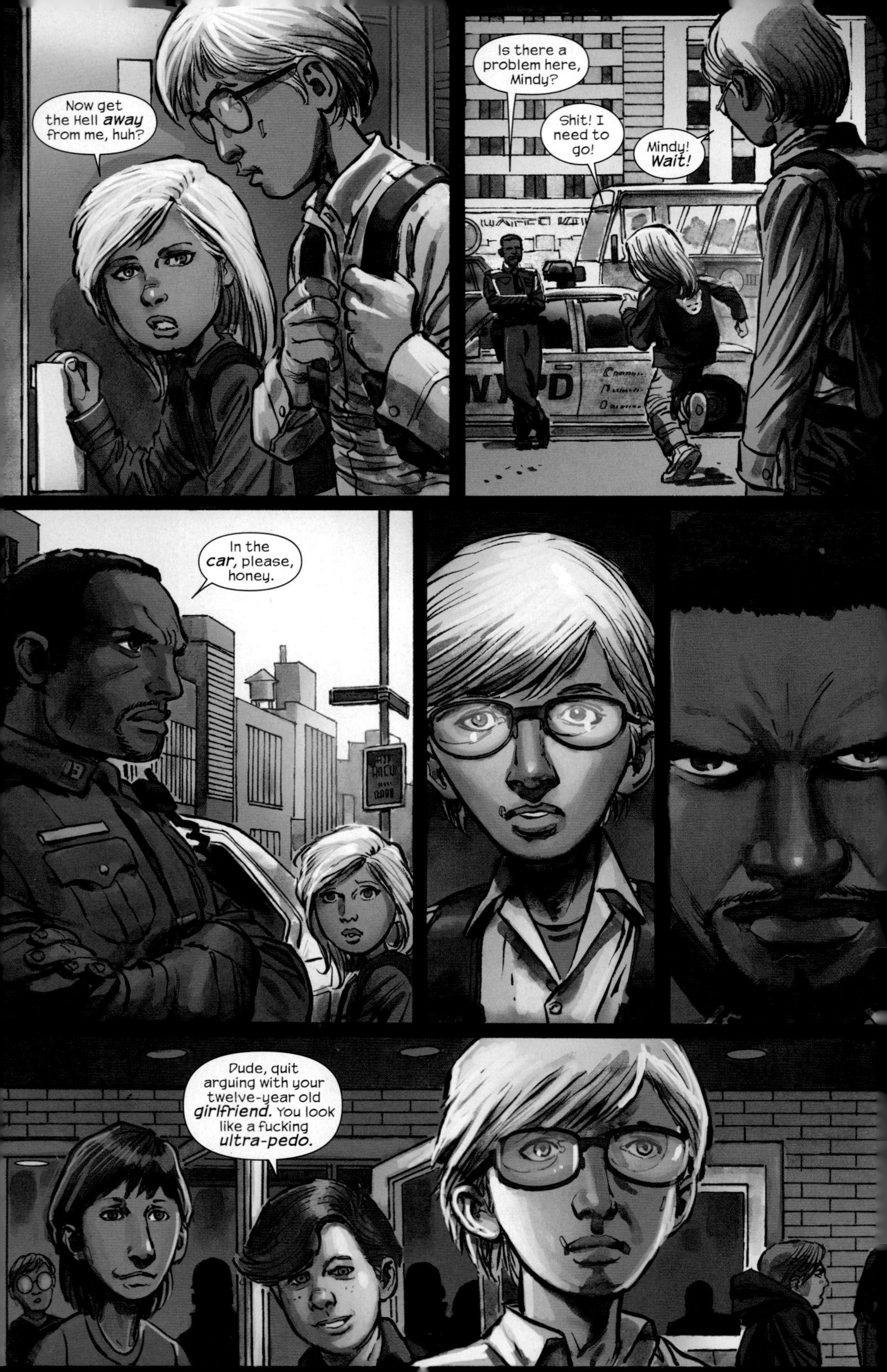

Now get the Hell *away* from me, huh?
Is there a problem here, Mindy?
Shit! I need to go!
Mindy! *Wait!*
NYPD
In the *car*, please, honey.
Dude, quit arguing with your twelve-year old *girlfriend.* You look like a fucking *ultra-pedo.*

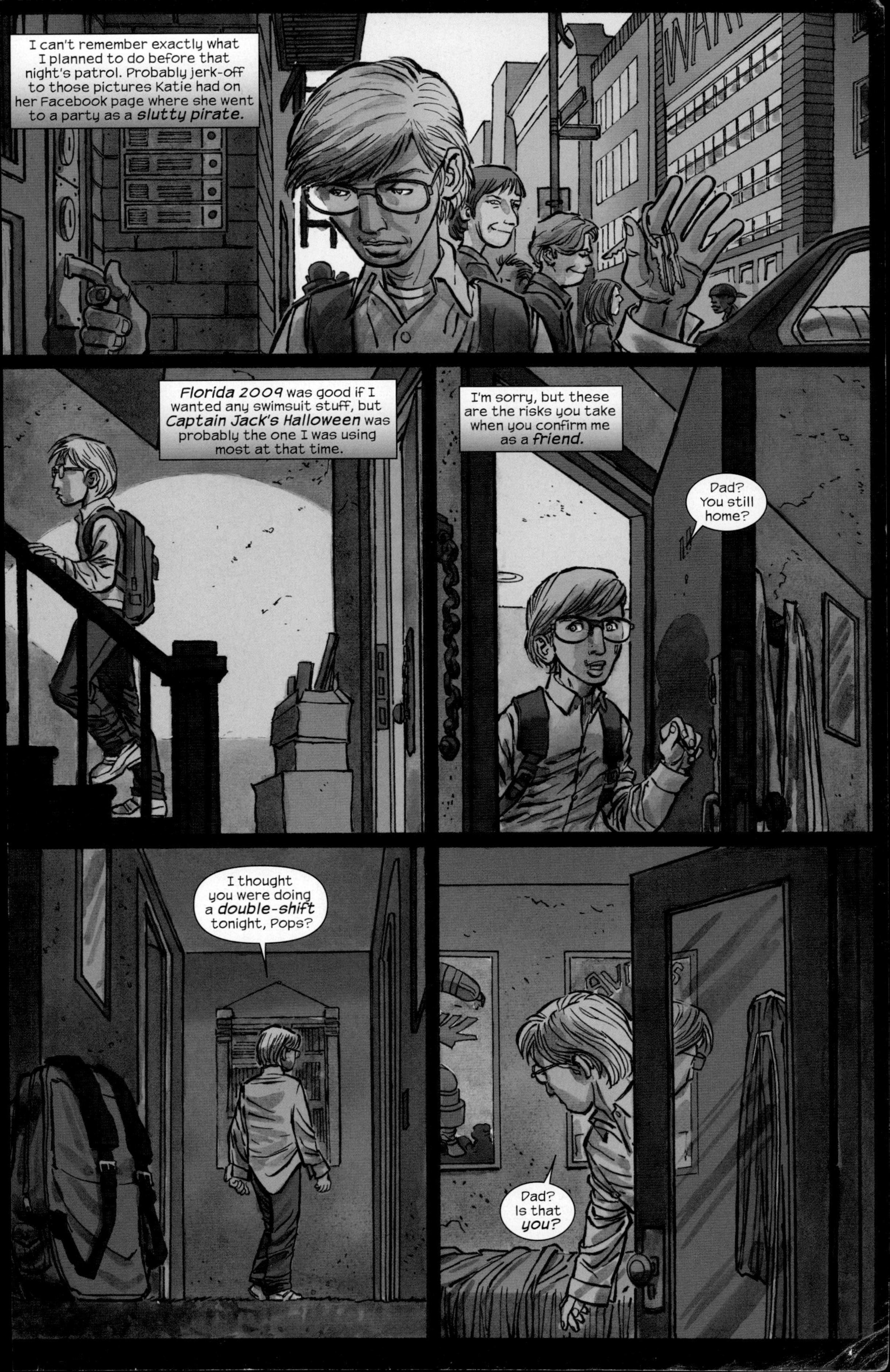
I can't remember exactly what I planned to do before that night's patrol. Probably jerk-off to those pictures Katie had on her Facebook page where she went to a party as a *slutty pirate.*
Florida 2009 was good if I wanted any swimsuit stuff, but *Captain Jack's Halloween* was probably the one I was using most at that time.
I'm sorry, but these are the risks you take when you confirm me as a *friend.*
Dad? You still home?
I thought you were doing a *double-shift* tonight, Pops?
Dad? Is that *you?*

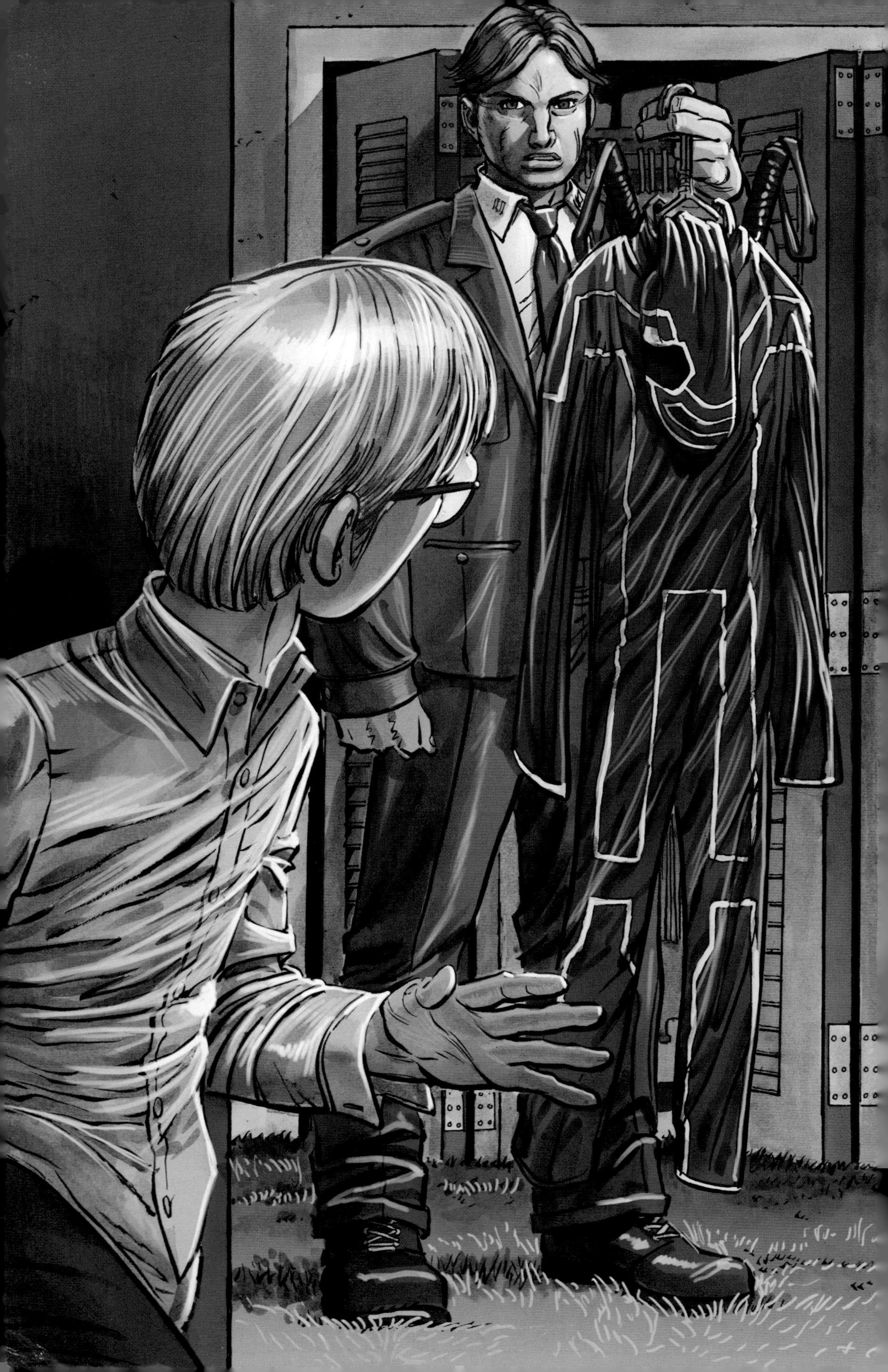

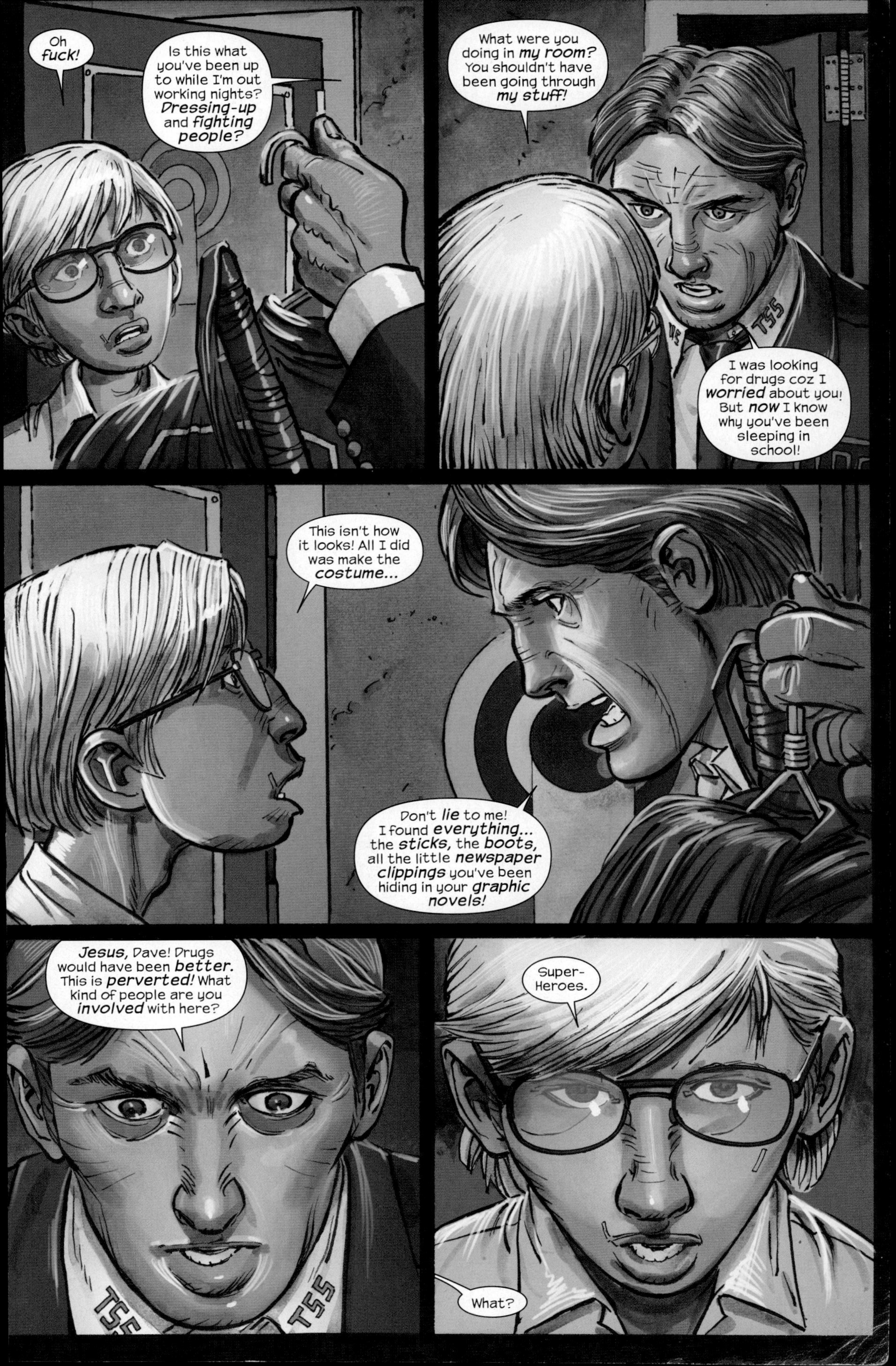
Oh *fuck!*
Is this what you've been up to while I'm out working nights? *Dressing-up* and *fighting people?*
What were you doing in *my room?* You shouldn't have been going through *my stuff!*
I was looking for drugs coz I *worried* about you! But *now* I know why you've been sleeping in school!
This isn't how it looks! All I did was make the *costume...*
Don't *lie* to me! I found *everything...* the *sticks,* the *boots,* all the little *newspaper clippings* you've been hiding in your *graphic novels!*
Jesus, Dave! Drugs would have been *better.* This is *perverted!* What kind of people are you *involved* with here?
Super-Heroes.
What?
TSS

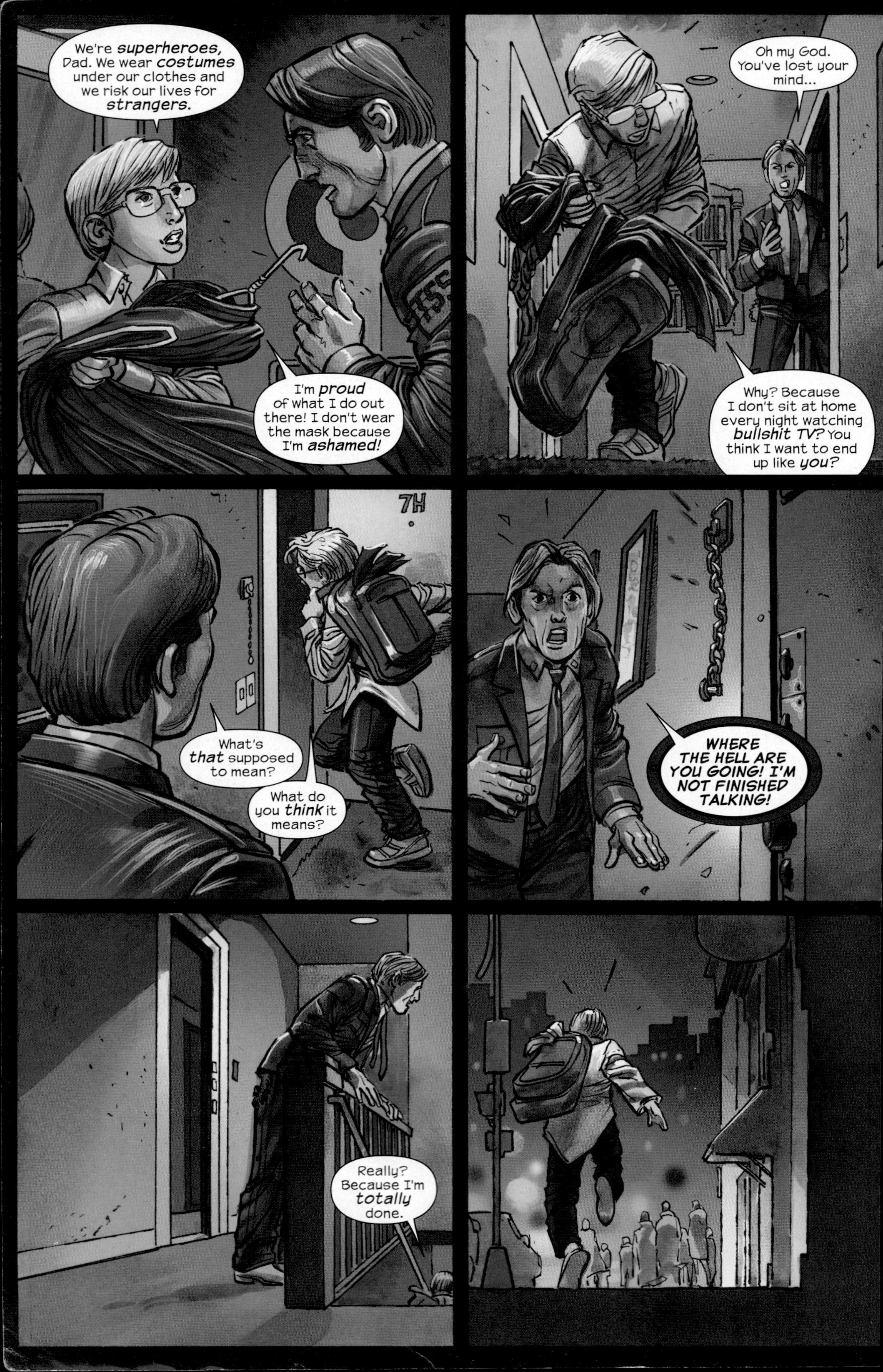
We're superheroes, Dad. We wear costumes under our clothes and we risk our lives for strangers.
I'm proud of what I do out there! I don't wear the mask because I'm ashamed!
Oh my God. You've lost your mind...
Why? Because I don't sit at home every night watching bullshit TV? You think I want to end up like you?
7H
What's that supposed to mean?
What do you think it means?
WHERE THE HELL ARE YOU GOING! I'M NOT FINISHED TALKING!
Really? Because I'm totally done.

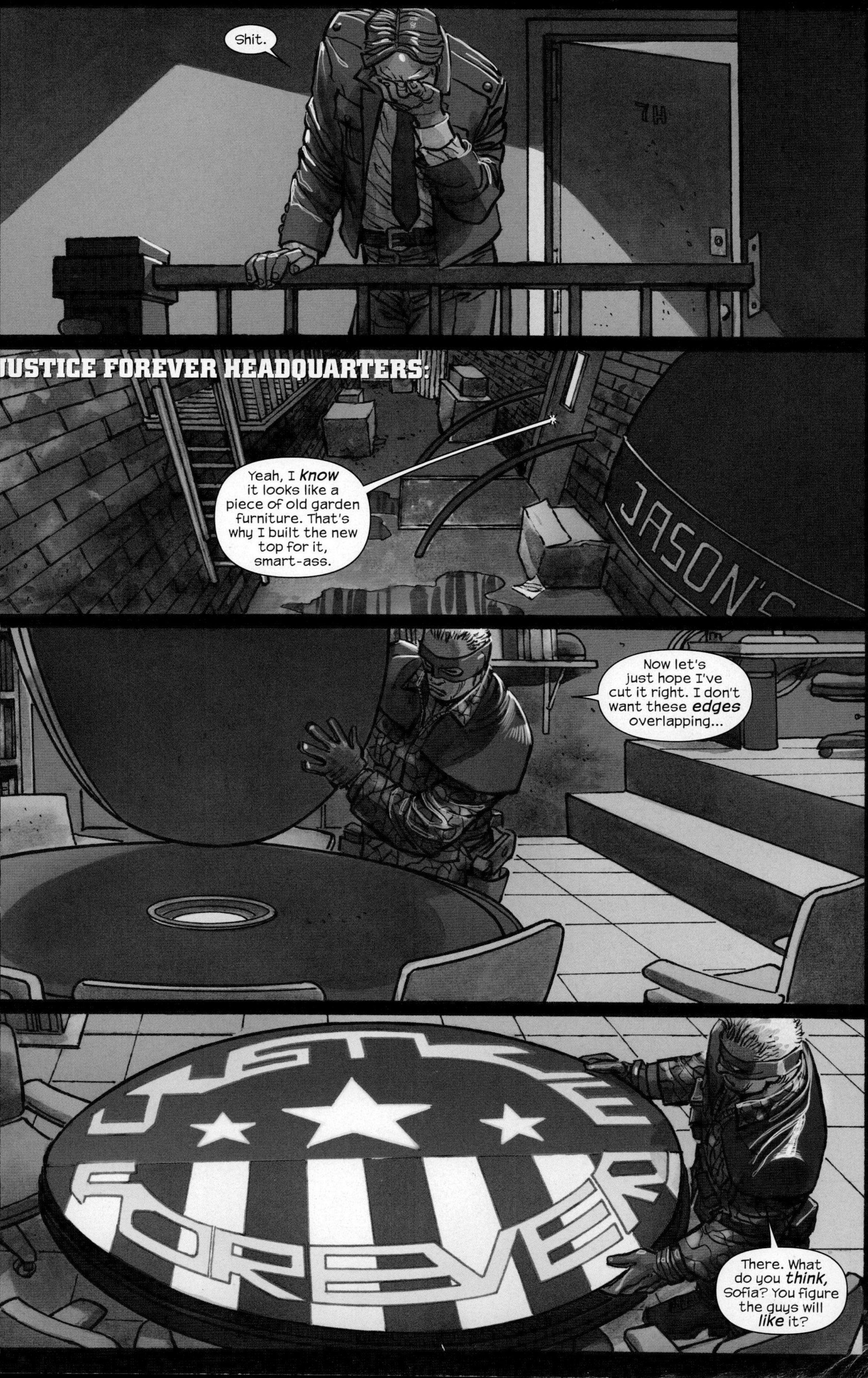
Shit.
7H
JUSTICE FOREVER HEADQUARTERS:
Yeah, I *know* it looks like a piece of old garden furniture. That's why I built the new top for it, smart-ass.
JASON'S
Now let's just hope I've cut it right. I don't want these *edges* overlapping...
JUSTICE FOREVER
There. What do you *think,* Sofia? You figure the guys will *like* it?

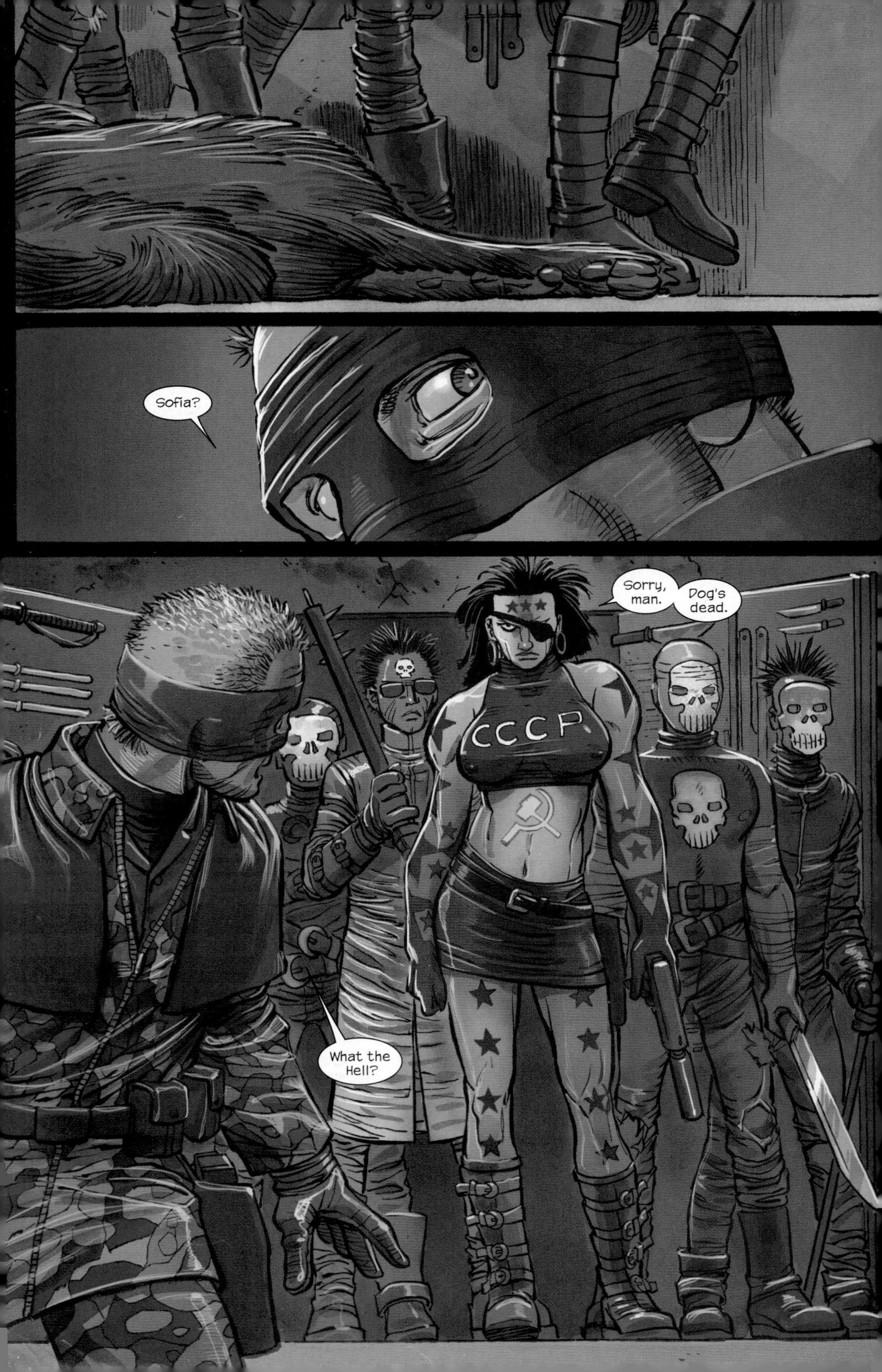
Sofia?
Sorry, man.
Dog's dead.
What the Hell?

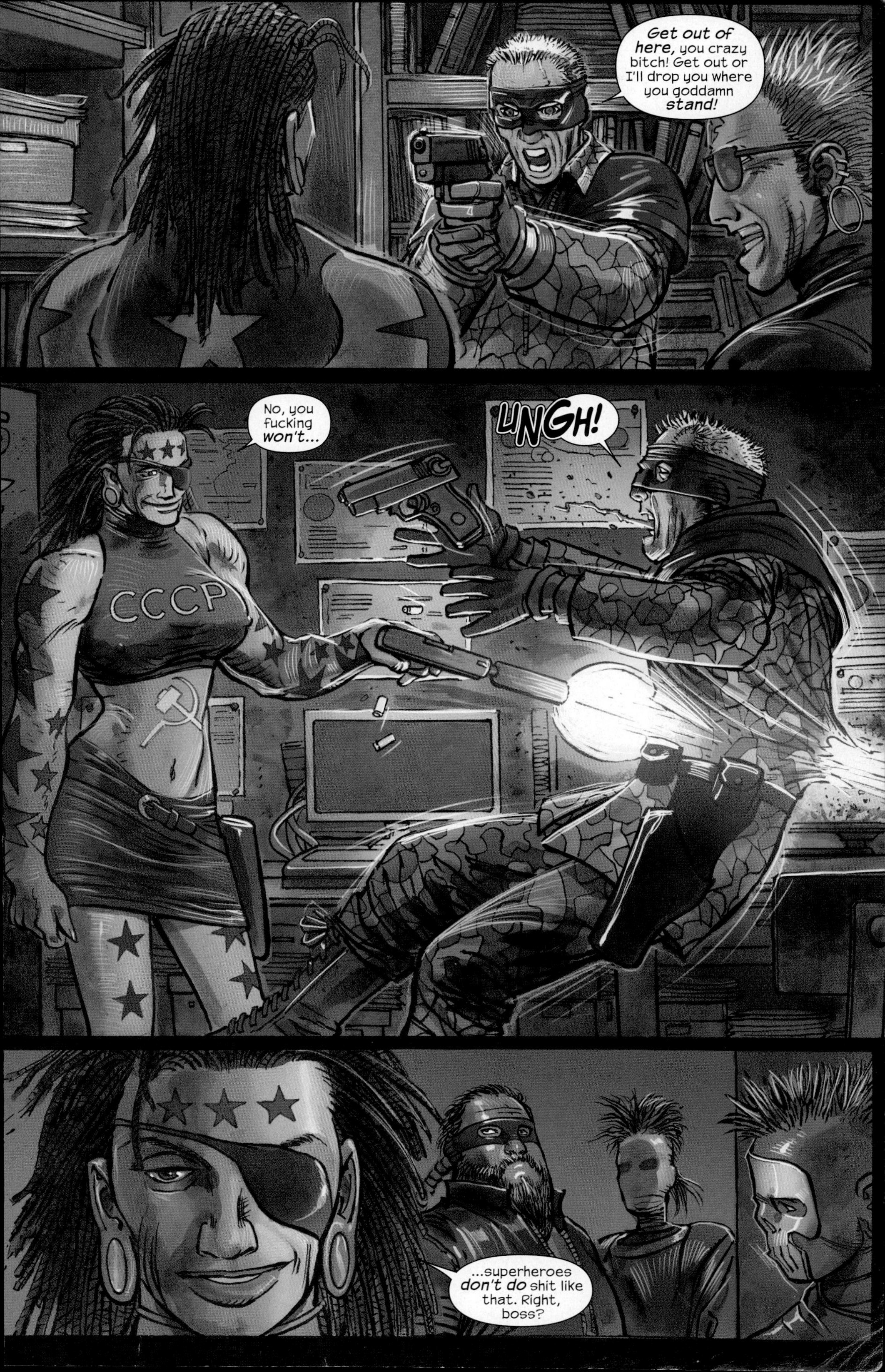
Get out of here, you crazy bitch! Get out or I'll drop you where you goddamn stand!
No, you fucking won't...
UNGH!
CCCP
...superheroes don't do shit like that. Right, boss?

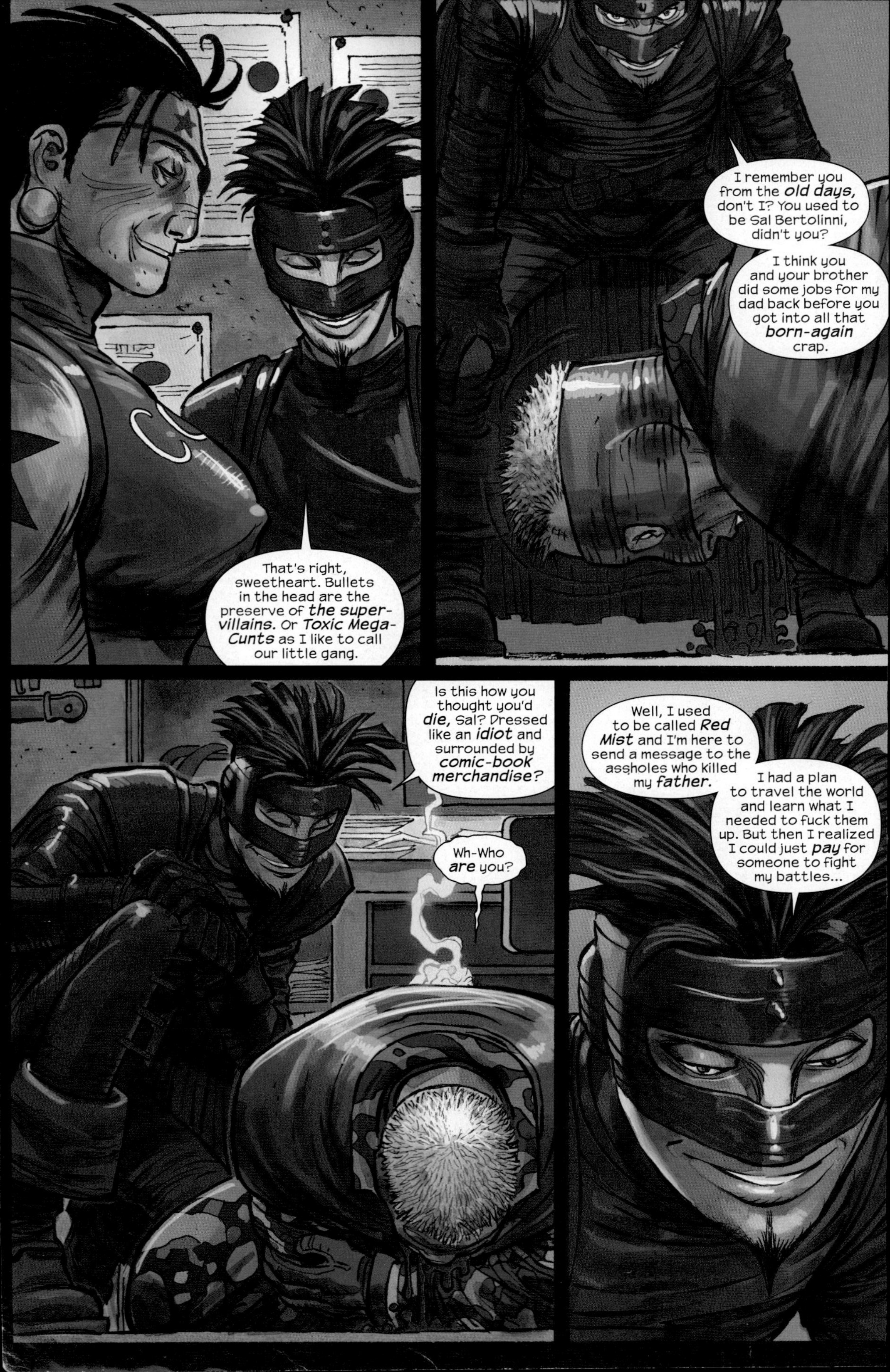
That's right, sweetheart. Bullets in the head are the preserve of *the super-villains.* Or *Toxic Mega-Cunts* as I like to call our little gang.
I remember you from the *old days,* don't I? You used to be Sal Bertolinni, didn't you?
I think you and your brother did some jobs for my dad back before you got into all that *born-again* crap.
Is this how you thought you'd *die,* Sal? Dressed like an *idiot* and surrounded by *comic-book merchandise?*
Wh-Who *are* you?
Well, I used to be called *Red Mist* and I'm here to send a message to the assholes who killed my *father.*
I had a plan to travel the world and learn what I needed to fuck them up. But then I realized I could just *pay* for someone to fight my battles...

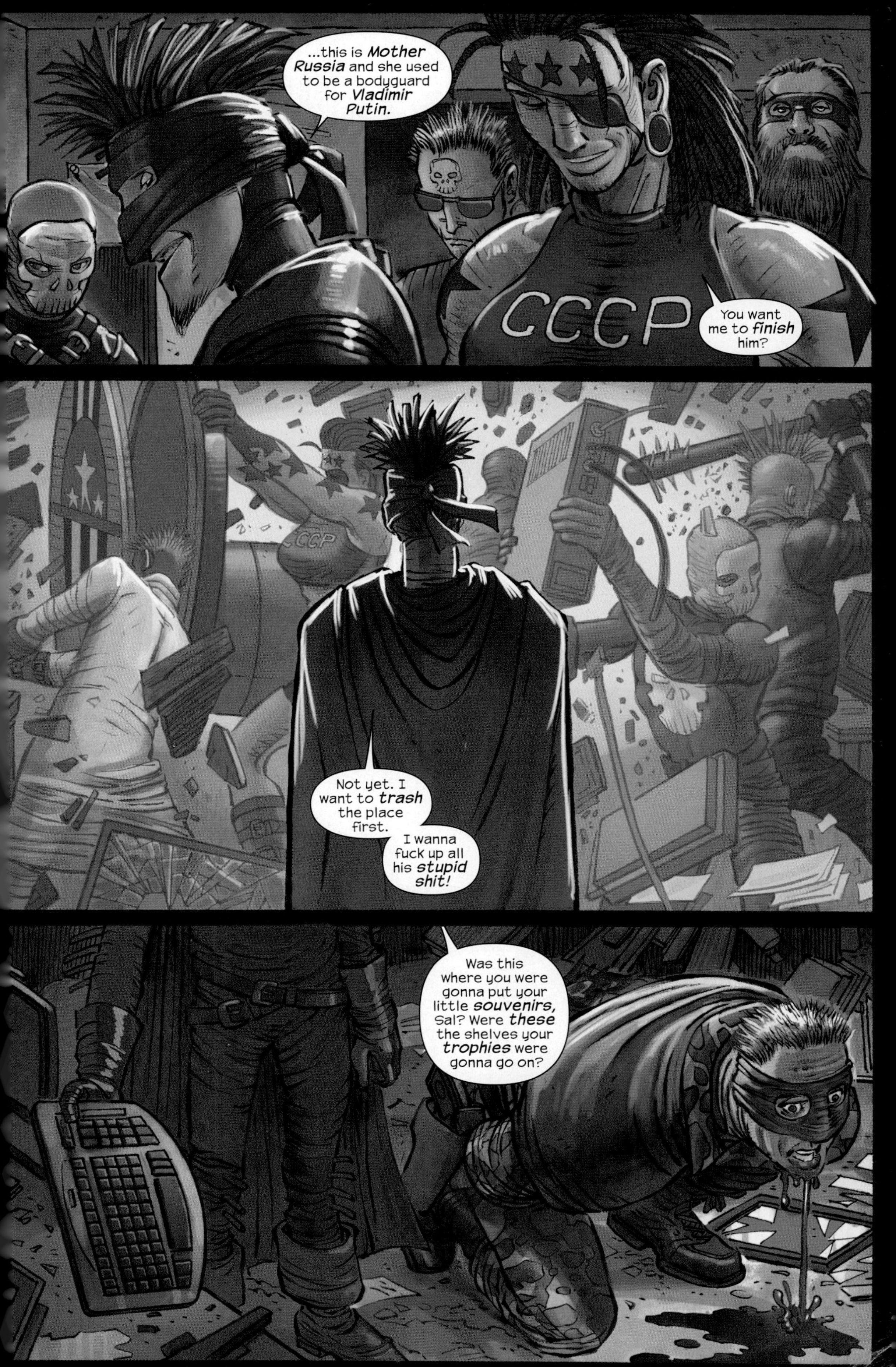
...this is *Mother Russia* and she used to be a bodyguard for *Vladimir Putin.*
CCCP
You want me to *finish* him?
CCCP
Not yet. I want to *trash* the place first.
I wanna fuck up all his *stupid shit!*
Was this where you were gonna put your little *souvenirs,* Sal? Were *these* the shelves your *trophies* were gonna go on?

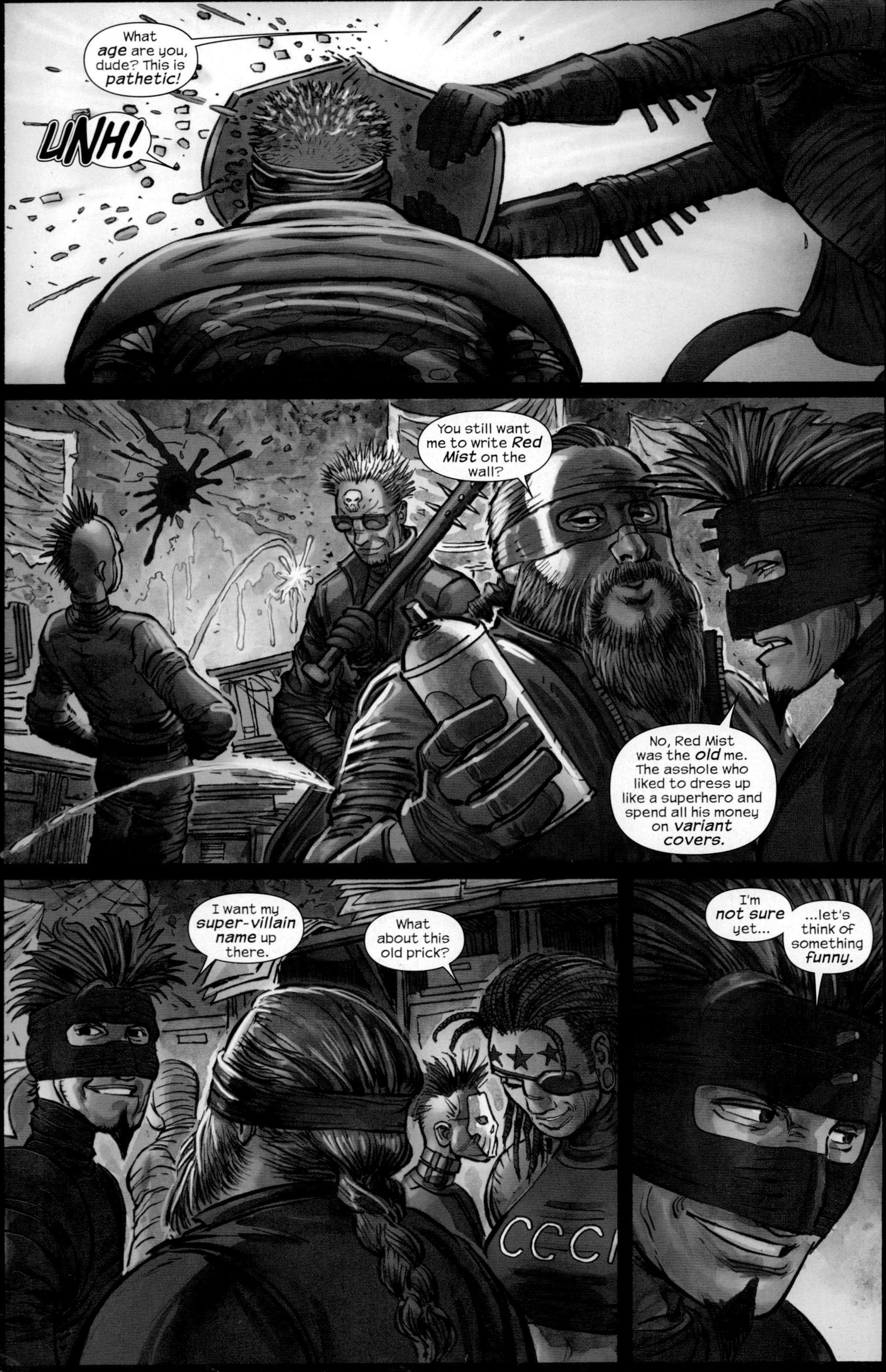
What age are you, dude? This is pathetic!
UNH!
You still want me to write Red Mist on the wall?
No, Red Mist was the old me. The asshole who liked to dress up like a superhero and spend all his money on variant covers.
I want my super-villain name up there.
What about this old prick?
I'm not sure yet...
...let's think of something funny.
CCC

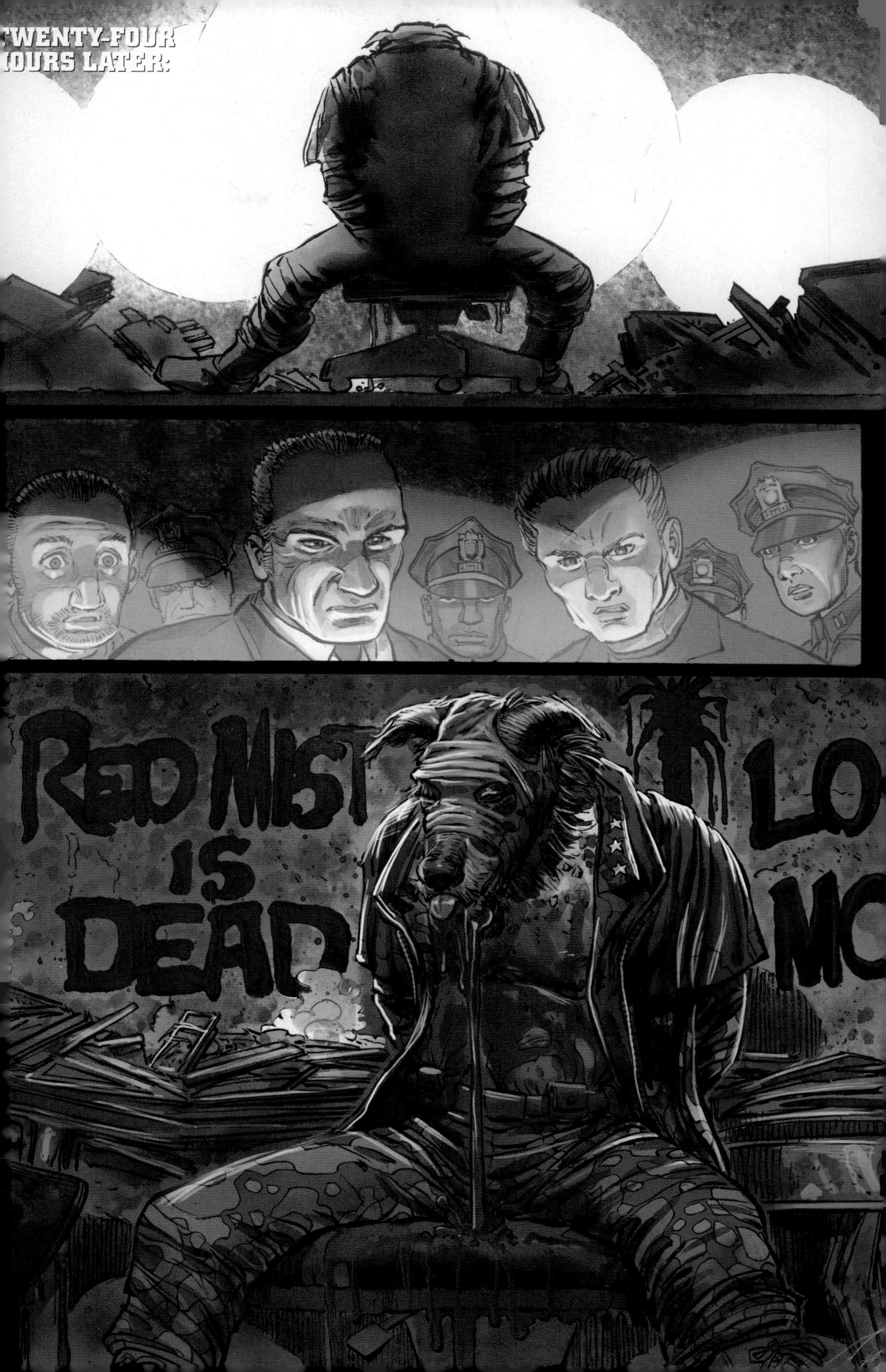
WENTY-FOUR
OURS LATER:
RED MIST
IS
DEAD
LO
MO

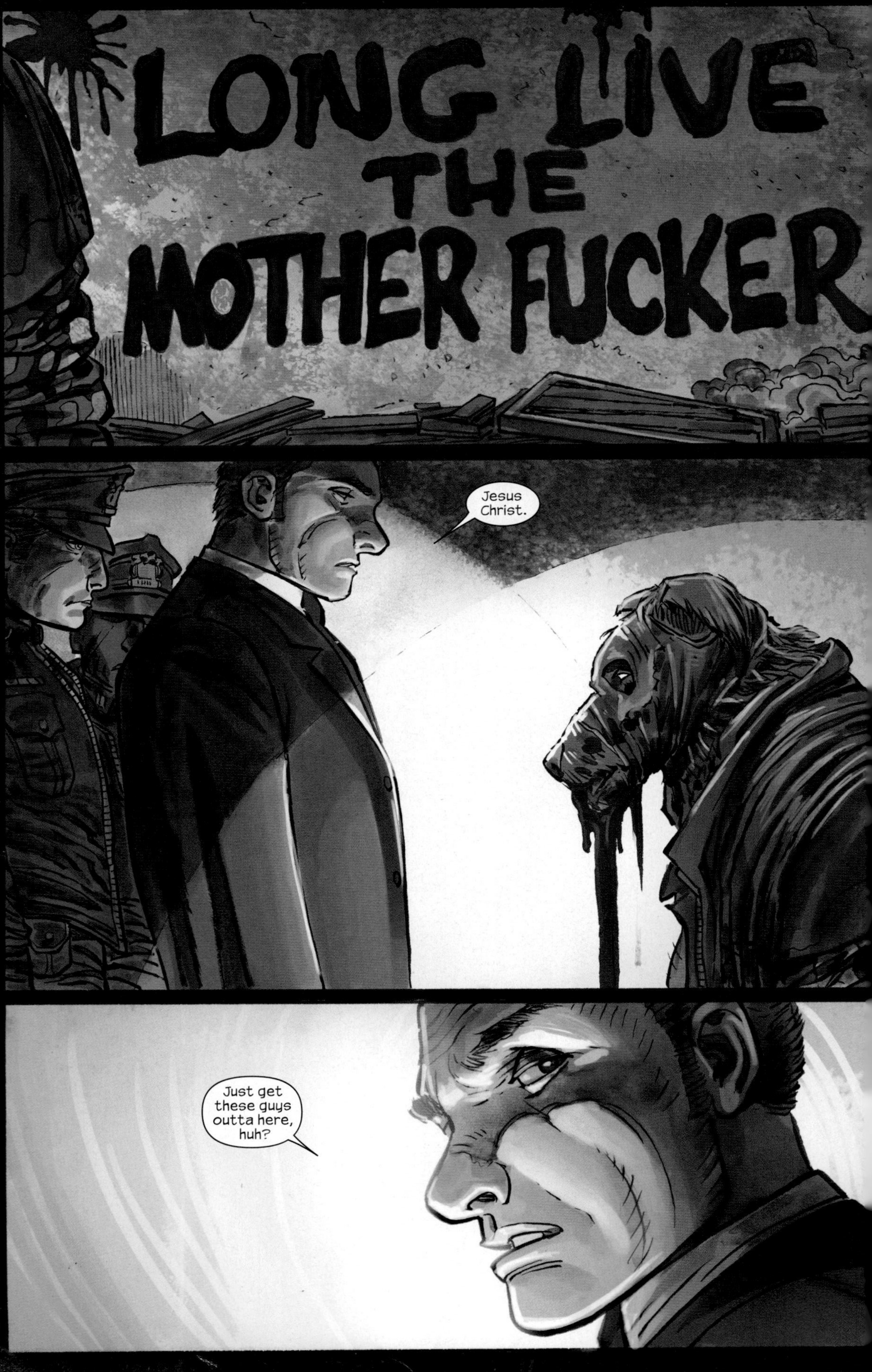
LONG LIVE THE MOTHER FUCKER
Jesus Christ.
Just get these guys outta here, huh?

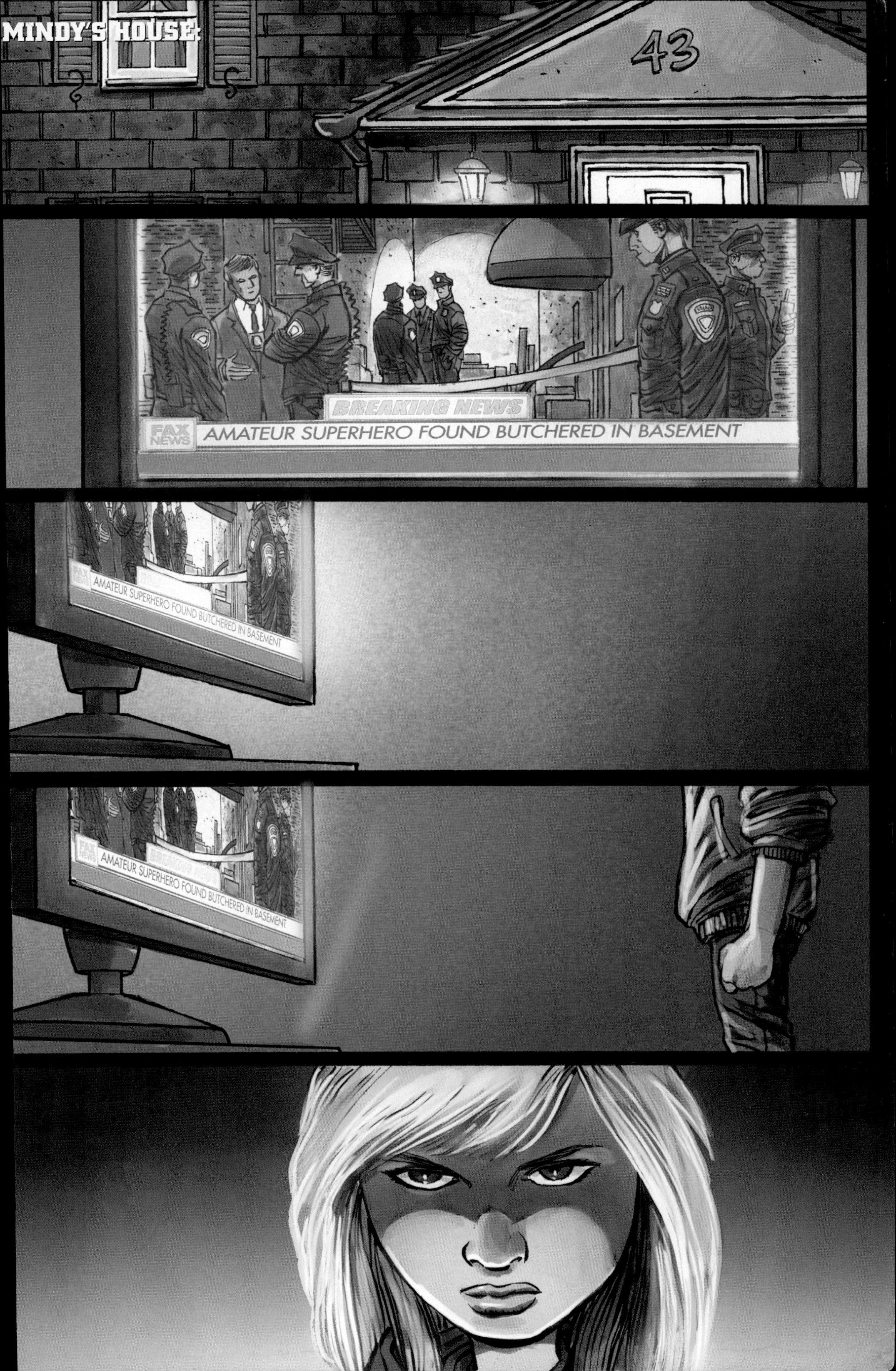
MINDY'S HOUSE:
43
BREAKING NEWS
FAX NEWS
AMATEUR SUPERHERO FOUND BUTCHERED IN BASEMENT
FAX NEWS
AMATEUR SUPERHERO FOUND BUTCHERED IN BASEMENT
FAX NEWS
AMATEUR SUPERHERO FOUND BUTCHERED IN BASEMENT

FOUR

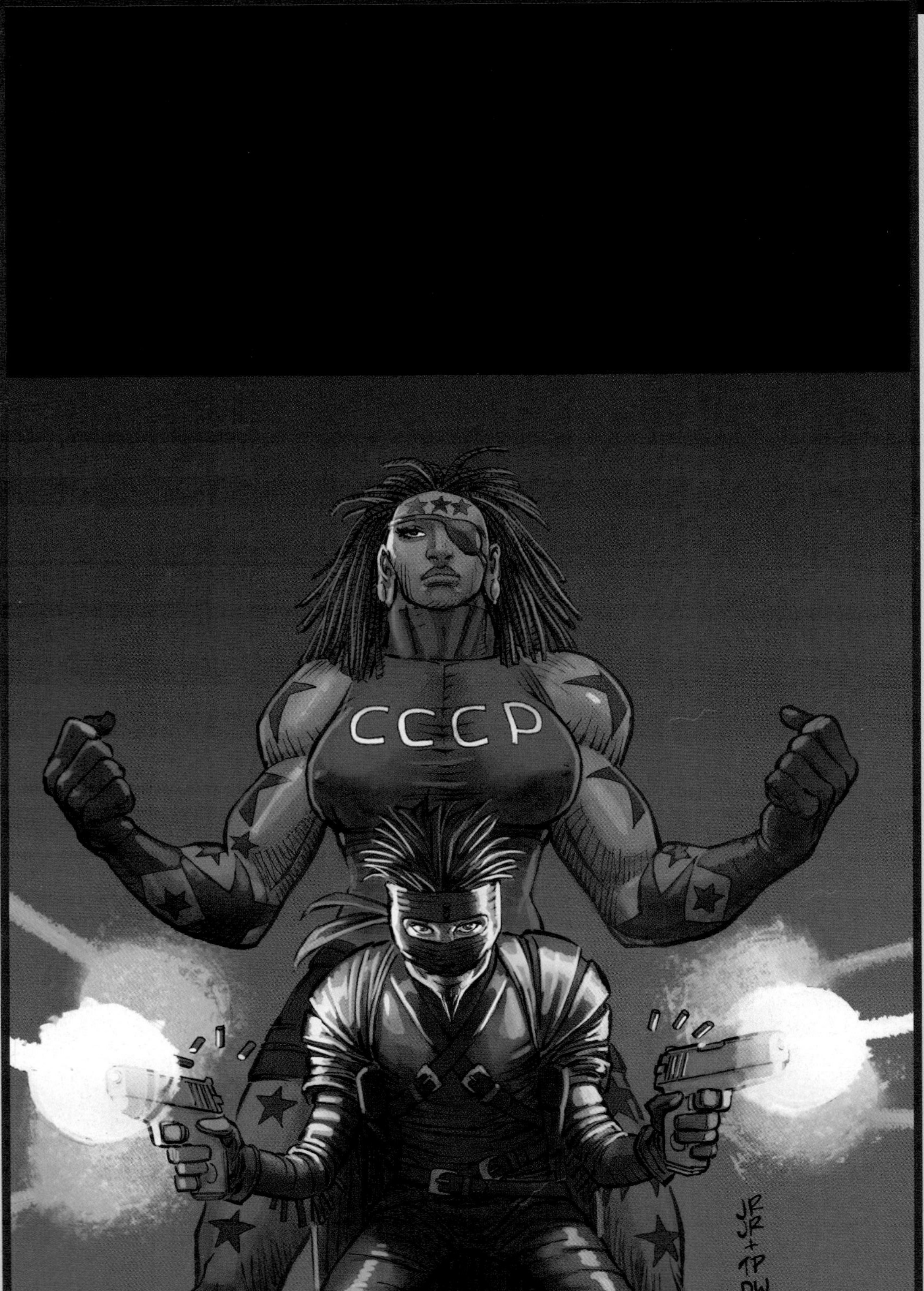
CCCP
JR JR + TP DW

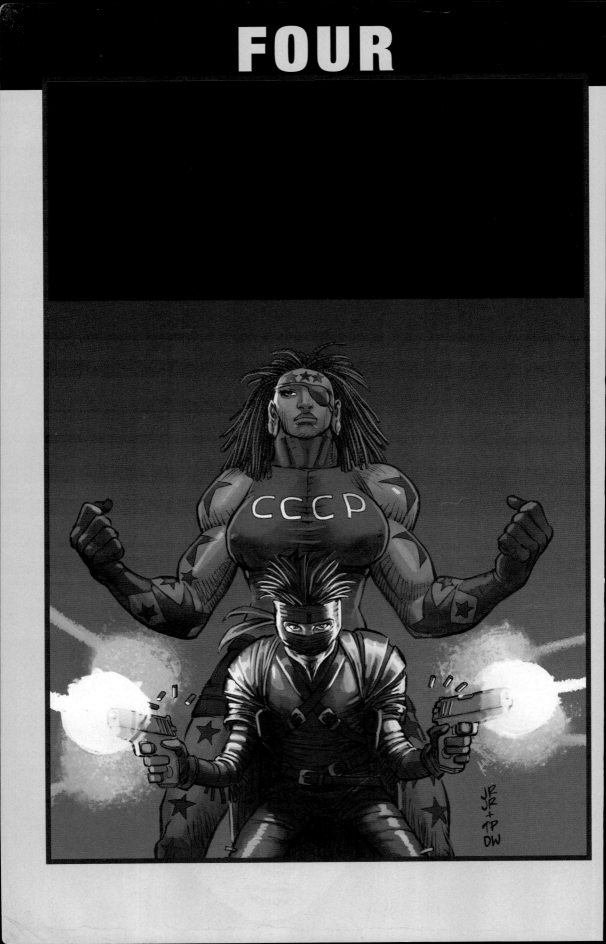

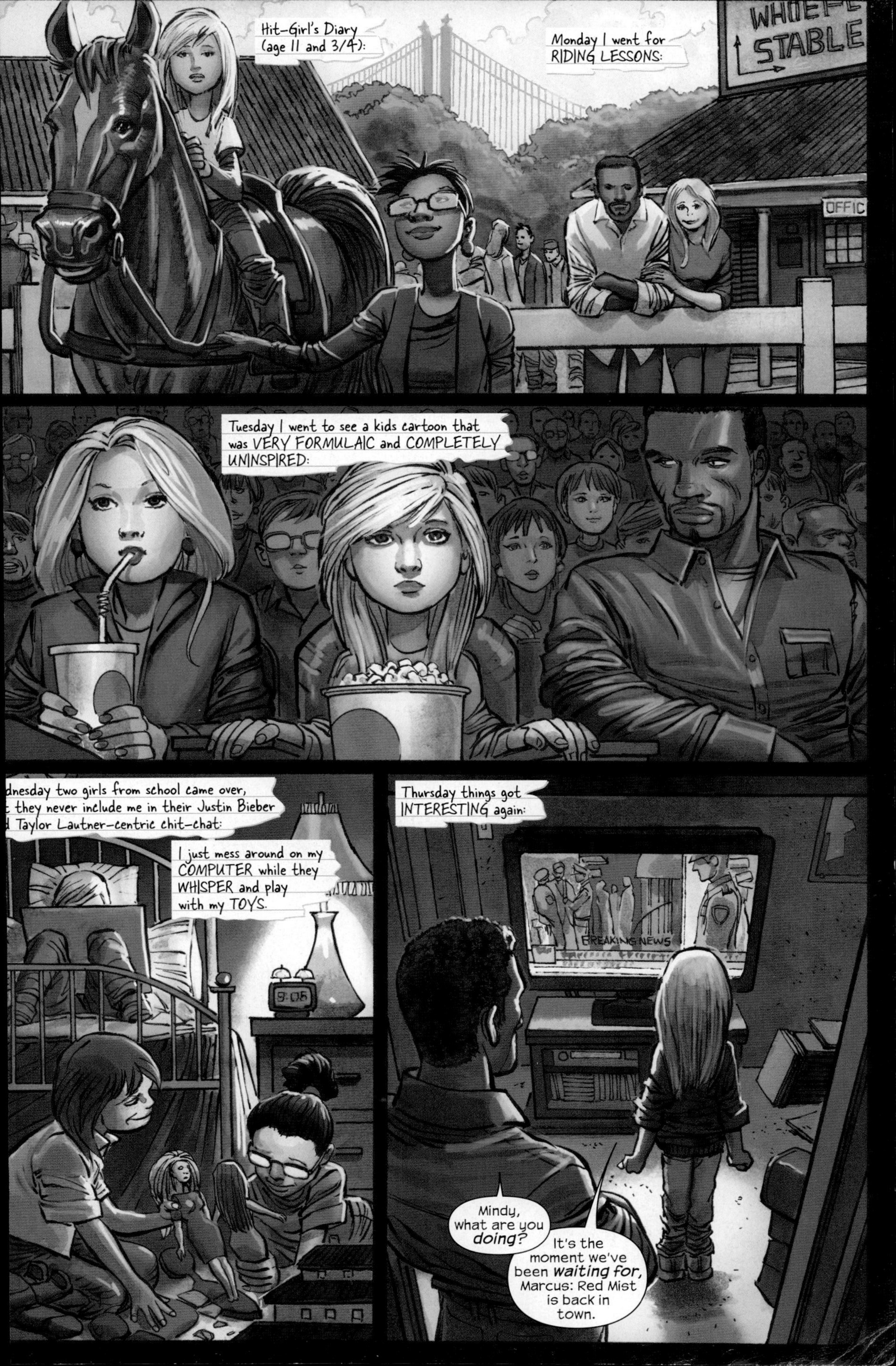
Hit-Girl's Diary
(age 11 and 3/4):
Monday I went for RIDING LESSONS:
STABLE
OFFIC
Tuesday I went to see a kids cartoon that was VERY FORMULAIC and COMPLETELY UNINSPIRED:
dnesday two girls from school came over,
t they never include me in their Justin Bieber
d Taylor Lautner-centric chit-chat:
I just mess around on my COMPUTER while they WHISPER and play with my TOYS.
9:05
Thursday things got INTERESTING again:
BREAKING NEWS
Mindy, what are you *doing?*
It's the moment we've been *waiting for,* Marcus: Red Mist is back in town.

We need to hunt this fucker *down* and make him wish his dad had finished on his *mother's tits.*

We need to hit him *hard* and *fast* and send a *message* to these *cocksuckers* that New York's superheroes are not to be *fucked with.*

Honey, I know your dad used to let you watch all those action movies and you think that kind of talk is *normal.*

But I don't want you *using* those words anymore...and you are absolutely *forbidden* from being Hit-Girl again.

They cut a guy's *head off,* for God's sake. *Who else* is going to stop them? Kick-Ass? *The rest* of those pussies he hangs around with?

Jeez, Mindy. You're an eleven-year old *child.* What makes you think this is *your* responsibility?

The cops are handling this an you've got *homewo* to do. Now switch off the news and g to your room. You kn Mom gets *upset* wh there's bad stuff on

Now

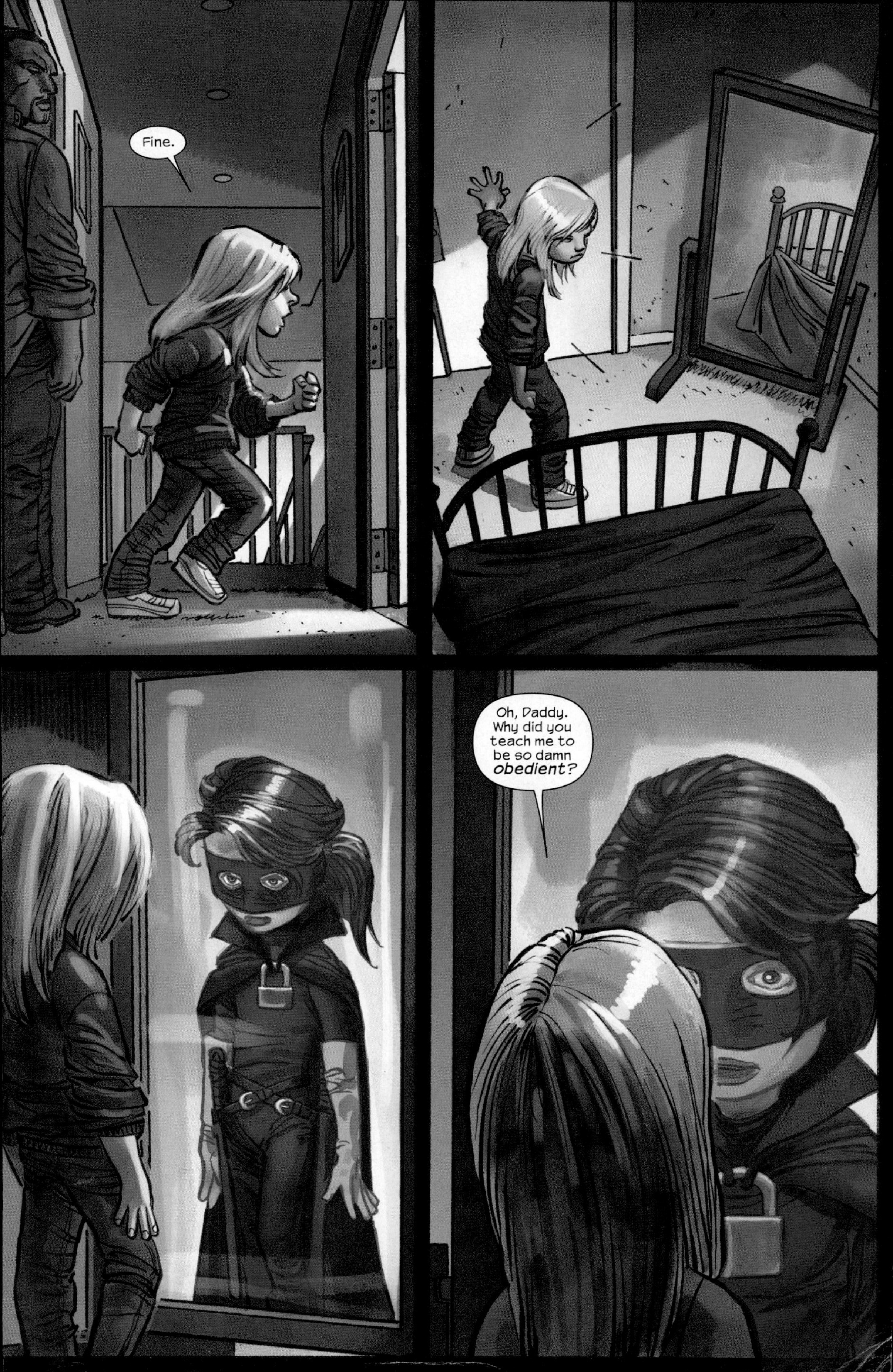
Fine.
Oh, Daddy. Why did you teach me to be so damn *obedient*?

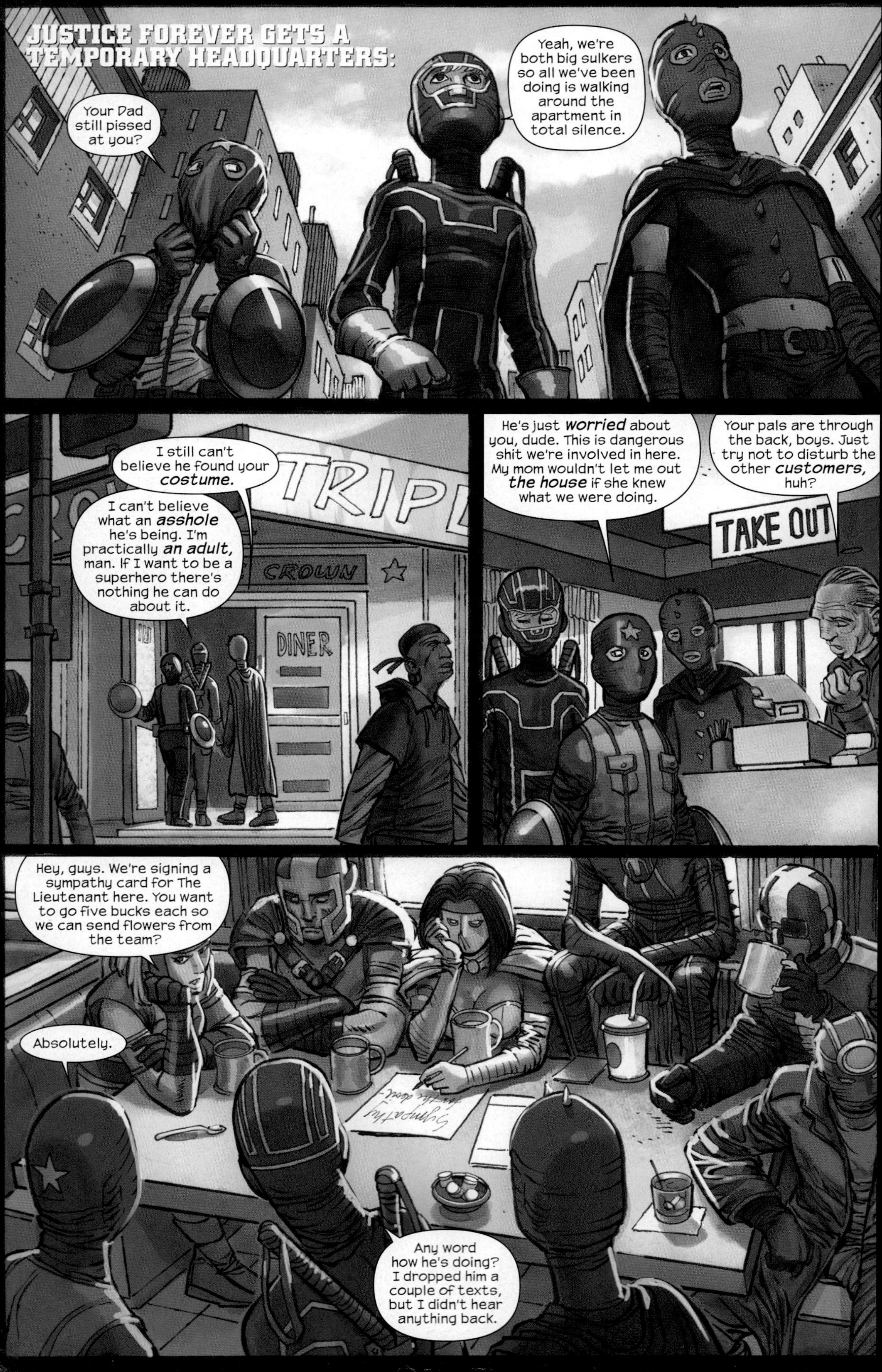
JUSTICE FOREVER GETS A TEMPORARY HEADQUARTERS:
Your Dad still pissed at you?
Yeah, we're both big sulkers so all we've been doing is walking around the apartment in total silence.
I still can't believe he found your *costume.*
I can't believe what an ***asshole*** he's being. I'm practically ***an adult,*** man. If I want to be a superhero there's nothing he can do about it.
TRIPL
CROWN
DINER
He's just ***worried*** about you, dude. This is dangerous shit we're involved in here. My mom wouldn't let me out ***the house*** if she knew what we were doing.
Your pals are through the back, boys. Just try not to disturb the other ***customers,*** huh?
TAKE OUT
Hey, guys. We're signing a sympathy card for The Lieutenant here. You want to go five bucks each so we can send flowers from the team?
Absolutely.
Any word how he's doing? I dropped him a couple of texts, but I didn't hear anything back.

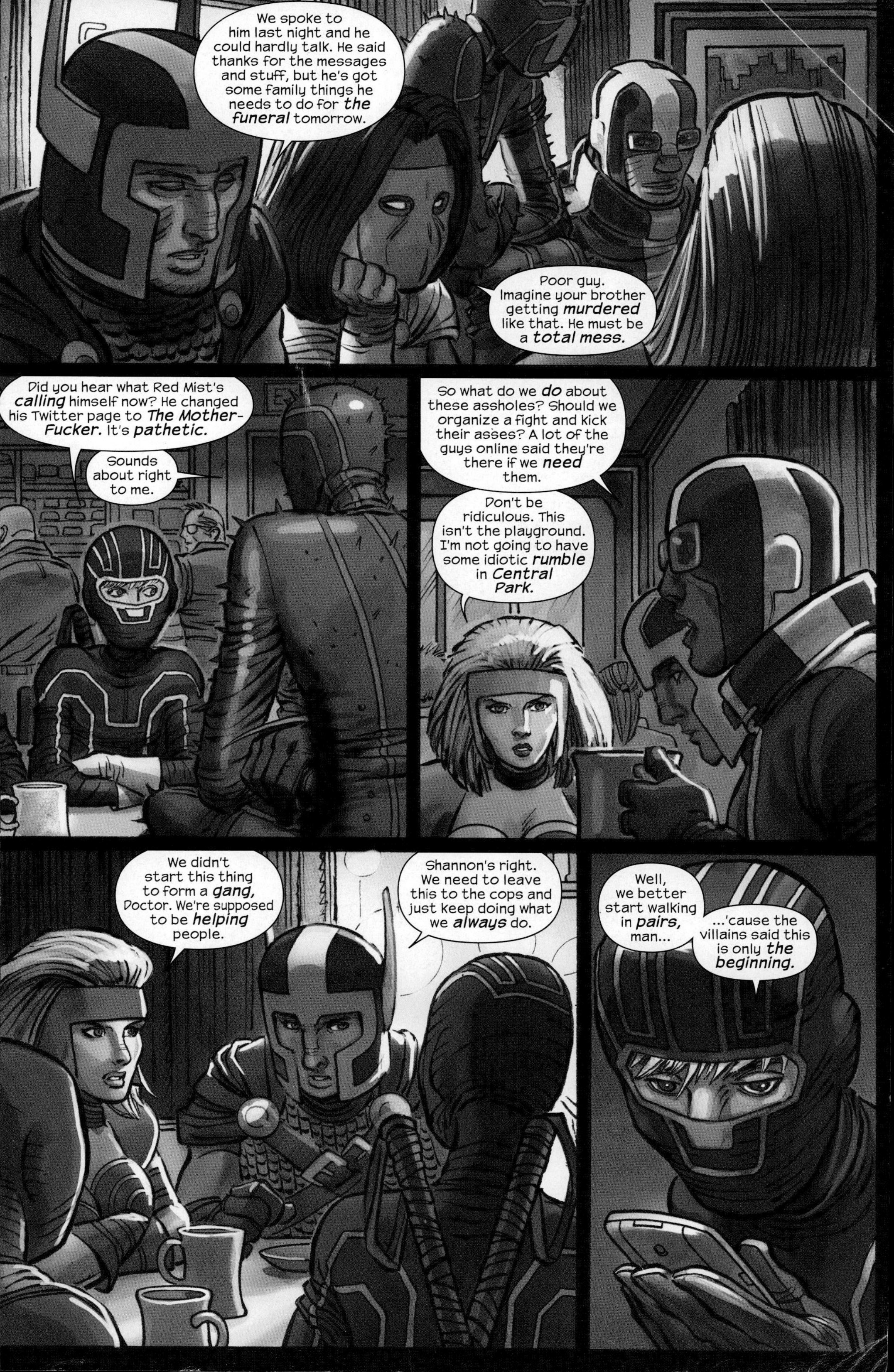
We spoke to him last night and he could hardly talk. He said thanks for the messages and stuff, but he's got some family things he needs to do for *the funeral* tomorrow.
Poor guy. Imagine your brother getting *murdered* like that. He must be a *total mess.*
Did you hear what Red Mist's *calling* himself now? He changed his Twitter page to *The Mother-Fucker*. It's *pathetic.*
Sounds about right to me.
So what do we *do* about these assholes? Should we organize a fight and kick their asses? A lot of the guys online said they're there if we *need* them.
Don't be ridiculous. This isn't the playground. I'm not going to have some idiotic *rumble* in *Central Park.*
We didn't start this thing to form a *gang,* Doctor. We're supposed to be *helping* people.
Shannon's right. We need to leave this to the cops and just keep doing what we *always* do.
Well, we better start walking in *pairs,* man...
...'cause the villains said this is only *the beginning.*

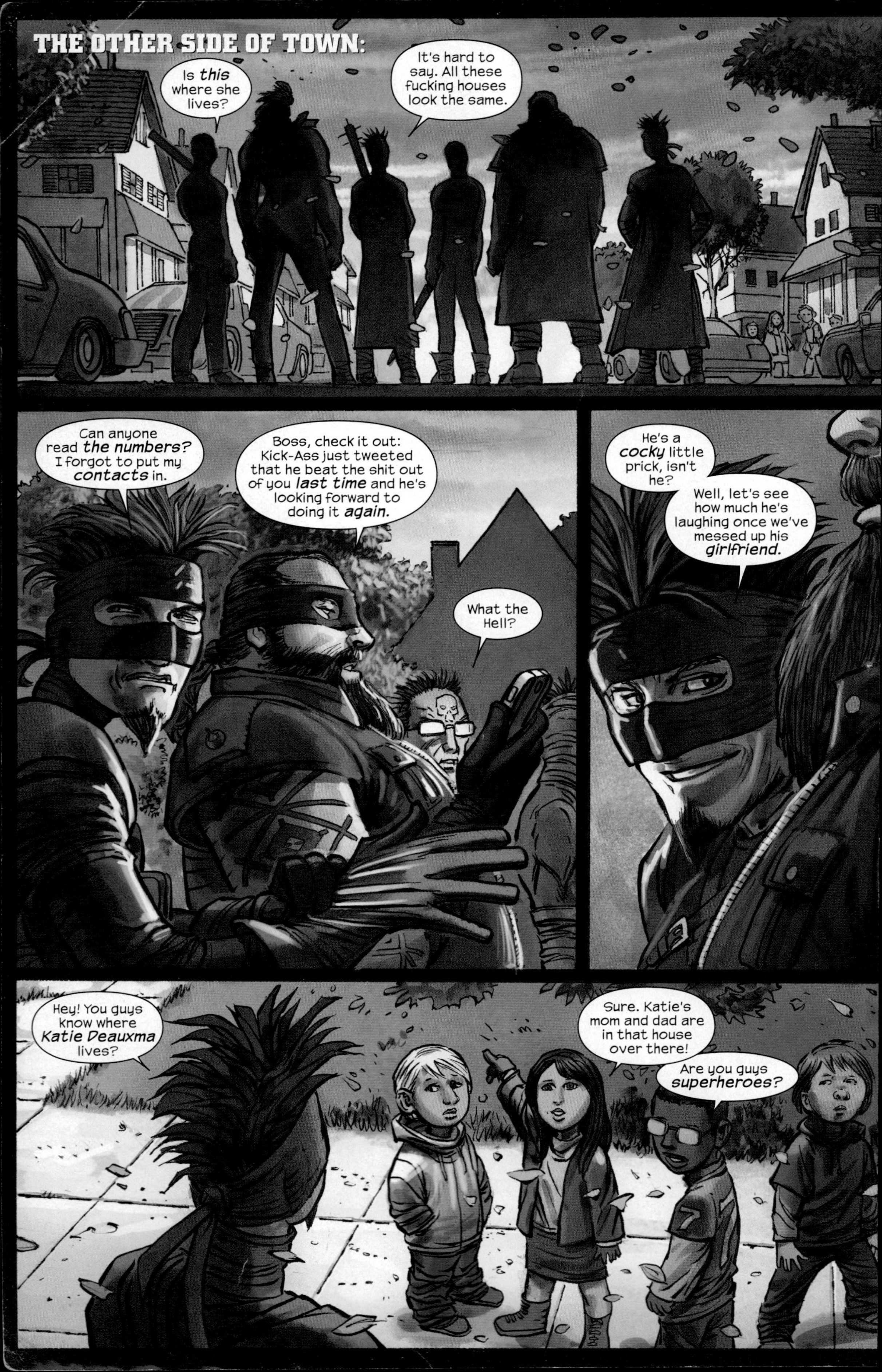
THE OTHER SIDE OF TOWN:
Is this where she lives?
It's hard to say. All these fucking houses look the same.
Can anyone read the numbers? I forgot to put my contacts in.
Boss, check it out: Kick-Ass just tweeted that he beat the shit out of you last time and he's looking forward to doing it again.
What the Hell?
He's a cocky little prick, isn't he?
Well, let's see how much he's laughing once we've messed up his girlfriend.
Hey! You guys know where Katie Deauxma lives?
Sure. Katie's mom and dad are in that house over there!
Are you guys superheroes?

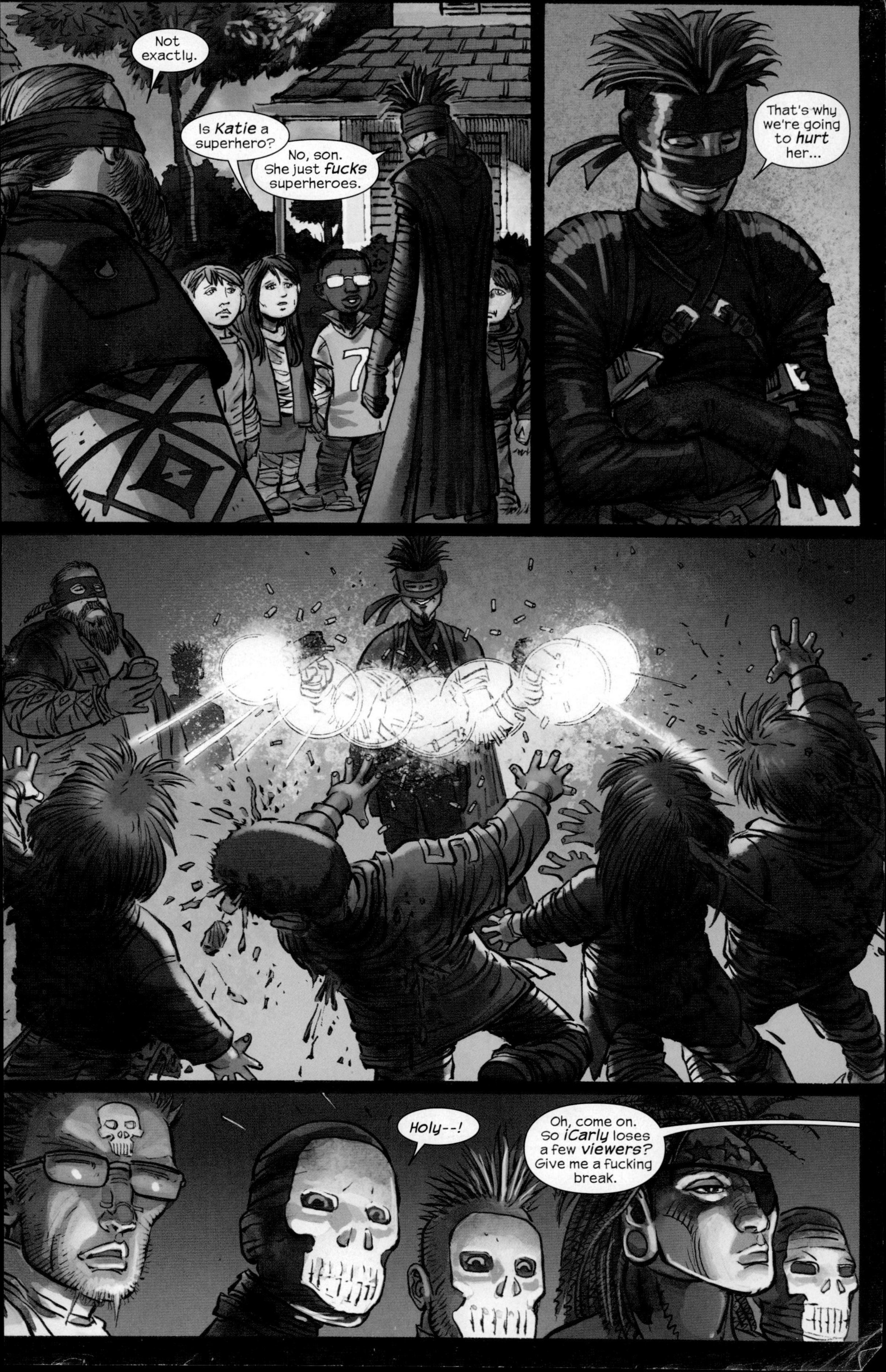
Not exactly.
Is *Katie* a superhero?
No, son. She just ***fucks*** superheroes.
That's why we're going to ***hurt*** her...
Holy--!
Oh, come on. So *iCarly* loses a few ***viewers?*** Give me a fucking break.

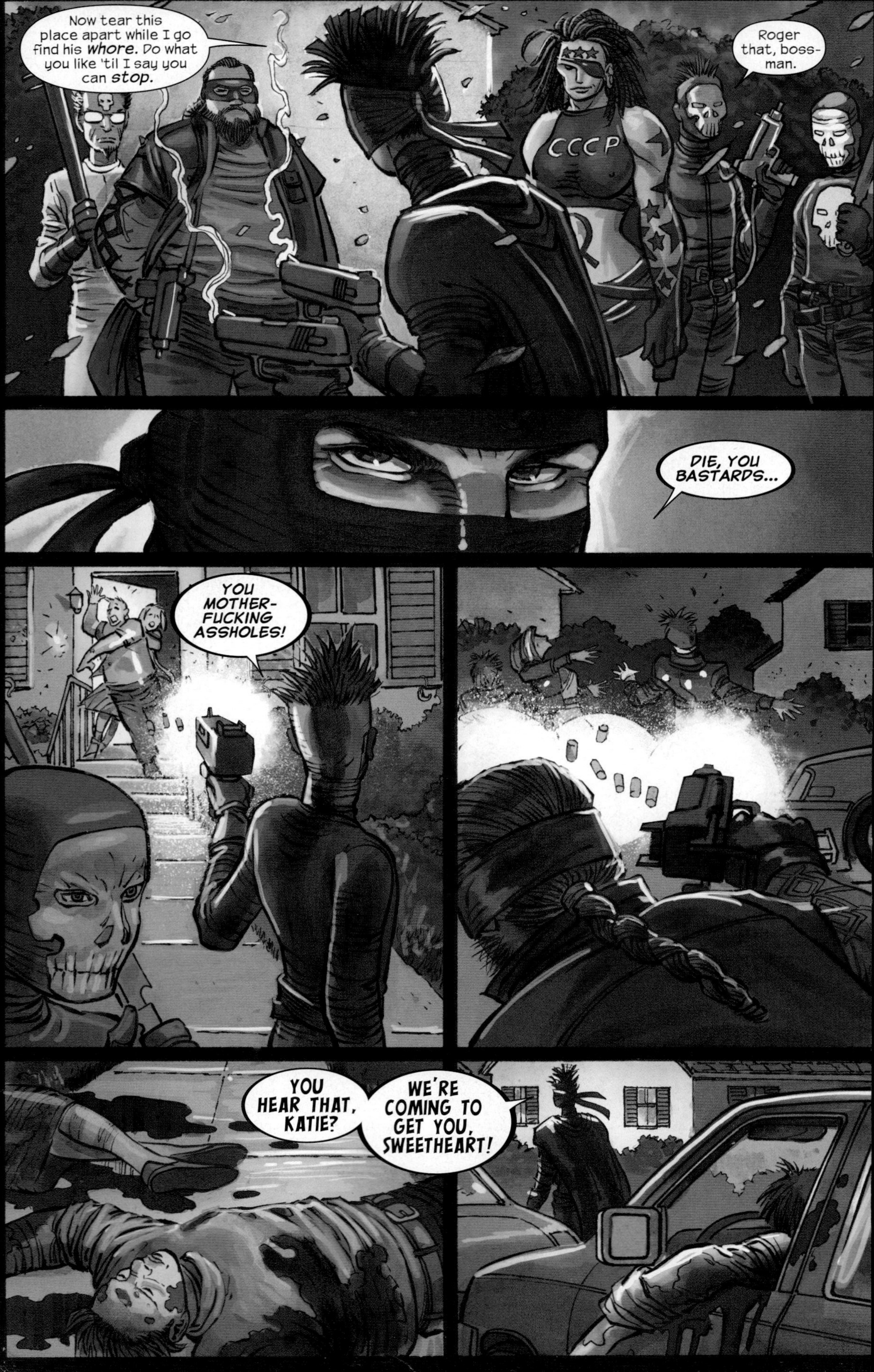
Now tear this place apart while I go find his whore. Do what you like 'til I say you can stop.
Roger that, boss-man.
CCCP
DIE, YOU BASTARDS...
YOU MOTHER-FUCKING ASSHOLES!
YOU HEAR THAT, KATIE?
WE'RE COMING TO GET YOU, SWEETHEART!

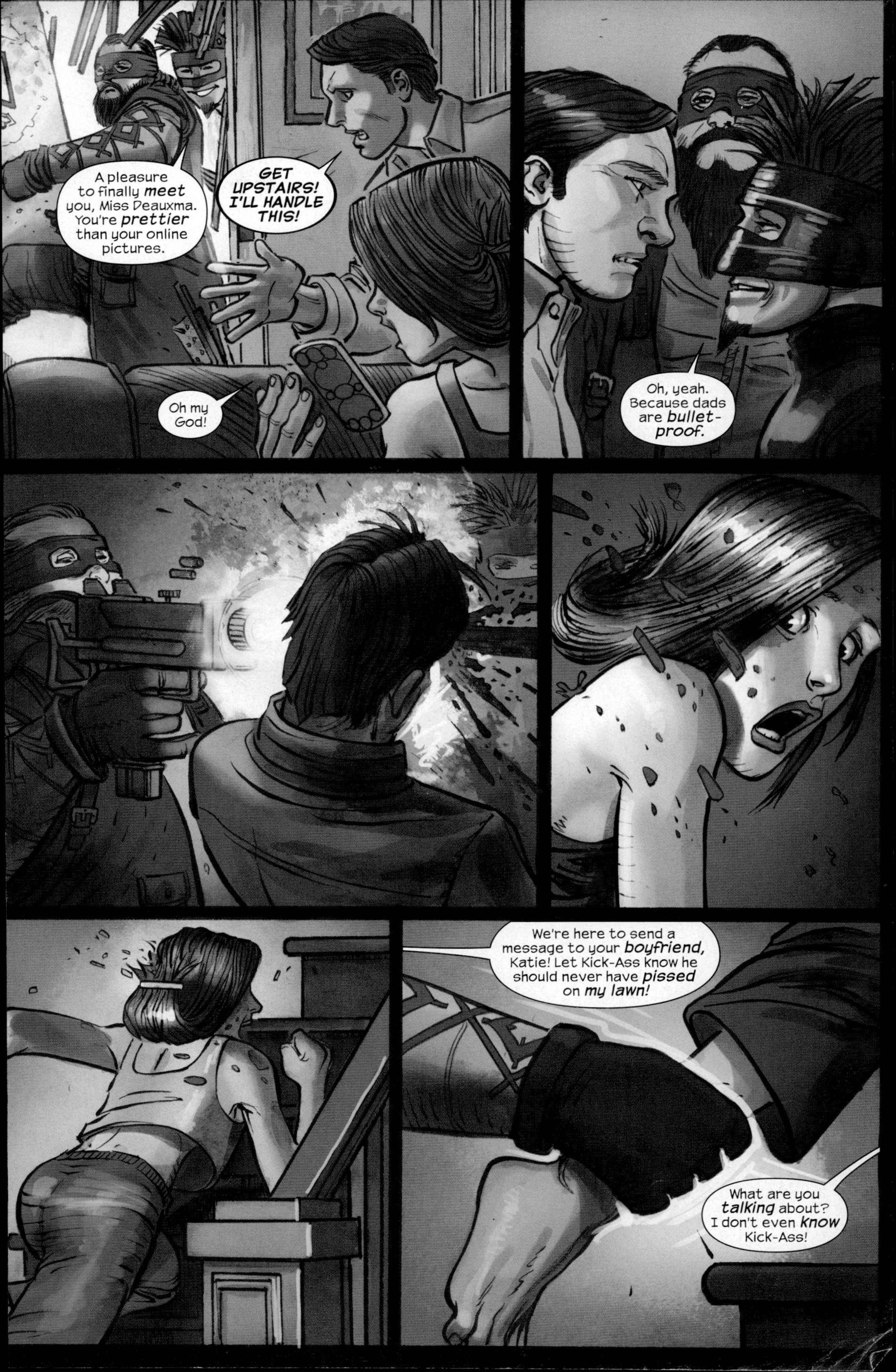
A pleasure to finally *meet* you, Miss Deauxma. You're *prettier* than your online pictures.
GET UPSTAIRS! I'LL HANDLE THIS!
Oh my God!
Oh, yeah. Because dads are *bullet-proof*.
We're here to send a message to your *boyfriend*, Katie! Let Kick-Ass know he should never have *pissed* on *my lawn!*
What are you *talking* about? I don't even *know* Kick-Ass!

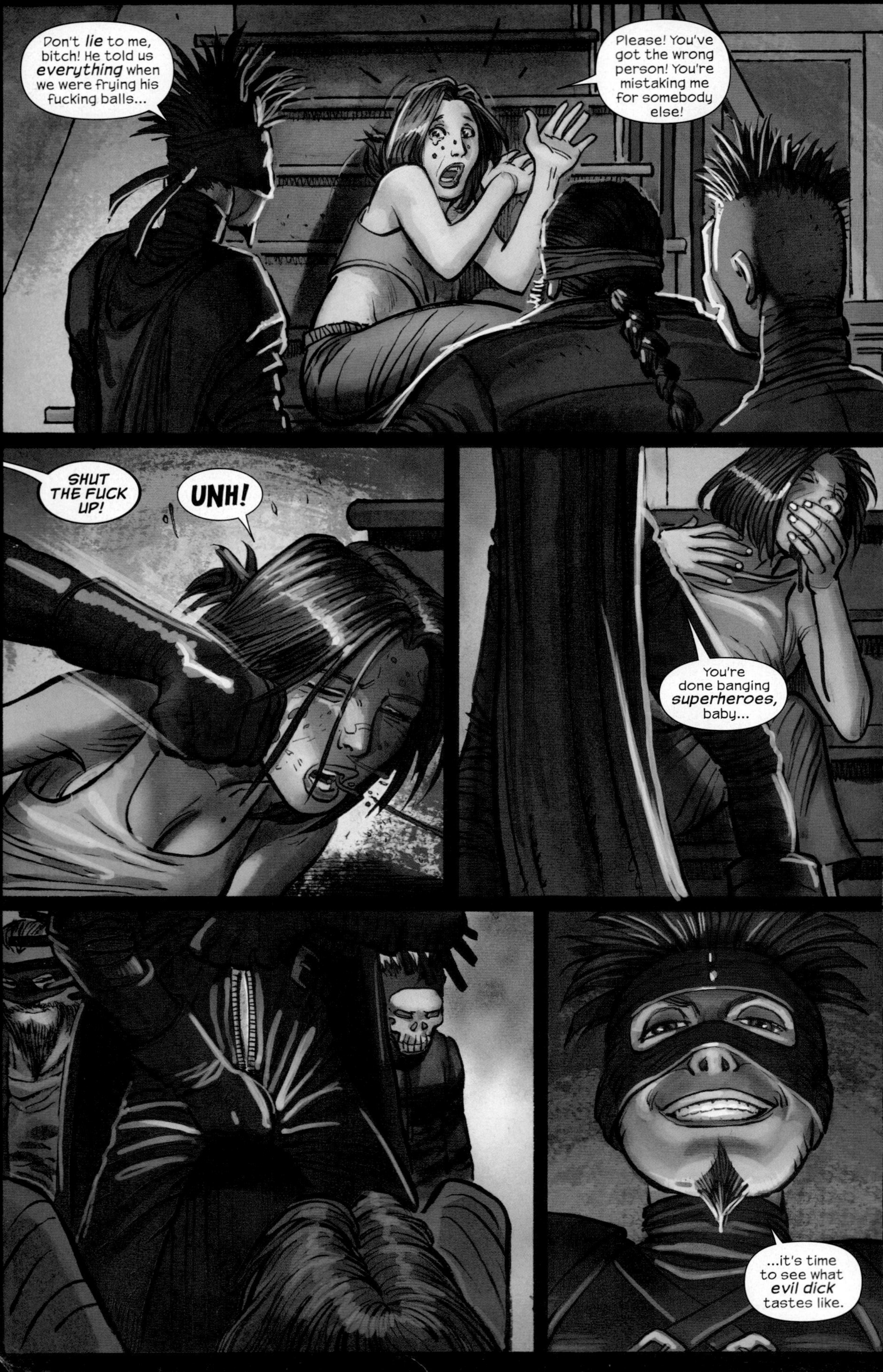
Don't lie to me, bitch! He told us everything when we were frying his fucking balls...
Please! You've got the wrong person! You're mistaking me for somebody else!
SHUT THE FUCK UP!
UNH!
You're done banging superheroes, baby...
...it's time to see what evil dick tastes like.

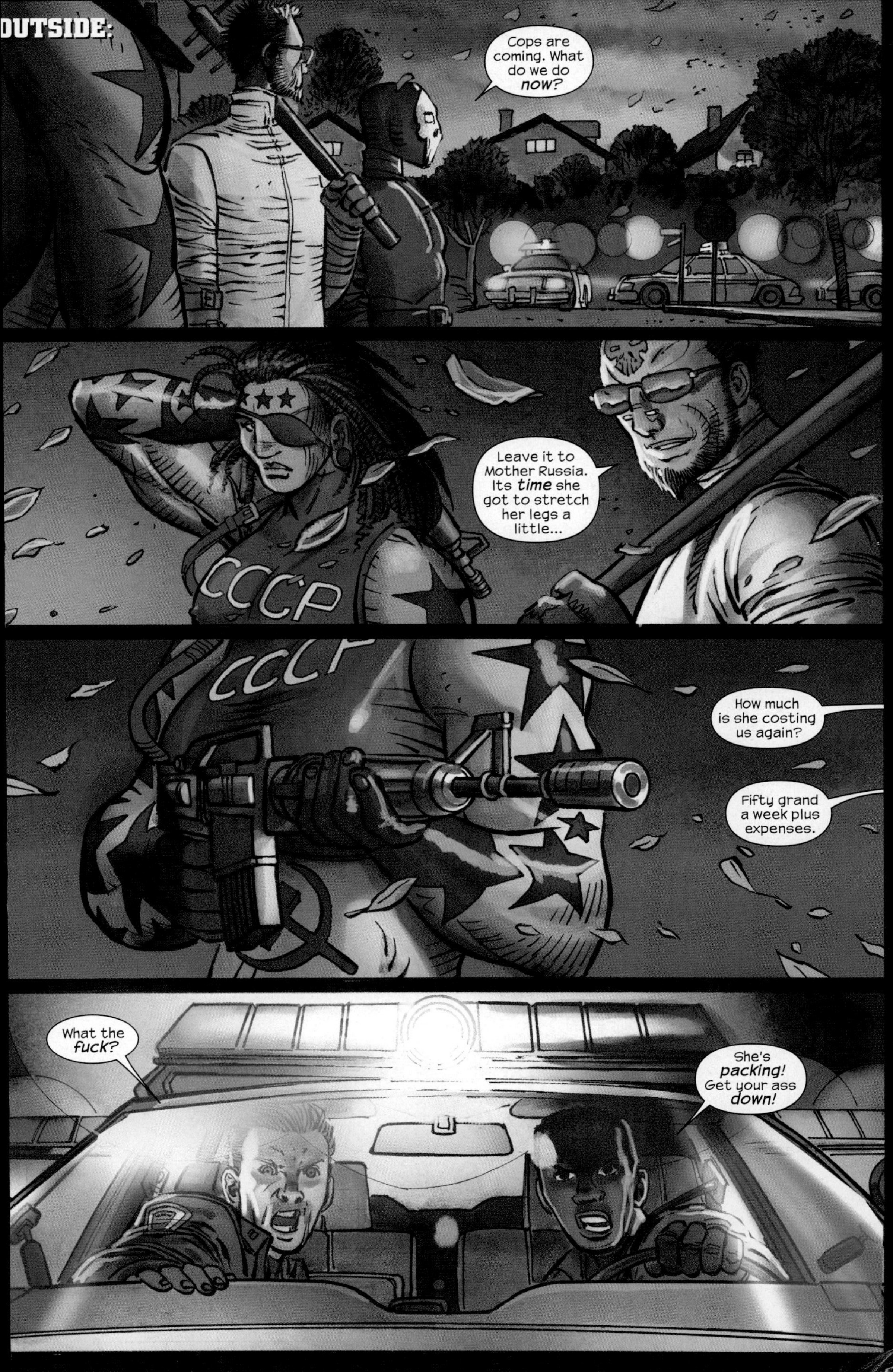
OUTSIDE:
Cops are coming. What do we do *now?*
Leave it to Mother Russia. Its *time* she got to stretch her legs a little...
CCCP
CCCP
How much is she costing us again?
Fifty grand a week plus expenses.
What the *fuck?*
She's *packing!* Get your ass *down!*

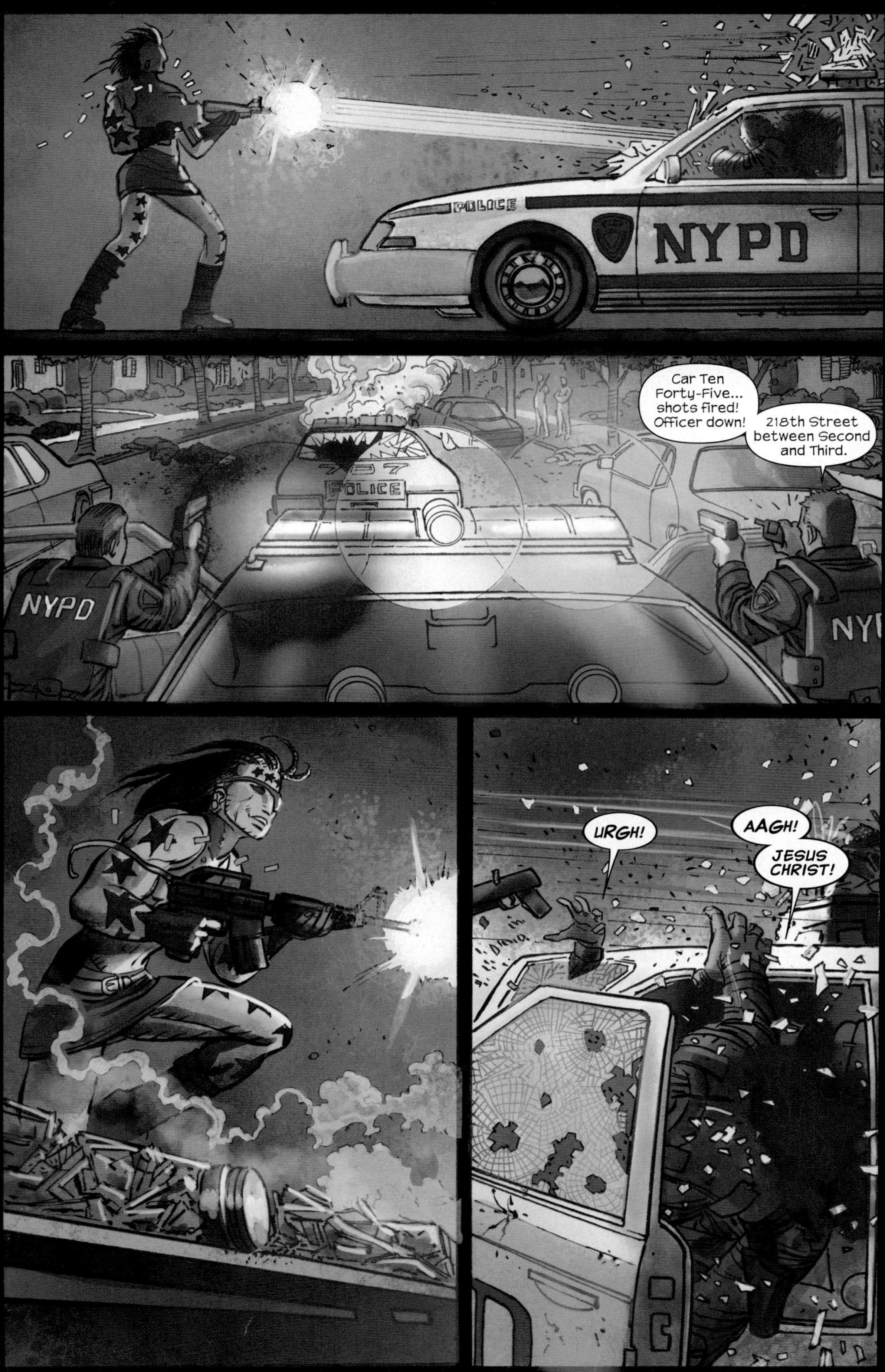

NYPD
POLICE
Car Ten Forty-Five... shots fired! Officer down!
218th Street between Second and Third.
POLICE
NYPD
URGH!
AAGH! JESUS CHRIST!

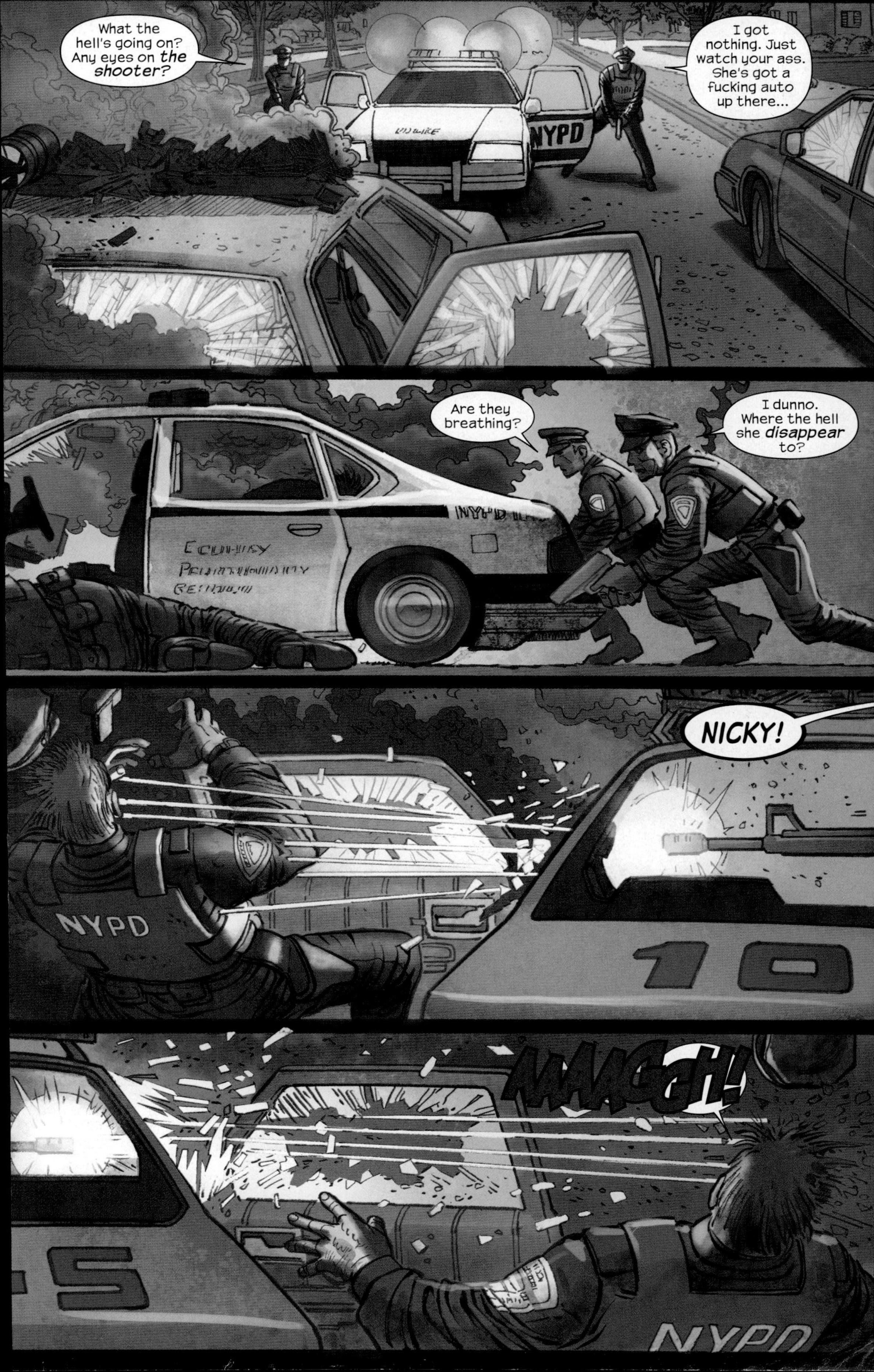
What the hell's going on? Any eyes on *the shooter*?
I got nothing. Just watch your ass. She's got a fucking auto up there...
NYPD
Are they breathing?
I dunno. Where the hell she *disappear* to?
NICKY!
NYPD
10
MAAGGH!
NYPD

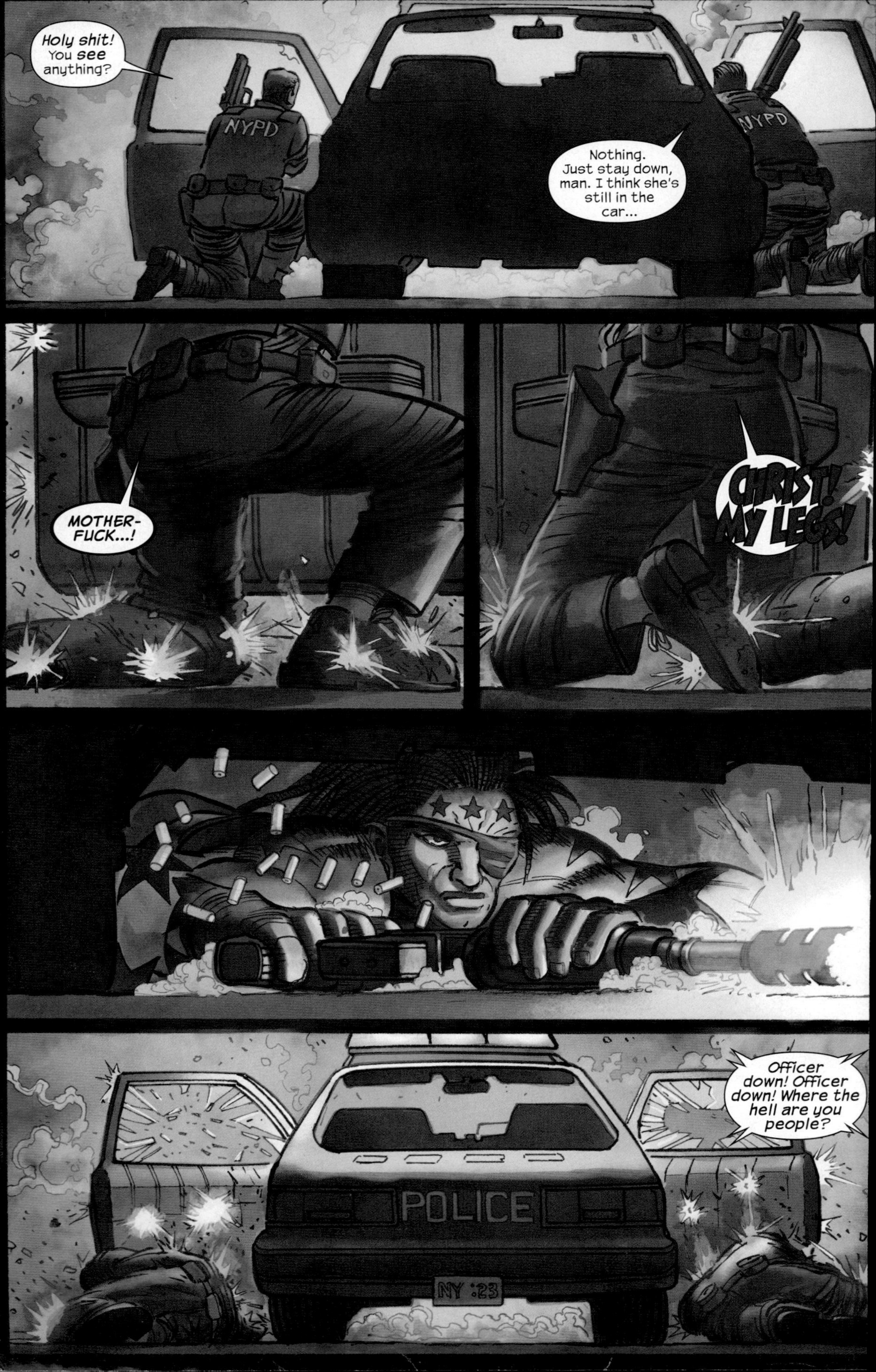
Holy shit! You see anything?
Nothing. Just stay down, man. I think she's still in the car...
MOTHER-FUCK...!
CHRIST! MY LEGS!
Officer down! Officer down! Where the hell are you people?
POLICE
NY :23

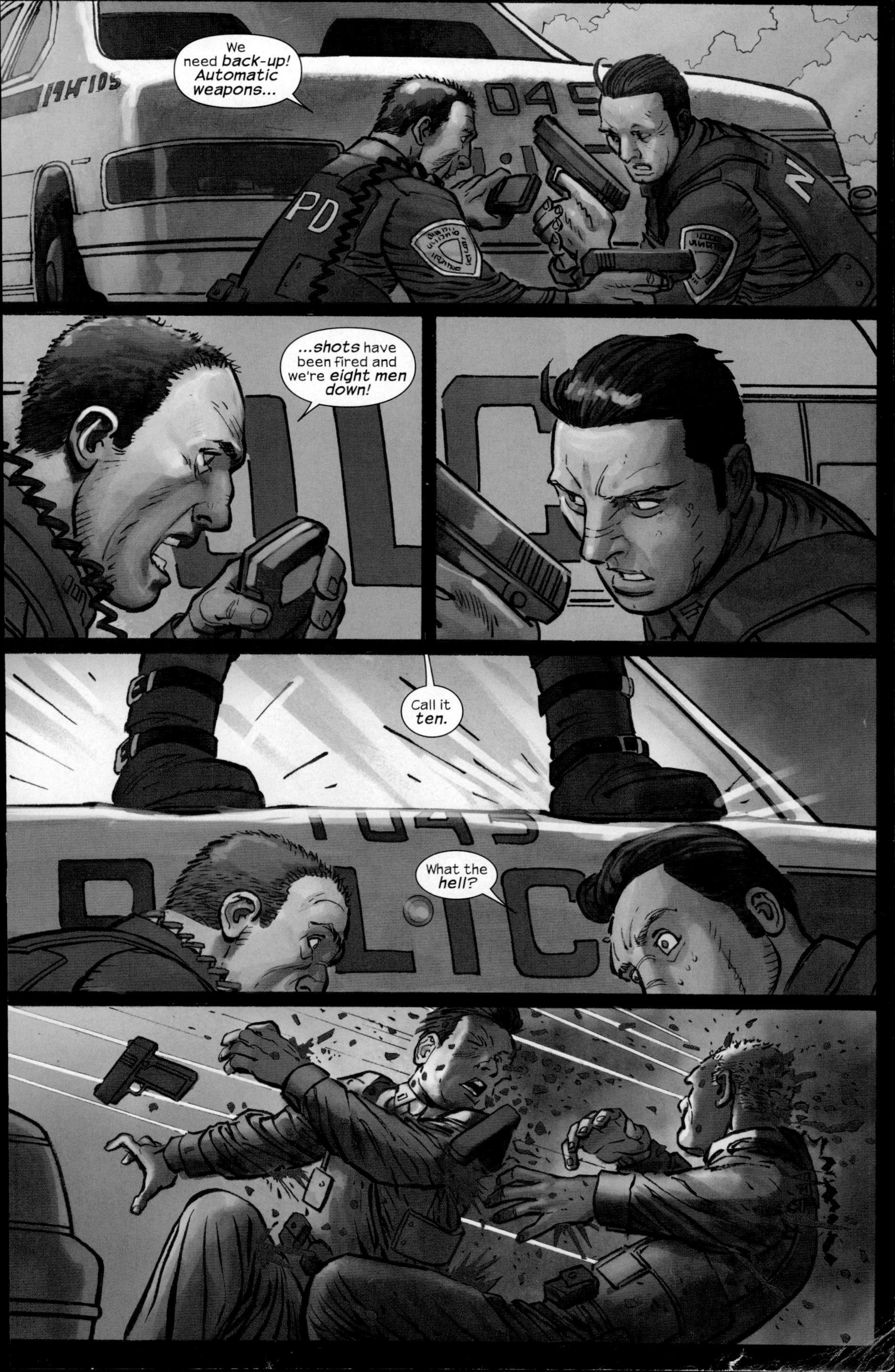
We need back-up! Automatic weapons...
...shots have been fired and we're eight men down!
Call it ten.
What the hell?

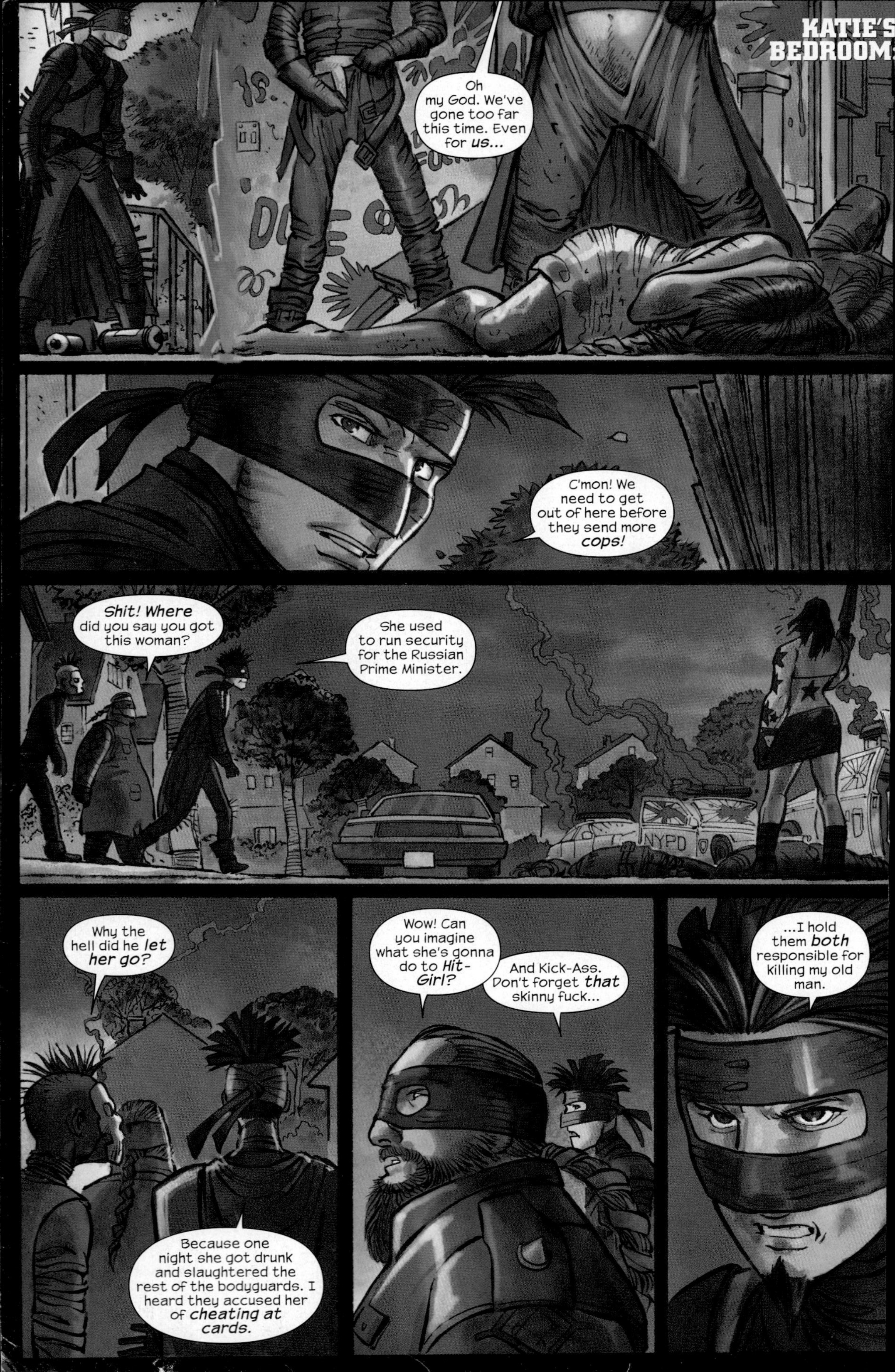
KATIE'S BEDROOM:
Oh my God. We've gone too far this time. Even for us...
C'mon! We need to get out of here before they send more cops!
Shit! Where did you say you got this woman?
She used to run security for the Russian Prime Minister.
NYPD
Why the hell did he let her go?
Because one night she got drunk and slaughtered the rest of the bodyguards. I heard they accused her of cheating at cards.
Wow! Can you imagine what she's gonna do to Hit-Girl?
And Kick-Ass. Don't forget that skinny fuck...
...I hold them both responsible for killing my old man.

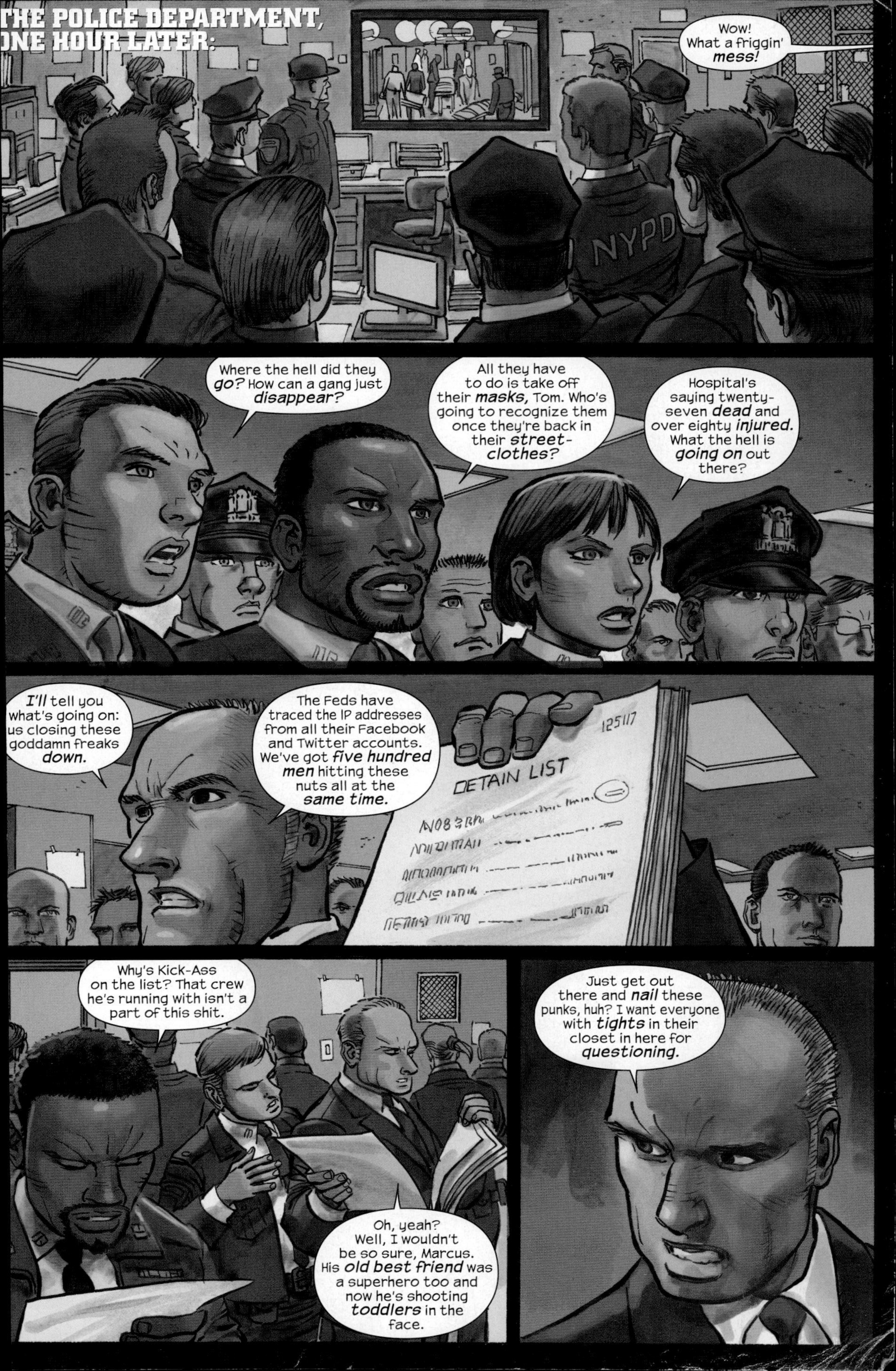

THE POLICE DEPARTMENT, ONE HOUR LATER:
Wow! What a friggin' mess!
Where the hell did they go? How can a gang just disappear?
All they have to do is take off their masks, Tom. Who's going to recognize them once they're back in their street-clothes?
Hospital's saying twenty-seven dead and over eighty injured. What the hell is going on out there?
I'll tell you what's going on: us closing these goddamn freaks down.
The Feds have traced the IP addresses from all their Facebook and Twitter accounts. We've got five hundred men hitting these nuts all at the same time.
125117
DETAIN LIST
Why's Kick-Ass on the list? That crew he's running with isn't a part of this shit.
Oh, yeah? Well, I wouldn't be so sure, Marcus. His old best friend was a superhero too and now he's shooting toddlers in the face.
Just get out there and nail these punks, huh? I want everyone with tights in their closet in here for questioning.

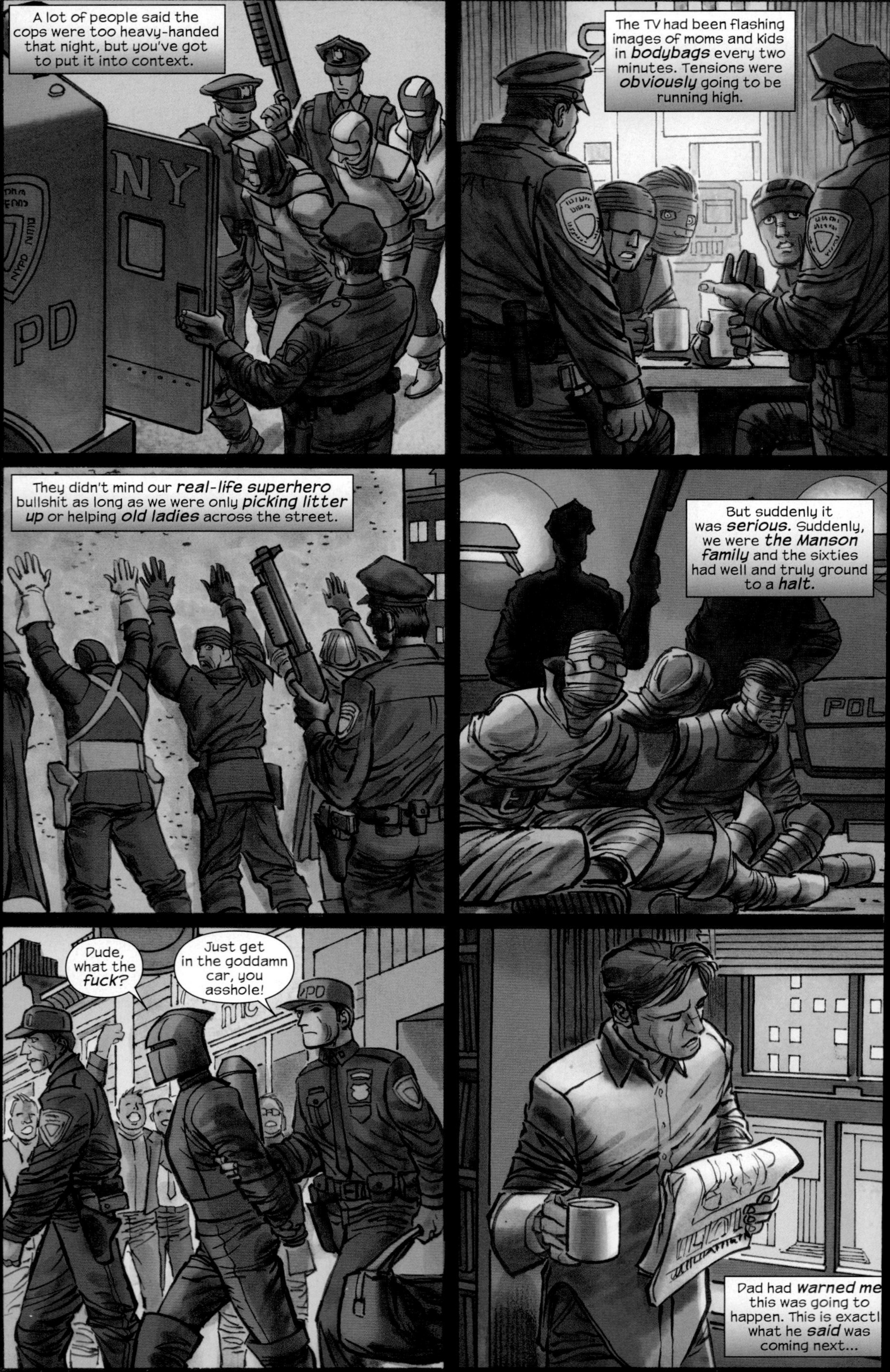
A lot of people said the cops were too heavy-handed that night, but you've got to put it into context.
The TV had been flashing images of moms and kids in *bodybags* every two minutes. Tensions were *obviously* going to be running high.
They didn't mind our *real-life superhero* bullshit as long as we were only *picking litter up* or helping *old ladies* across the street.
But suddenly it was *serious.* Suddenly, we were *the Manson family* and the sixties had well and truly ground to a *halt.*
Dude, what the *fuck?*
Just get in the goddamn car, you asshole!
Dad had *warned me* this was going to happen. This is exactl what he *said* was coming next...

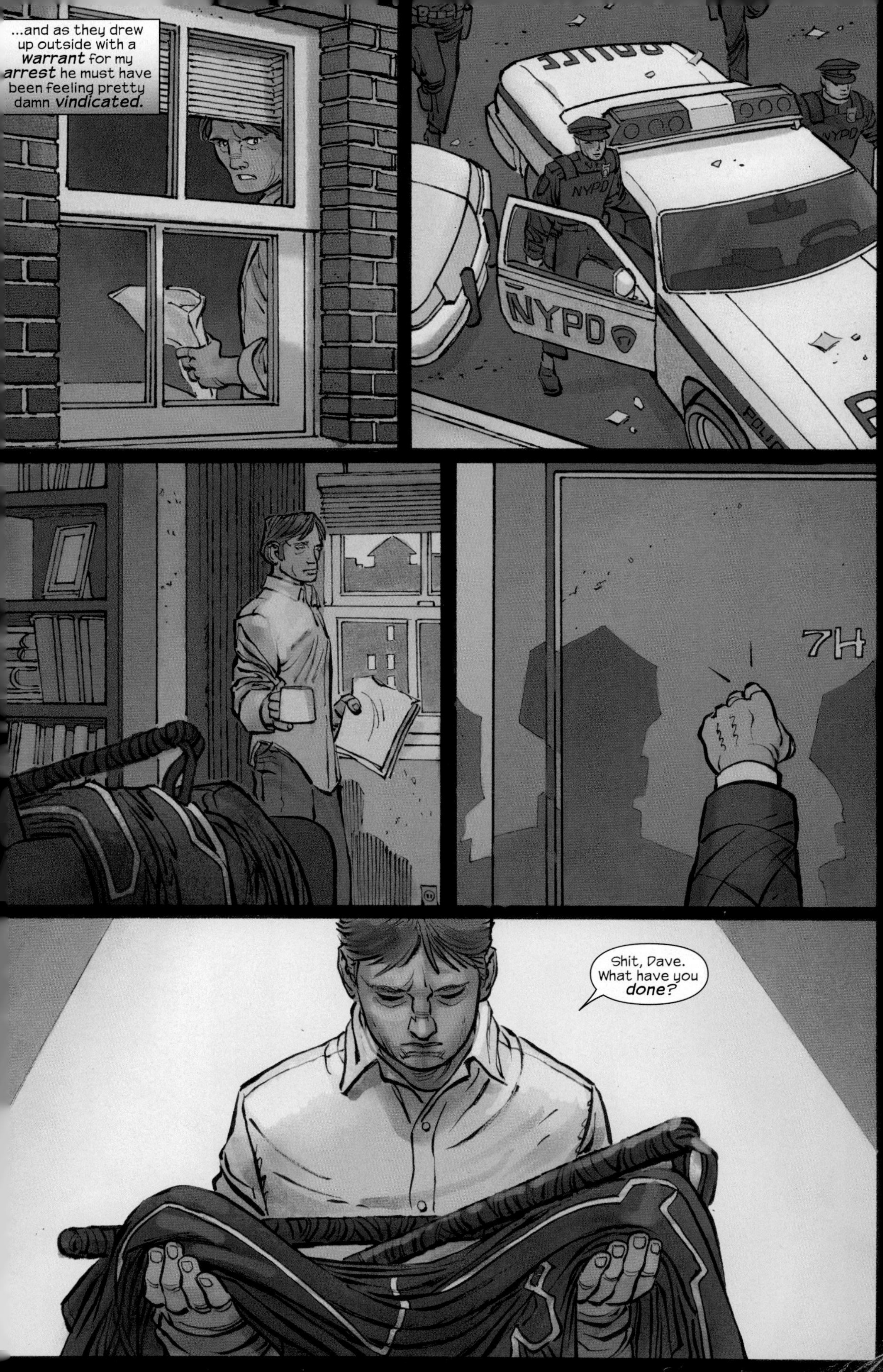
...and as they drew up outside with a *warrant* for my *arrest* he must have been feeling pretty damn *vindicated.*
POLICE
NYPD
NYPD
NYPD
7H
Shit, Dave. What have you *done*?

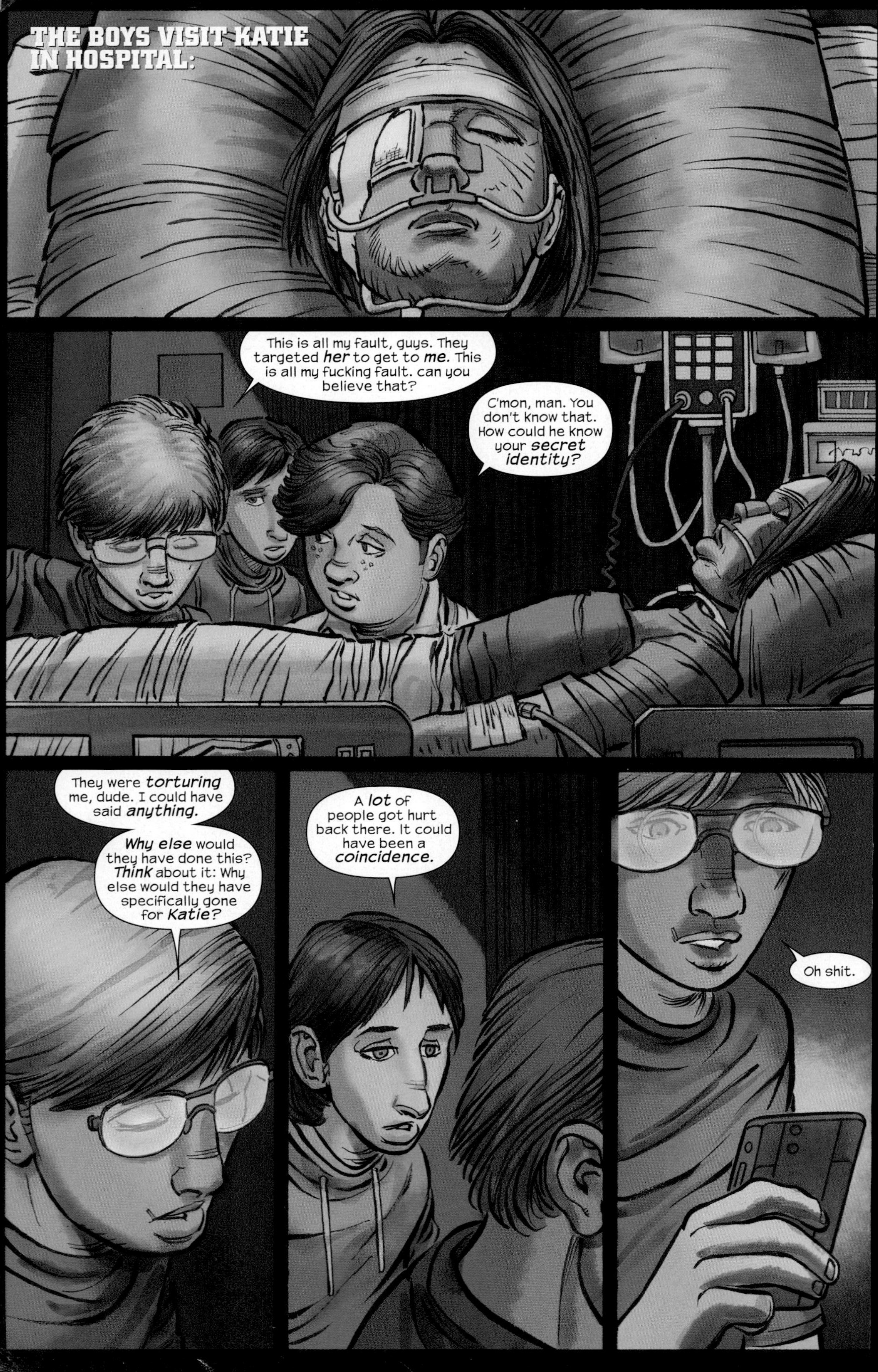
THE BOYS VISIT KATIE IN HOSPITAL:
This is all my fault, guys. They targeted *her* to get to *me.* This is all my fucking fault. can you believe that?
C'mon, man. You don't know that. How could he know your *secret identity?*
They were *torturing* me, dude. I could have said *anything.*
Why else would they have done this? *Think* about it: Why else would they have specifically gone for *Katie?*
A *lot* of people got hurt back there. It could have been a *coincidence.*
Oh shit.

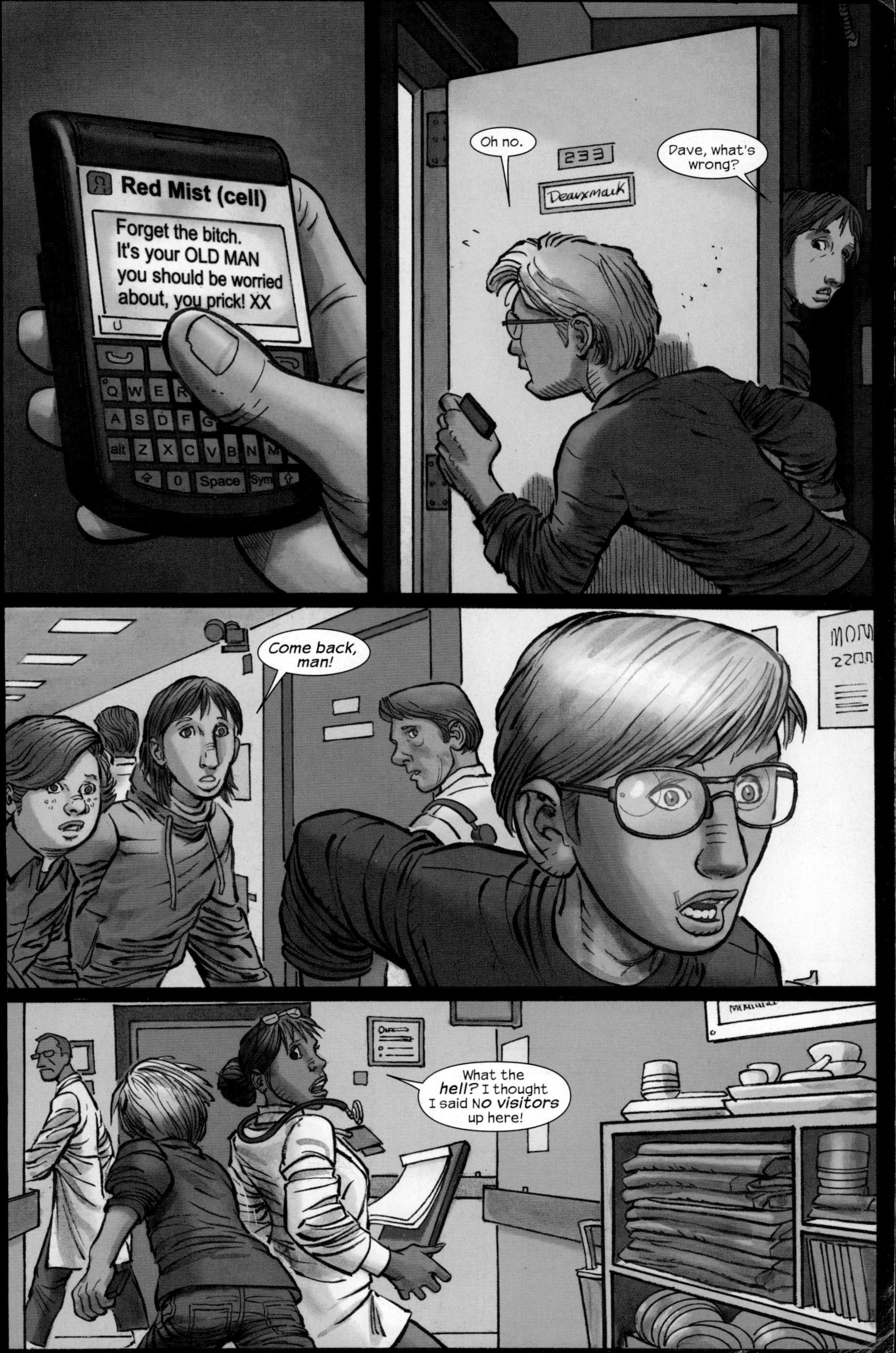
Red Mist (cell)
Forget the bitch. It's your OLD MAN you should be worried about, you prick! XX
Oh no.
233
Deauxmark
Dave, what's wrong?
Come back, man!
What the *hell?* I thought I said NO *visitors* up here!

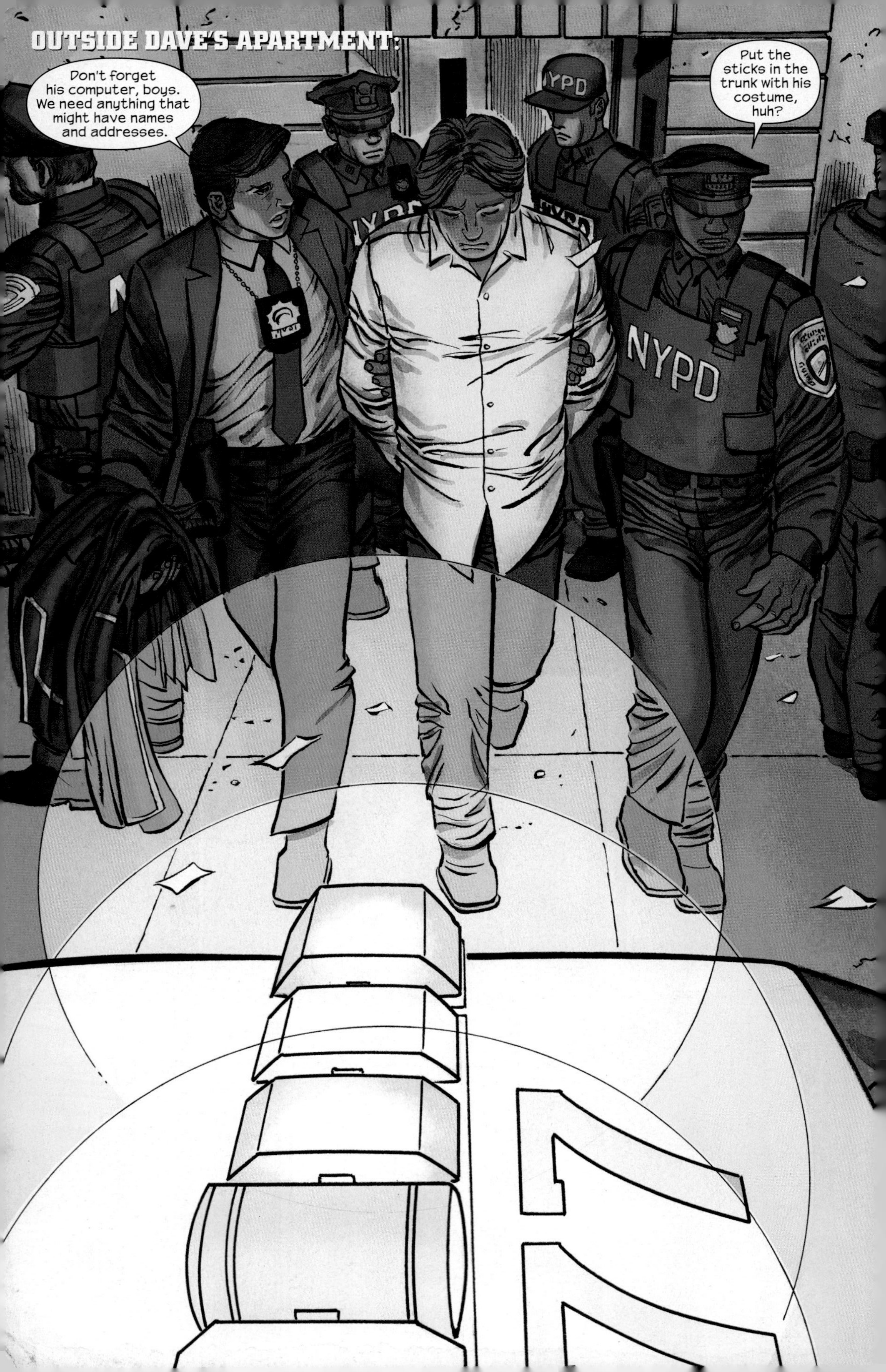
OUTSIDE DAVE'S APARTMENT:
Don't forget his computer, boys. We need anything that might have names and addresses.
Put the sticks in the trunk with his costume, huh?
NYPD

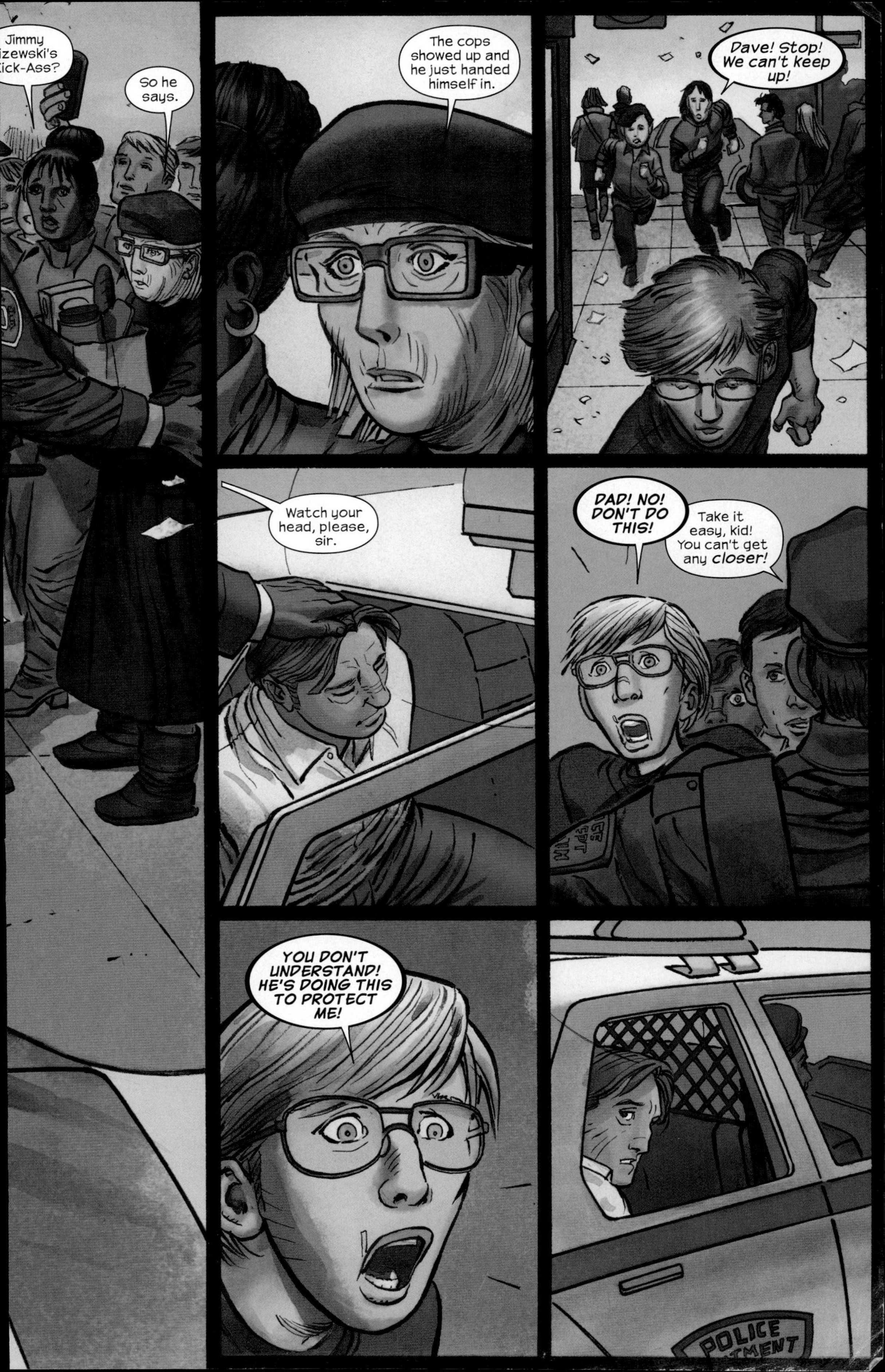

Jimmy
izewski's
Kick-Ass?
So he says.
The cops showed up and he just handed himself in.
Dave! Stop! We can't keep up!
Watch your head, please, sir.
DAD! NO! DON'T DO THIS!
Take it easy, kid! You can't get any closer!
YOU DON'T UNDERSTAND! HE'S DOING THIS TO PROTECT ME!
POLICE
TMENT

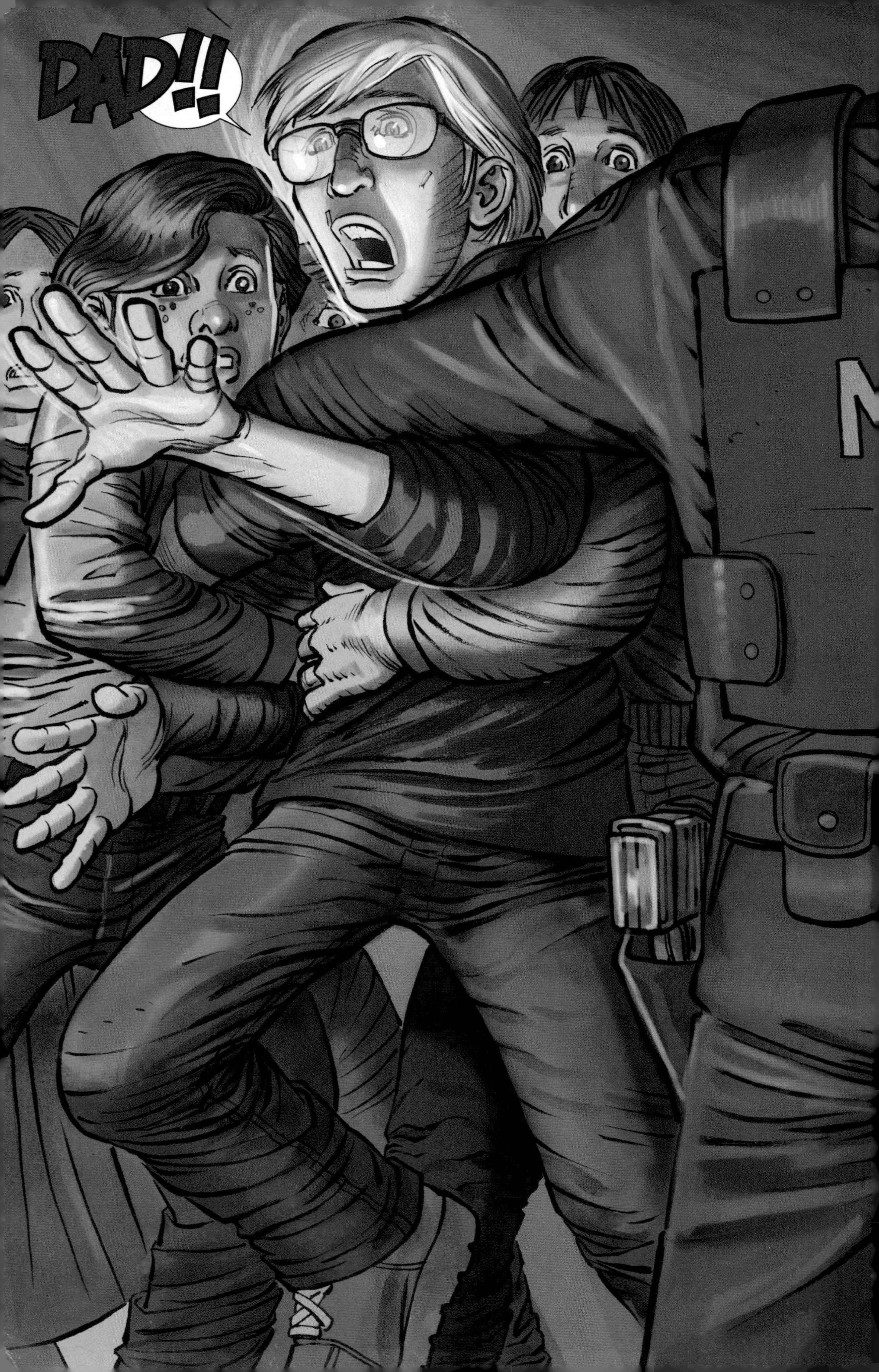
DAD!!

FIVE

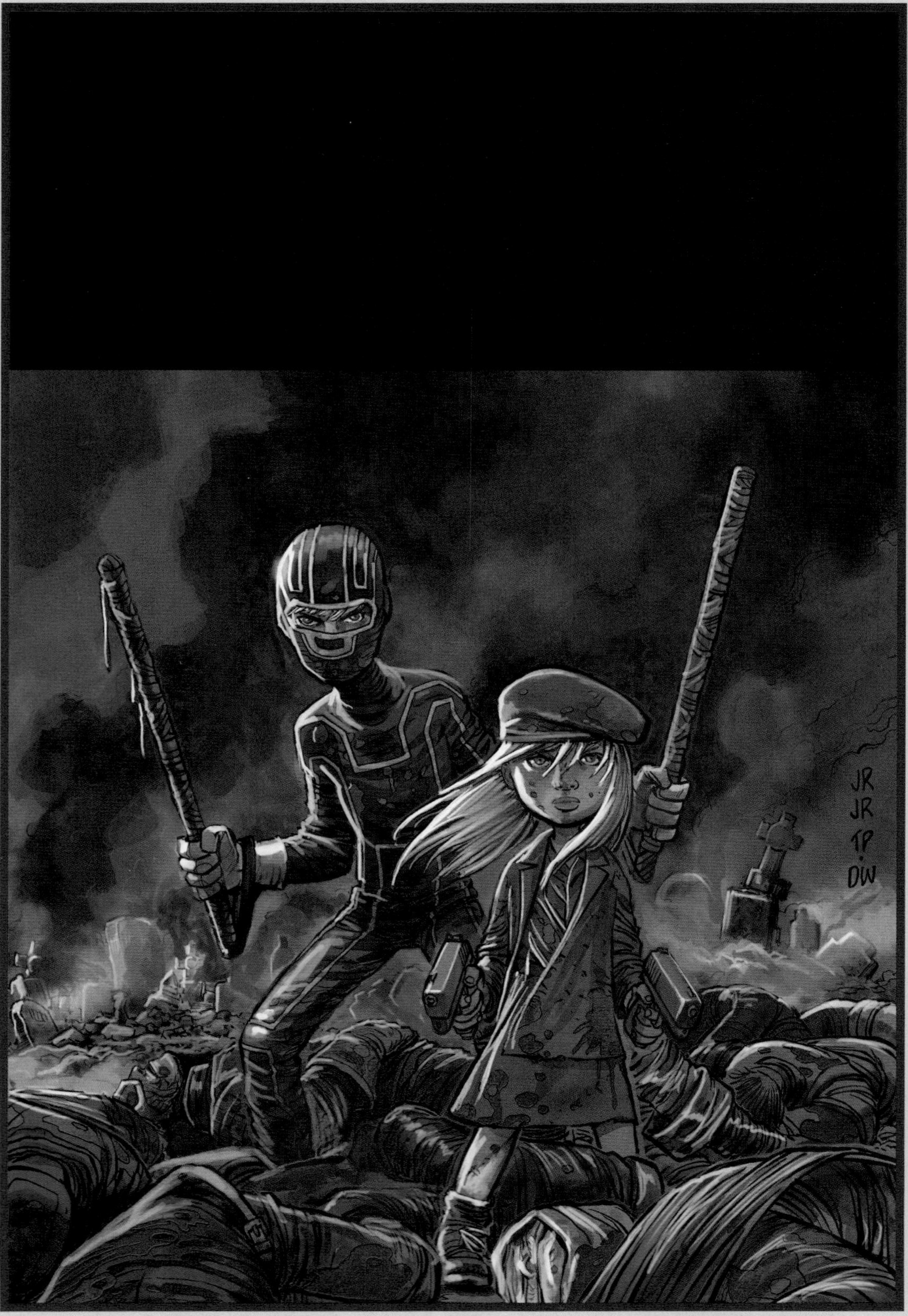
JR
JR
TP
DW

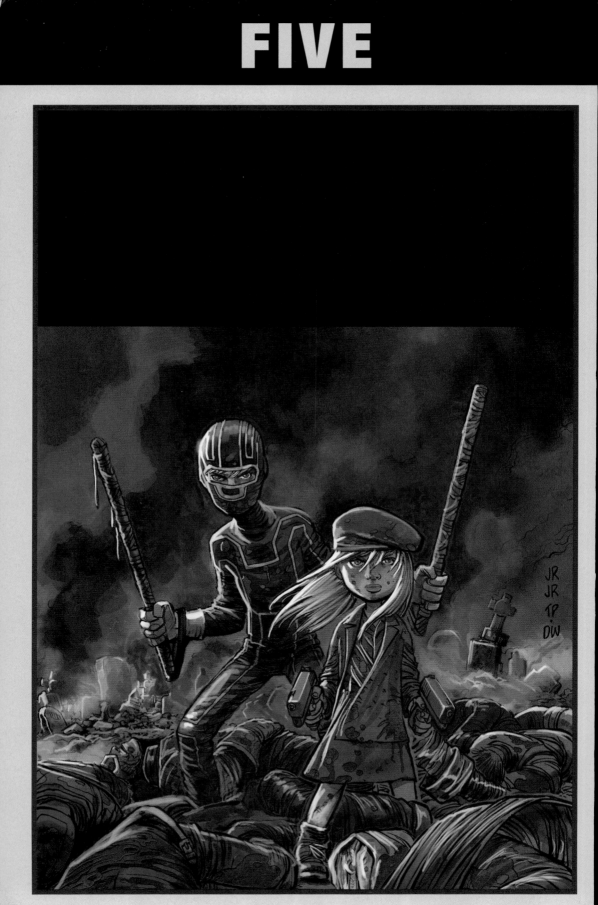

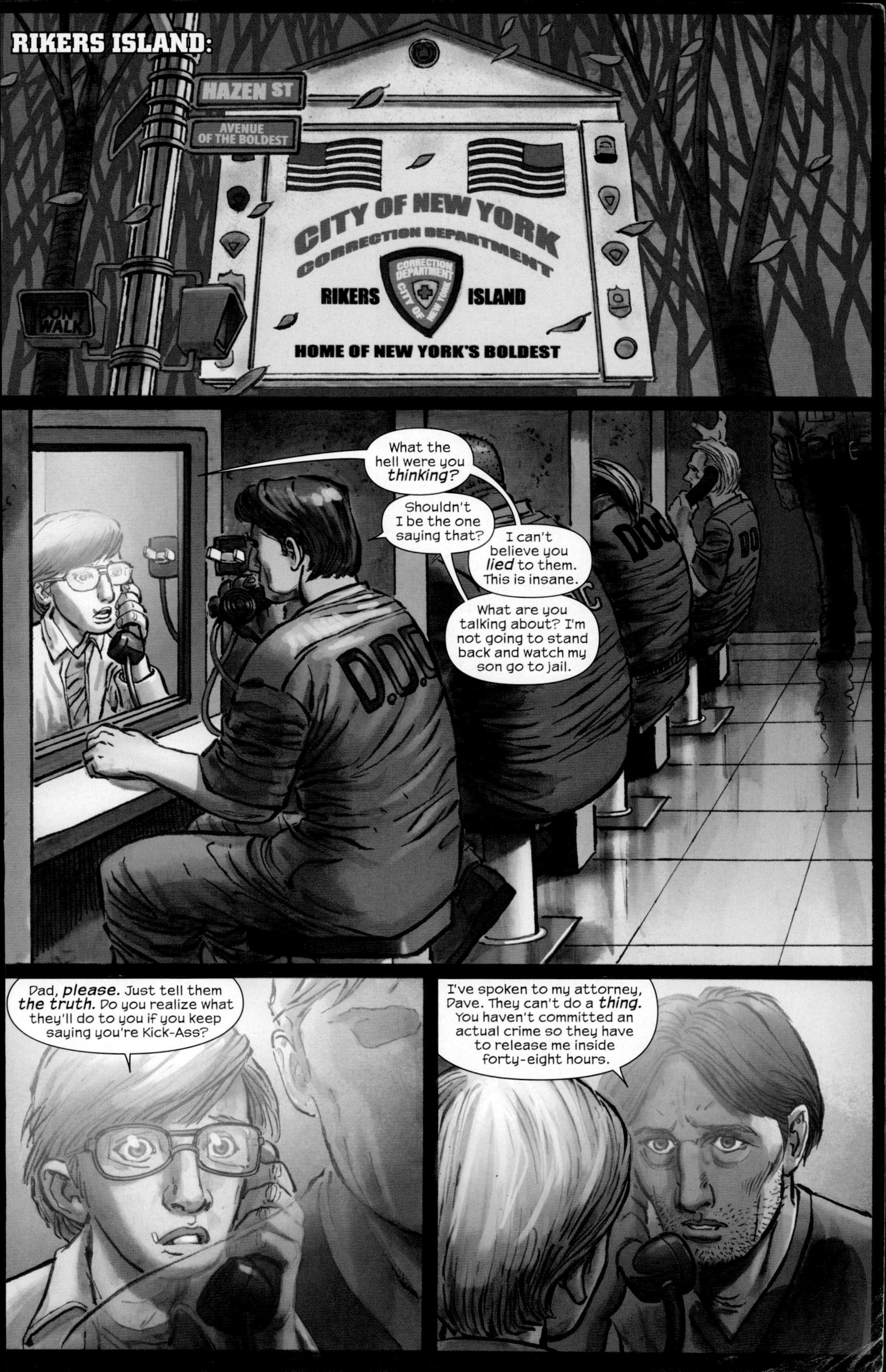
RIKERS ISLAND:
HAZEN ST
AVENUE OF THE BOLDEST
DON'T WALK
CITY OF NEW YORK
CORRECTION DEPARTMENT
CORRECTION DEPARTMENT CITY OF NEW YORK
RIKERS ISLAND
HOME OF NEW YORK'S BOLDEST
What the hell were you *thinking?*
Shouldn't I be the one saying that?
I can't believe you *lied* to them. This is insane.
What are you talking about? I'm not going to stand back and watch my son go to jail.
Dad, ***please.*** Just tell them ***the truth.*** Do you realize what they'll do to you if you keep saying you're Kick-Ass?
I've spoken to my attorney, Dave. They can't do a ***thing.*** You haven't committed an actual crime so they have to release me inside forty-eight hours.

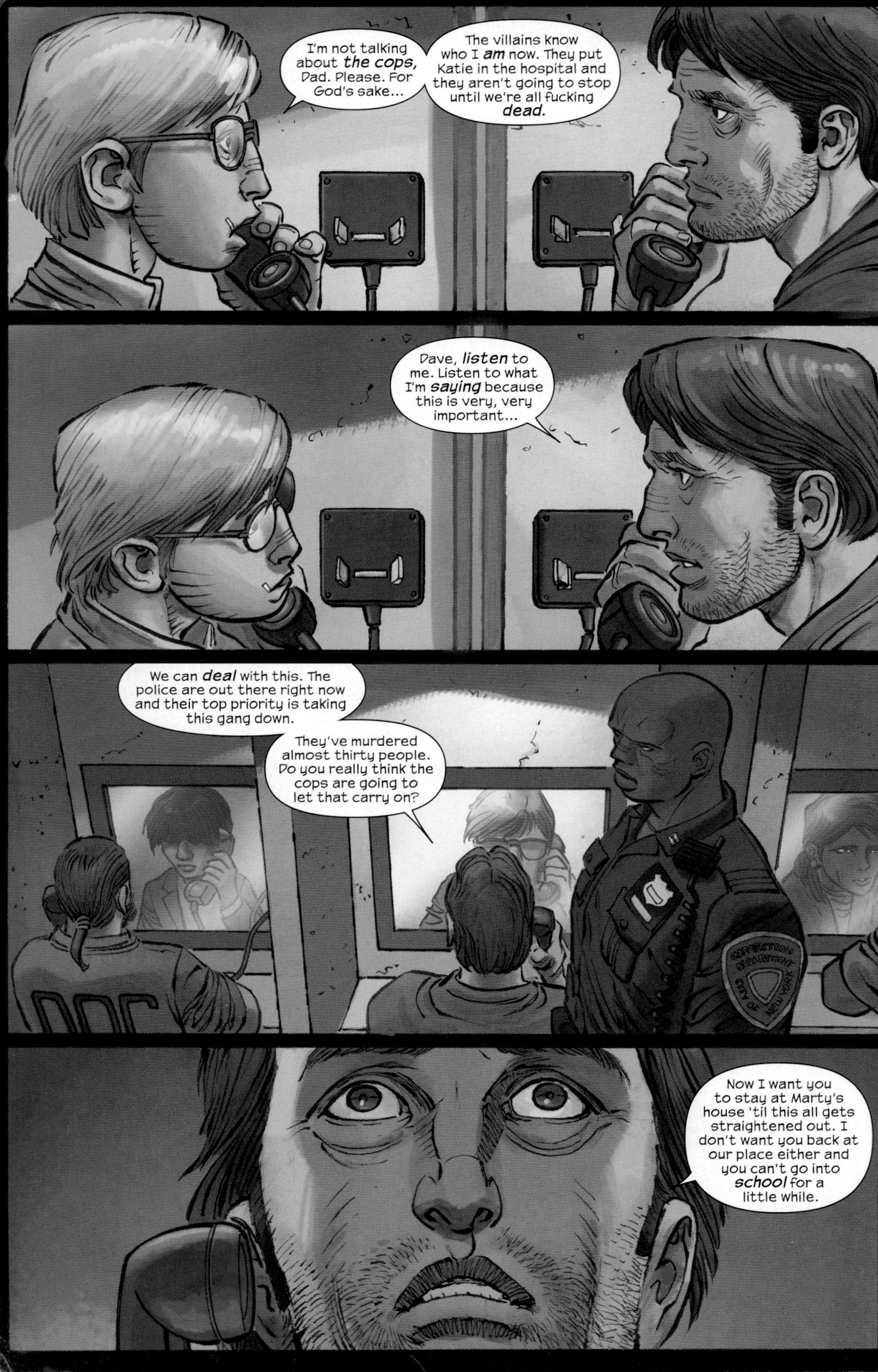
I'm not talking about the cops, Dad. Please. For God's sake...
The villains know who I am now. They put Katie in the hospital and they aren't going to stop until we're all fucking dead.
Dave, listen to me. Listen to what I'm saying because this is very, very important...
We can deal with this. The police are out there right now and their top priority is taking this gang down.
They've murdered almost thirty people. Do you really think the cops are going to let that carry on?
CORRECTION DEPARTMENT CITY OF NEW YORK
Now I want you to stay at Marty's house 'til this all gets straightened out. I don't want you back at our place either and you can't go into school for a little while.

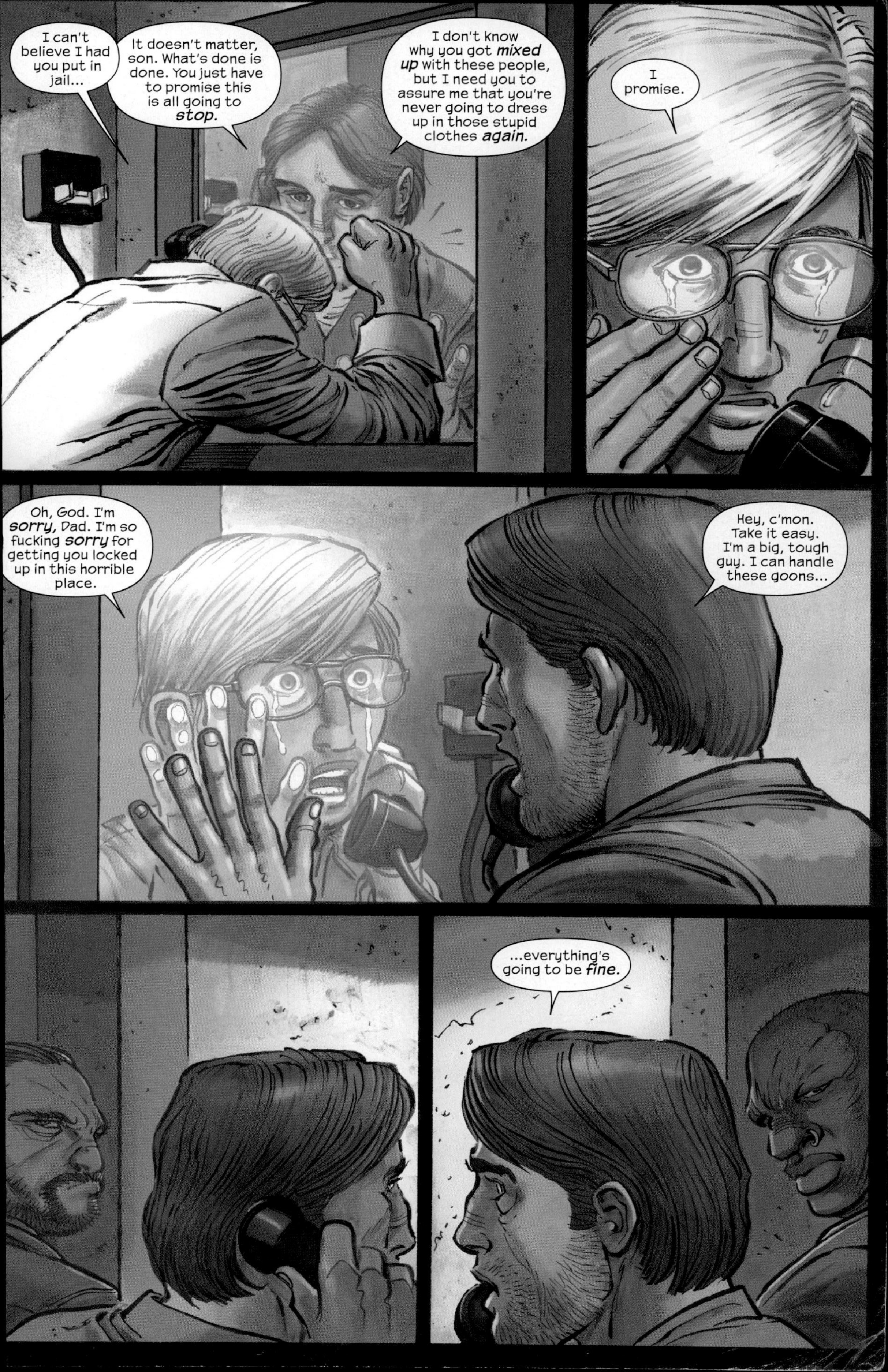
I can't believe I had you put in jail...
It doesn't matter, son. What's done is done. You just have to promise this is all going to *stop.*
I don't know why you got *mixed up* with these people, but I need you to assure me that you're never going to dress up in those stupid clothes *again.*
I promise.
Oh, God. I'm *sorry,* Dad. I'm so fucking *sorry* for getting you locked up in this horrible place.
Hey, c'mon. Take it easy. I'm a big, tough guy. I can handle these goons...
...everything's going to be *fine.*

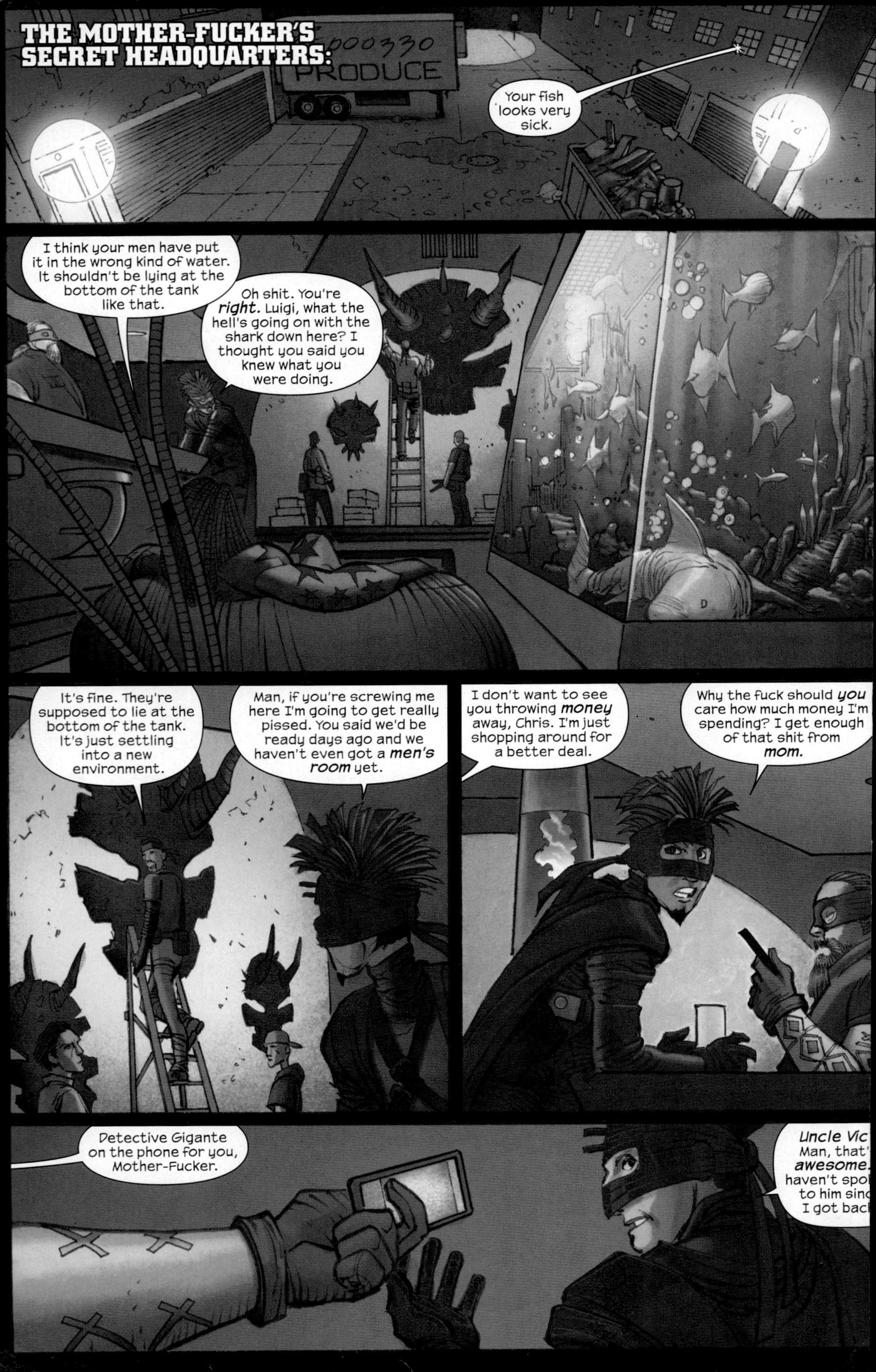
THE MOTHER-FUCKER'S SECRET HEADQUARTERS:
000330
PRODUCE
Your fish looks very sick.
I think your men have put it in the wrong kind of water. It shouldn't be lying at the bottom of the tank like that.
Oh shit. You're *right.* Luigi, what the hell's going on with the shark down here? I thought you said you knew what you were doing.
It's fine. They're supposed to lie at the bottom of the tank. It's just settling into a new environment.
Man, if you're screwing me here I'm going to get really pissed. You said we'd be ready days ago and we haven't even got a *men's room* yet.
I don't want to see you throwing *money* away, Chris. I'm just shopping around for a better deal.
Why the fuck should *you* care how much money I'm spending? I get enough of that shit from *mom.*
Detective Gigante on the phone for you, Mother-Fucker.
Uncle Vic
Man, that'
awesome.
haven't spo
to him sinc
I got bac

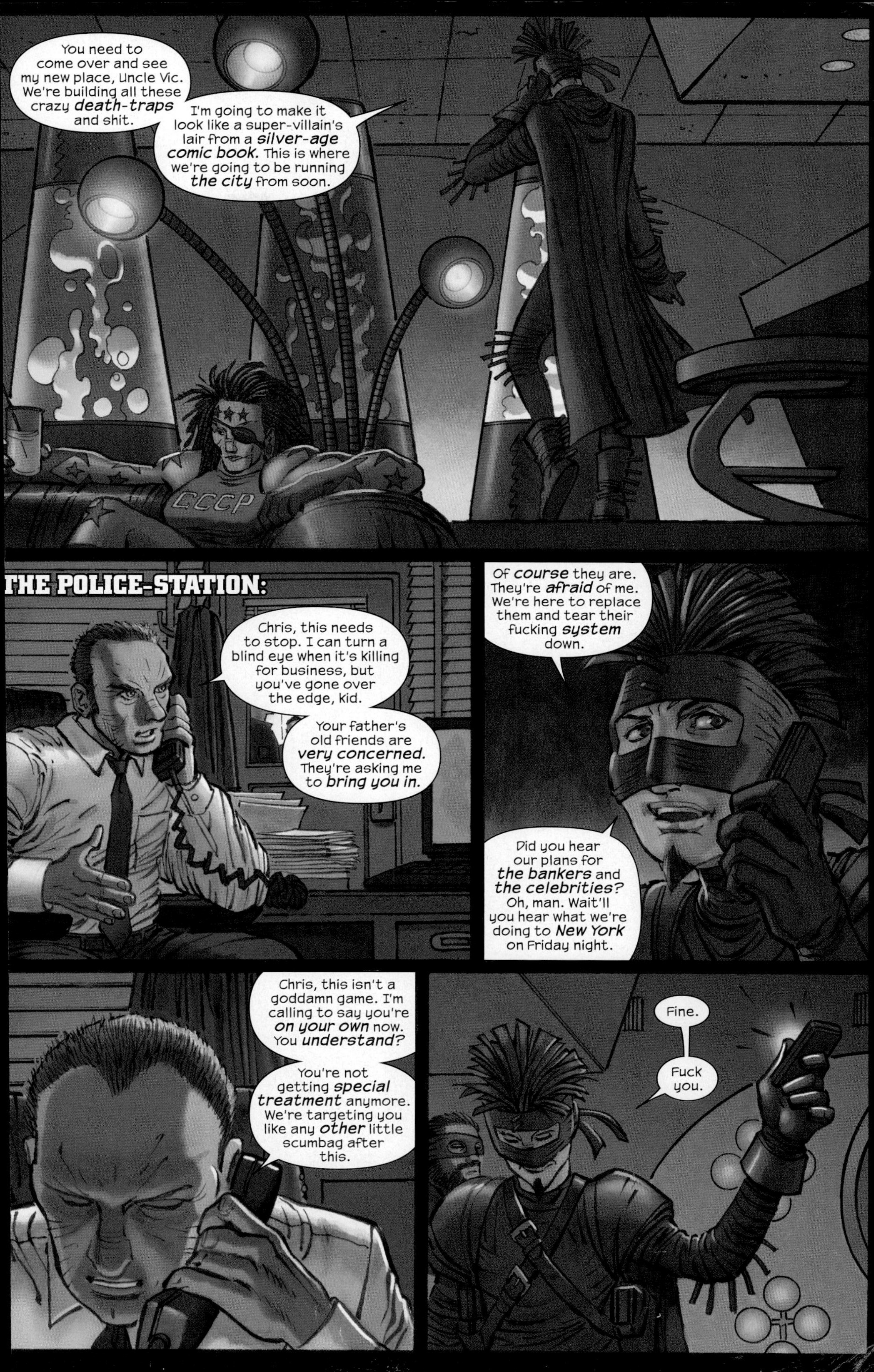
You need to come over and see my new place, Uncle Vic. We're building all these crazy *death-traps* and shit.
I'm going to make it look like a super-villain's lair from a *silver-age comic book.* This is where we're going to be running *the city* from soon.
CCCP
THE POLICE-STATION:
Chris, this needs to stop. I can turn a blind eye when it's killing for business, but you've gone over the edge, kid.
Your father's old friends are *very concerned.* They're asking me to *bring you in.*
Of *course* they are. They're *afraid* of me. We're here to replace them and tear their fucking *system* down.
Did you hear our plans for *the bankers* and *the celebrities?* Oh, man. Wait'll you hear what we're doing to *New York* on Friday night.
Chris, this isn't a goddamn game. I'm calling to say you're *on your own* now. You *understand?*
You're not getting *special treatment* anymore. We're targeting you like any *other* little scumbag after this.
Fine.
Fuck you.

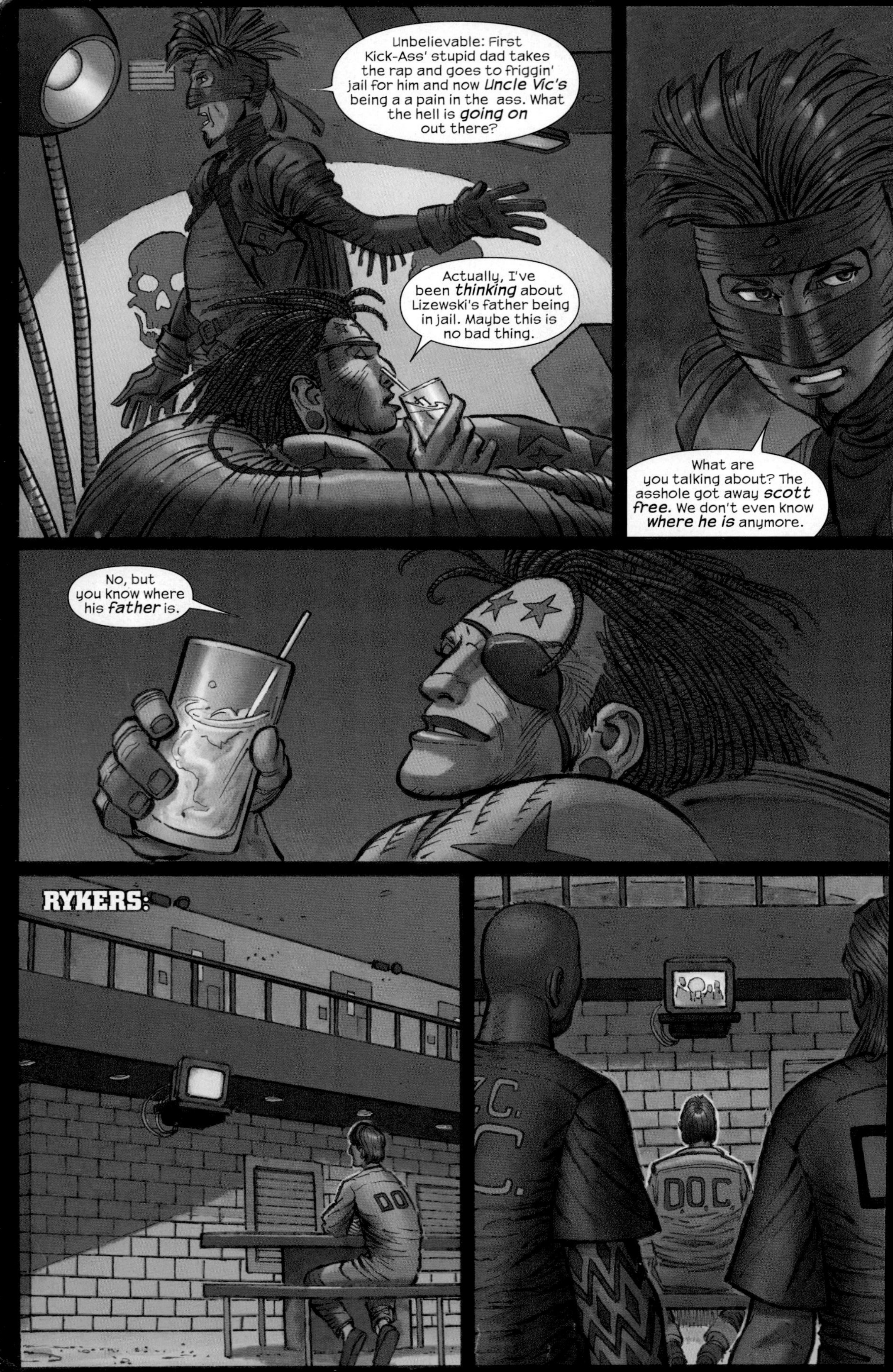
Unbelievable: First Kick-Ass' stupid dad takes the rap and goes to friggin' jail for him and now *Uncle Vic's* being a a pain in the ass. What the hell is *going on* out there?
Actually, I've been *thinking* about Lizewski's father being in jail. Maybe this is no bad thing.
What are you talking about? The asshole got away *scott free.* We don't even know *where he is* anymore.
No, but you know where his *father* is.
RYKERS:
DO
D.O.C.

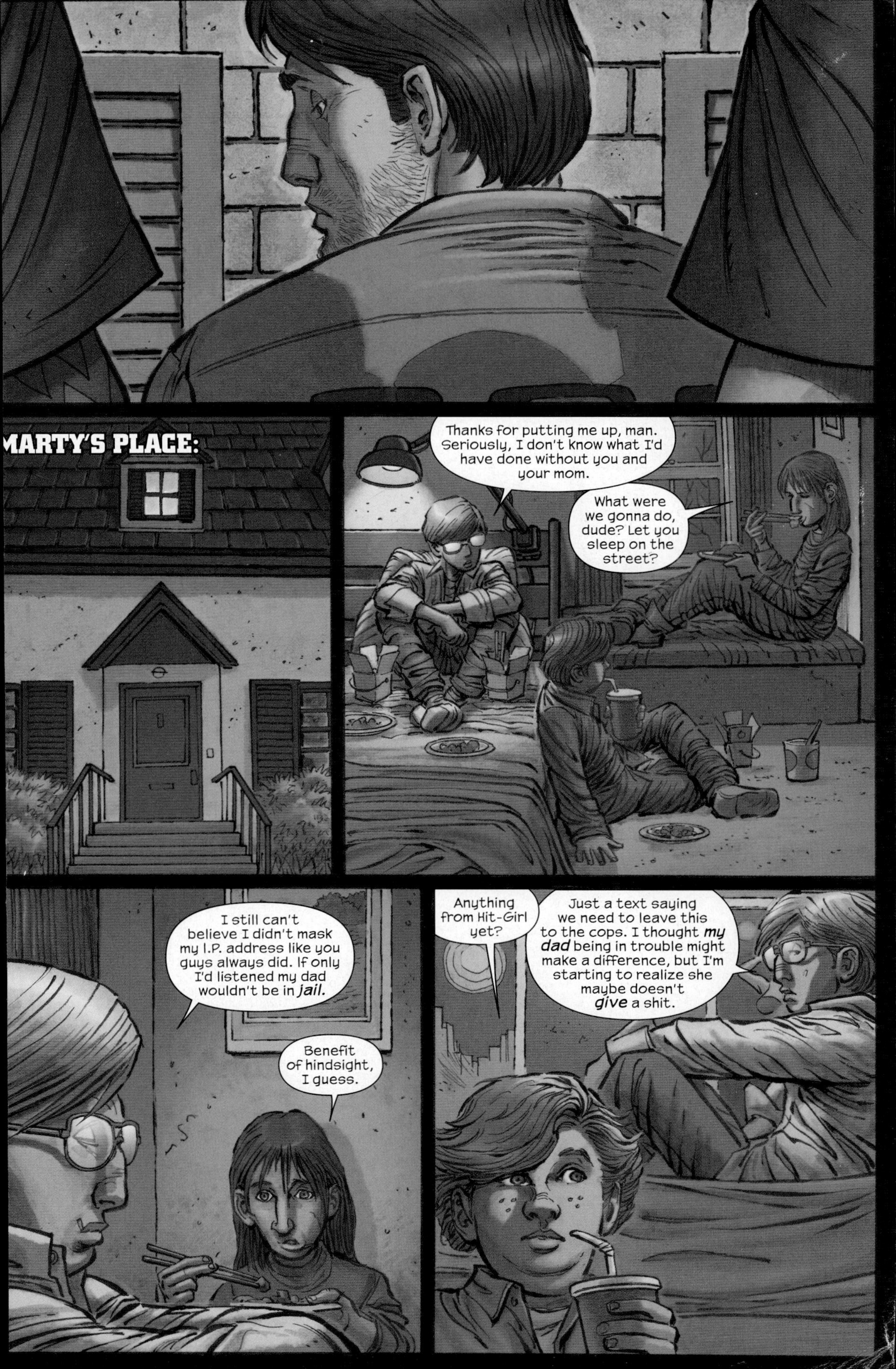
MARTY'S PLACE:
Thanks for putting me up, man. Seriously, I don't know what I'd have done without you and your mom.
What were we gonna do, dude? Let you sleep on the street?
I still can't believe I didn't mask my I.P. address like you guys always did. If only I'd listened my dad wouldn't be in *jail*.
Benefit of hindsight, I guess.
Anything from Hit-Girl yet?
Just a text saying we need to leave this to the cops. I thought *my dad* being in trouble might make a difference, but I'm starting to realize she maybe doesn't *give* a shit.

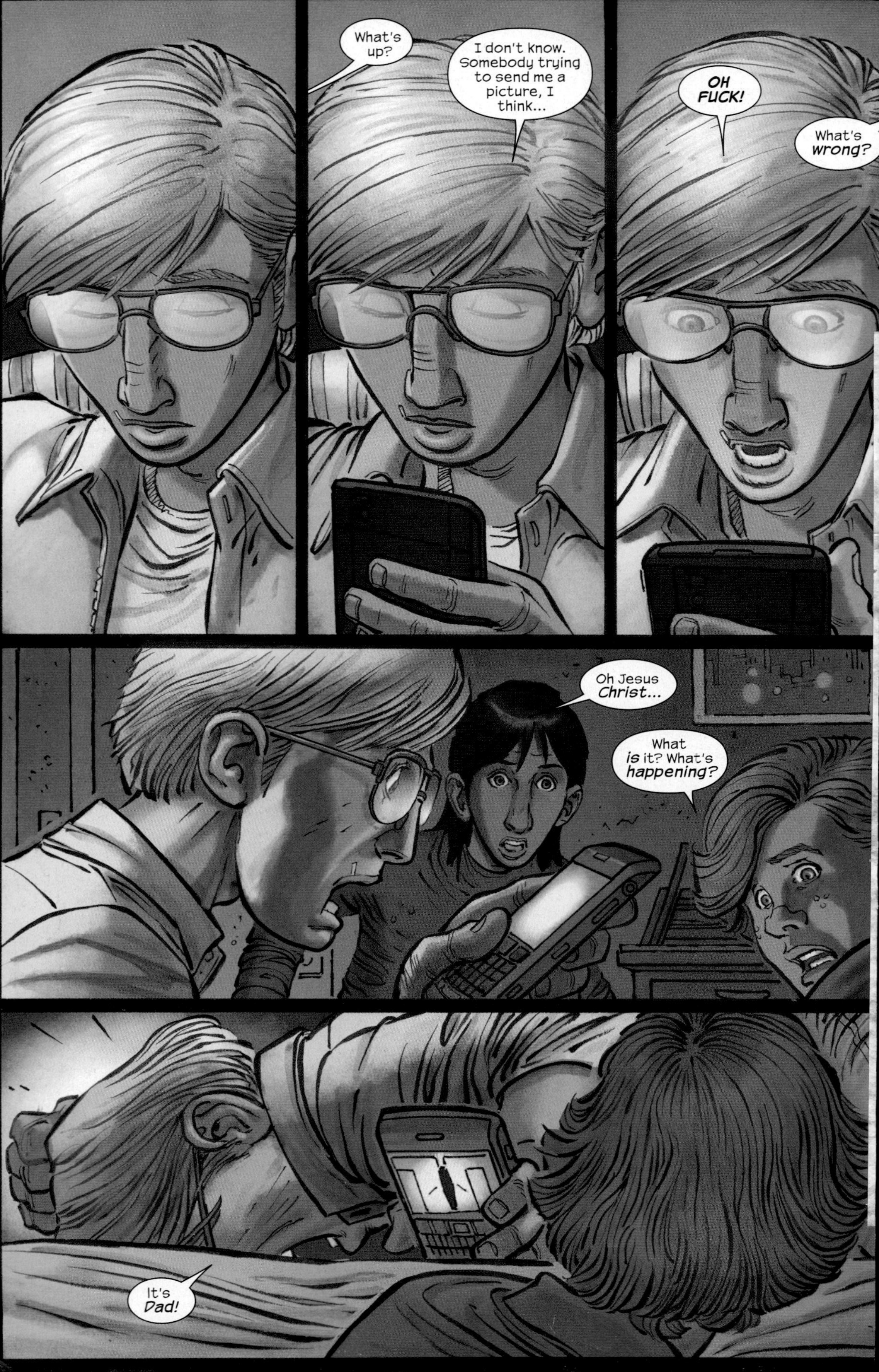
What's up?
I don't know. Somebody trying to send me a picture, I think...
OH FUCK!
What's wrong?
Oh Jesus Christ...
What is it? What's happening?
It's Dad!

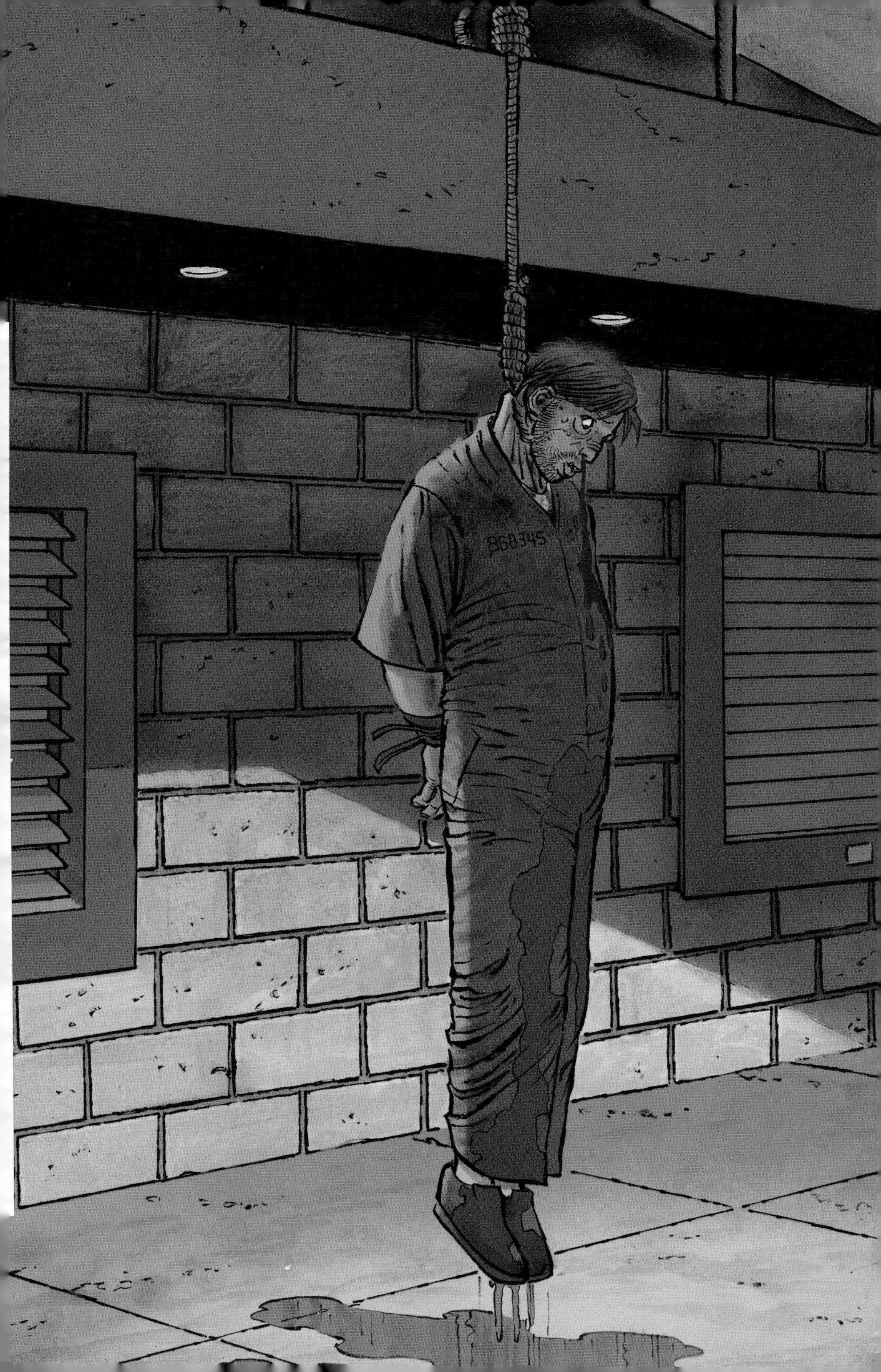
868345

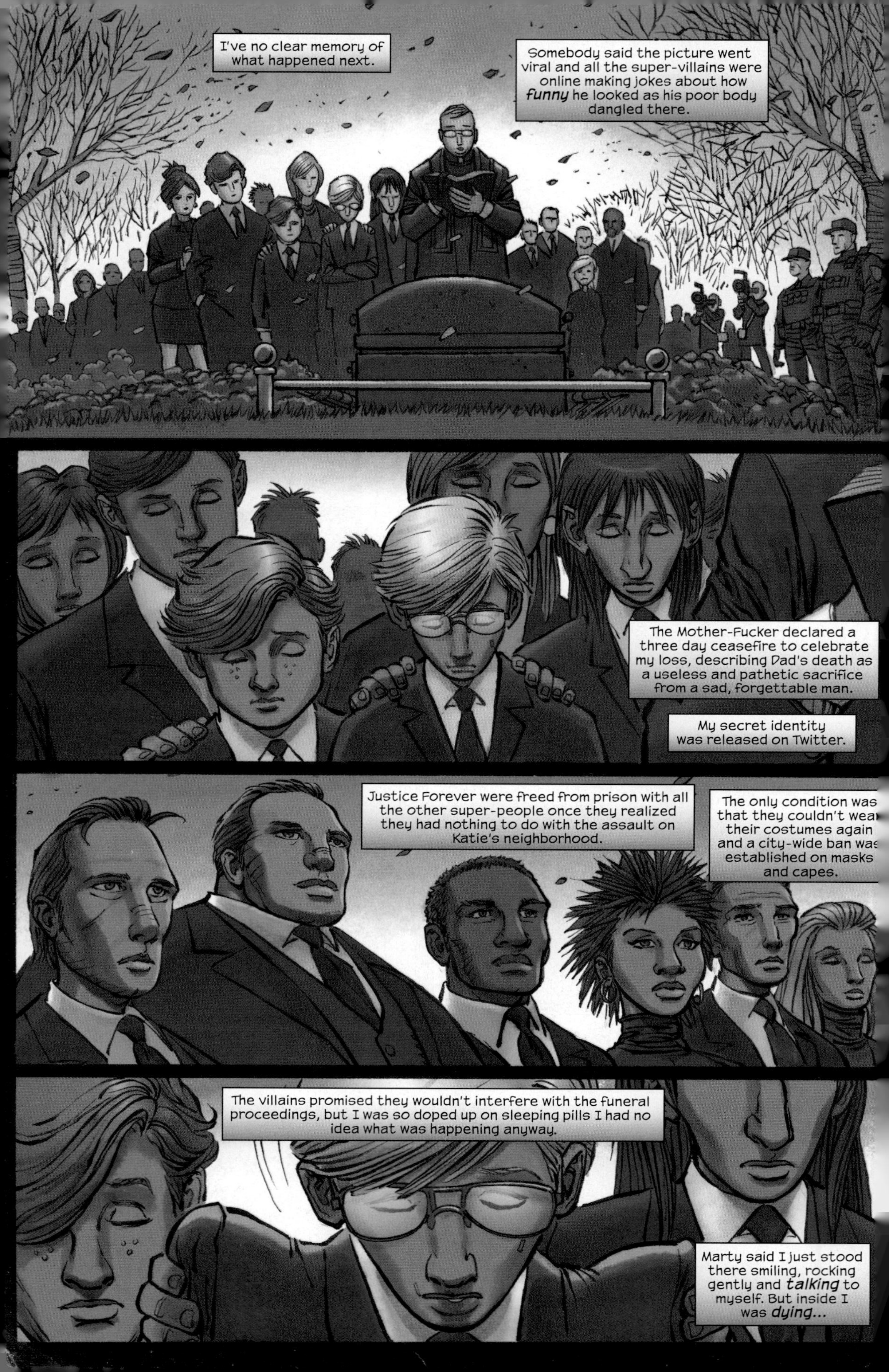
I've no clear memory of what happened next.
Somebody said the picture went viral and all the super-villains were online making jokes about how *funny* he looked as his poor body dangled there.
The Mother-Fucker declared a three day ceasefire to celebrate my loss, describing Dad's death as a useless and pathetic sacrifice from a sad, forgettable man.
My secret identity was released on Twitter.
Justice Forever were freed from prison with all the other super-people once they realized they had nothing to do with the assault on Katie's neighborhood.
The only condition was that they couldn't wear their costumes again and a city-wide ban was established on masks and capes.
The villains promised they wouldn't interfere with the funeral proceedings, but I was so doped up on sleeping pills I had no idea what was happening anyway.
Marty said I just stood there smiling, rocking gently and *talking* to myself. But inside I was *dying*...

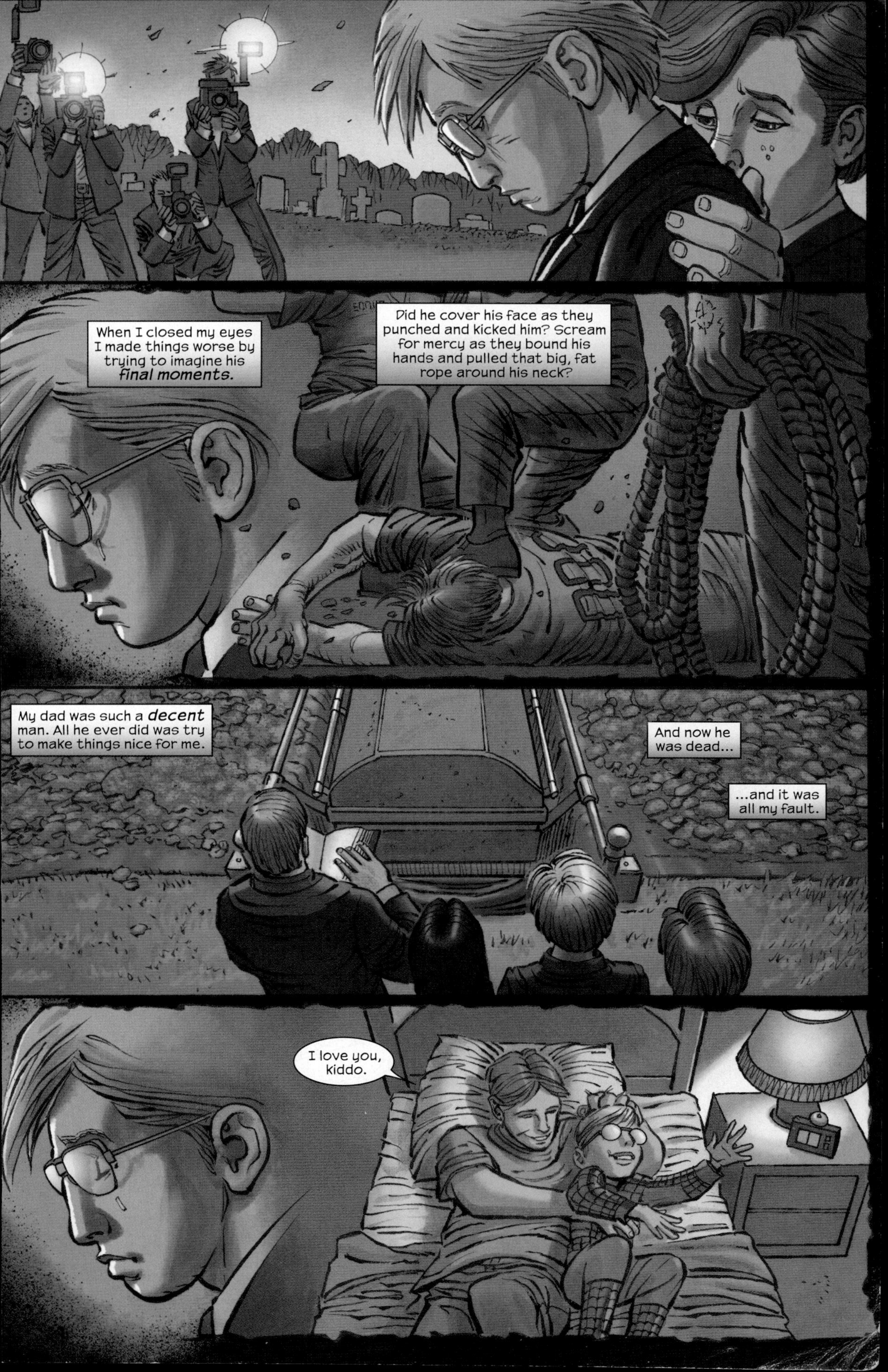
When I closed my eyes I made things worse by trying to imagine his *final moments.*
Did he cover his face as they punched and kicked him? Scream for mercy as they bound his hands and pulled that big, fat rope around his neck?
My dad was such a *decent* man. All he ever did was try to make things nice for me.
And now he was dead...
...and it was all my fault.
I love you, kiddo.

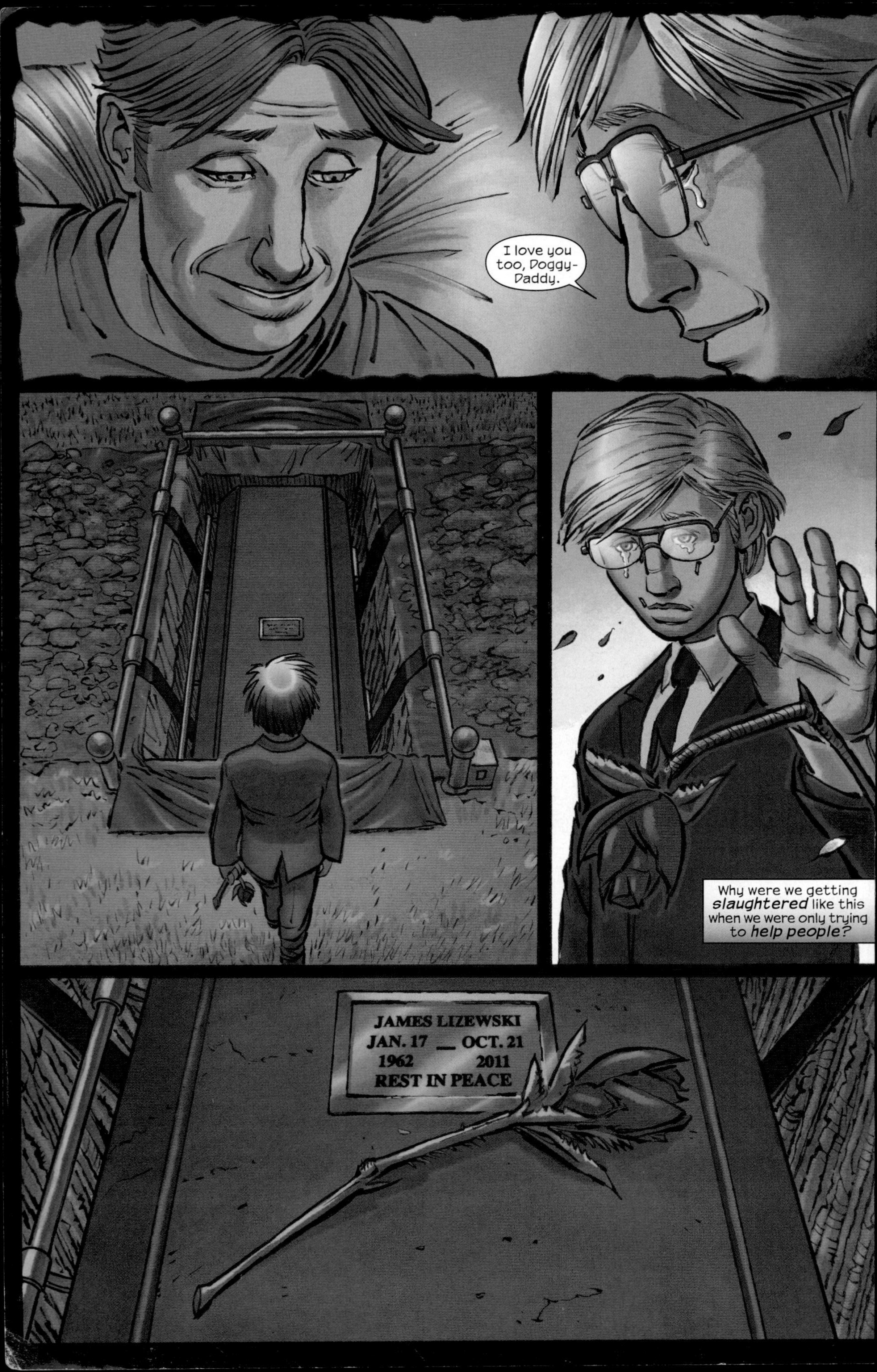
I love you too, Doggy-Daddy.
Why were we getting slaughtered like this when we were only trying to help people?
JAMES LIZEWSKI
JAN. 17 — OCT. 21
1962 2011
REST IN PEACE

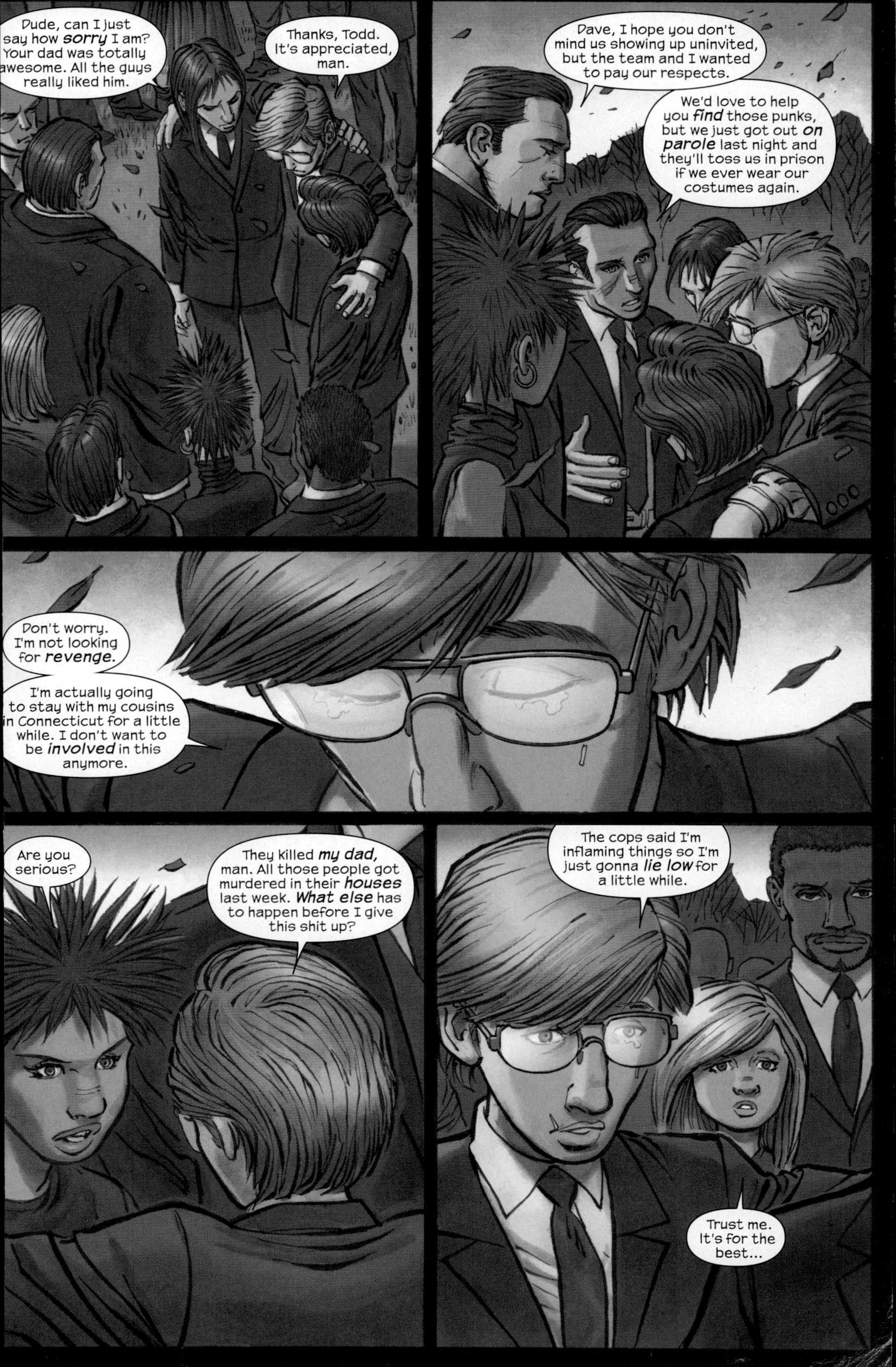
Dude, can I just say how *sorry* I am? Your dad was totally awesome. All the guys really liked him.
Thanks, Todd. It's appreciated, man.
Dave, I hope you don't mind us showing up uninvited, but the team and I wanted to pay our respects.
We'd love to help you *find* those punks, but we just got out *on parole* last night and they'll toss us in prison if we ever wear our costumes again.
Don't worry. I'm not looking for *revenge*.
I'm actually going to stay with my cousins in Connecticut for a little while. I don't want to be *involved* in this anymore.
Are you serious?
They killed *my dad,* man. All those people got murdered in their *houses* last week. *What else* has to happen before I give this shit up?
The cops said I'm inflaming things so I'm just gonna *lie low* for a little while.
Trust me. It's for the best...

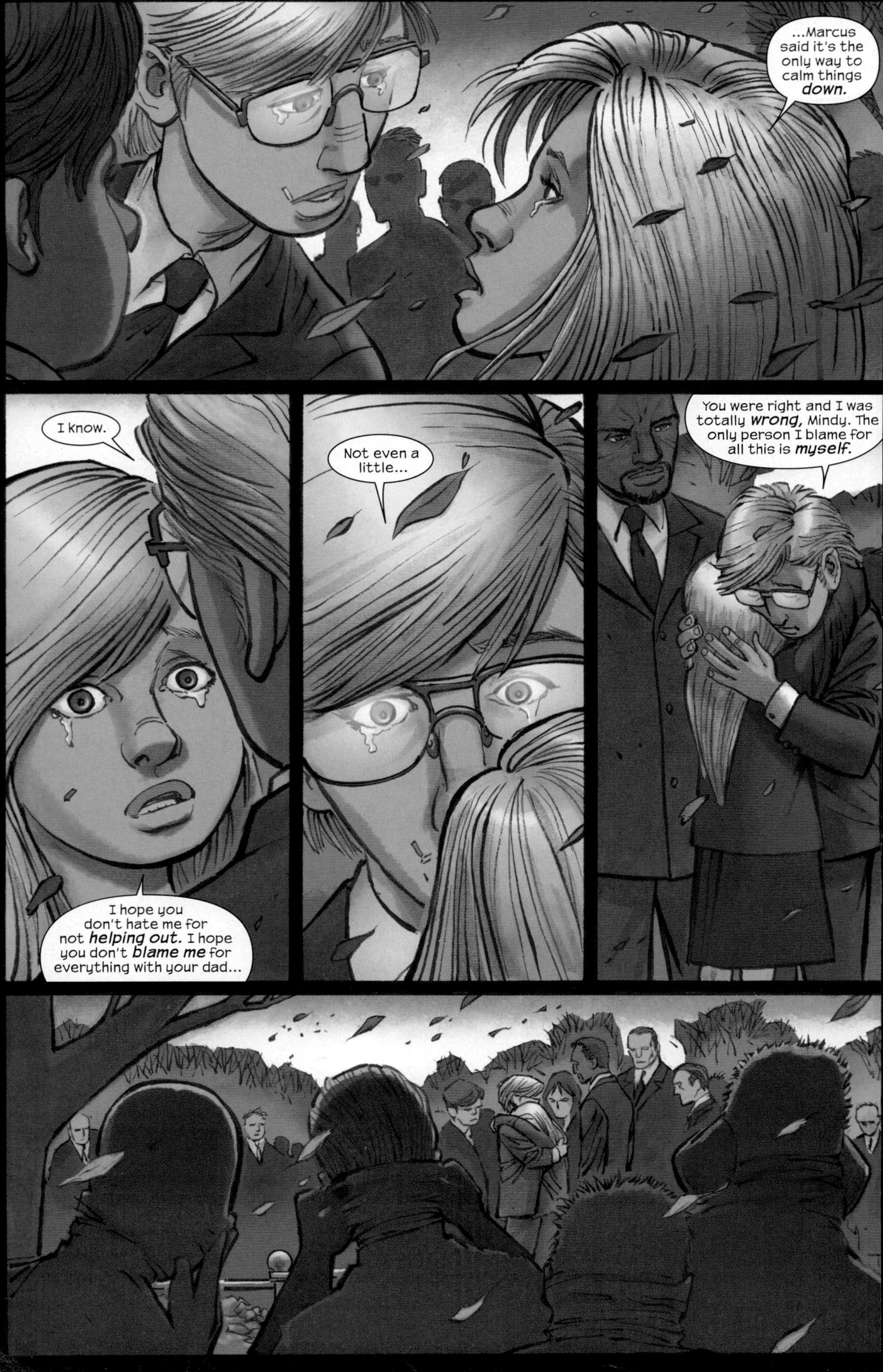
...Marcus said it's the only way to calm things *down.*
I know.
I hope you don't hate me for not ***helping out.*** I hope you don't ***blame me*** for everything with your dad...
Not even a little...
You were right and I was totally ***wrong,*** Mindy. The only person I blame for all this is ***myself.***

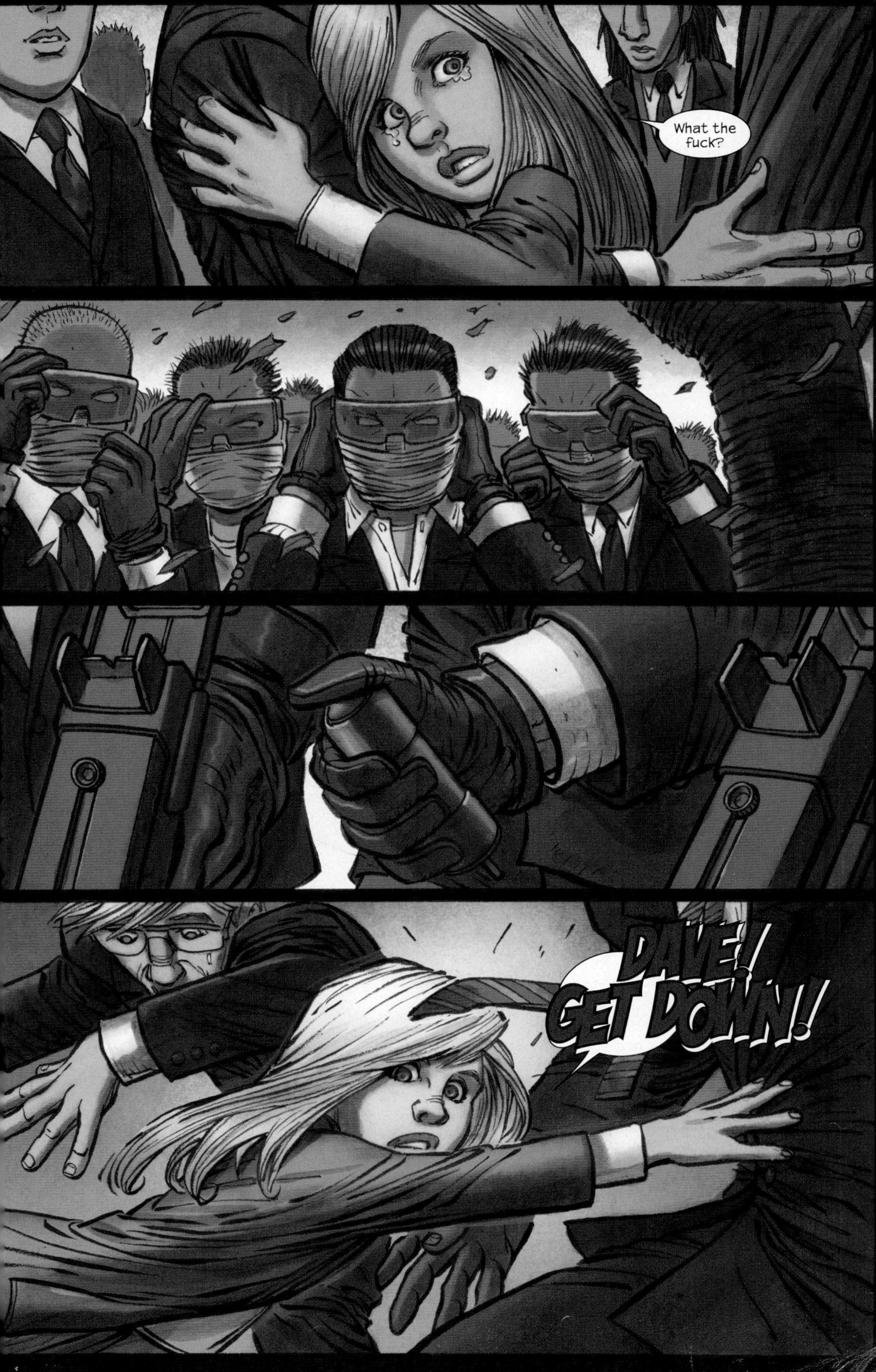
What the fuck?
DAVE! GET DOWN!

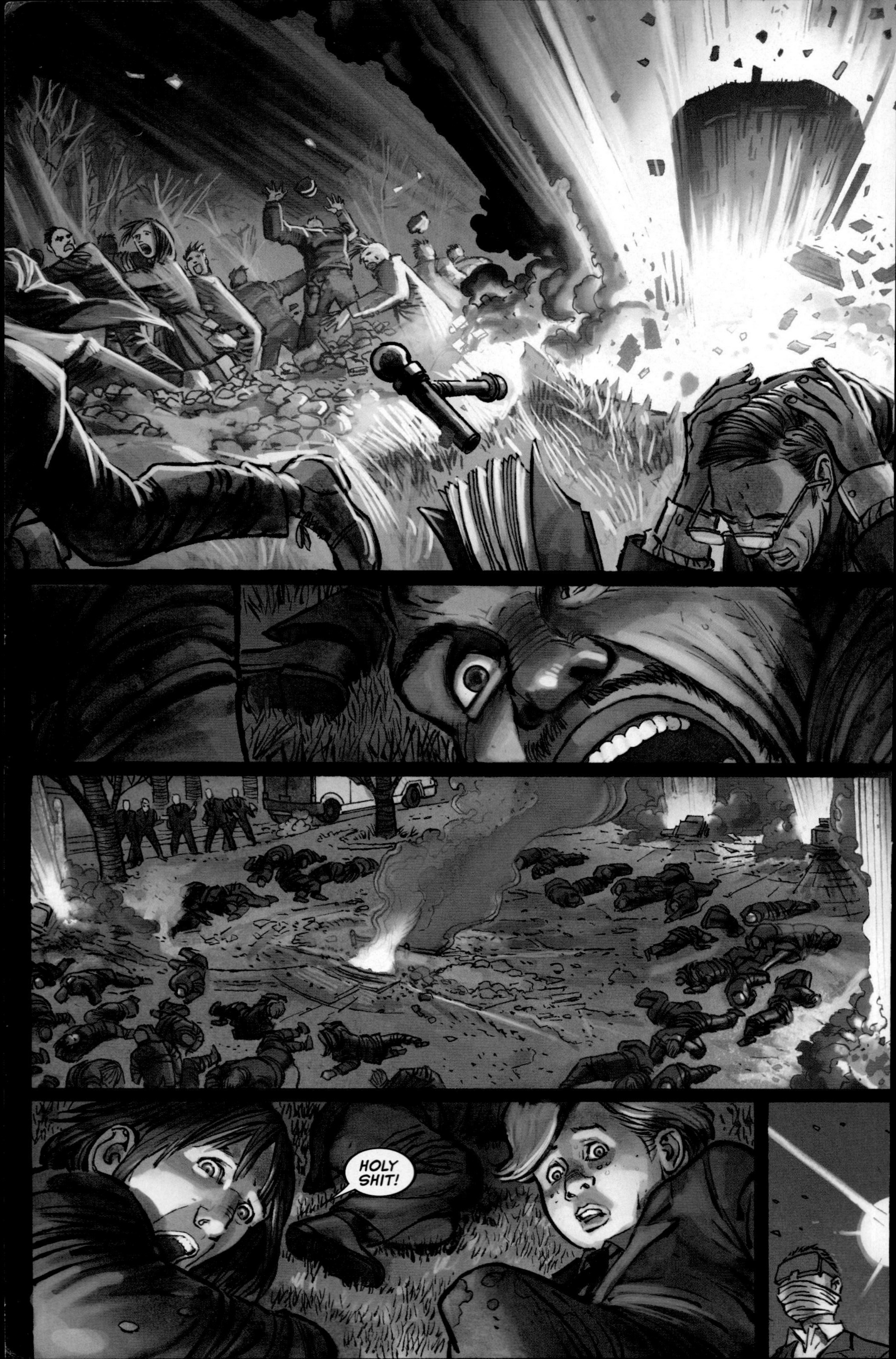
HOLY SHIT!

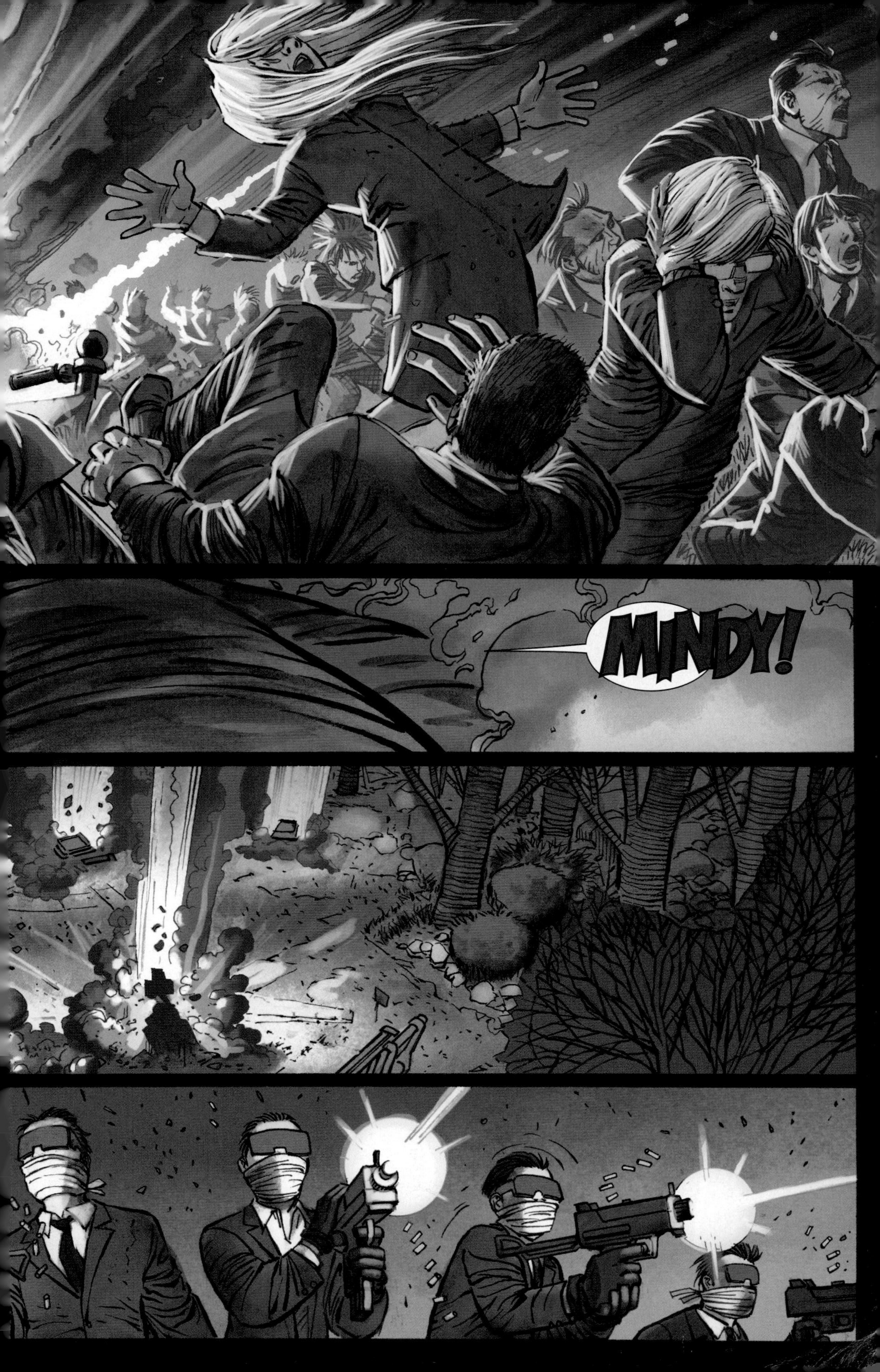
MINDY!

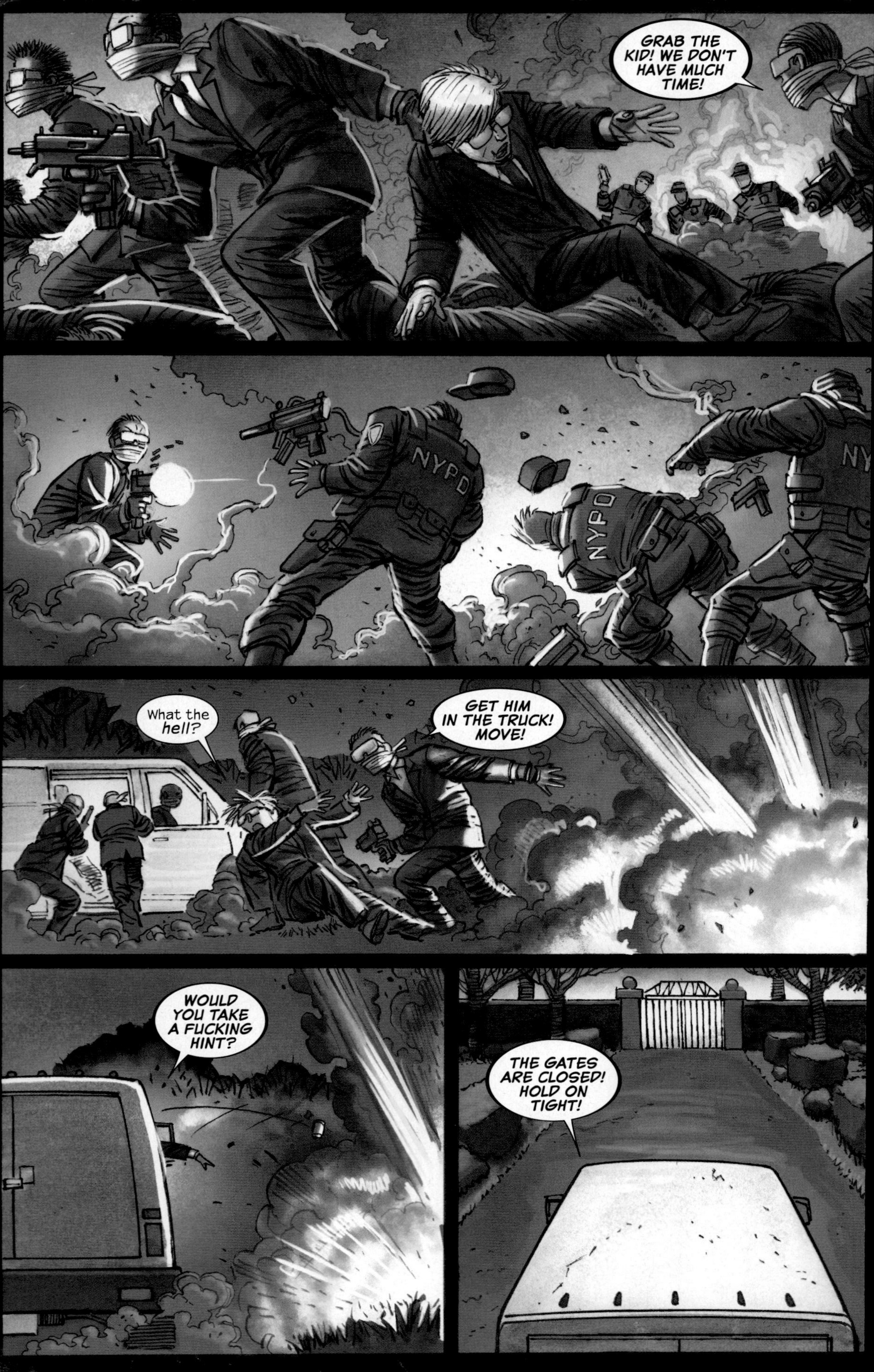
GRAB THE KID! WE DON'T HAVE MUCH TIME!
NYPD
NYPD
What the *hell*?
GET HIM IN THE TRUCK! MOVE!
WOULD YOU TAKE A FUCKING HINT?
THE GATES ARE CLOSED! HOLD ON TIGHT!

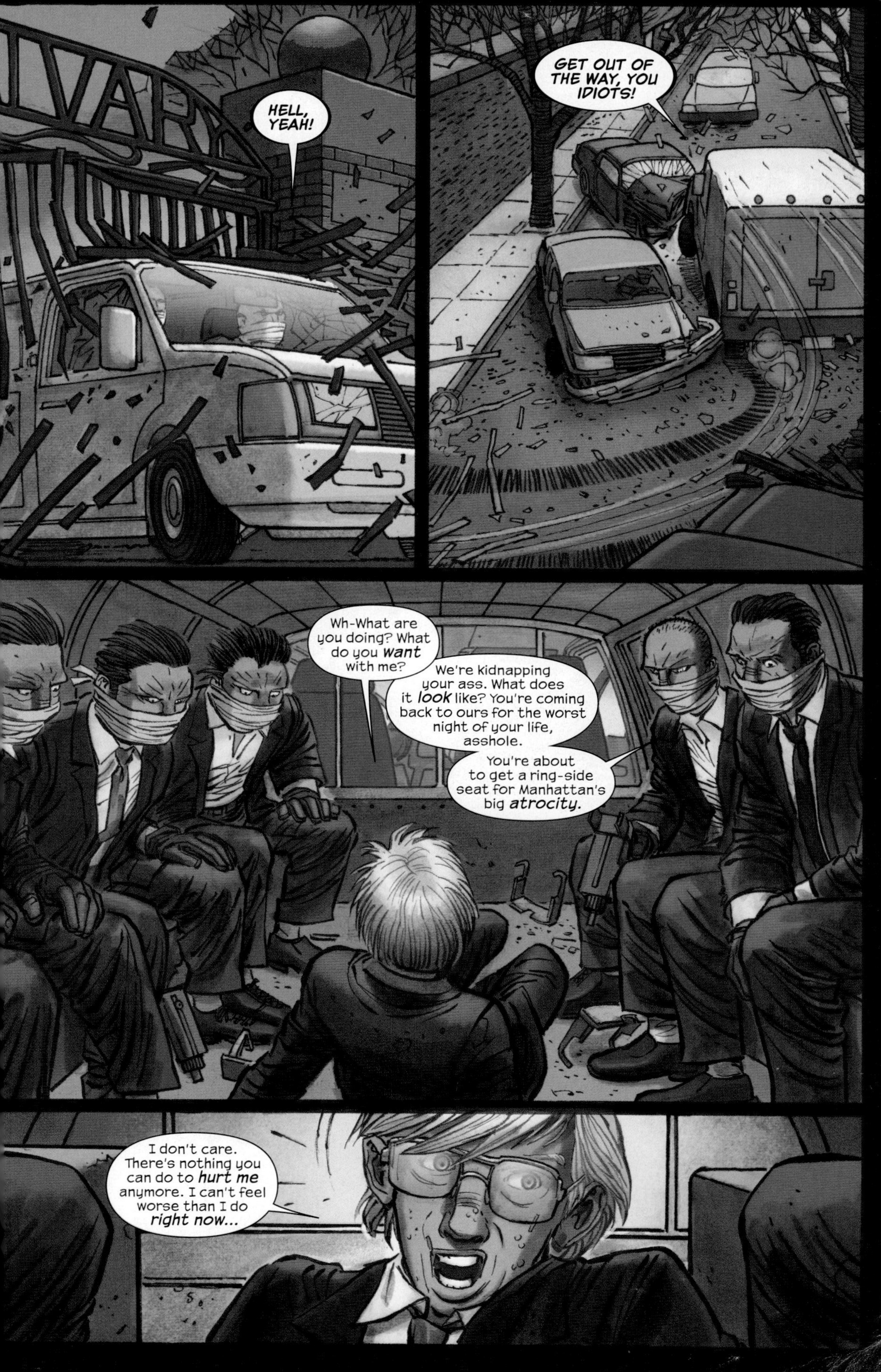
HELL, YEAH!
GET OUT OF THE WAY, YOU IDIOTS!
Wh-What are you doing? What do you *want* with me?
We're kidnapping your ass. What does it *look* like? You're coming back to ours for the worst night of your life, asshole.
You're about to get a ring-side seat for Manhattan's big *atrocity*.
I don't care. There's nothing you can do to *hurt me* anymore. I can't feel worse than I do *right now...*

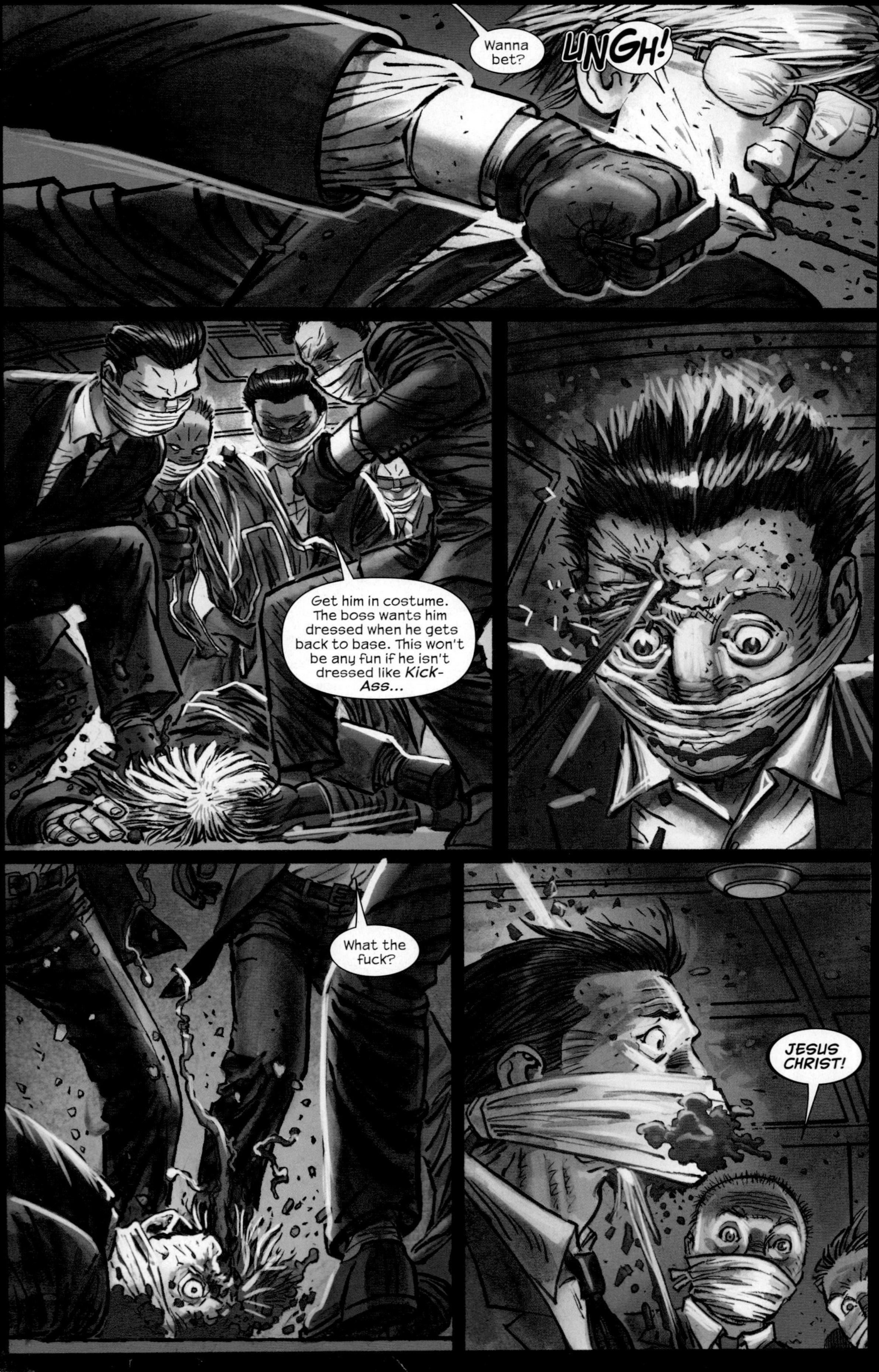
Wanna bet?
UNGH!
Get him in costume. The boss wants him dressed when he gets back to base. This won't be any fun if he isn't dressed like Kick-Ass...
What the fuck?
JESUS CHRIST!

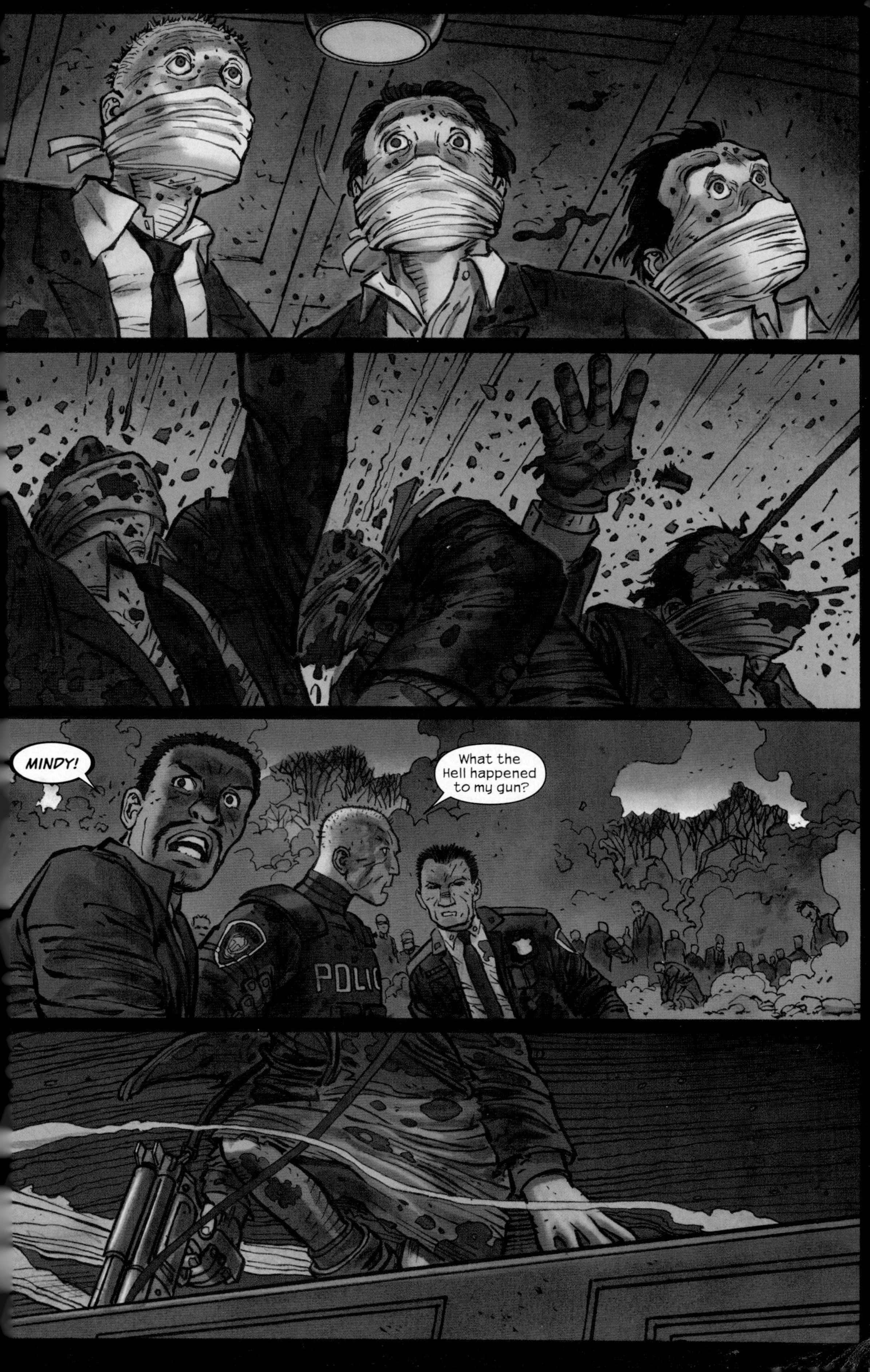
MINDY!
What the Hell happened to my gun?
POLIC

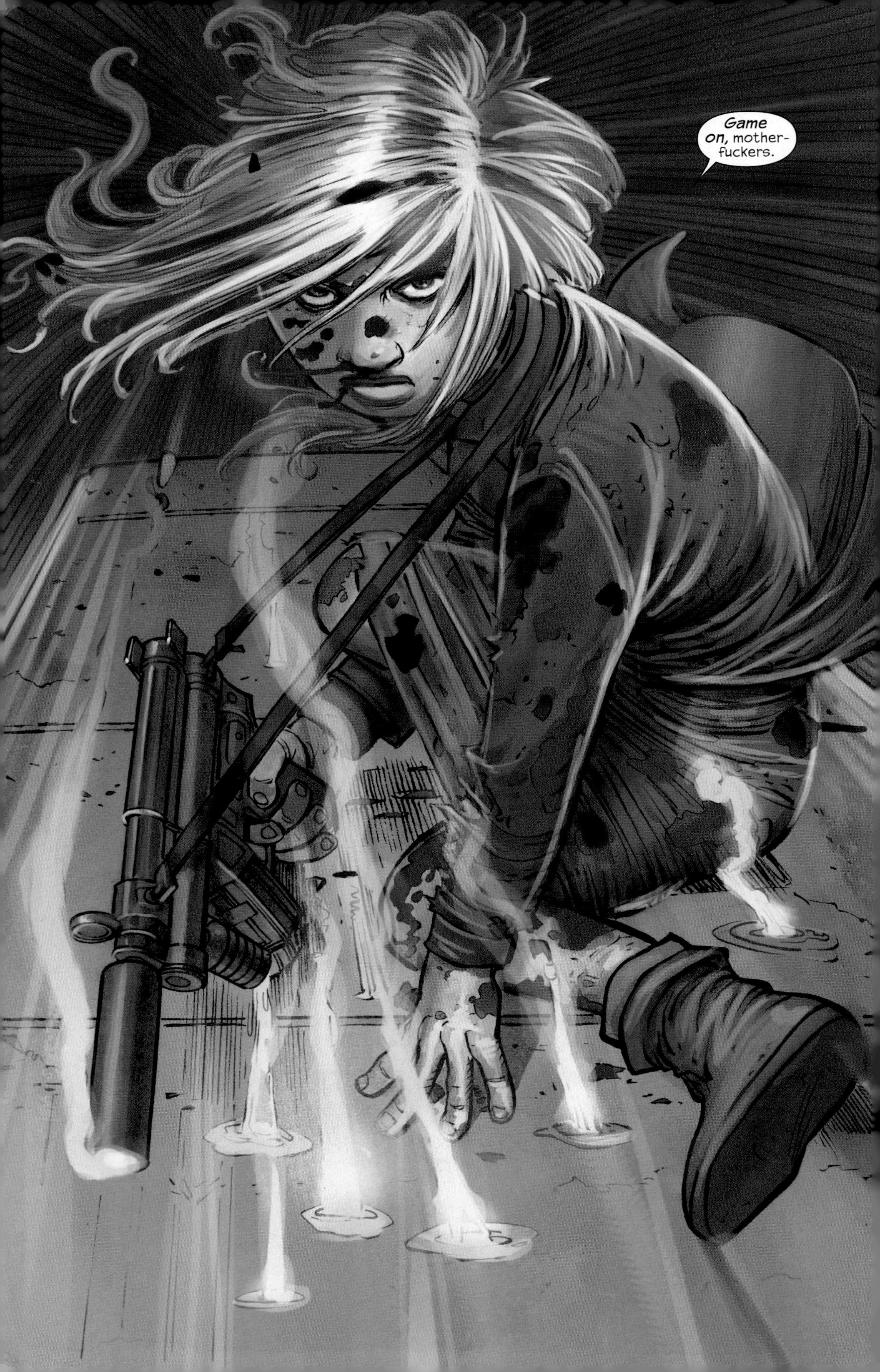
Game on, mother-fuckers.

SIX

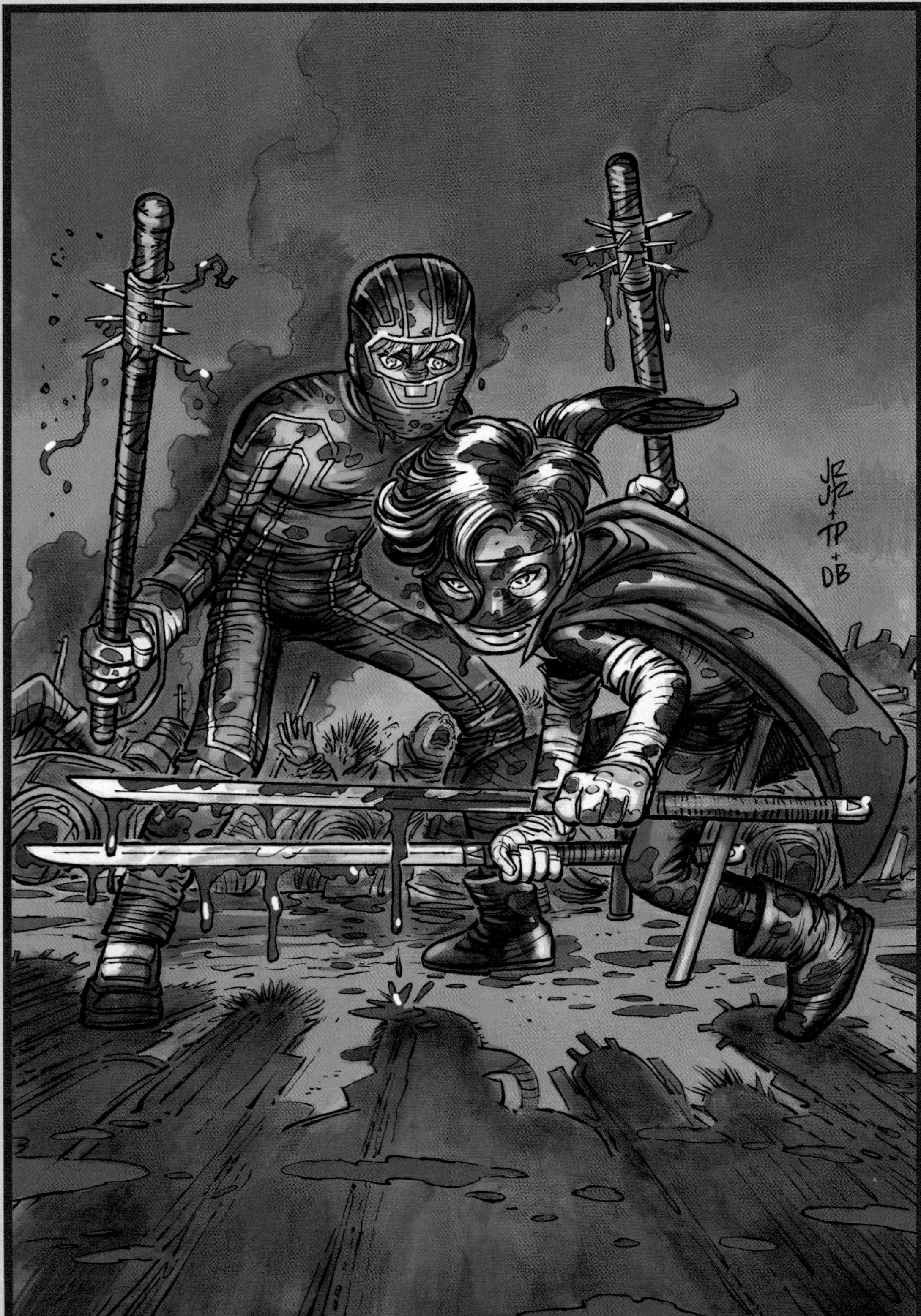
JRJR + TP + DB

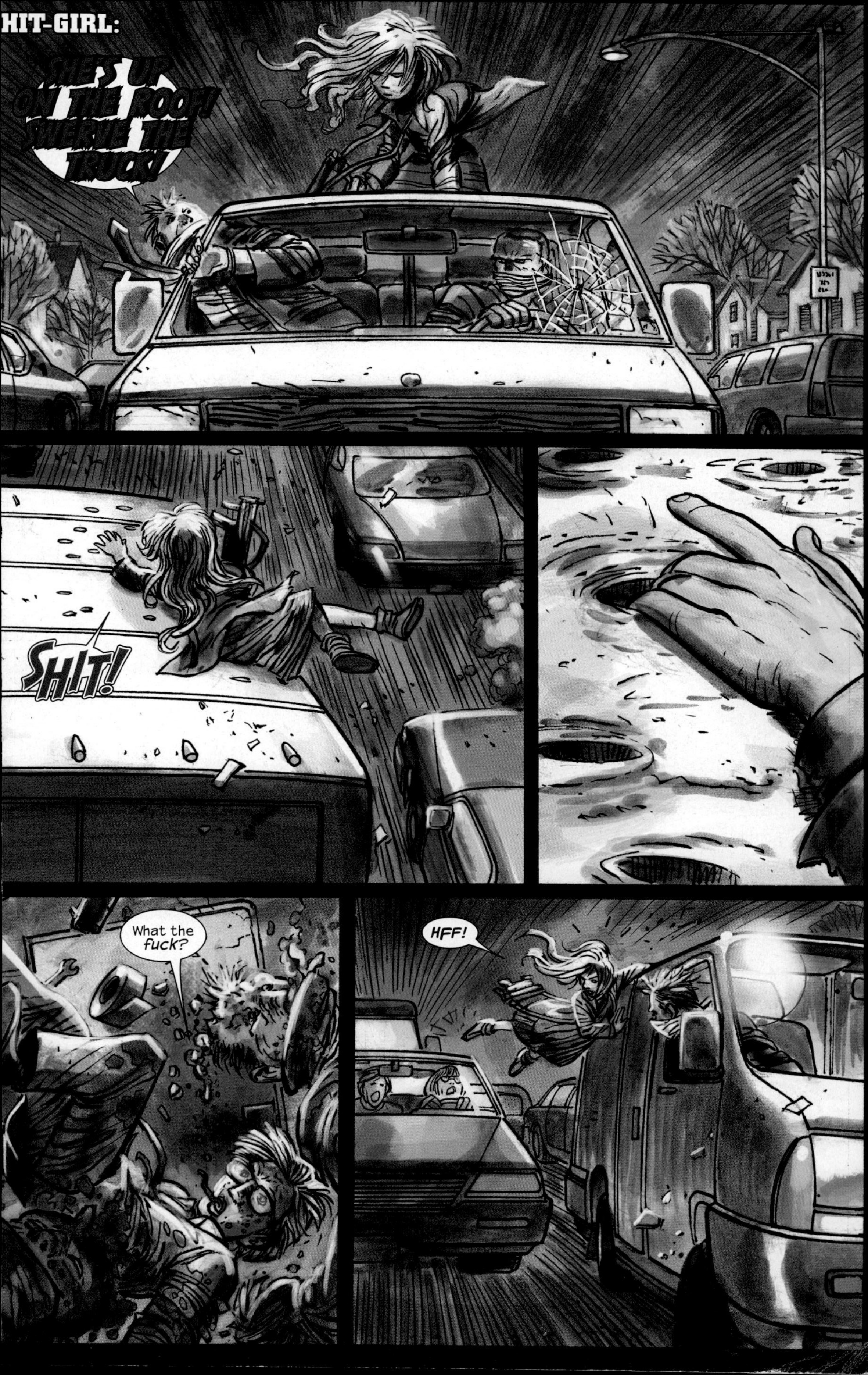
HIT-GIRL:
SHE'S UP ON THE ROOF! SWERVE THE TRUCK!
SHIT!
What the fuck?
HFF!

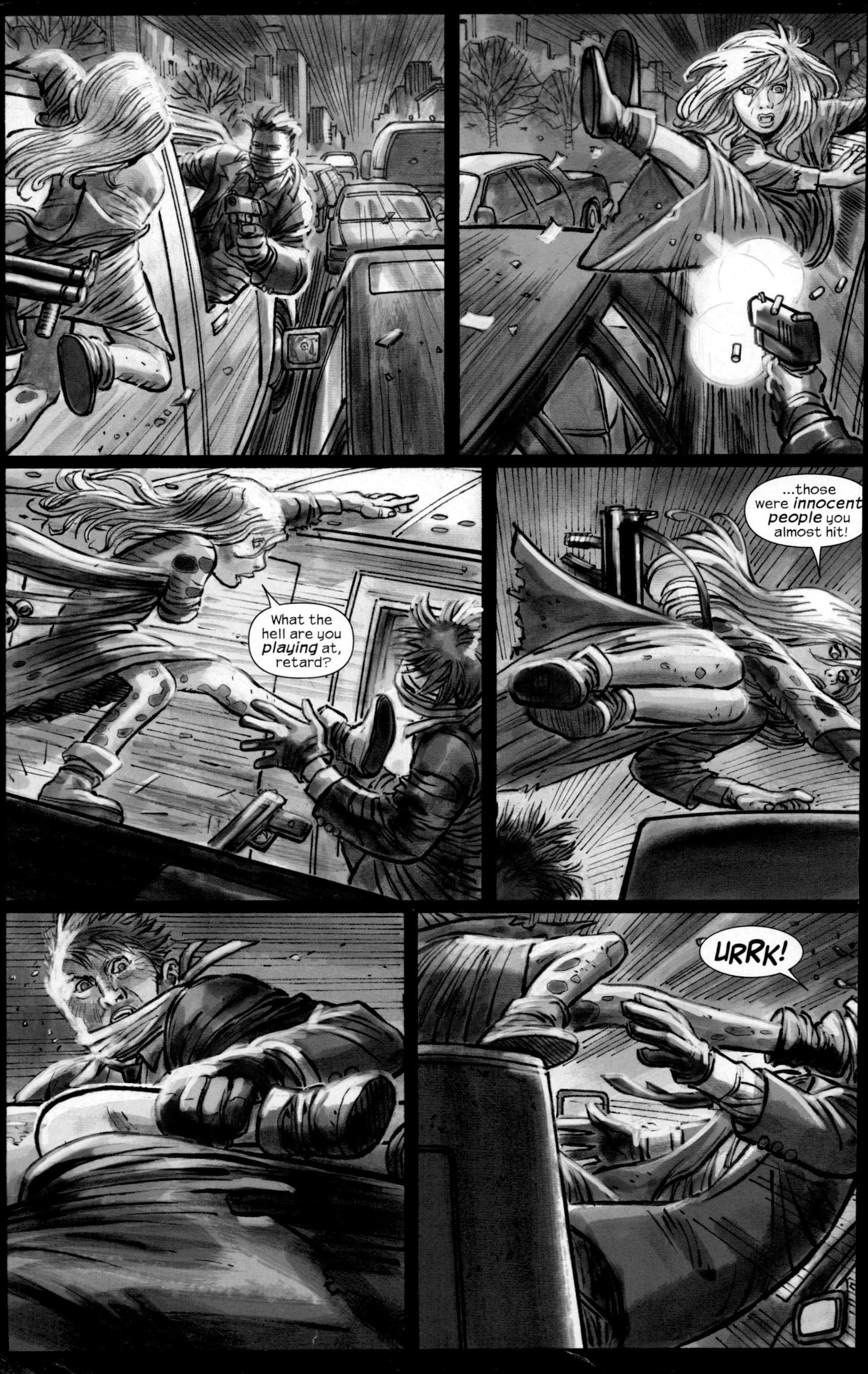
What the hell are you *playing* at, retard?
...those were *innocent people* you almost hit!
URRK!

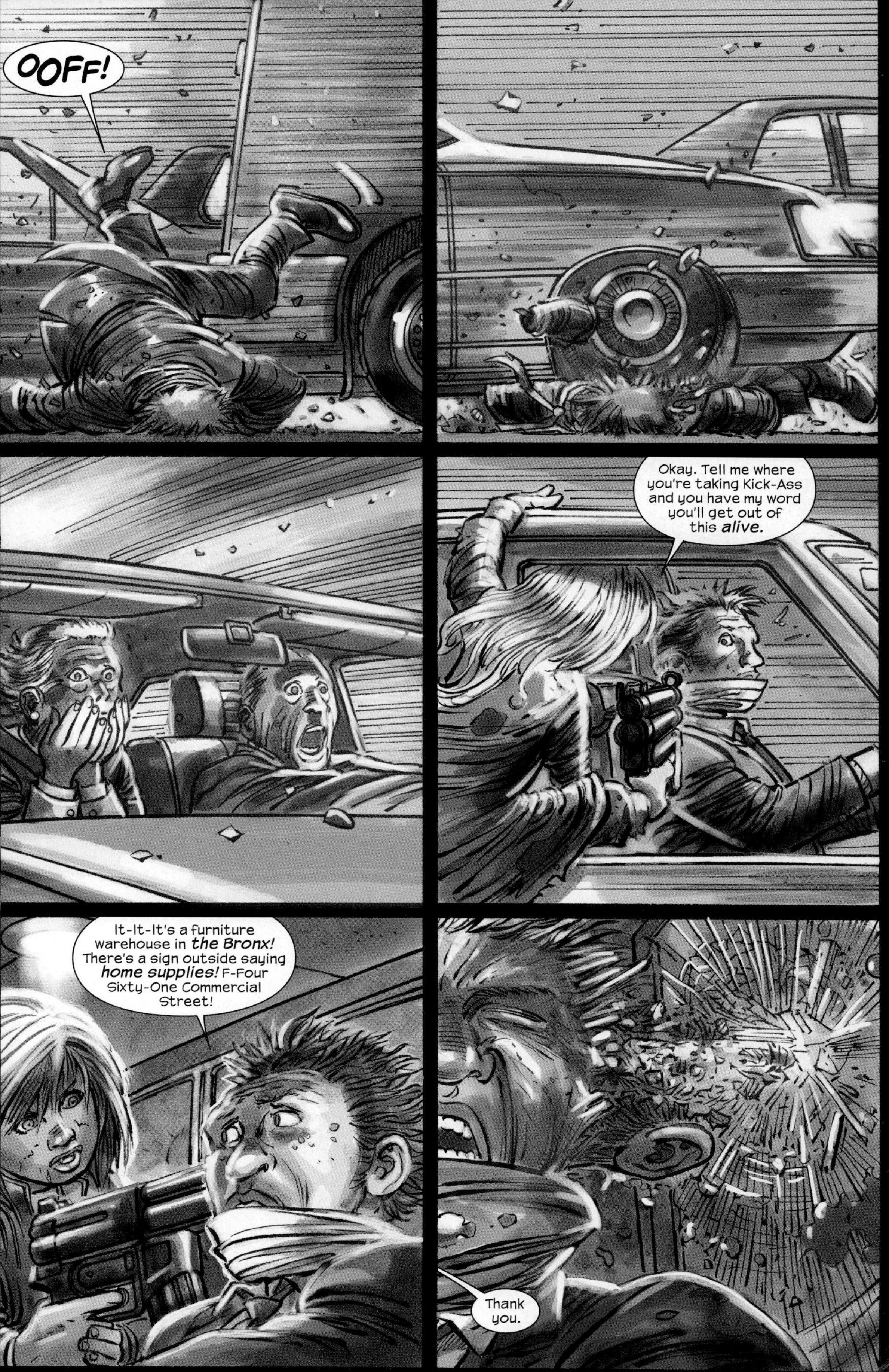
OOFF!
Okay. Tell me where you're taking Kick-Ass and you have my word you'll get out of this *alive.*
It-It-It's a furniture warehouse in ***the Bronx!*** There's a sign outside saying ***home supplies!*** F-Four Sixty-One Commercial Street!
Thank you.

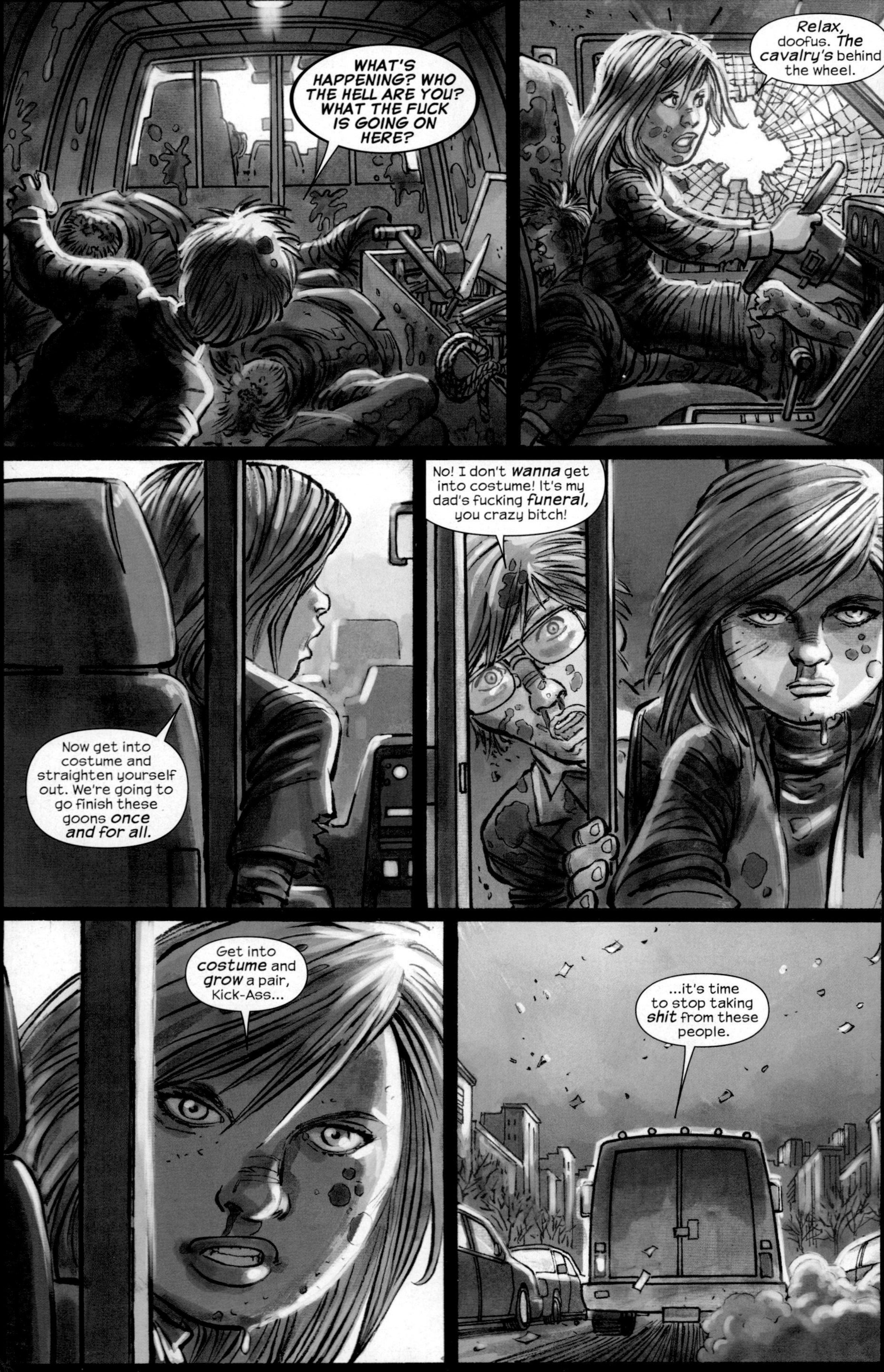
WHAT'S HAPPENING? WHO THE HELL ARE YOU? WHAT THE FUCK IS GOING ON HERE?
Relax, doofus. The cavalry's behind the wheel.
Now get into costume and straighten yourself out. We're going to go finish these goons once and for all.
No! I don't wanna get into costume! It's my dad's fucking funeral, you crazy bitch!
Get into costume and grow a pair, Kick-Ass...
...it's time to stop taking shit from these people.

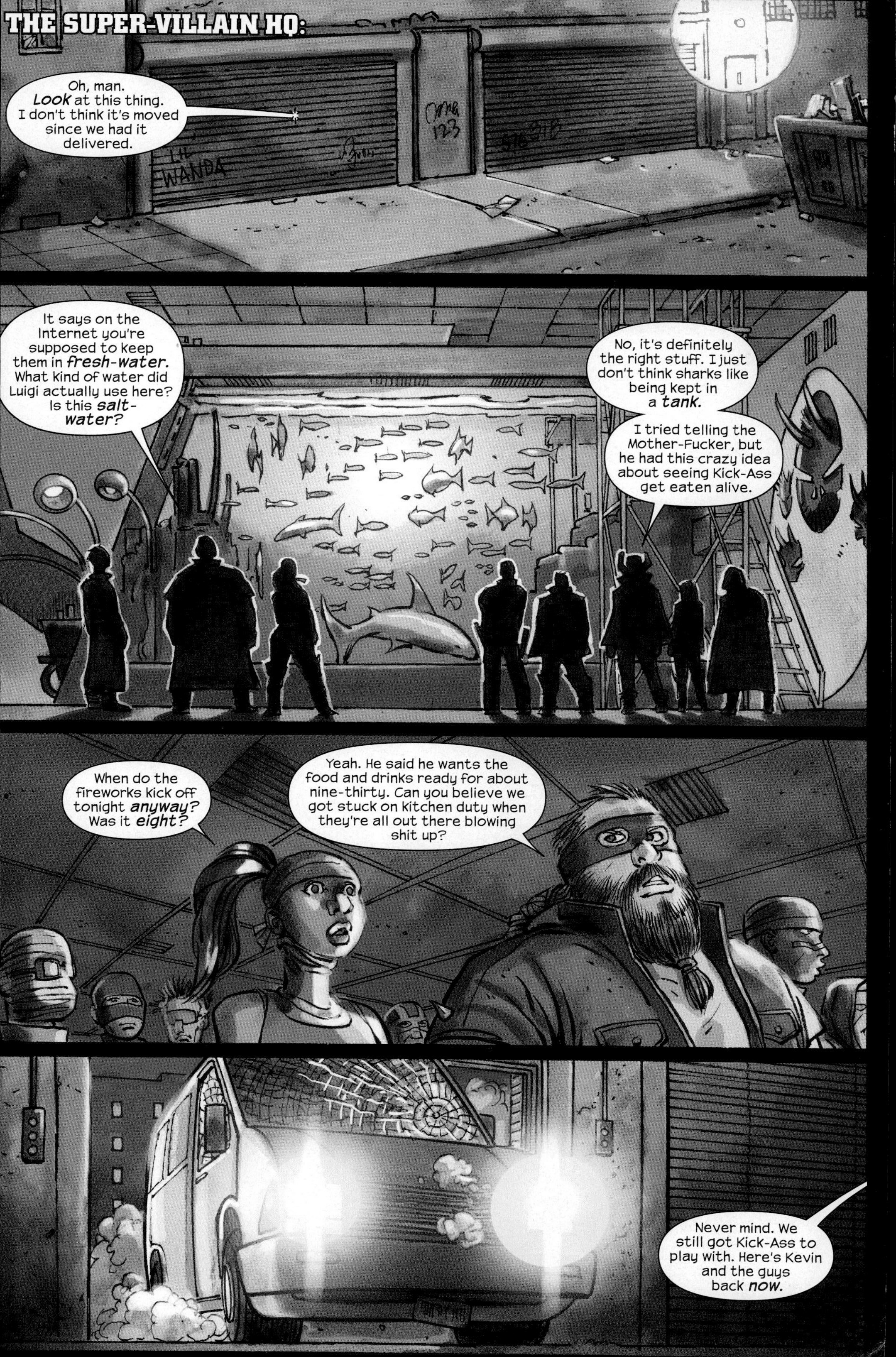
THE SUPER-VILLAIN HQ:
Oh, man. LOOK at this thing. I don't think it's moved since we had it delivered.
LIL WANDA
123
It says on the Internet you're supposed to keep them in fresh-water. What kind of water did Luigi actually use here? Is this salt-water?
No, it's definitely the right stuff. I just don't think sharks like being kept in a tank.
I tried telling the Mother-Fucker, but he had this crazy idea about seeing Kick-Ass get eaten alive.
When do the fireworks kick off tonight anyway? Was it eight?
Yeah. He said he wants the food and drinks ready for about nine-thirty. Can you believe we got stuck on kitchen duty when they're all out there blowing shit up?
Never mind. We still got Kick-Ass to play with. Here's Kevin and the guys back now.

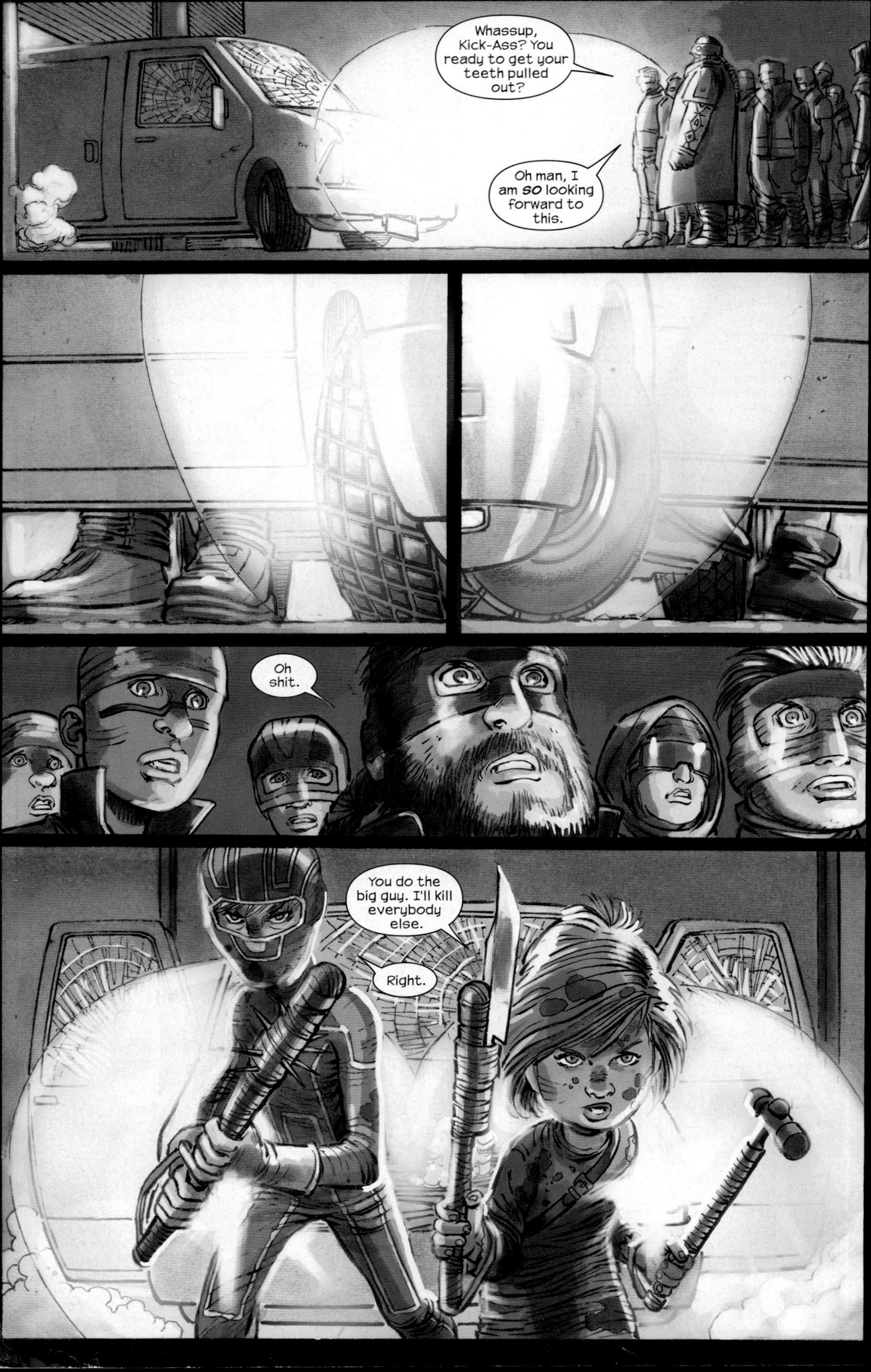
Whassup, Kick-Ass? You ready to get your teeth pulled out?
Oh man, I am SO looking forward to this.
Oh shit.
You do the big guy. I'll kill everybody else.
Right.

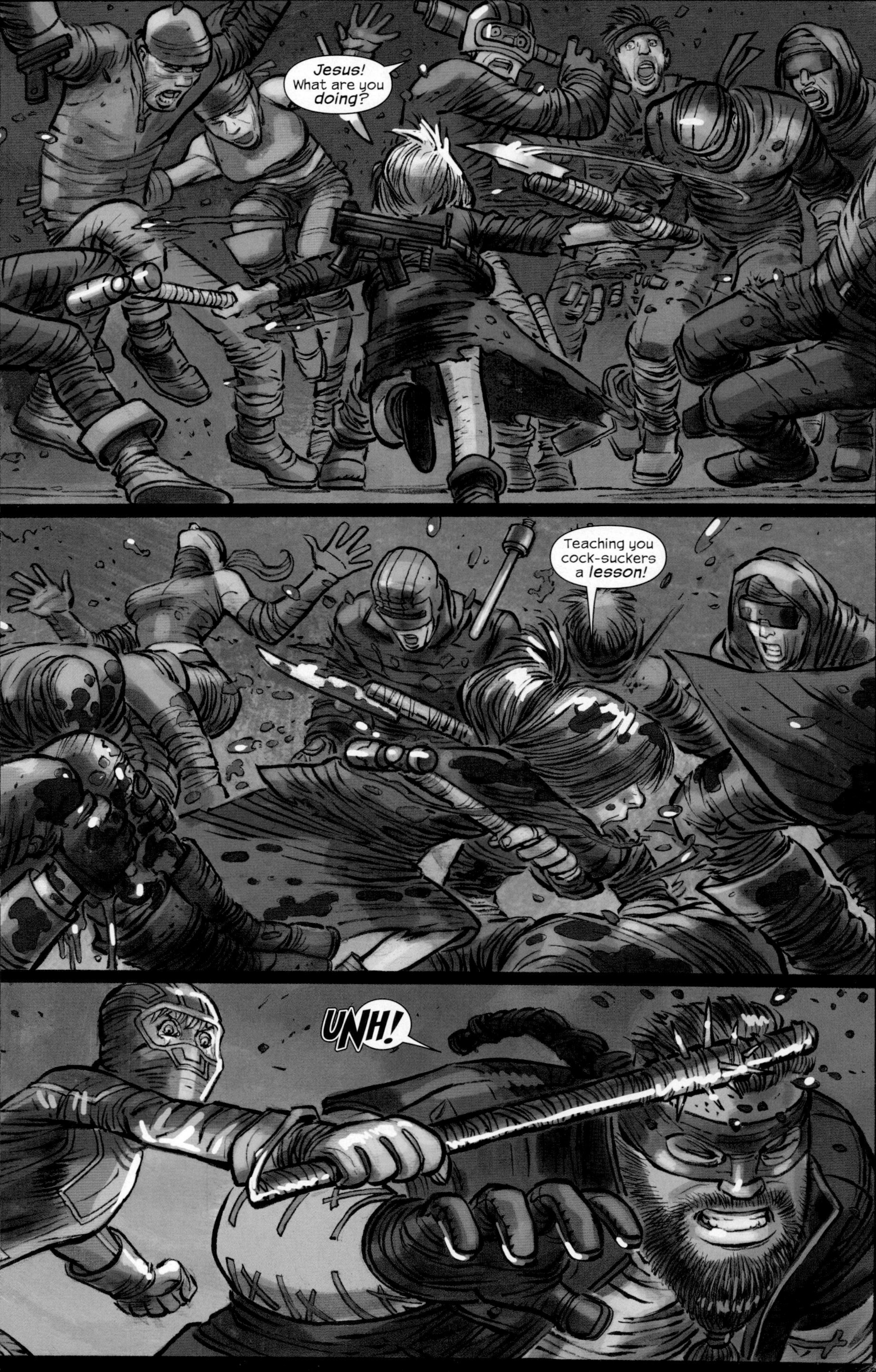
Jesus! What are you doing?
Teaching you cock-suckers a lesson!
UNH!

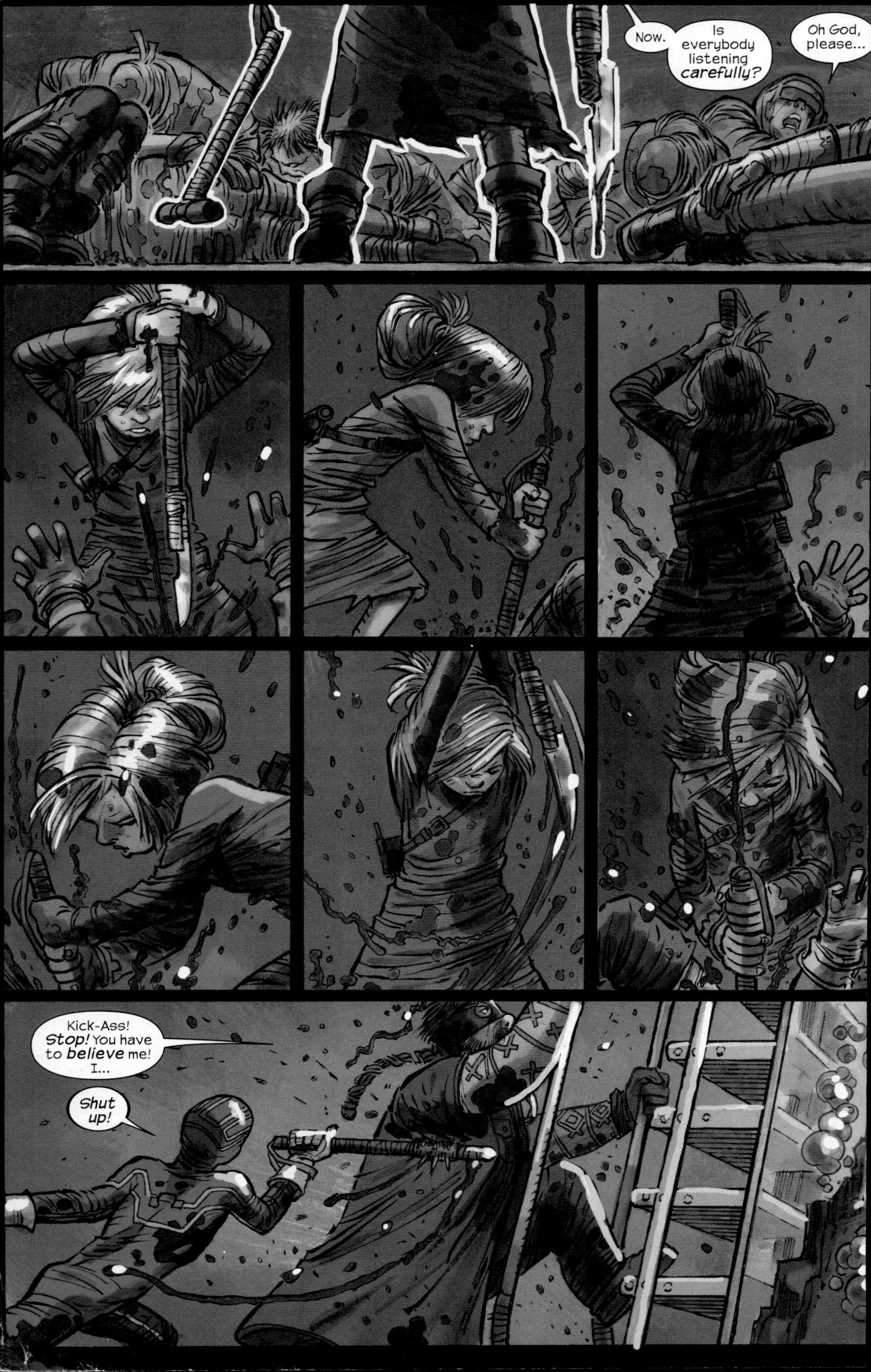
Now.
Is everybody listening *carefully?*
Oh God, please...
Kick-Ass! *Stop!* You have to *believe* me! I...
Shut up!

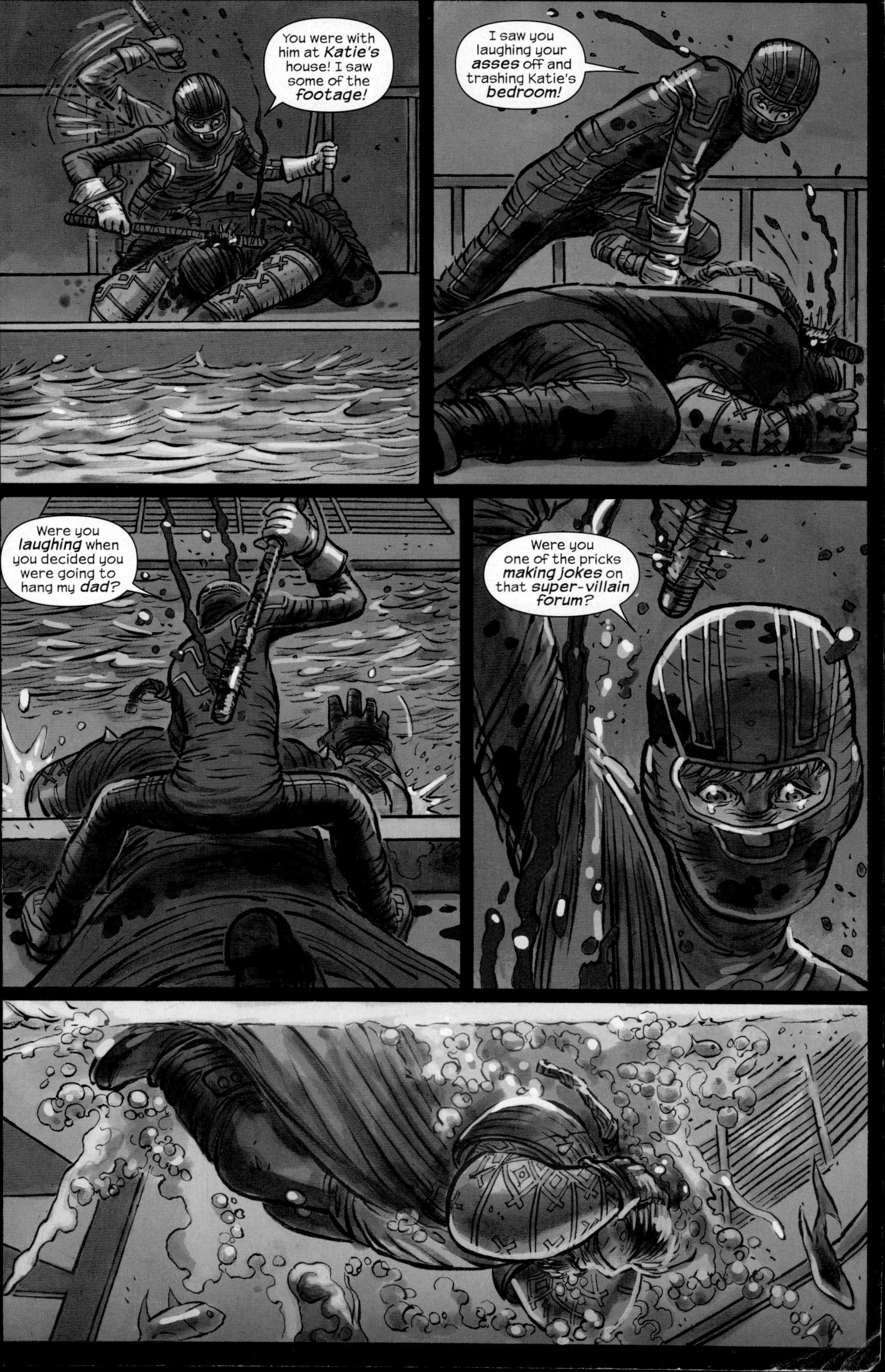
You were with him at *Katie's* house! I saw some of the *footage!*
I saw you laughing your ***asses*** off and trashing Katie's ***bedroom!***
Were you ***laughing*** when you decided you were going to hang my ***dad?***
Were you one of the pricks ***making jokes*** on that ***super-villain forum?***

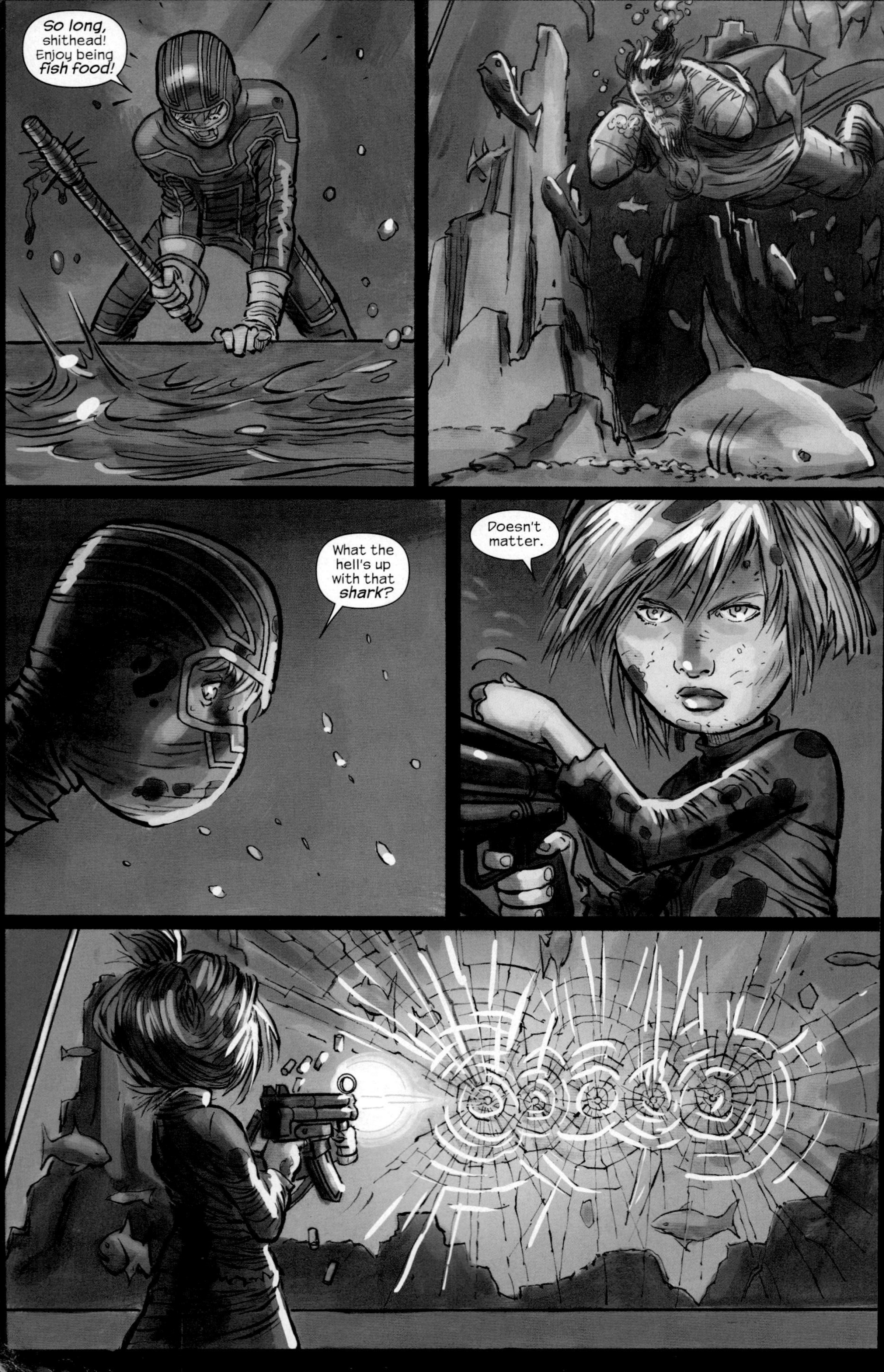
So long, shithead! Enjoy being fish food!
What the hell's up with that shark?
Doesn't matter.

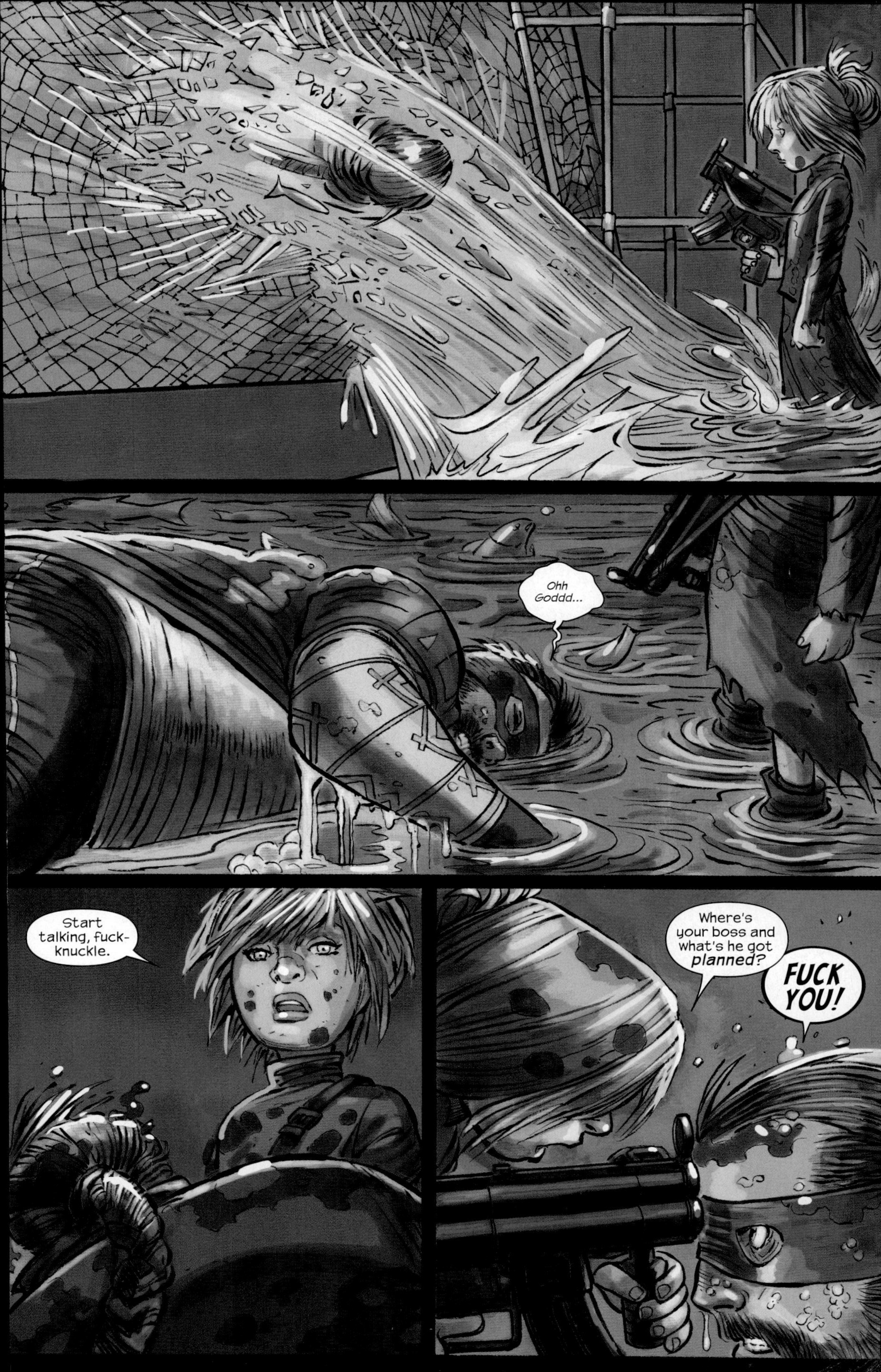
Ohh Goddd...
Start talking, fuck-knuckle.
Where's your boss and what's he got *planned*?
FUCK YOU!

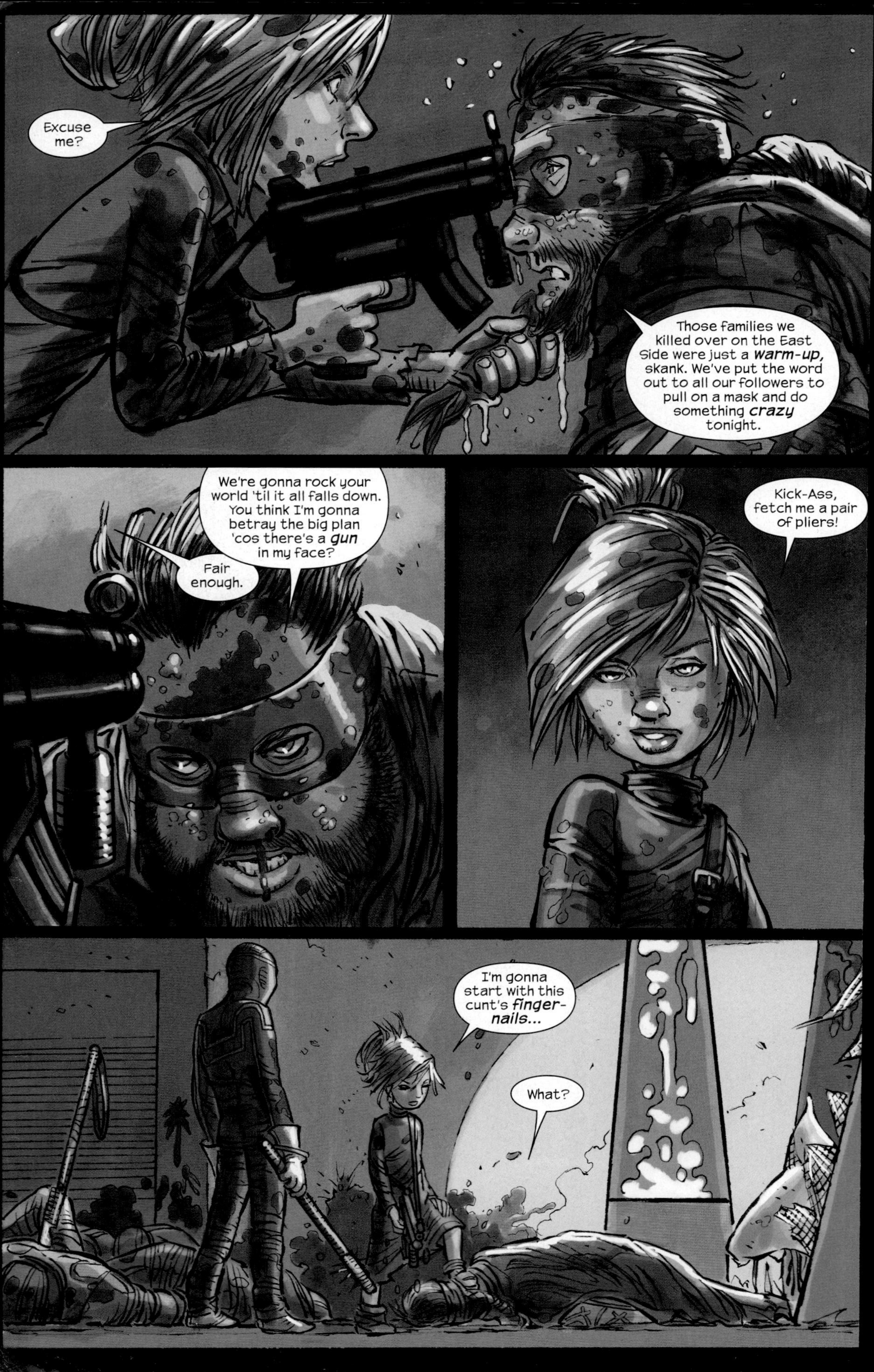
Excuse me?
Those families we killed over on the East Side were just a warm-up, skank. We've put the word out to all our followers to pull on a mask and do something crazy tonight.
We're gonna rock your world 'til it all falls down. You think I'm gonna betray the big plan 'cos there's a gun in my face?
Fair enough.
Kick-Ass, fetch me a pair of pliers!
I'm gonna start with this cunt's finger-nails...
What?

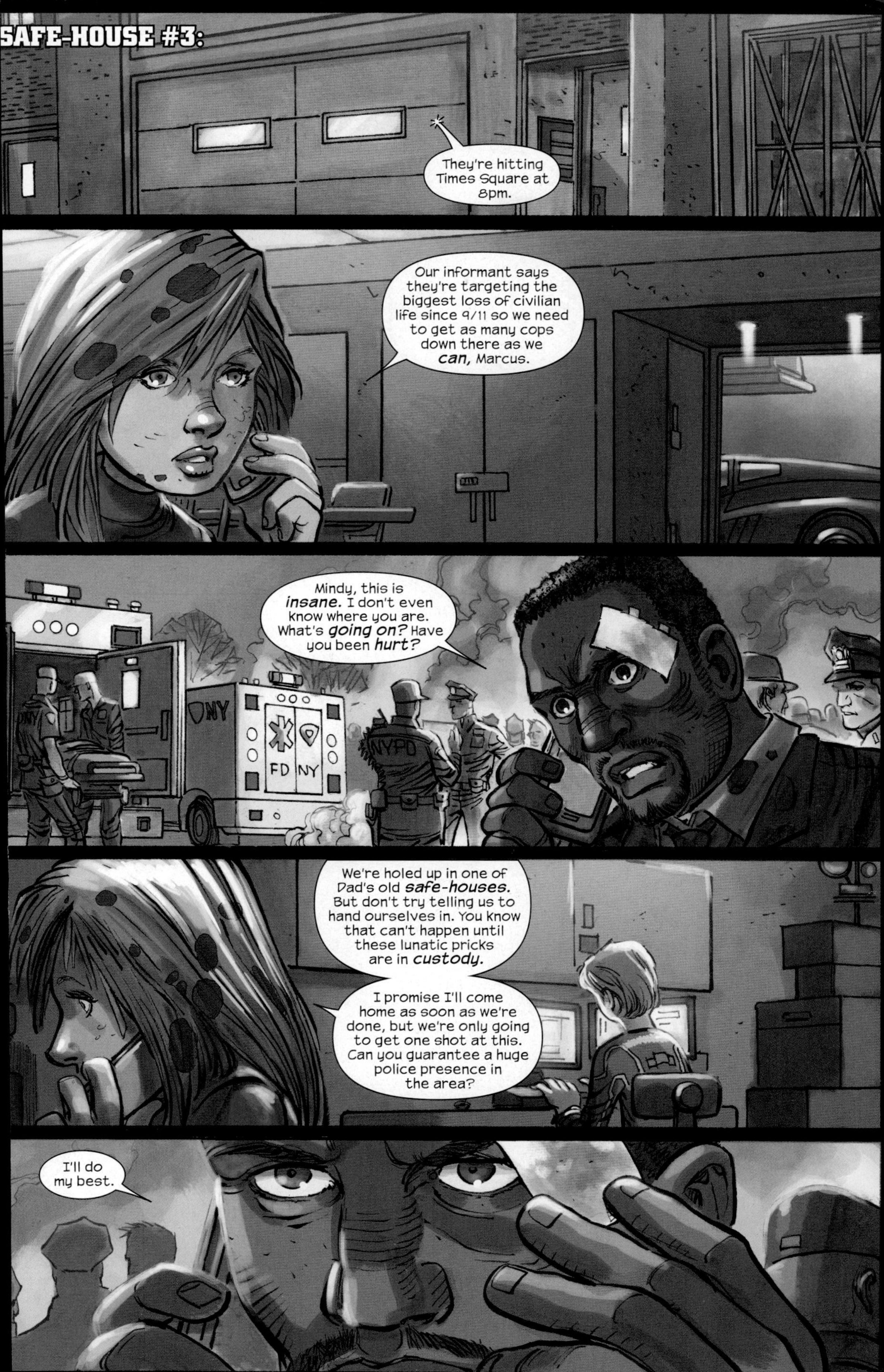
SAFE-HOUSE #3:
They're hitting Times Square at 8pm.
Our informant says they're targeting the biggest loss of civilian life since 9/11 so we need to get as many cops down there as we *can,* Marcus.
Mindy, this is *insane.* I don't even know where you are. What's *going on?* Have you been *hurt?*
NYPD
FD NY
We're holed up in one of Dad's old *safe-houses.* But don't try telling us to hand ourselves in. You know that can't happen until these lunatic pricks are in *custody.*
I promise I'll come home as soon as we're done, but we're only going to get one shot at this. Can you guarantee a huge police presence in the area?
I'll do my best.

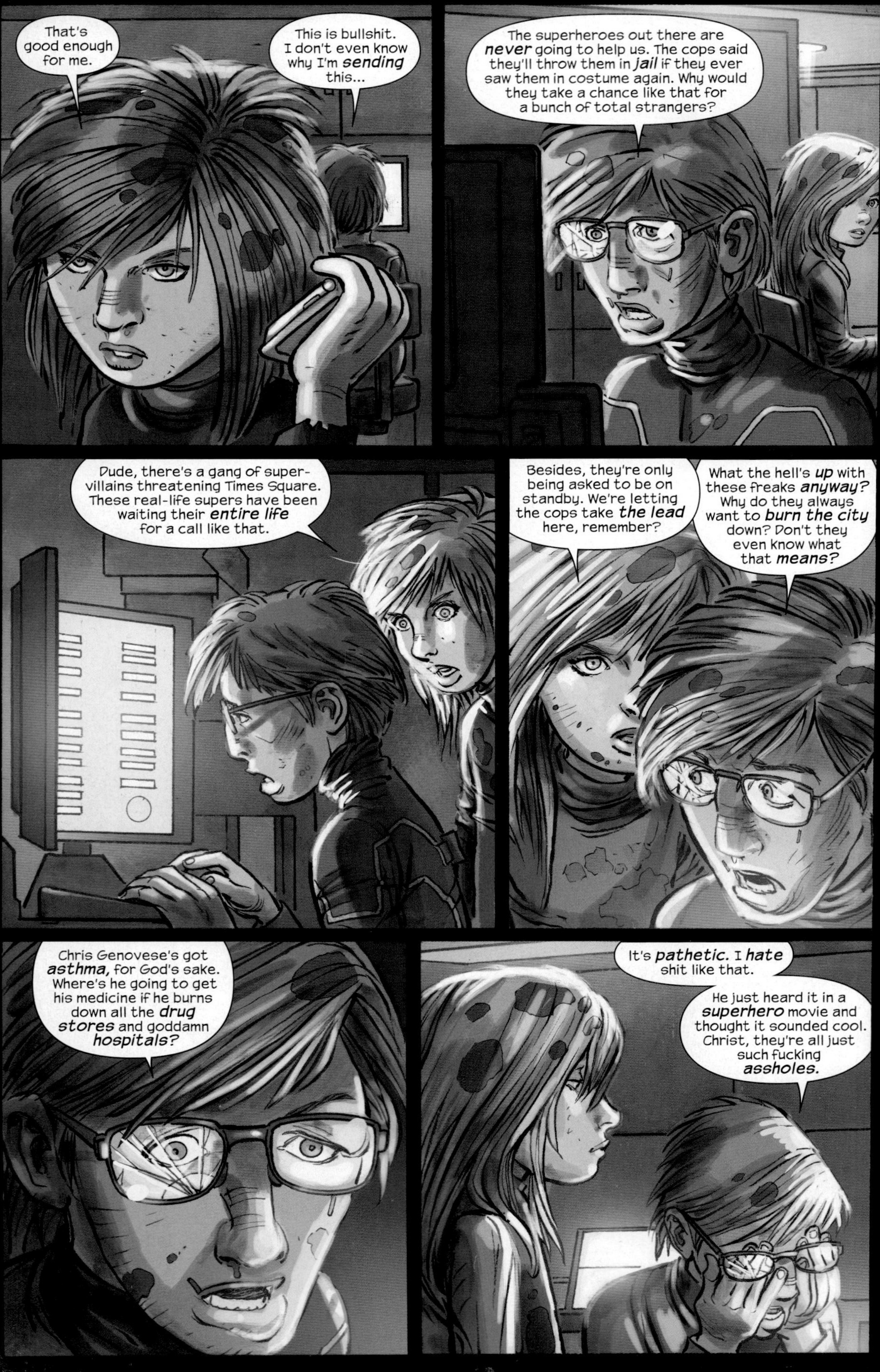
That's good enough for me.
This is bullshit. I don't even know why I'm *sending* this...
The superheroes out there are ***never*** going to help us. The cops said they'll throw them in ***jail*** if they ever saw them in costume again. Why would they take a chance like that for a bunch of total strangers?
Dude, there's a gang of super-villains threatening Times Square. These real-life supers have been waiting their ***entire life*** for a call like that.
Besides, they're only being asked to be on standby. We're letting the cops take ***the lead*** here, remember?
What the hell's ***up*** with these freaks ***anyway?*** Why do they always want to ***burn the city*** down? Don't they even know what that ***means?***
Chris Genovese's got ***asthma,*** for God's sake. Where's he going to get his medicine if he burns down all the ***drug stores*** and goddamn ***hospitals?***
It's ***pathetic.*** I ***hate*** shit like that.
He just heard it in a ***superhero*** movie and thought it sounded cool. Christ, they're all just such fucking ***assholes.***

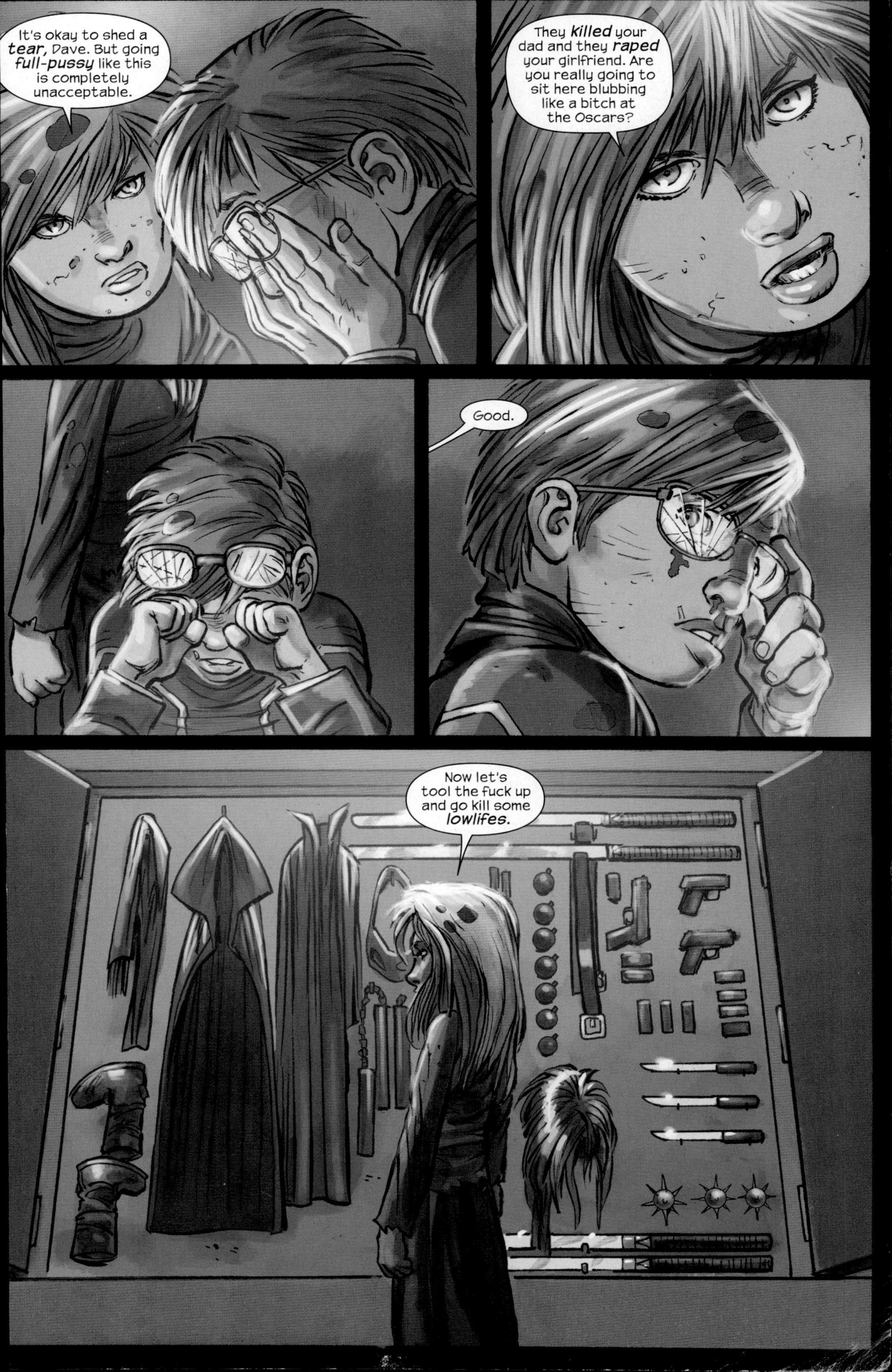
It's okay to shed a tear, Dave. But going full-pussy like this is completely unacceptable.
They killed your dad and they raped your girlfriend. Are you really going to sit here blubbing like a bitch at the Oscars?
Good.
Now let's tool the fuck up and go kill some lowlifes.

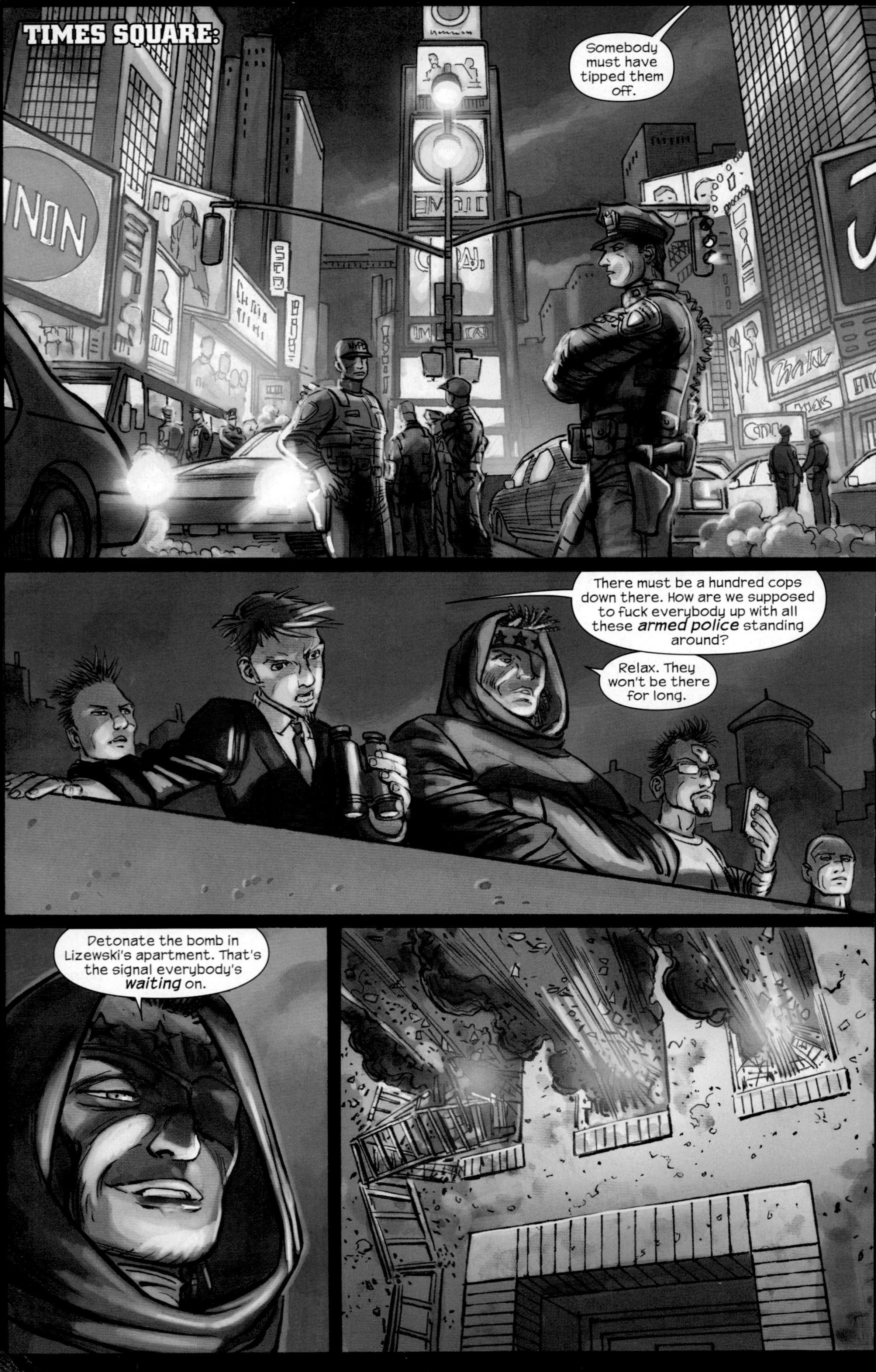
TIMES SQUARE:
Somebody must have tipped them off.
NYPD
There must be a hundred cops down there. How are we supposed to fuck everybody up with all these *armed police* standing around?
Relax. They won't be there for long.
Detonate the bomb in Lizewski's apartment. That's the signal everybody's *waiting* on.

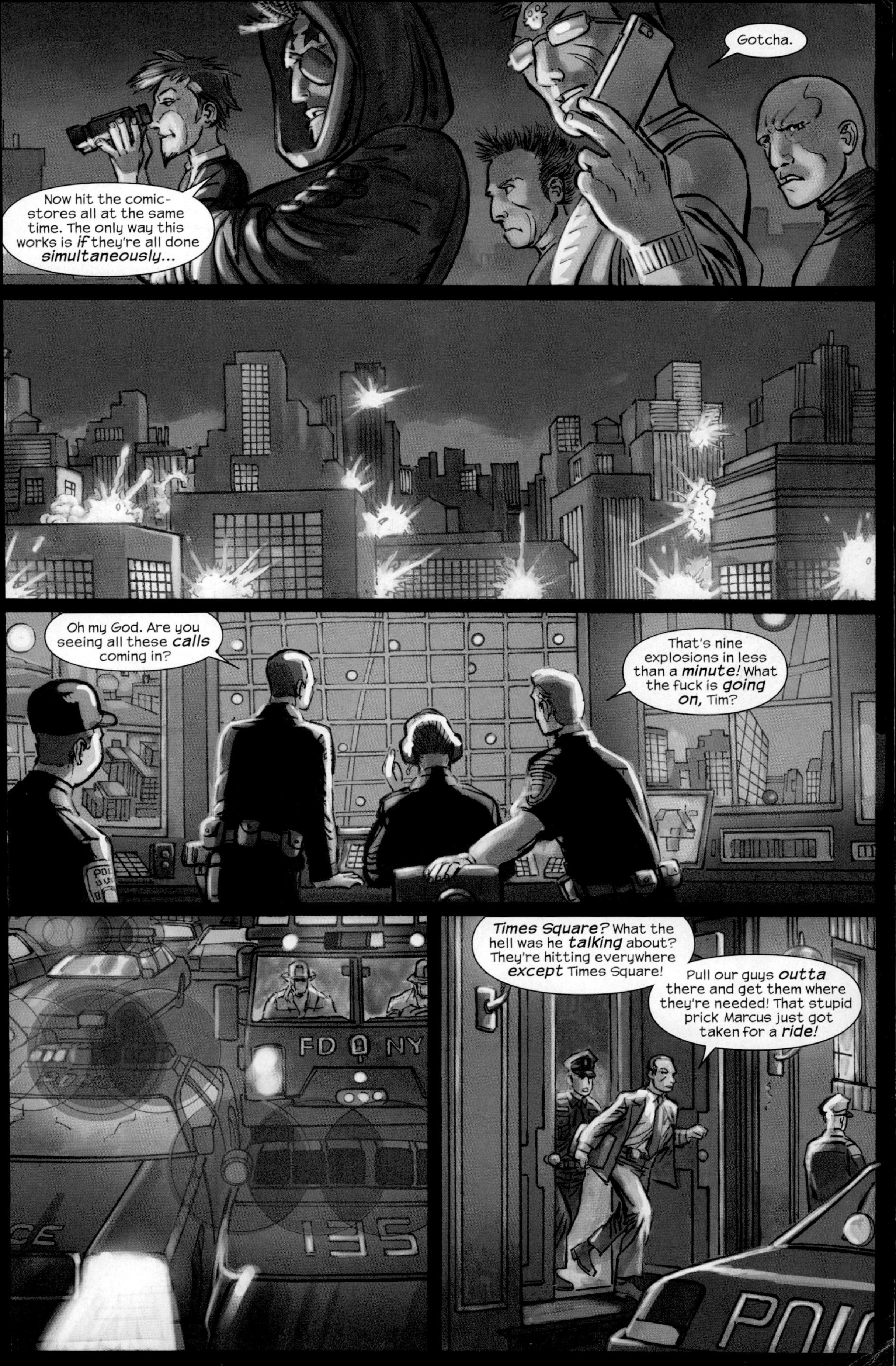
Now hit the comic-stores all at the same time. The only way this works is *if* they're all done *simultaneously...*
Gotcha.
Oh my God. Are you seeing all these *calls* coming in?
That's nine explosions in less than a *minute!* What the fuck is *going on,* Tim?
FD NY
135
Times Square? What the hell was he *talking* about? They're hitting everywhere *except* Times Square!
Pull our guys *outta* there and get them where they're needed! That stupid prick Marcus just got taken for a *ride!*

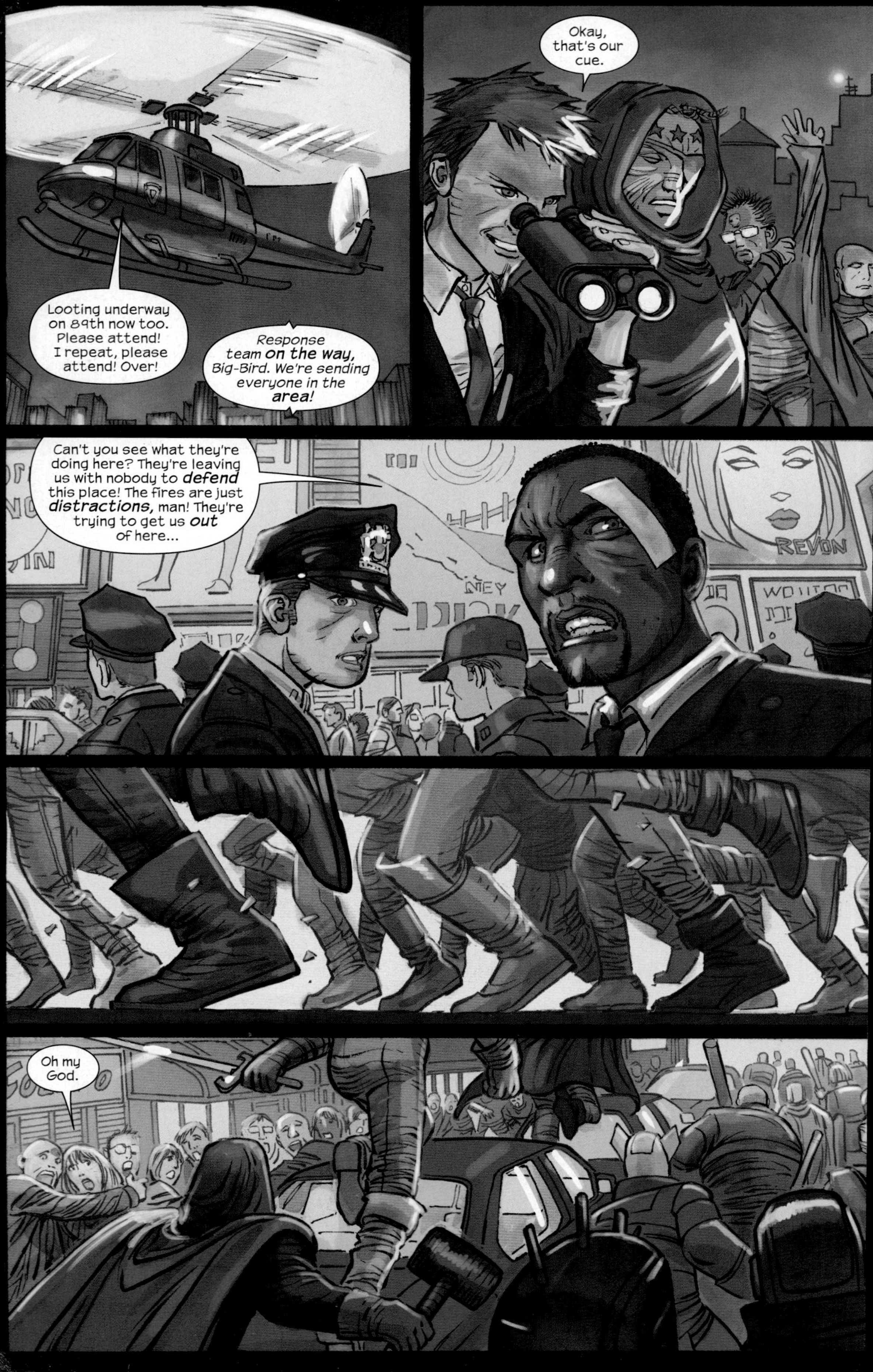

Looting underway on 89th now too. Please attend! I repeat, please attend! Over!
Response team on the way, Big-Bird. We're sending everyone in the area!
Okay, that's our cue.
Can't you see what they're doing here? They're leaving us with nobody to defend this place! The fires are just distractions, man! They're trying to get us out of here...
REVON
Oh my God.

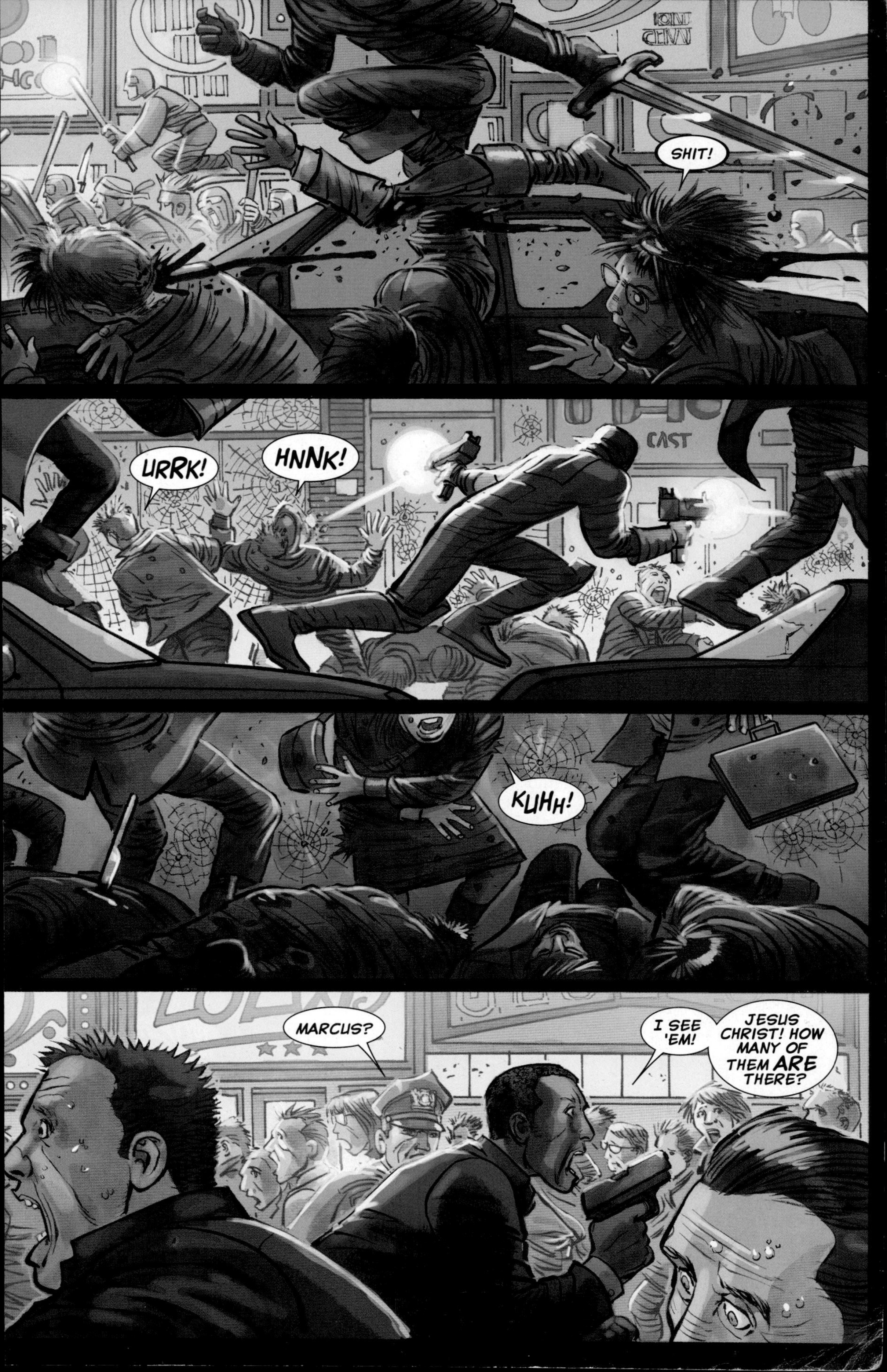
SHIT!
CAST
URRK!
HNNK!
KUHH!
MARCUS?
I SEE 'EM!
JESUS CHRIST! HOW MANY OF THEM ARE THERE?

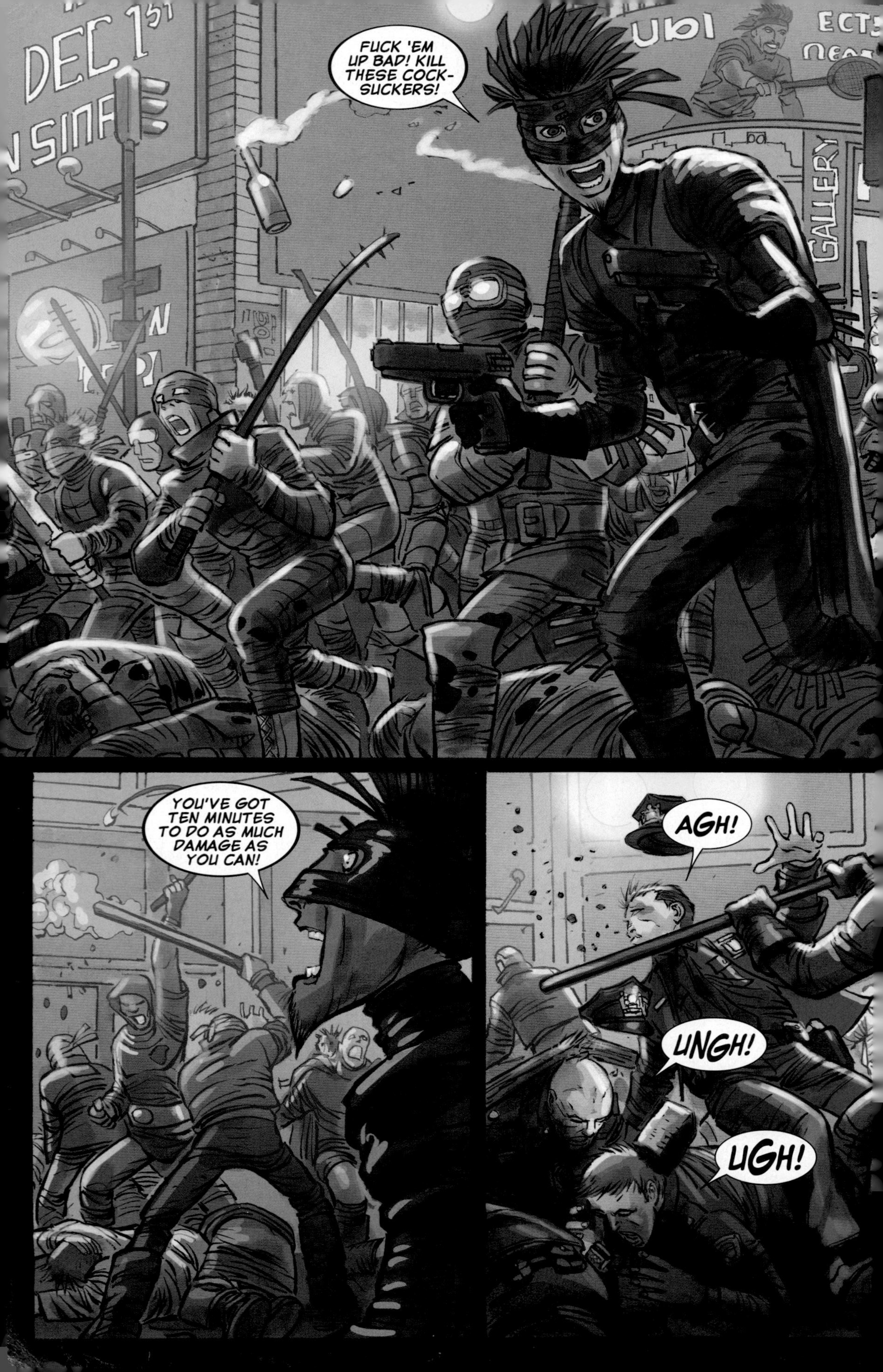

DEC 1ST
GALLERY
FUCK 'EM UP BAD! KILL THESE COCK-SUCKERS!
YOU'VE GOT TEN MINUTES TO DO AS MUCH DAMAGE AS YOU CAN!
AGH!
UNGH!
UGH!

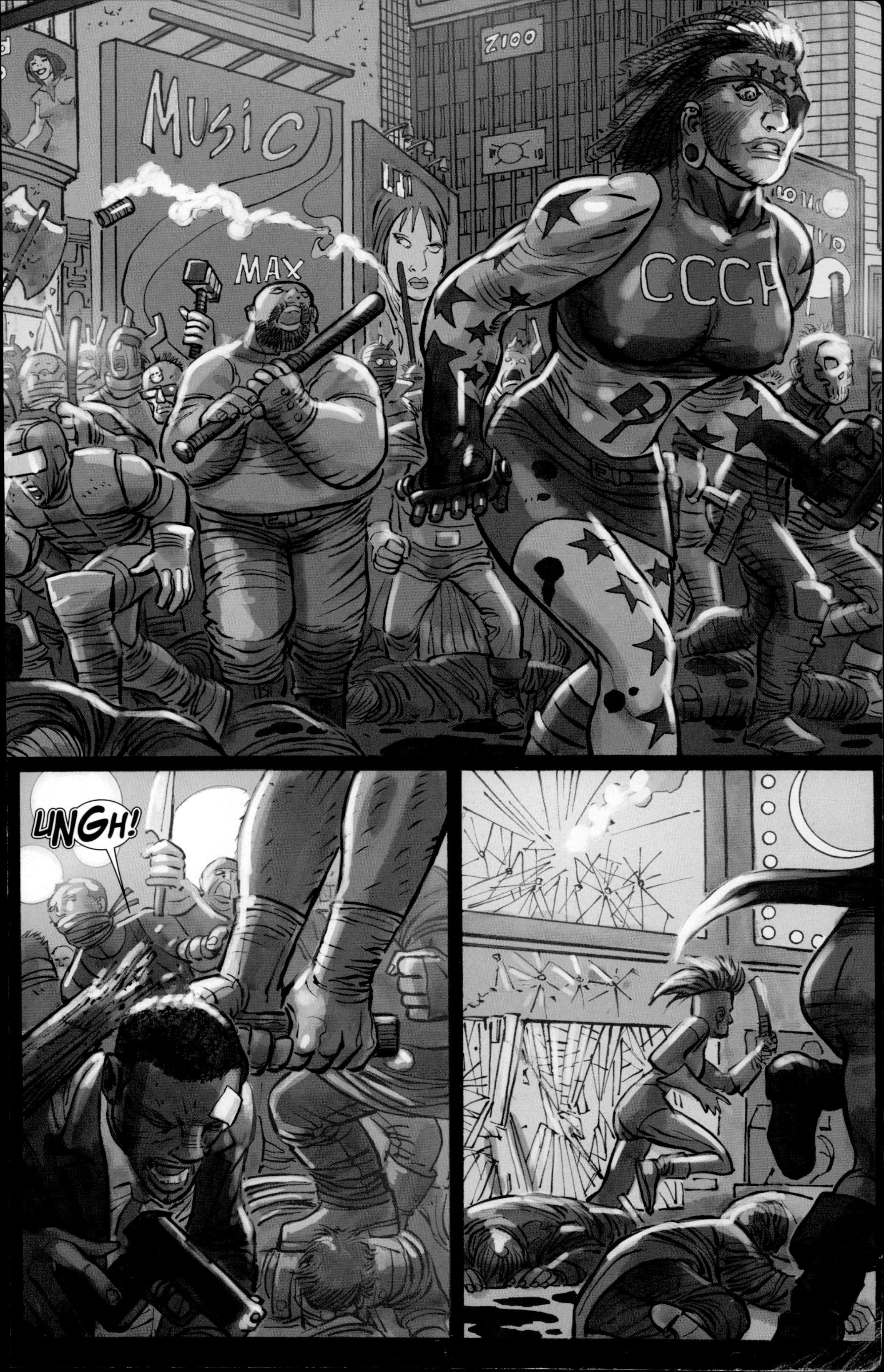
MUSIC
Z100
MAX
CCCP
UNGH!

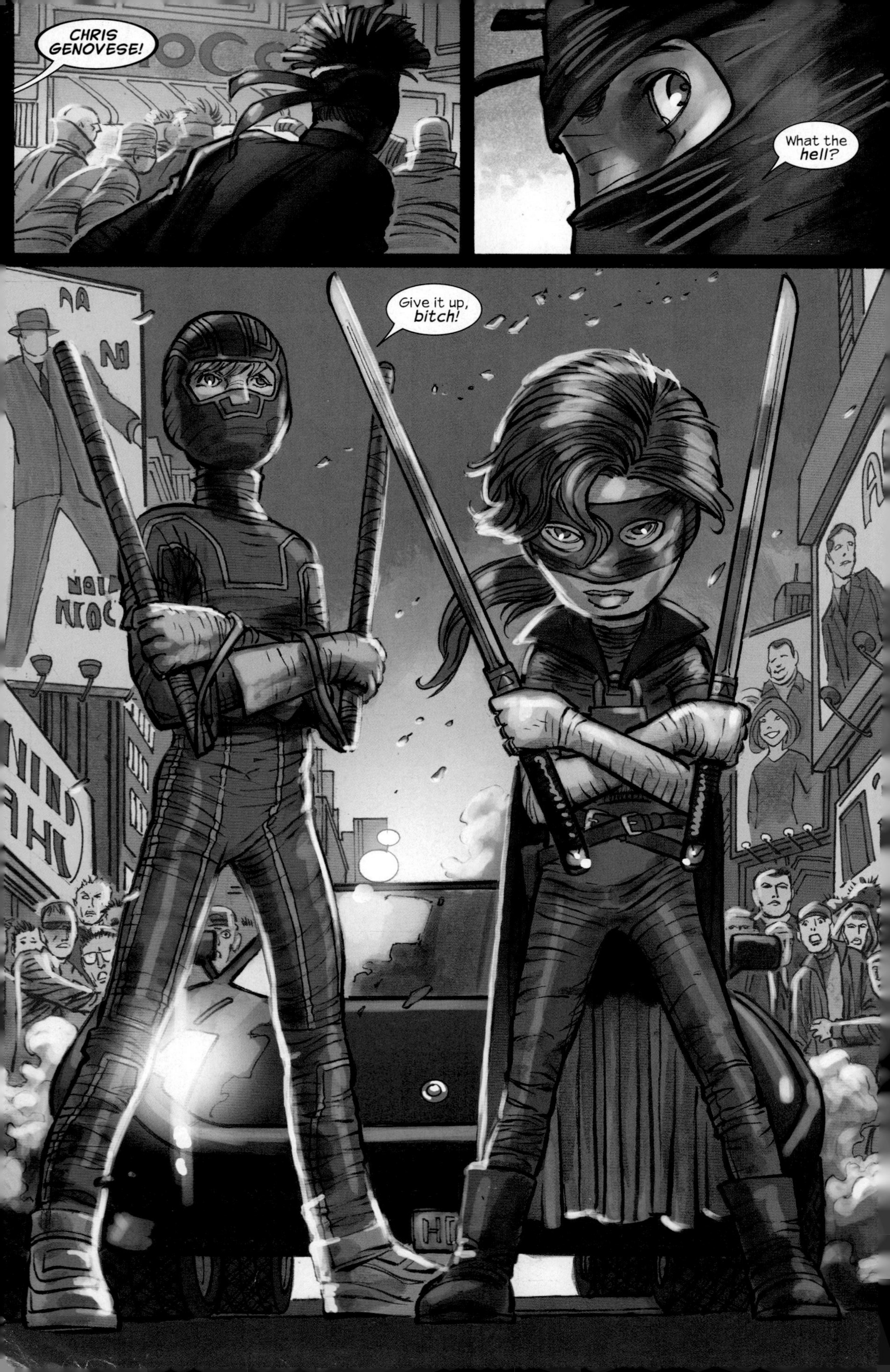
CHRIS GENOVESE!
What the hell?
Give it up, bitch!

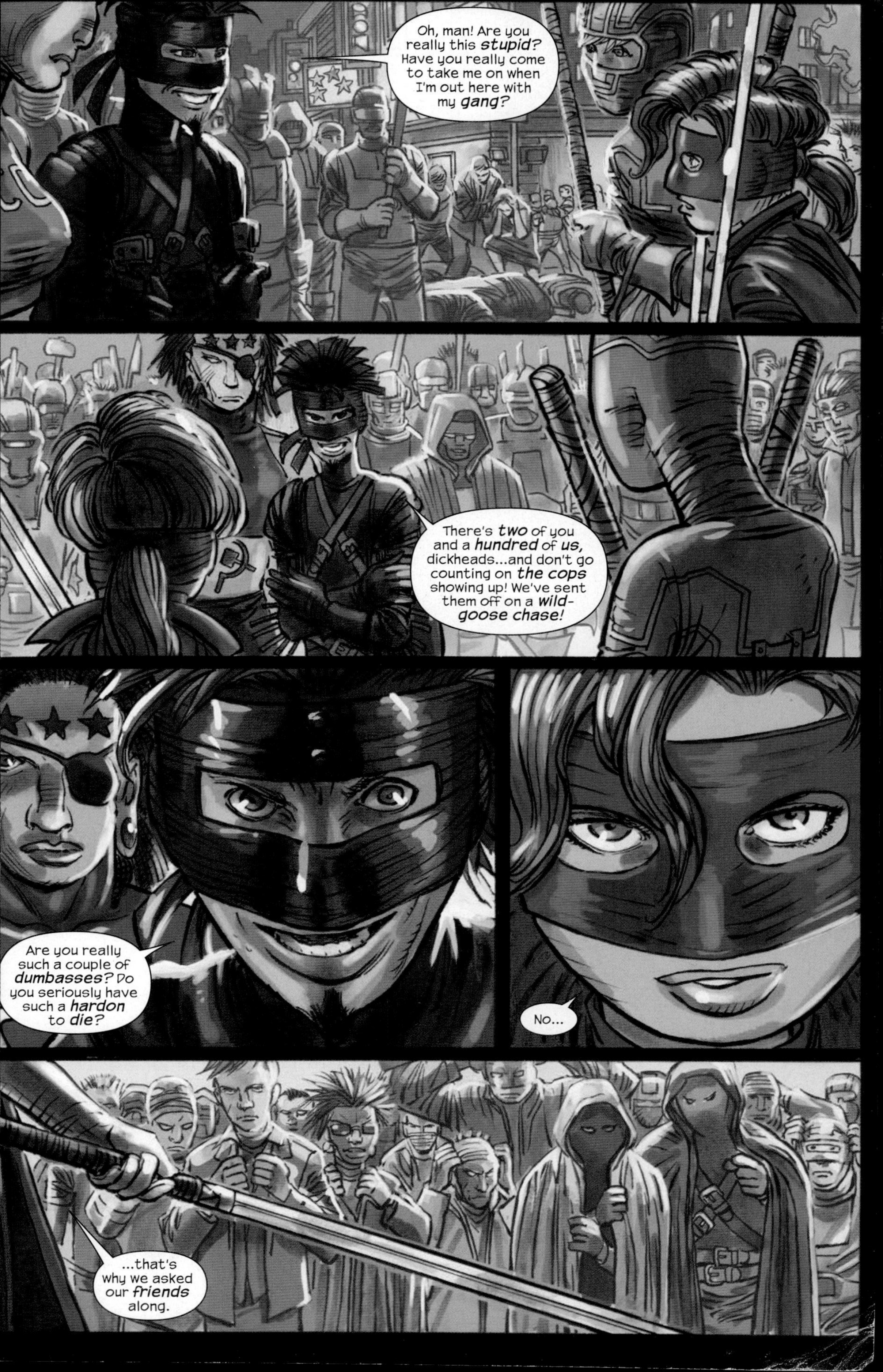
Oh, man! Are you really this *stupid*? Have you really come to take me on when I'm out here with my *gang*?
There's *two* of you and a *hundred* of *us,* dickheads...and don't go counting on *the cops* showing up! We've sent them off on a *wild-goose chase!*
Are you really such a couple of *dumbasses?* Do you seriously have such a *hardon* to *die*?
No...
...that's why we asked our *friends* along.

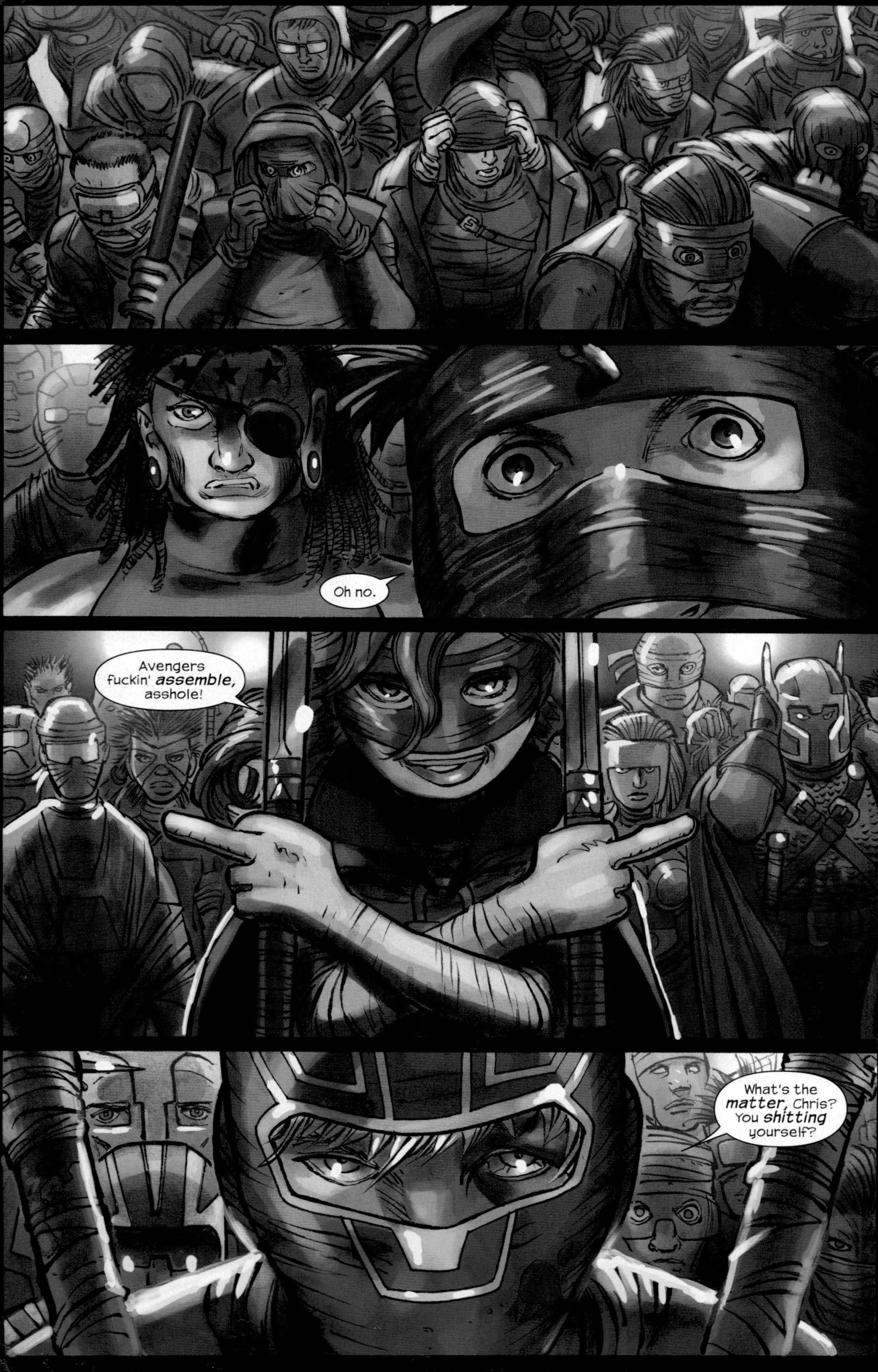
Oh no.
Avengers fuckin' *assemble,* asshole!
What's the *matter,* Chris? You *shitting* yourself?

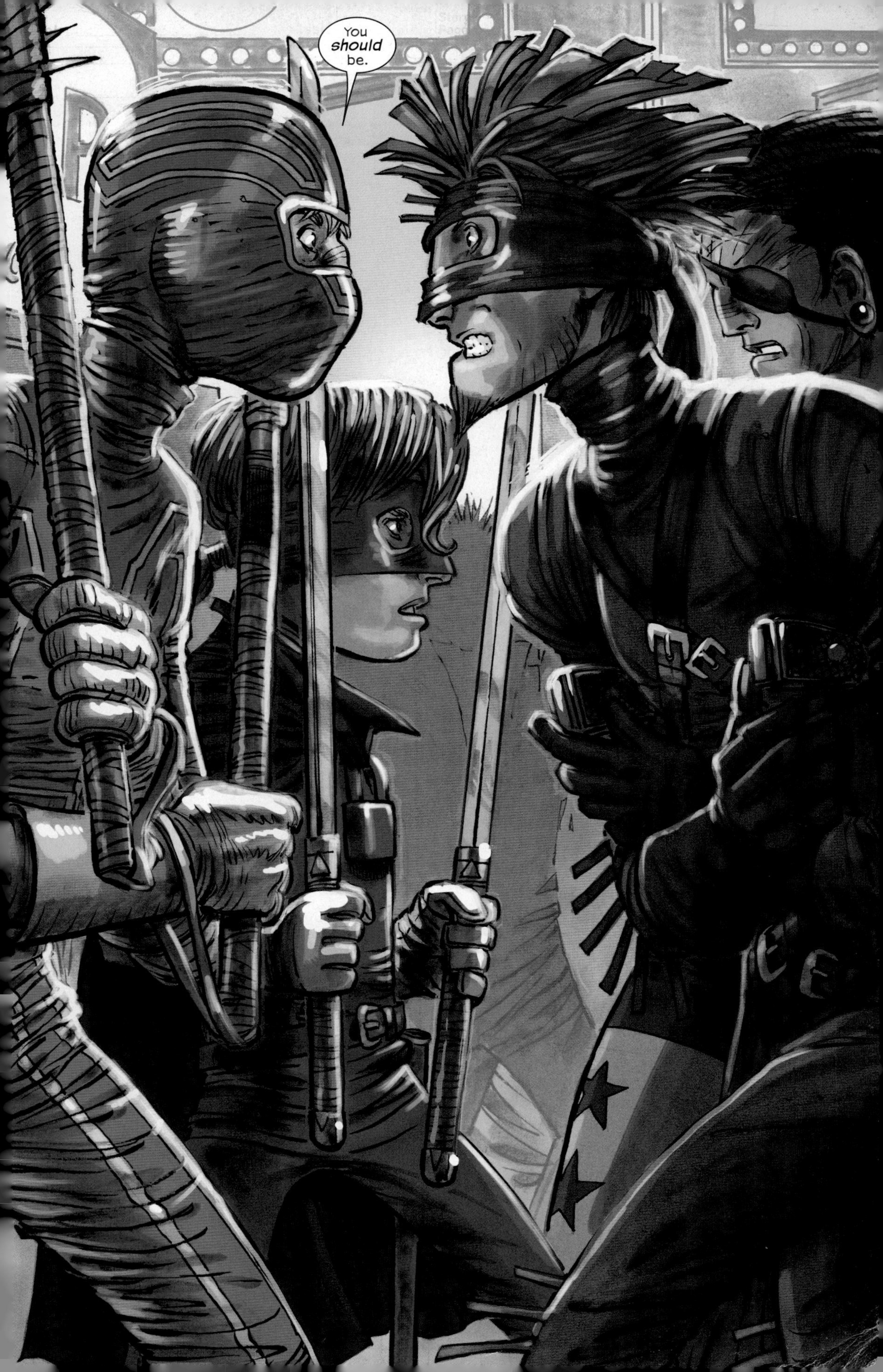
You *should* be.

SEVEN

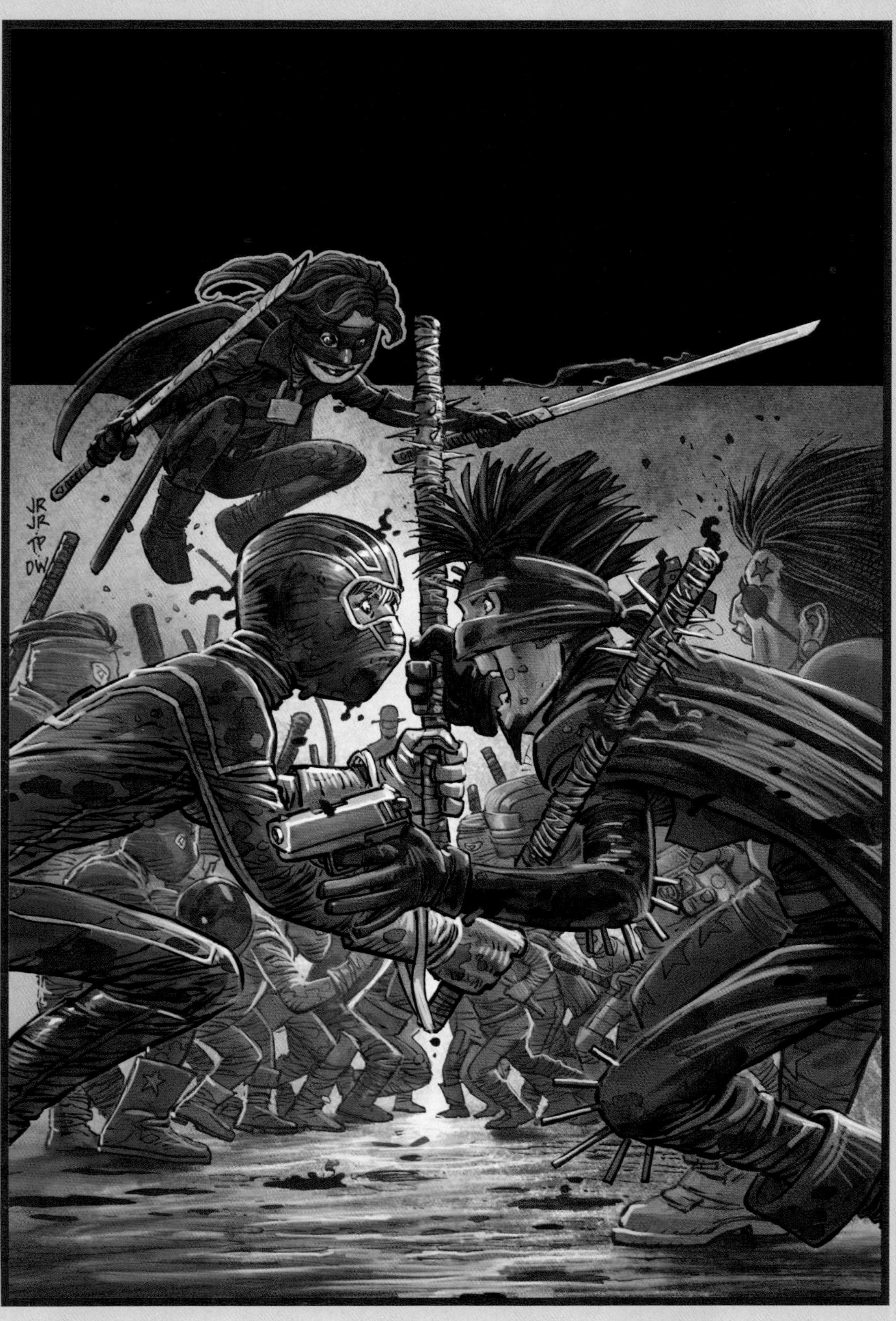
JR
JR
TP
DW

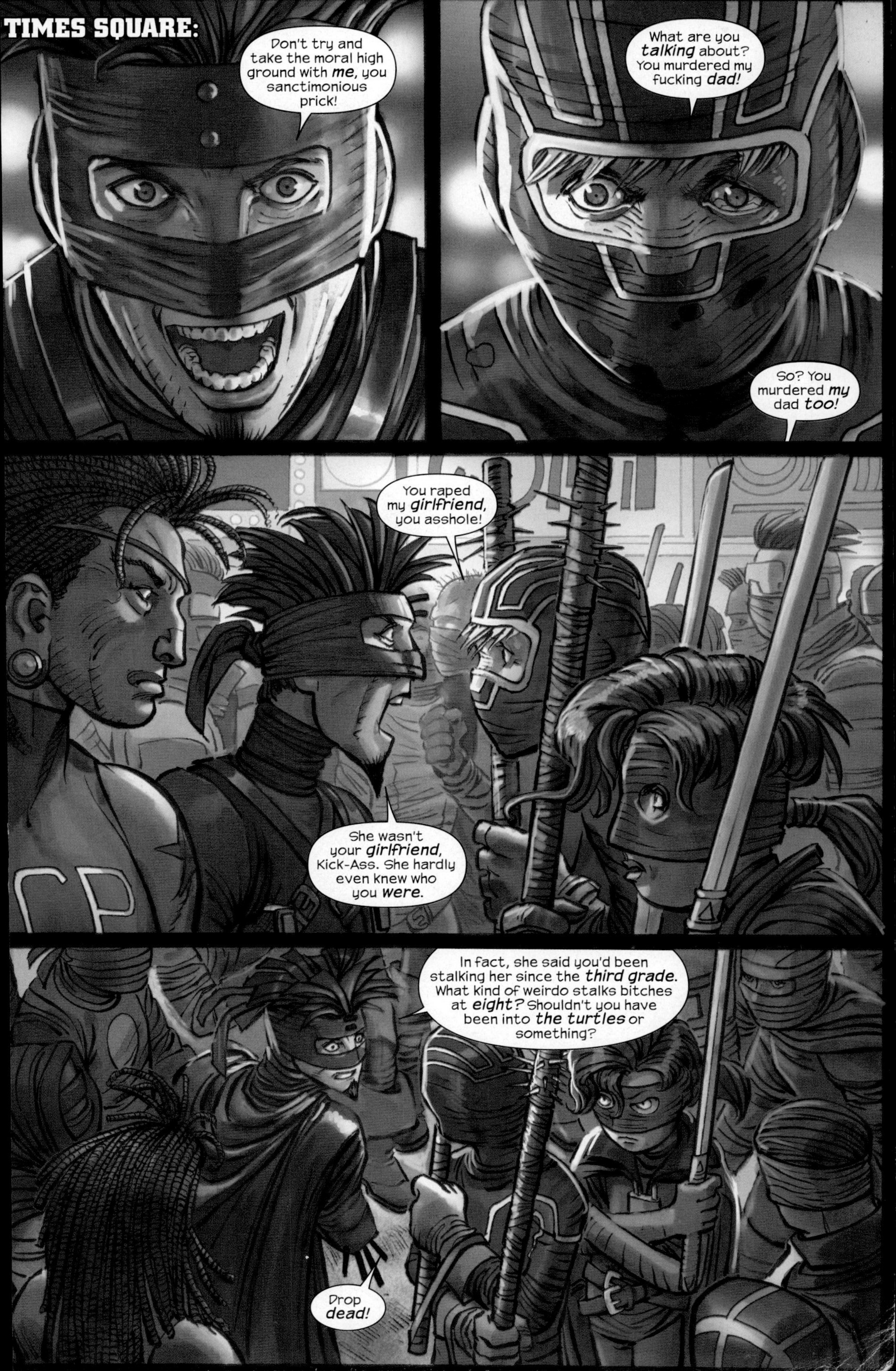

TIMES SQUARE:
Don't try and take the moral high ground with *me*, you sanctimonious prick!
What are you *talking* about? You murdered my fucking *dad!*
So? You murdered *my* dad *too!*
You raped my *girlfriend*, you asshole!
She wasn't your *girlfriend*, Kick-Ass. She hardly even knew who you *were*.
In fact, she said you'd been stalking her since the *third grade*. What kind of weirdo stalks bitches at *eight?* Shouldn't you have been into *the turtles* or something?
Drop *dead!*

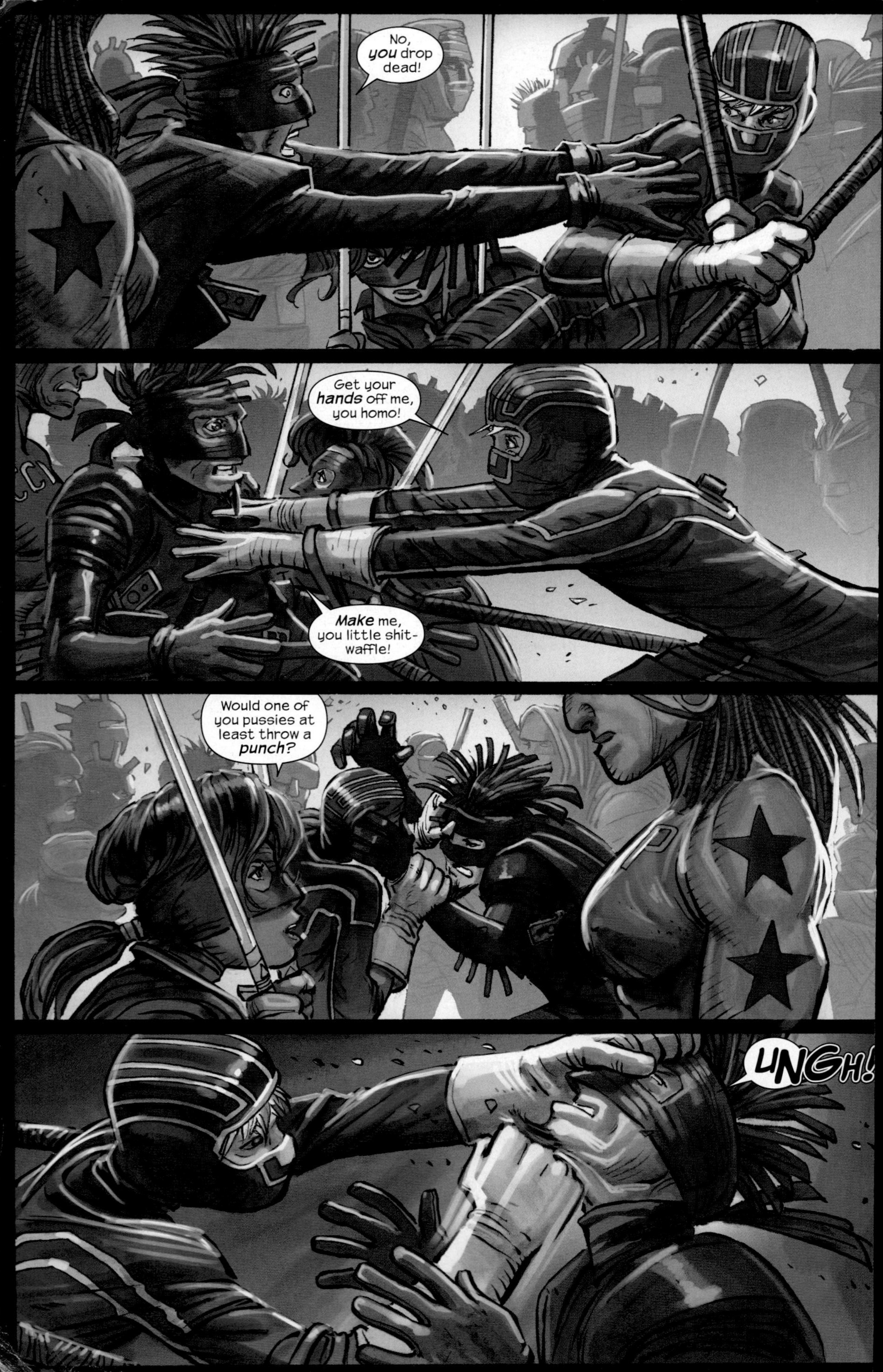

No, *you* drop dead!
Get your *hands* off me, you homo!
Make me, you little shit-waffle!
Would one of you pussies at least throw a *punch?*
UNGH!

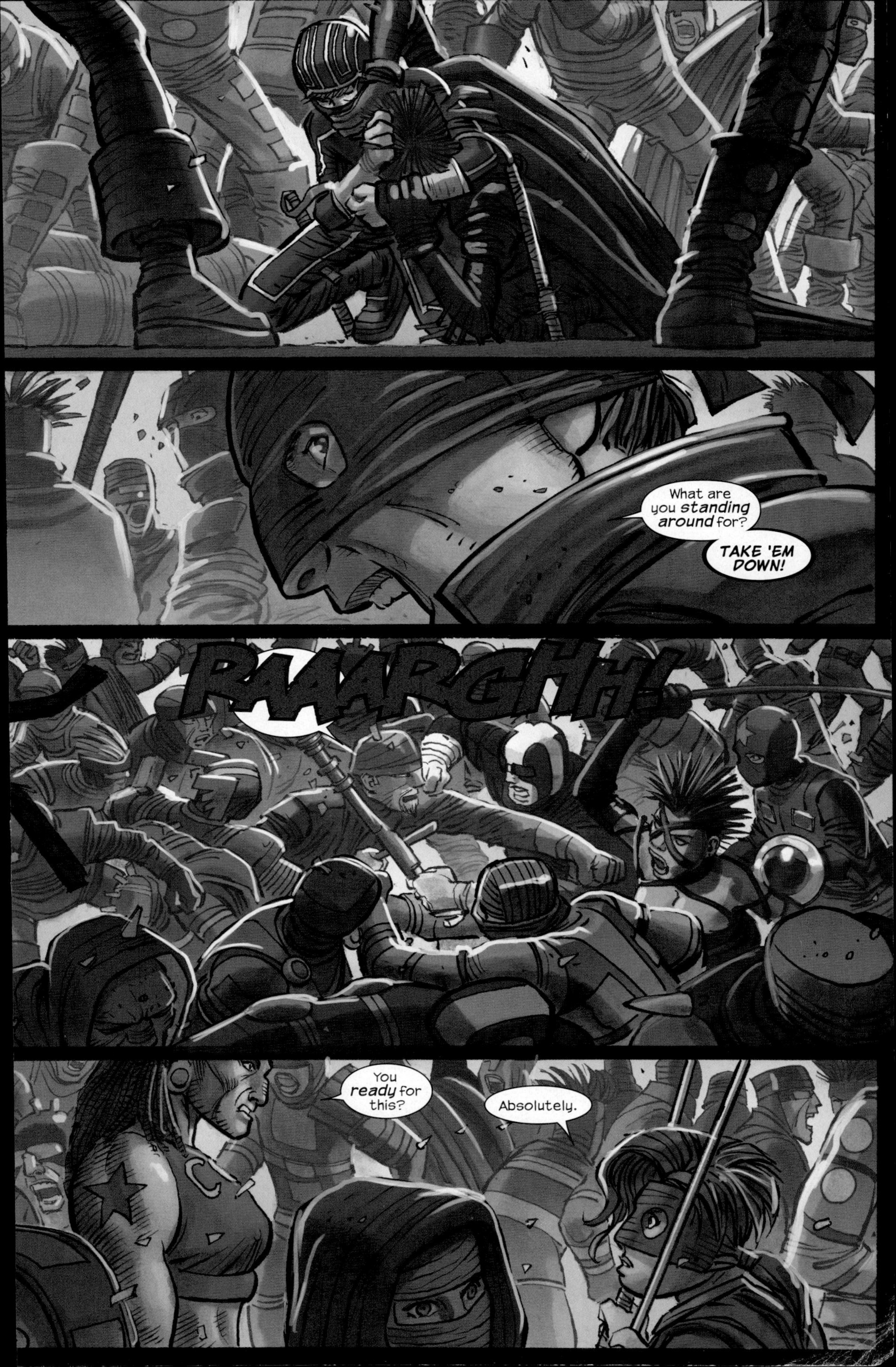
What are you standing around for?
TAKE 'EM DOWN!
RAAARCHH!
You ready for this?
Absolutely.

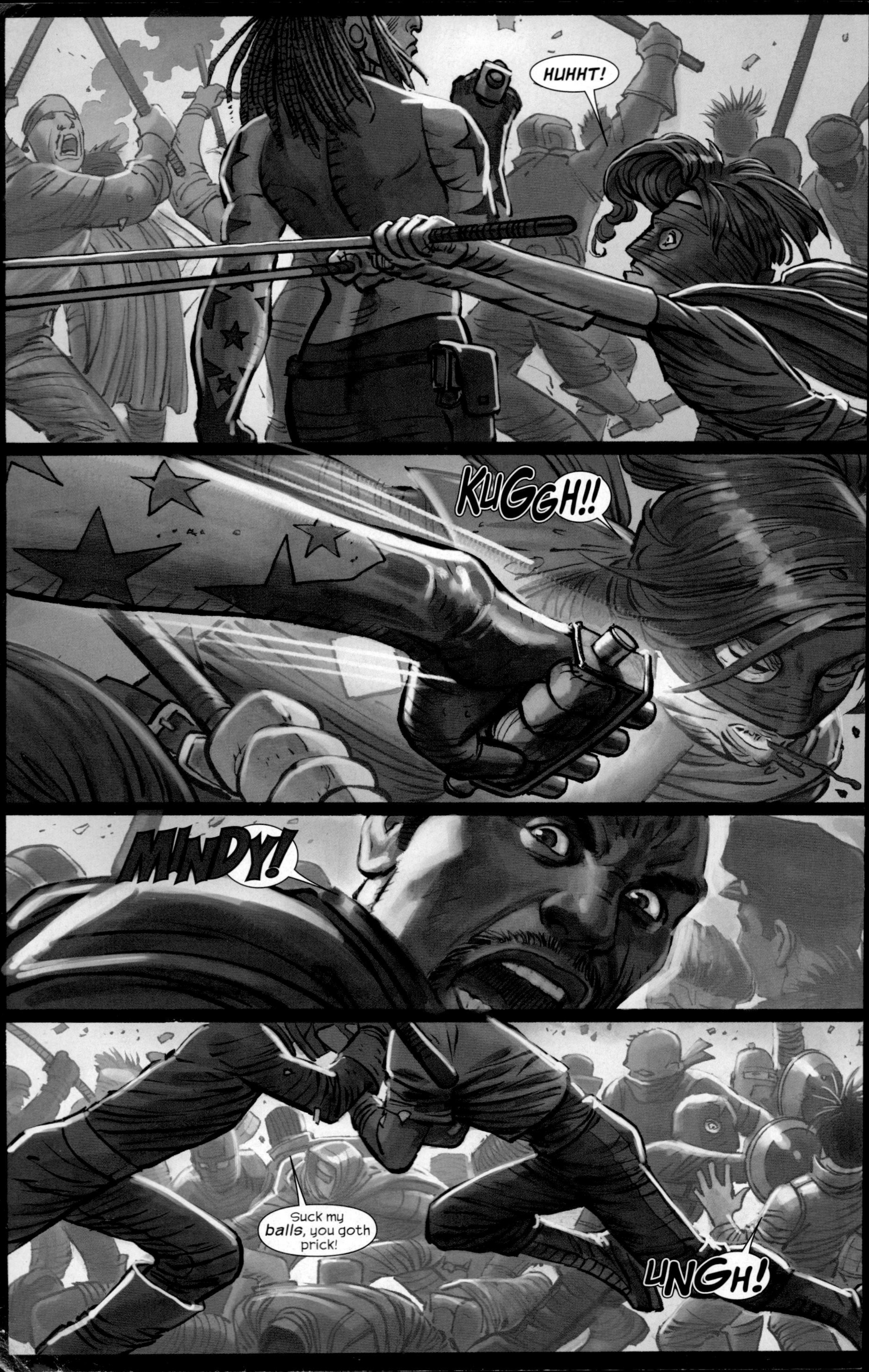
HUHHT!
KLUGGH!!
MINDY!
Suck my *balls*, you goth prick!
UNGH!

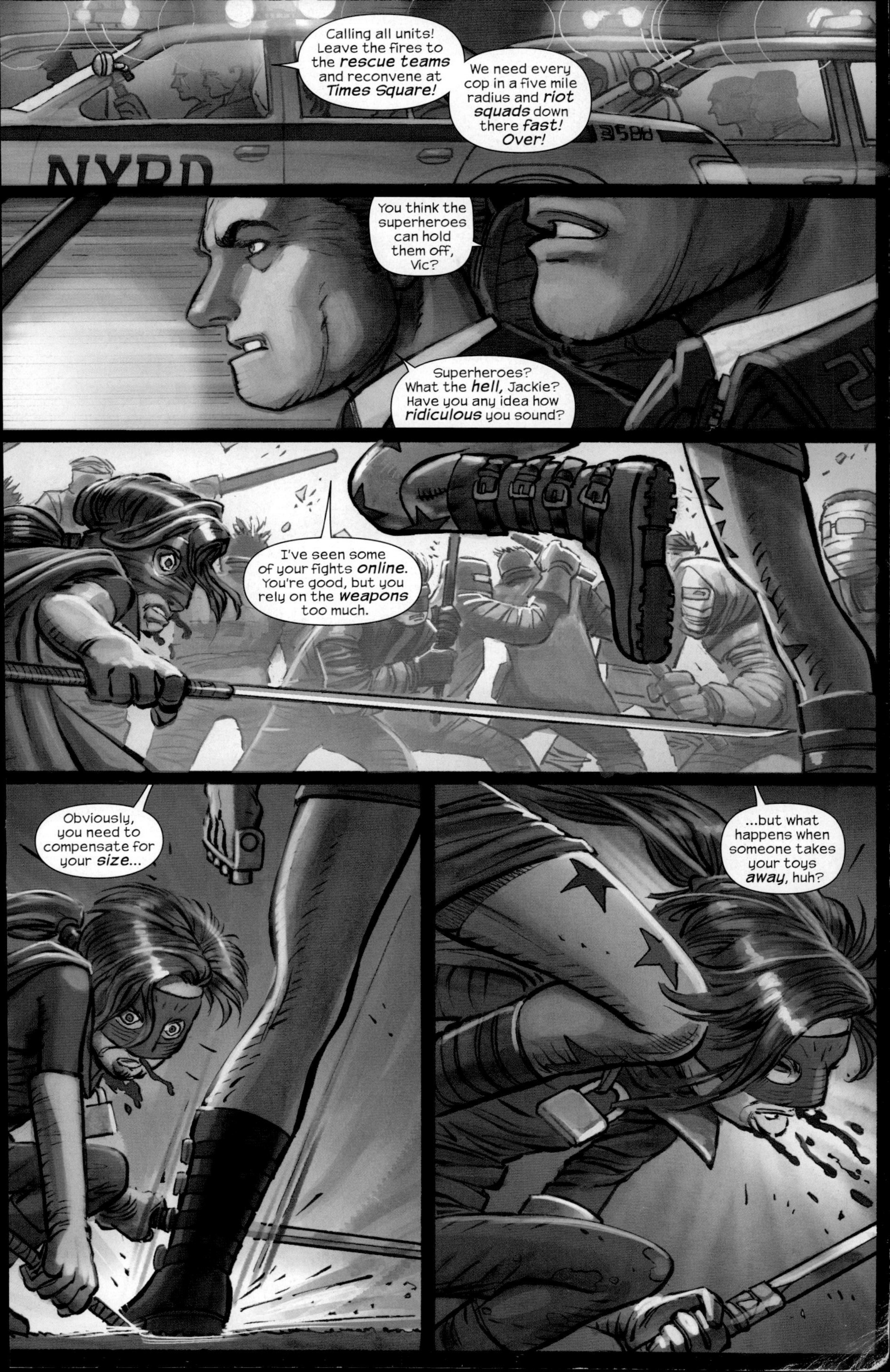
Calling all units! Leave the fires to the *rescue teams* and reconvene at *Times Square!*
We need every cop in a five mile radius and *riot squads* down there *fast! Over!*
NYPD
3588
You think the superheroes can hold them off, Vic?
Superheroes? What the *hell,* Jackie? Have you any idea how *ridiculous* you sound?
I've seen some of your fights *online*. You're good, but you rely on the *weapons* too much.
Obviously, you need to compensate for your *size*...
...but what happens when someone takes your toys *away*, huh?

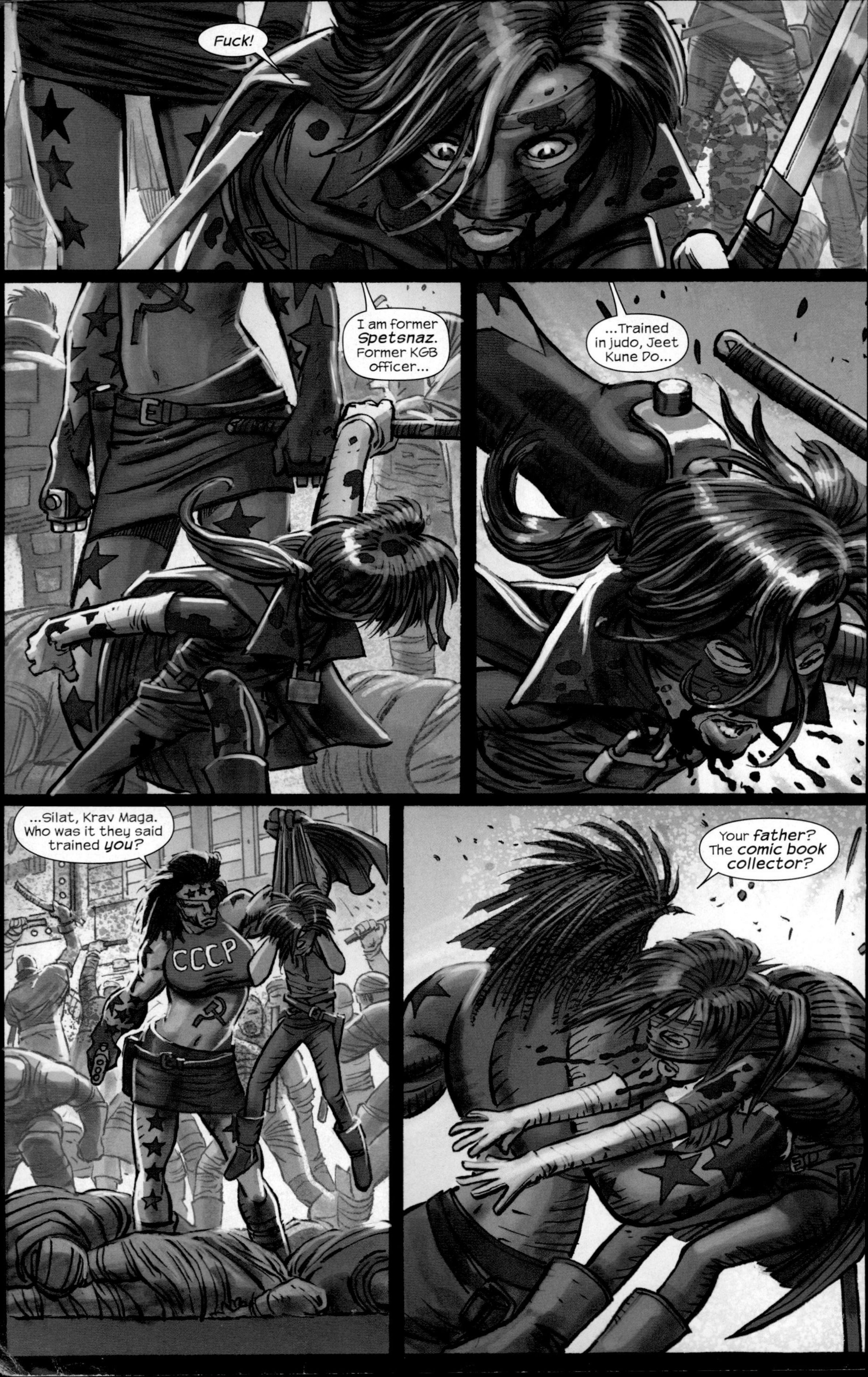
Fuck!
I am former Spetsnaz. Former KGB officer...
...Trained in judo, Jeet Kune Do...
...Silat, Krav Maga. Who was it they said trained you?
CCCP
Your father? The comic book collector?

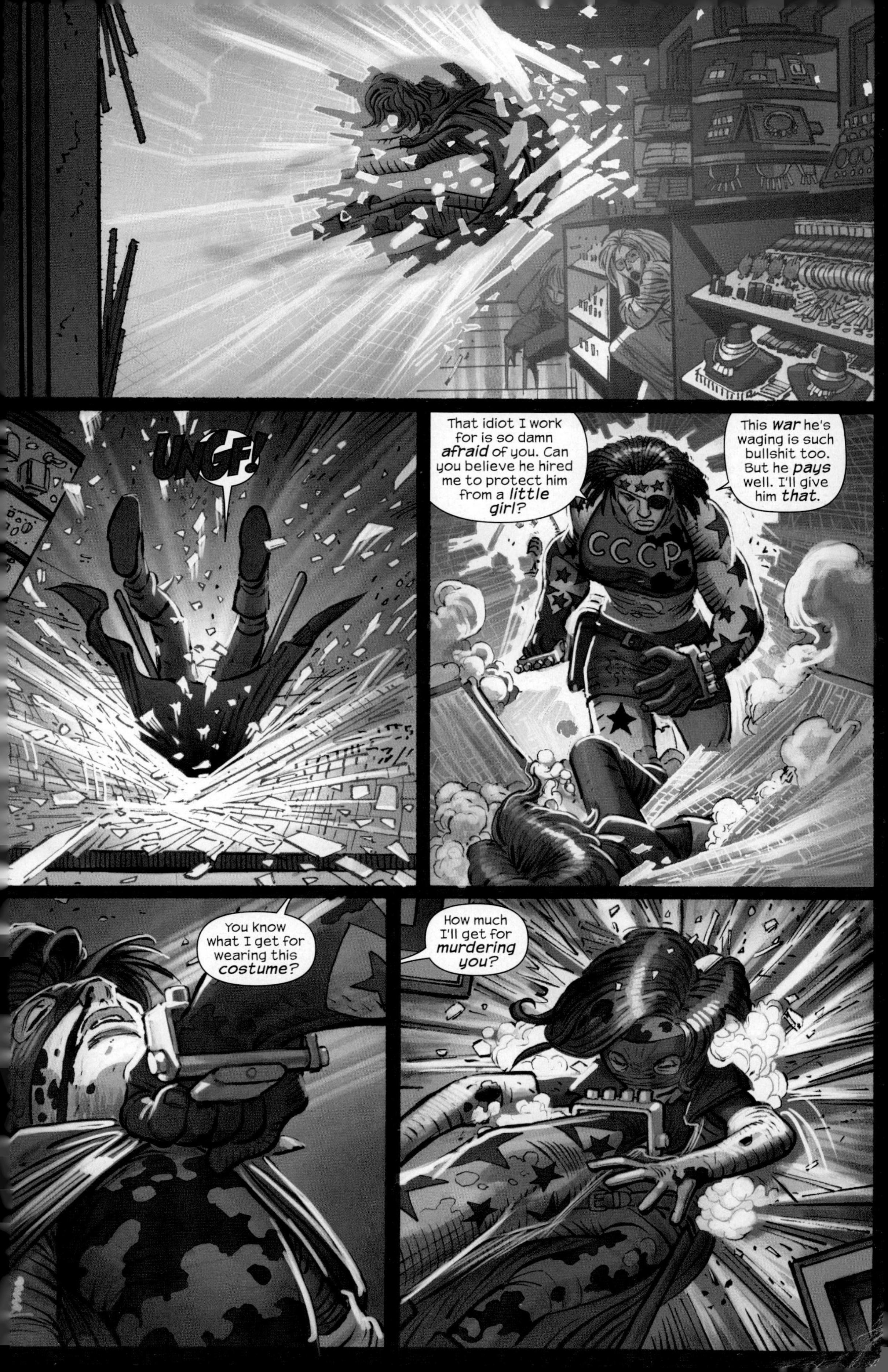
UNGF!
That idiot I work for is so damn *afraid* of you. Can you believe he hired me to protect him from a *little girl*?
This *war* he's waging is such bullshit too. But he *pays* well. I'll give him *that*.
You know what I get for wearing this *costume*?
How much I'll get for *murdering you*?

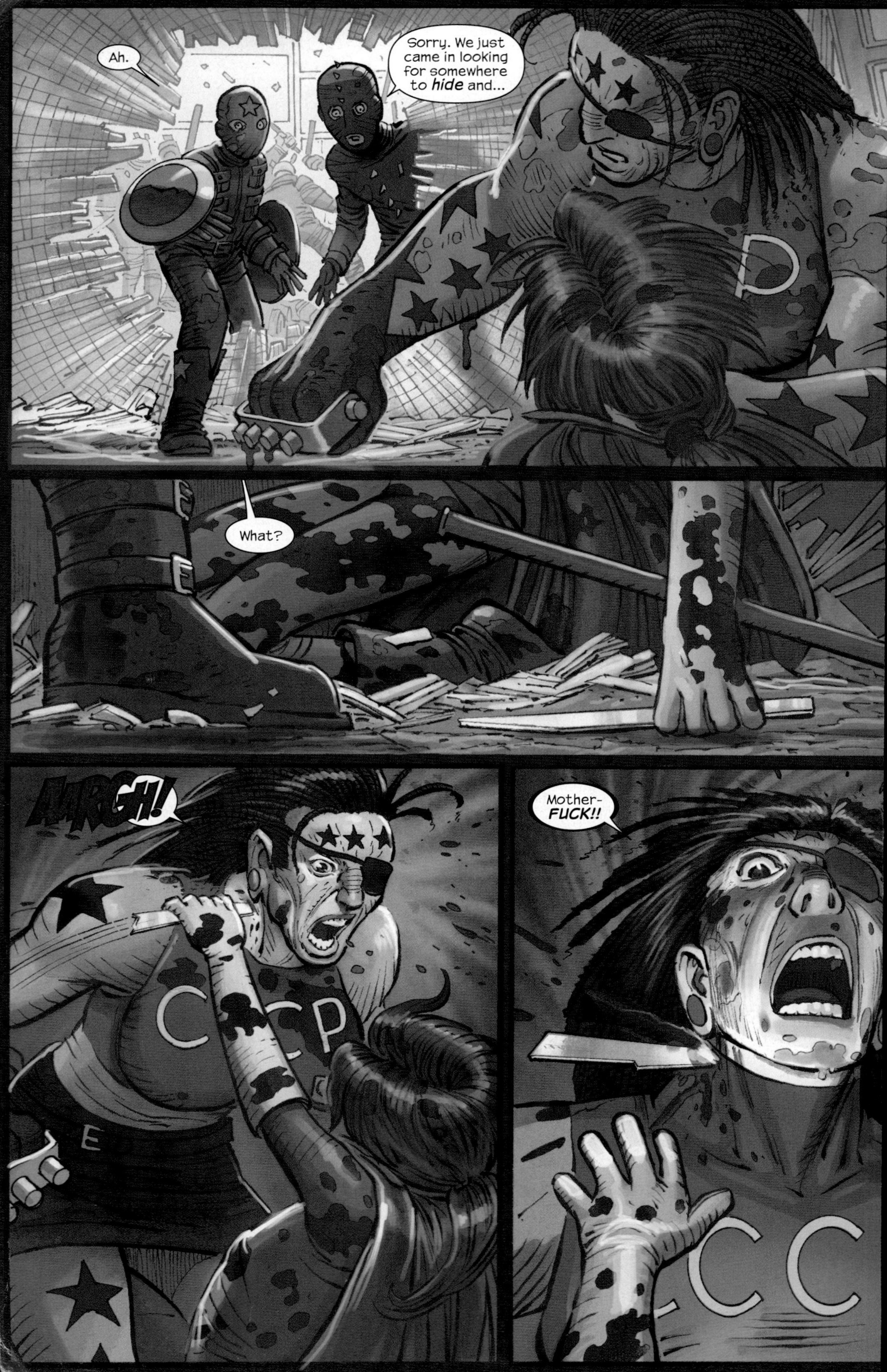
Ah.
Sorry. We just came in looking for somewhere to *hide* and...
What?
AARGH!
Mother-*FUCK!!*

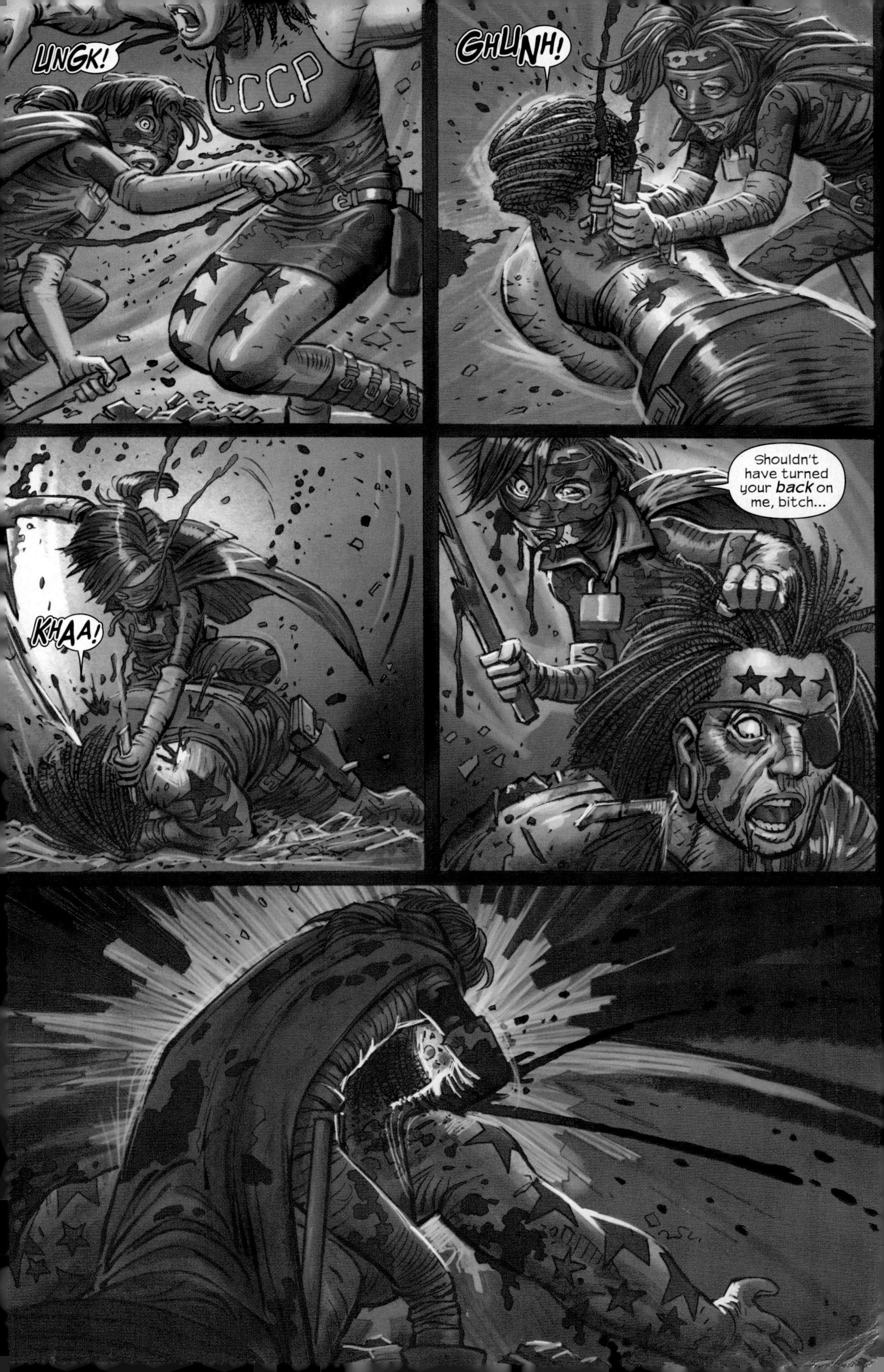
UNGK!
GHUNH!
KHAA!
Shouldn't have turned your back on me, bitch...

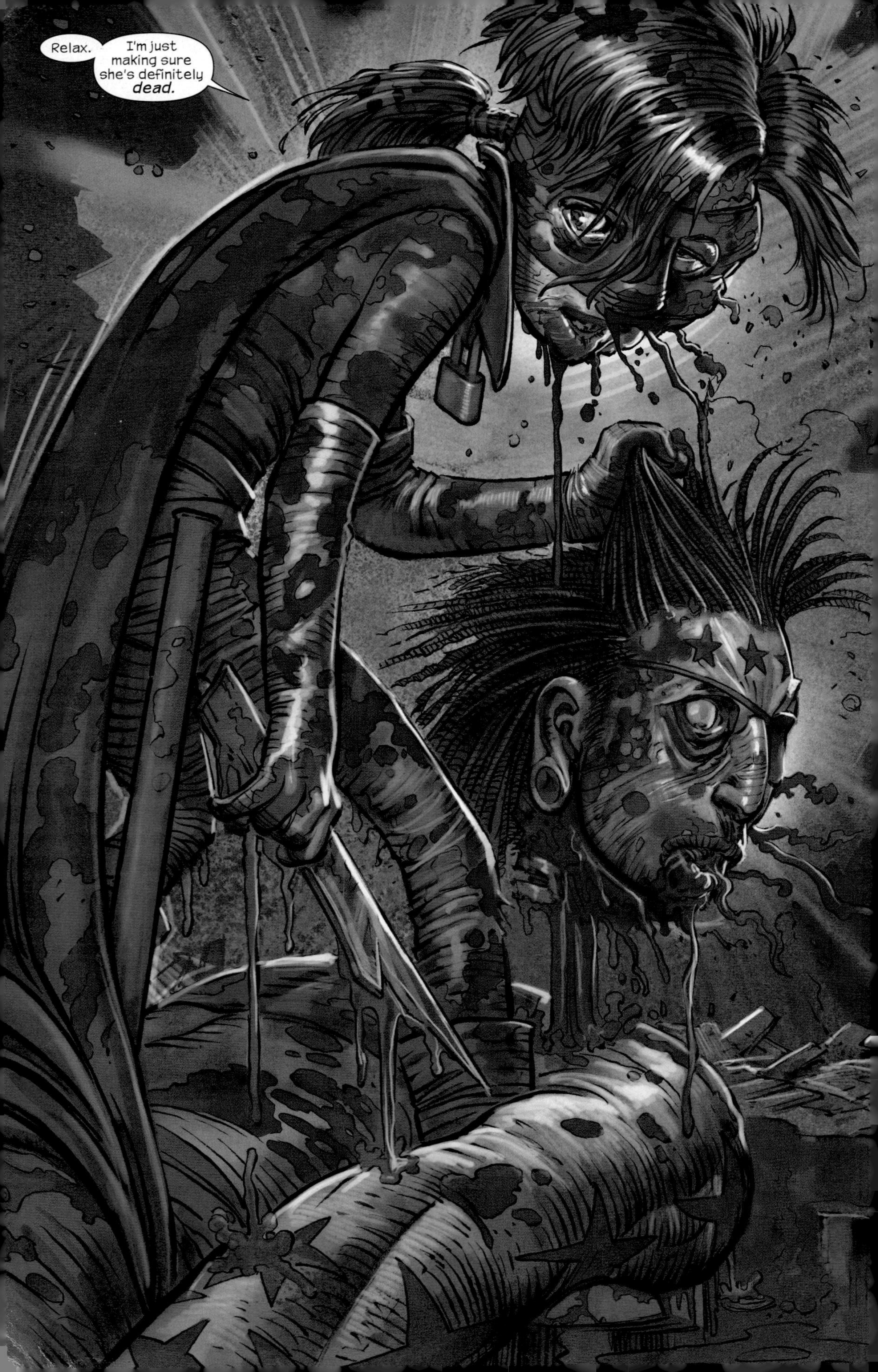
Relax.
I'm just making sure she's definitely *dead.*

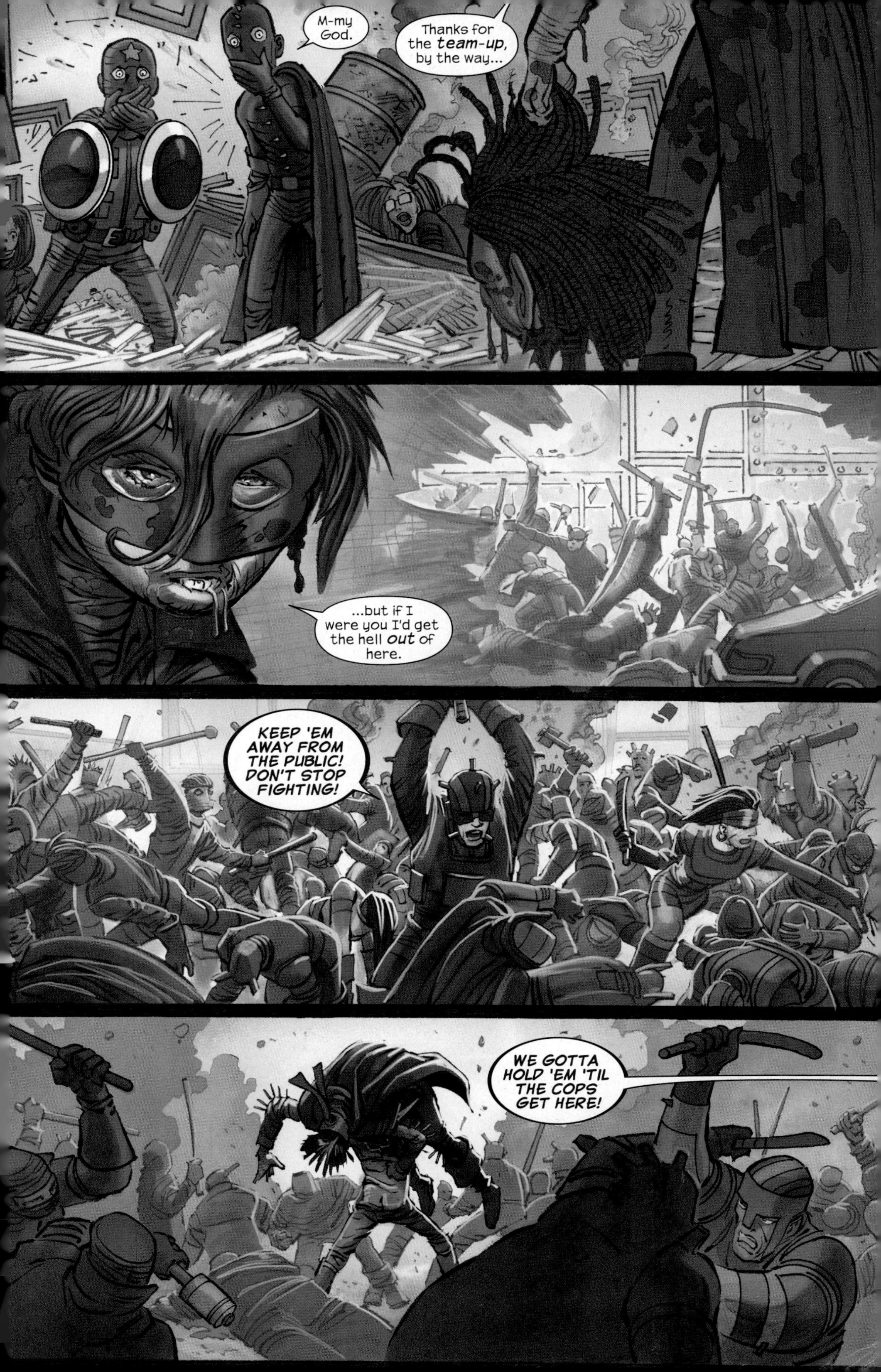
M-my God.
Thanks for the team-up, by the way...
...but if I were you I'd get the hell out of here.
KEEP 'EM AWAY FROM THE PUBLIC! DON'T STOP FIGHTING!
WE GOTTA HOLD 'EM 'TIL THE COPS GET HERE!

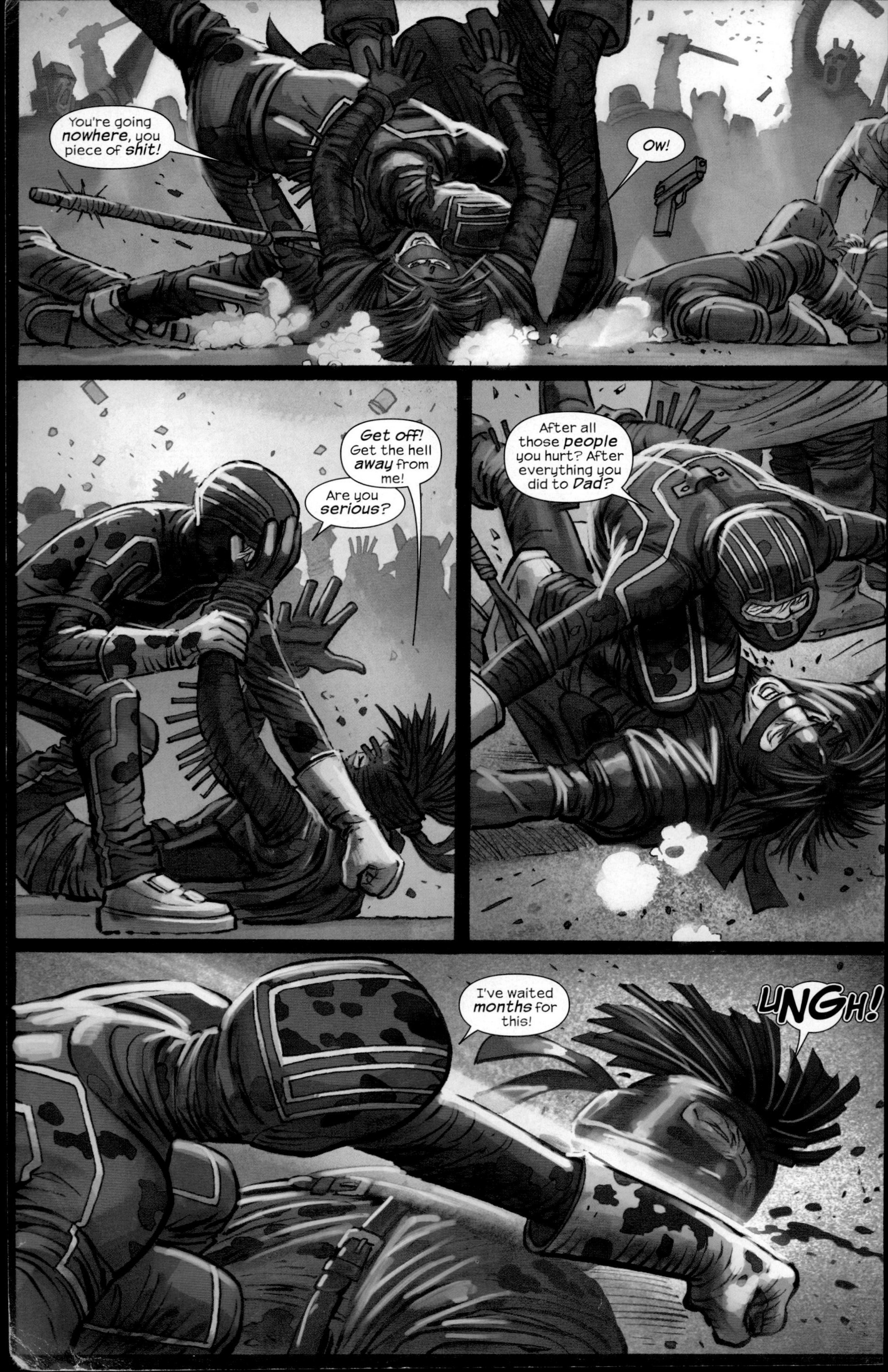
You're going *nowhere*, you piece of *shit!*
Ow!
Get off! Get the hell *away* from me!
Are you *serious?*
After all those *people* you hurt? After everything you did to *Dad?*
I've waited *months* for this!
UNGH!

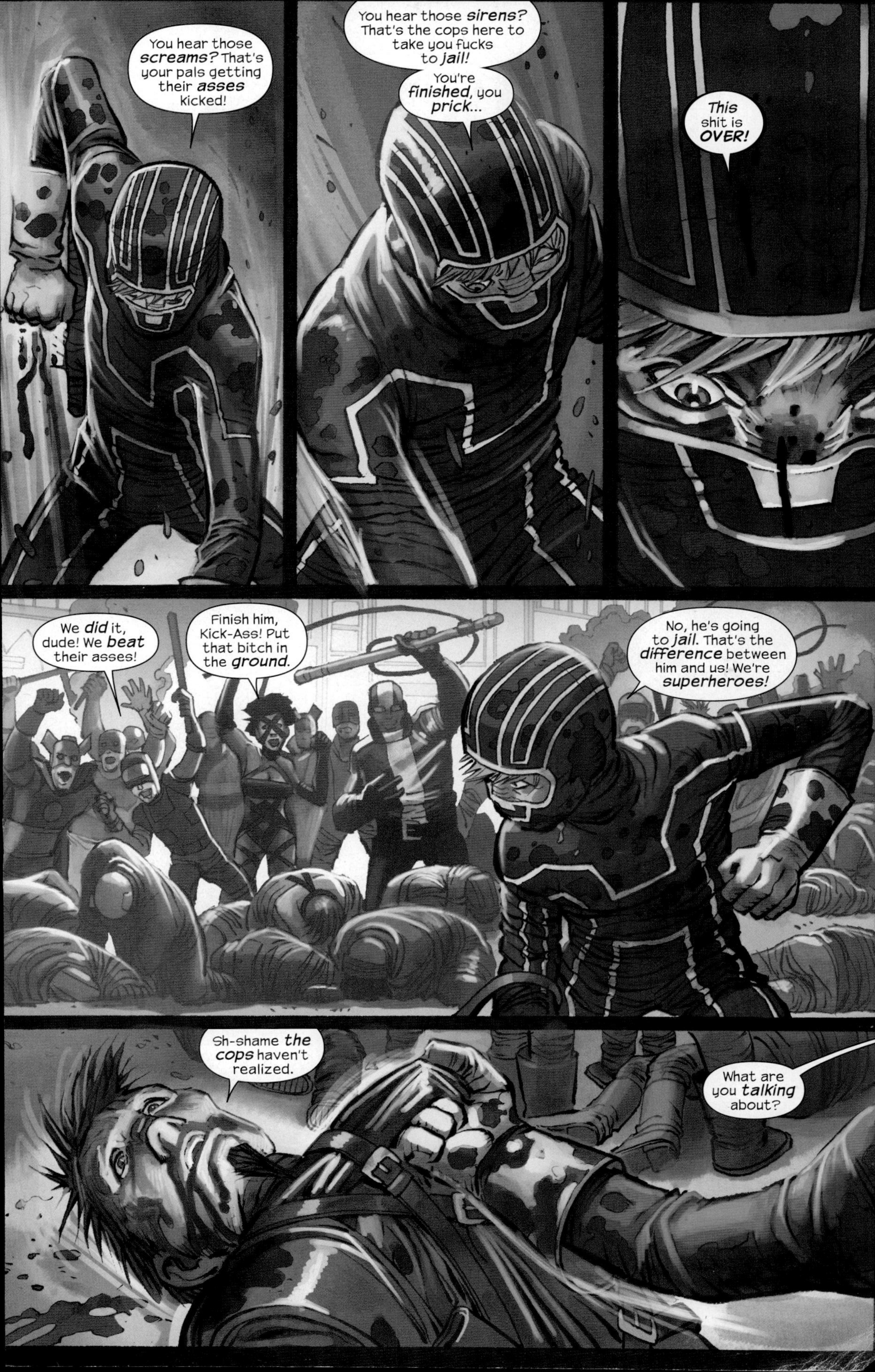
You hear those *screams?* That's your pals getting their *asses* kicked!
You hear those *sirens?* That's the cops here to take you fucks to *jail!*
You're *finished*, you *prick...*
This shit is *OVER!*
We *did* it, dude! We *beat* their asses!
Finish him, Kick-Ass! Put that bitch in the *ground*.
No, he's going to *jail*. That's the *difference* between him and us! We're *superheroes!*
Sh-shame *the cops* haven't realized.
What are you *talking* about?

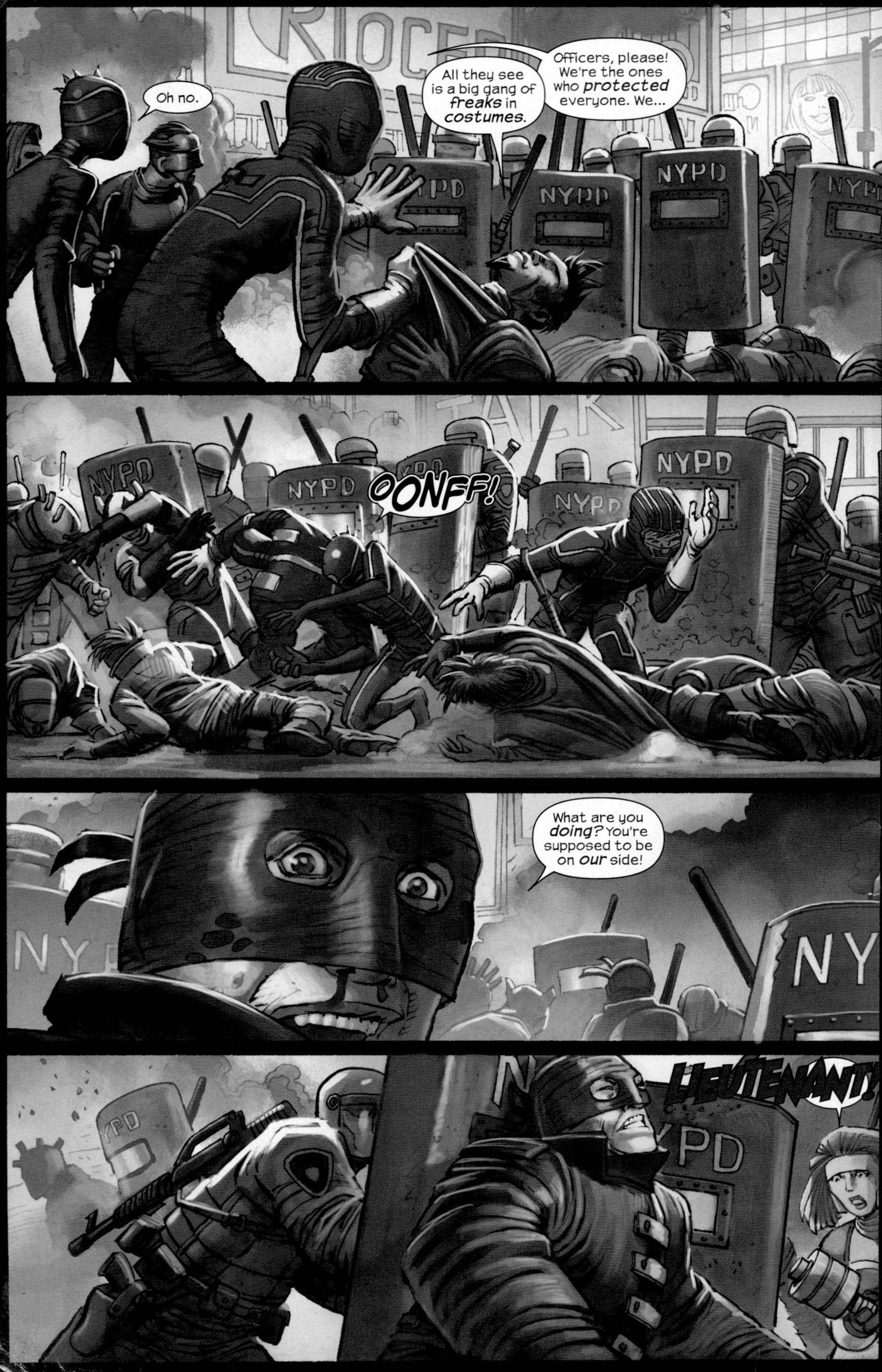

Oh no.
All they see is a big gang of freaks in costumes.
Officers, please! We're the ones who protected everyone. We...
NYPD
OONFF!
What are you doing? You're supposed to be on our side!
LIEUTENANT!

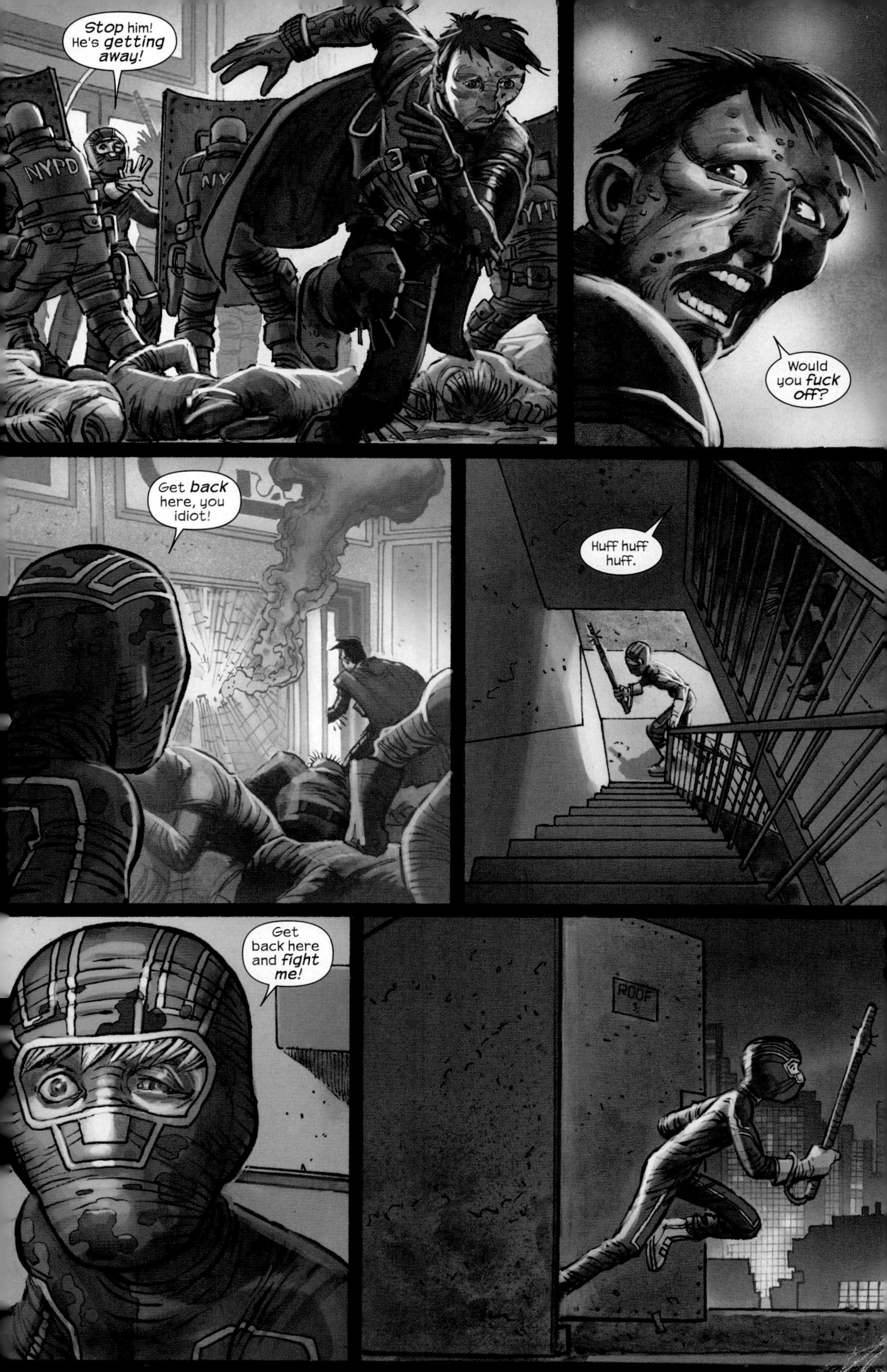
Stop him! He's getting away!
Would you fuck off?
Get back here, you idiot!
Huff huff huff.
Get back here and fight me!
ROOF

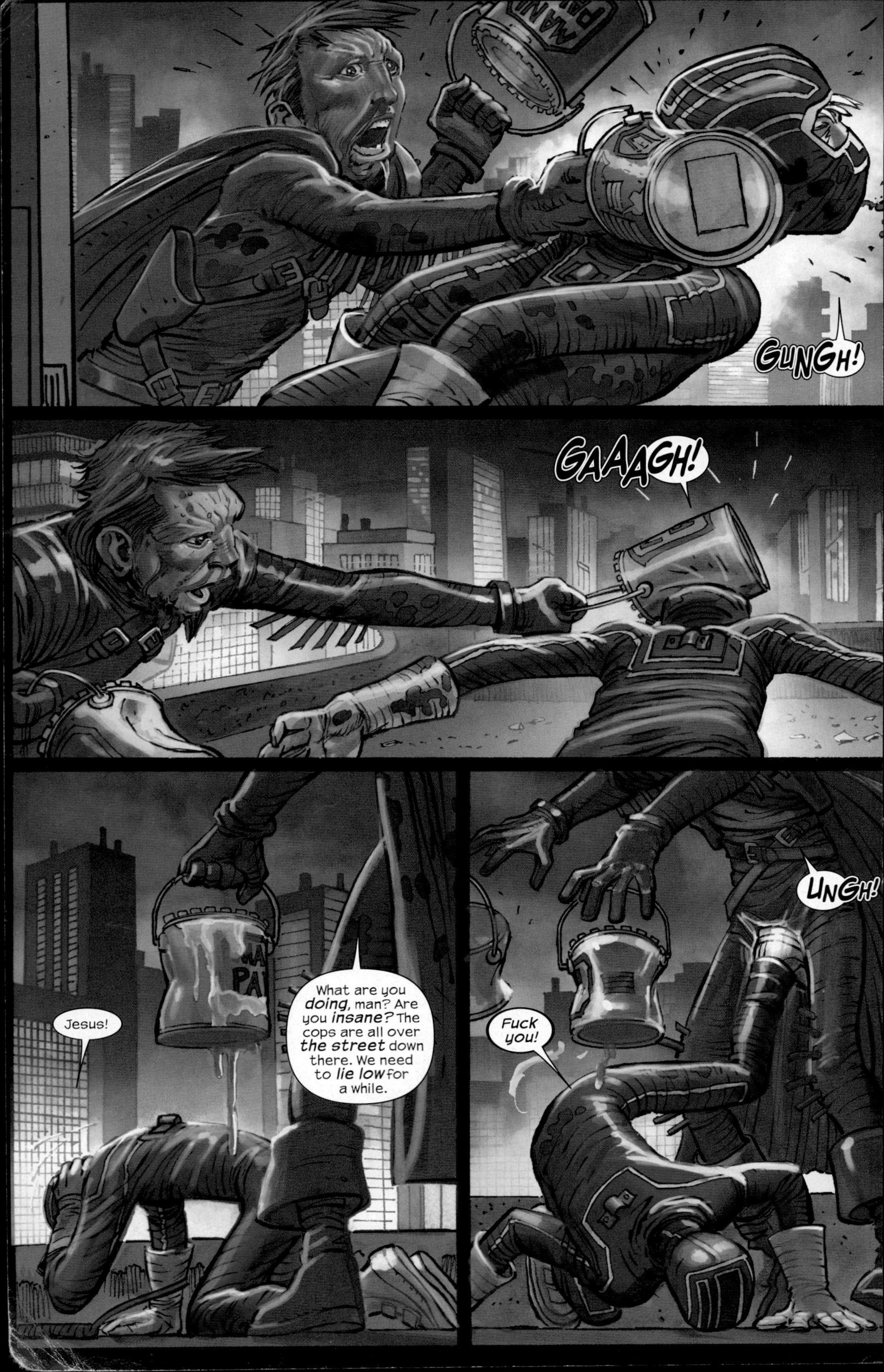
GUNGH!
GAAAGH!
Jesus!
What are you doing, man? Are you insane? The cops are all over the street down there. We need to lie low for a while.
UNGH!
Fuck you!

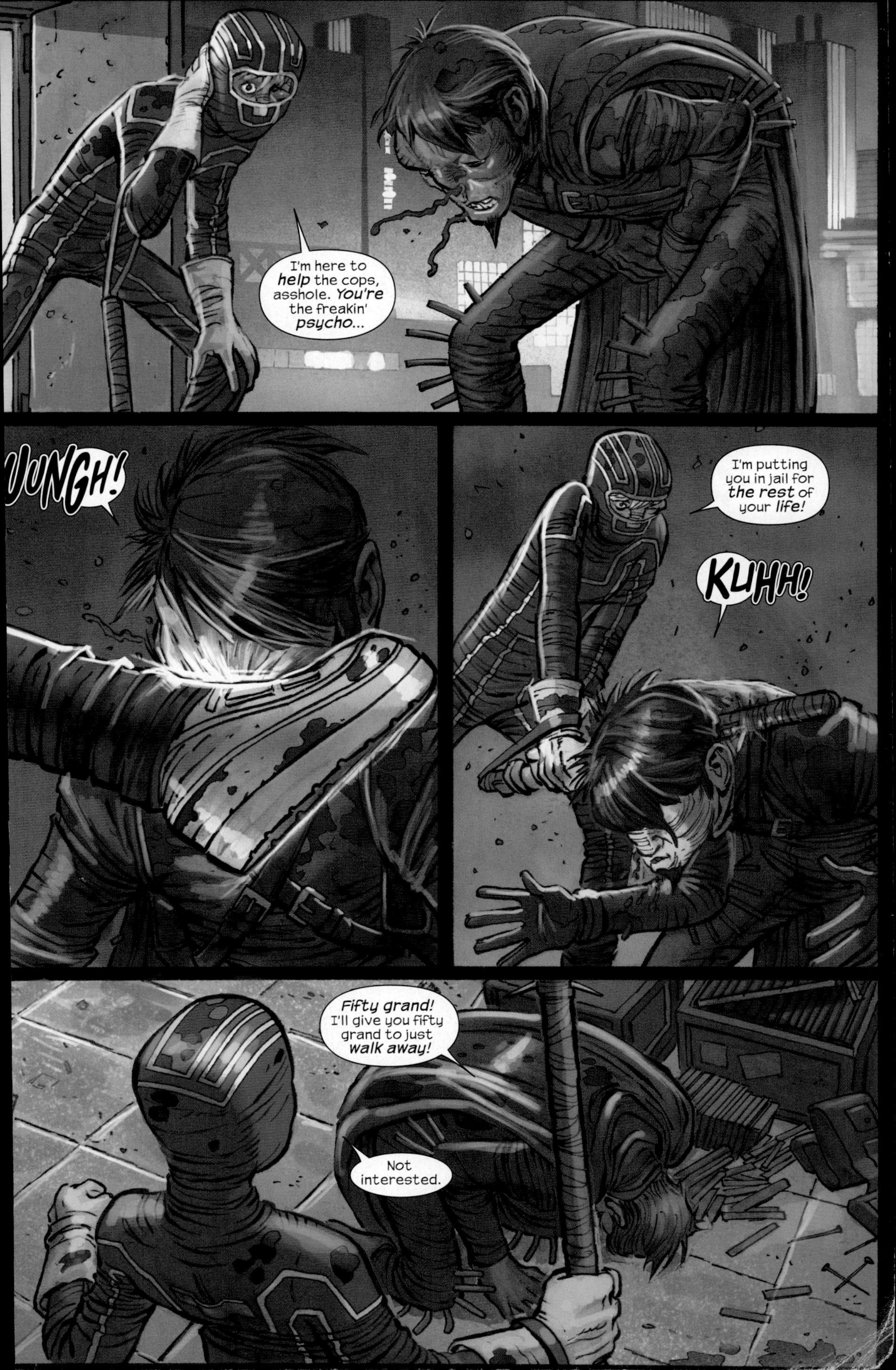
I'm here to *help* the cops, asshole. *You're* the freakin' *psycho*...
UUNGH!
I'm putting you in jail for *the rest* of your *life!*
KUHH!
Fifty grand! I'll give you fifty grand to just *walk away!*
Not interested.

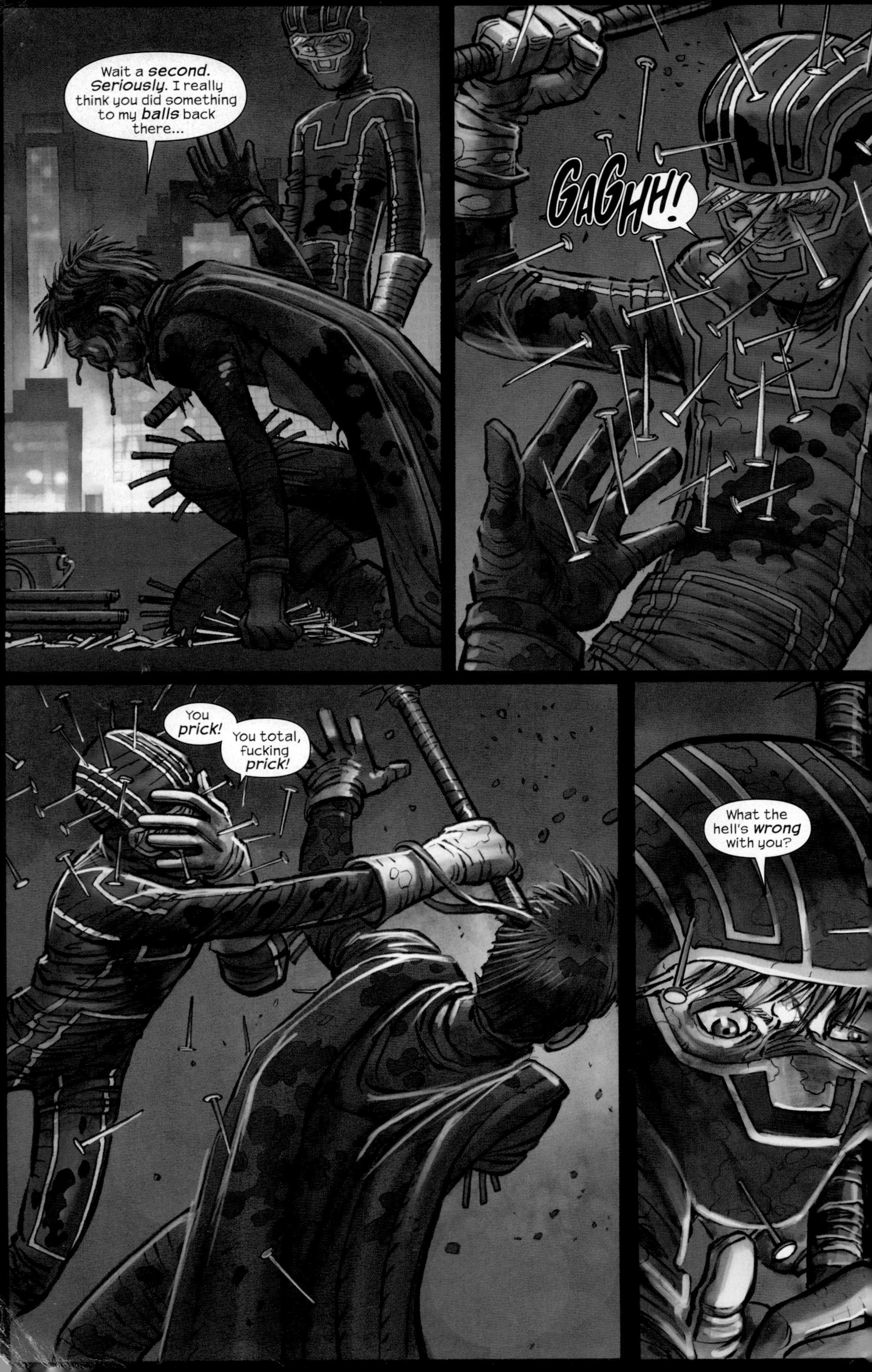
Wait a **second**. **Seriously**. I really think you did something to my **balls** back there...
GAGHH!
You **prick!**
You total, fucking **prick!**
What the hell's **wrong** with you?

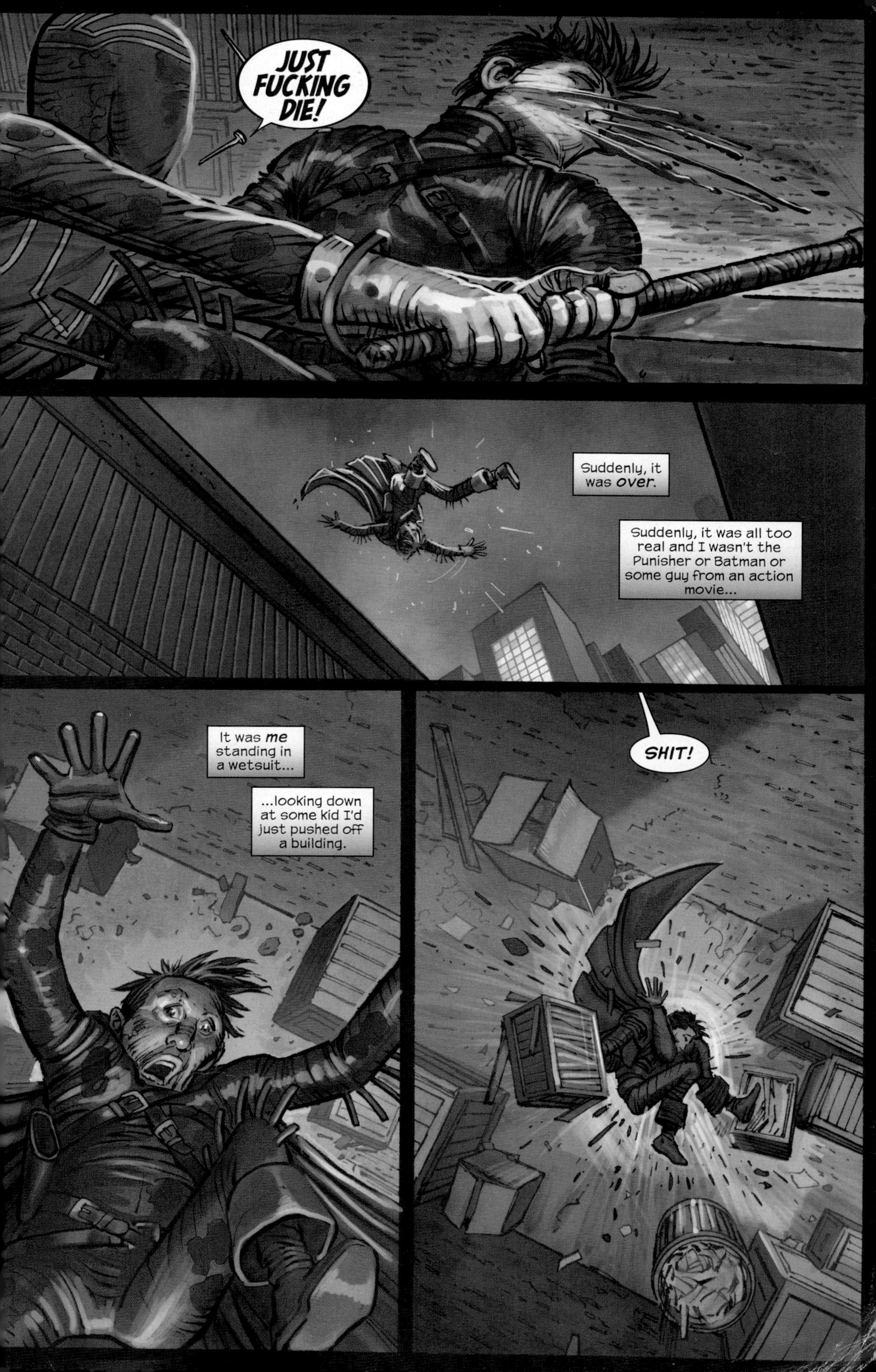
JUST FUCKING DIE!
Suddenly, it was *over*.
Suddenly, it was all too real and I wasn't the Punisher or Batman or some guy from an action movie...
It was *me* standing in a wetsuit...
...looking down at some kid I'd just pushed off a building.
SHIT!

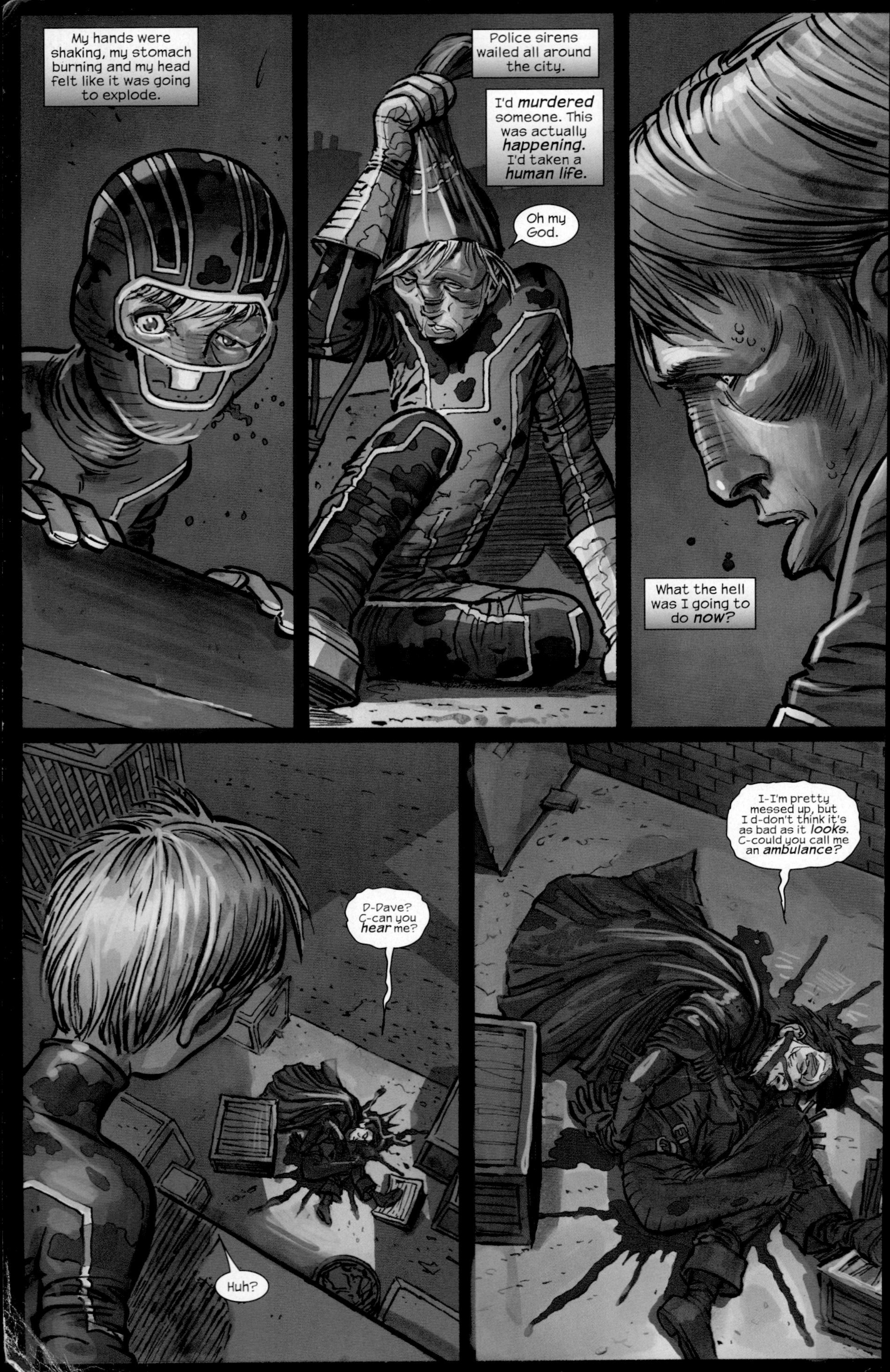
My hands were shaking, my stomach burning and my head felt like it was going to explode.
Police sirens wailed all around the city.
I'd *murdered* someone. This was actually *happening*. I'd taken a *human life*.
Oh my God.
What the hell was I going to do *now?*
D-Dave? C-can you *hear* me?
Huh?
I-I'm pretty messed up, but I d-don't think it's as bad as it *looks*. C-could you call me an *ambulance*?

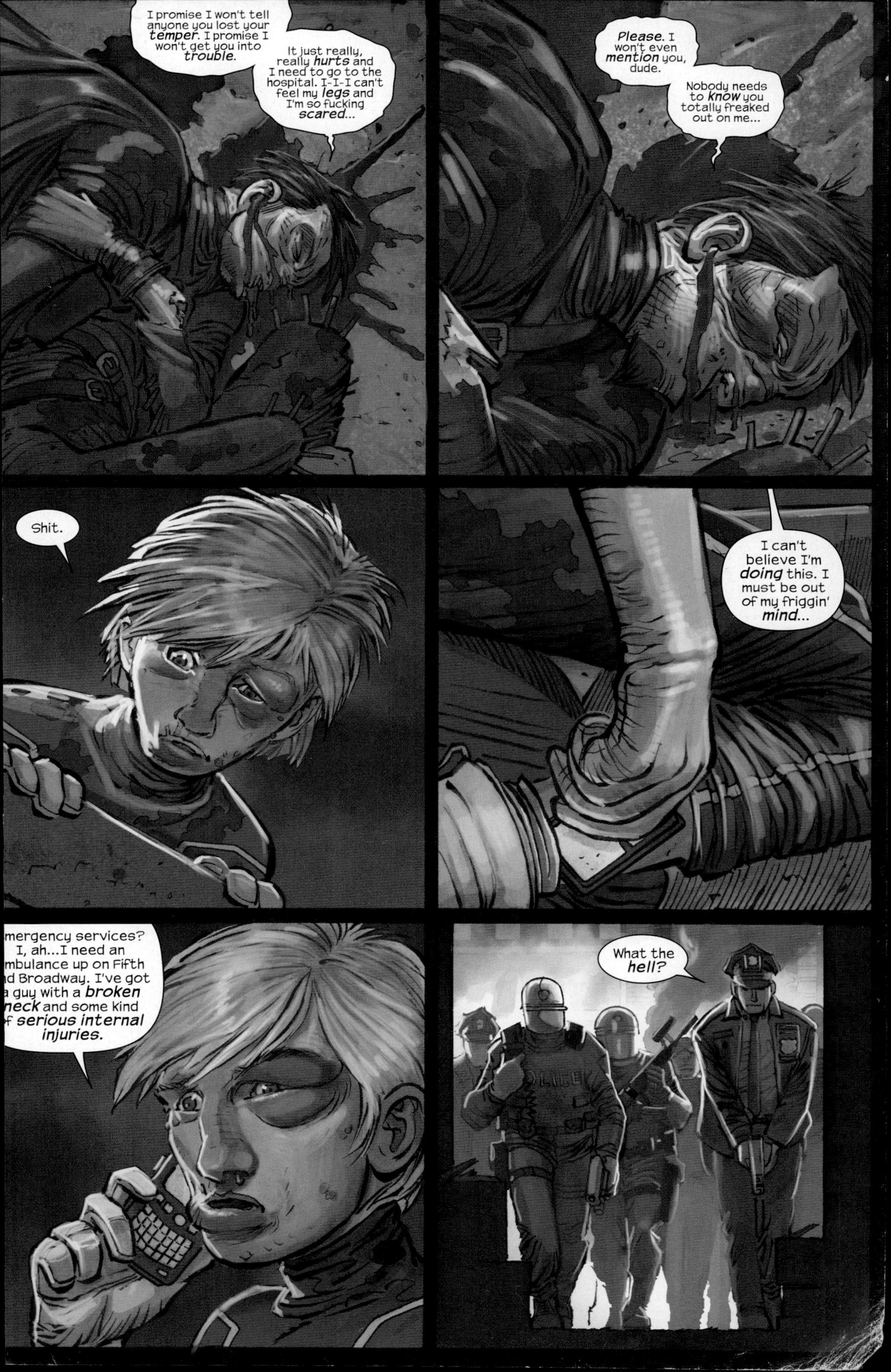
I promise I won't tell anyone you lost your *temper*. I promise I won't get you into *trouble*.
It just really, really *hurts* and I need to go to the hospital. I-I-I can't feel my *legs* and I'm so fucking *scared*...
Please. I won't even *mention* you, dude.
Nobody needs to *know* you totally freaked out on me...
Shit.
I can't believe I'm *doing* this. I must be out of my friggin' *mind*...
mergency services? I, ah...I need an mbulance up on Fifth d Broadway. I've got a guy with a *broken* neck and some kind f *serious internal injuries*.
What the *hell*?

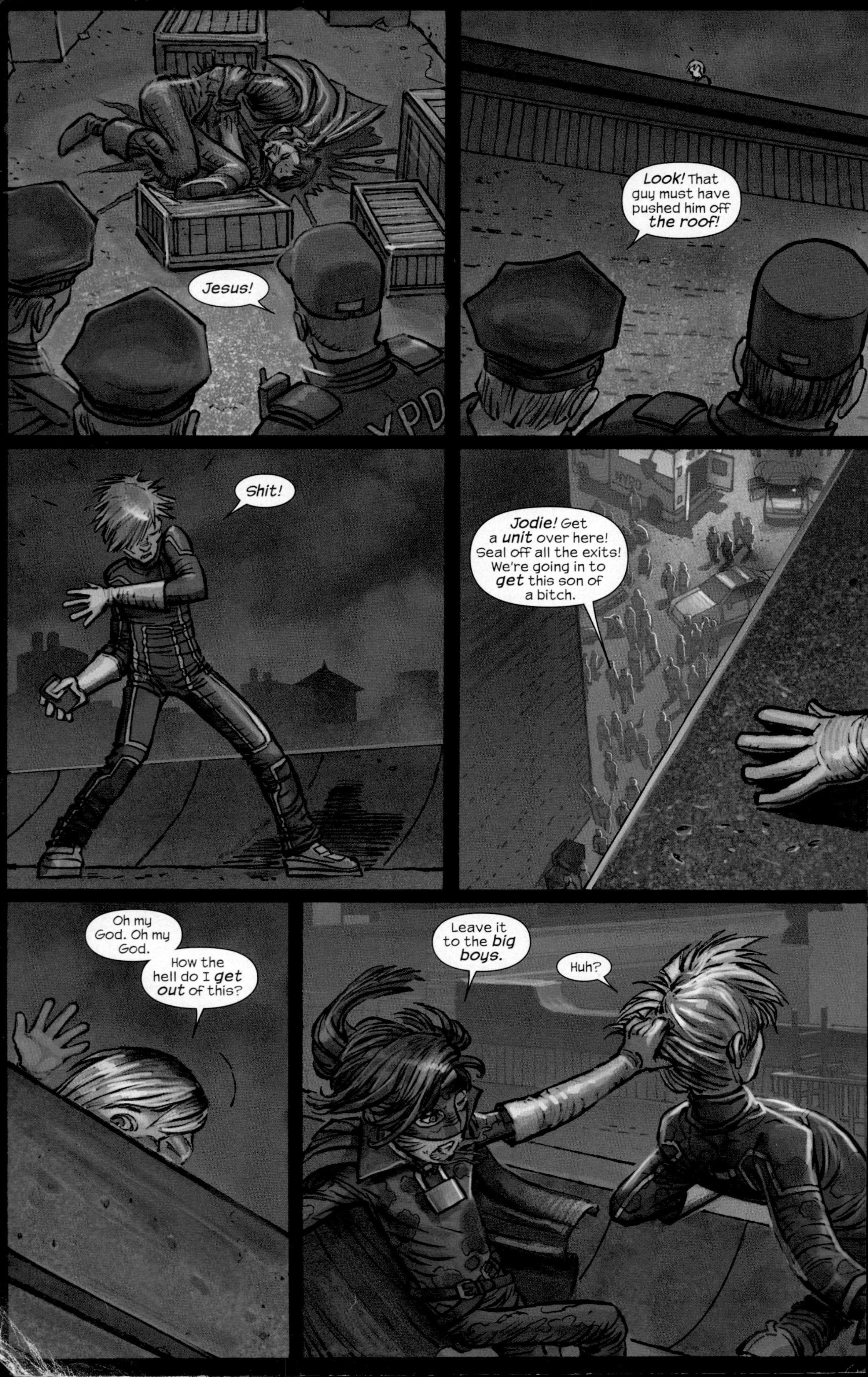
Jesus!
Look! That guy must have pushed him off the roof!
Shit!
Jodie! Get a unit over here! Seal off all the exits! We're going in to get this son of a bitch.
Oh my God. Oh my God.
How the hell do I get out of this?
Leave it to the big boys.
Huh?

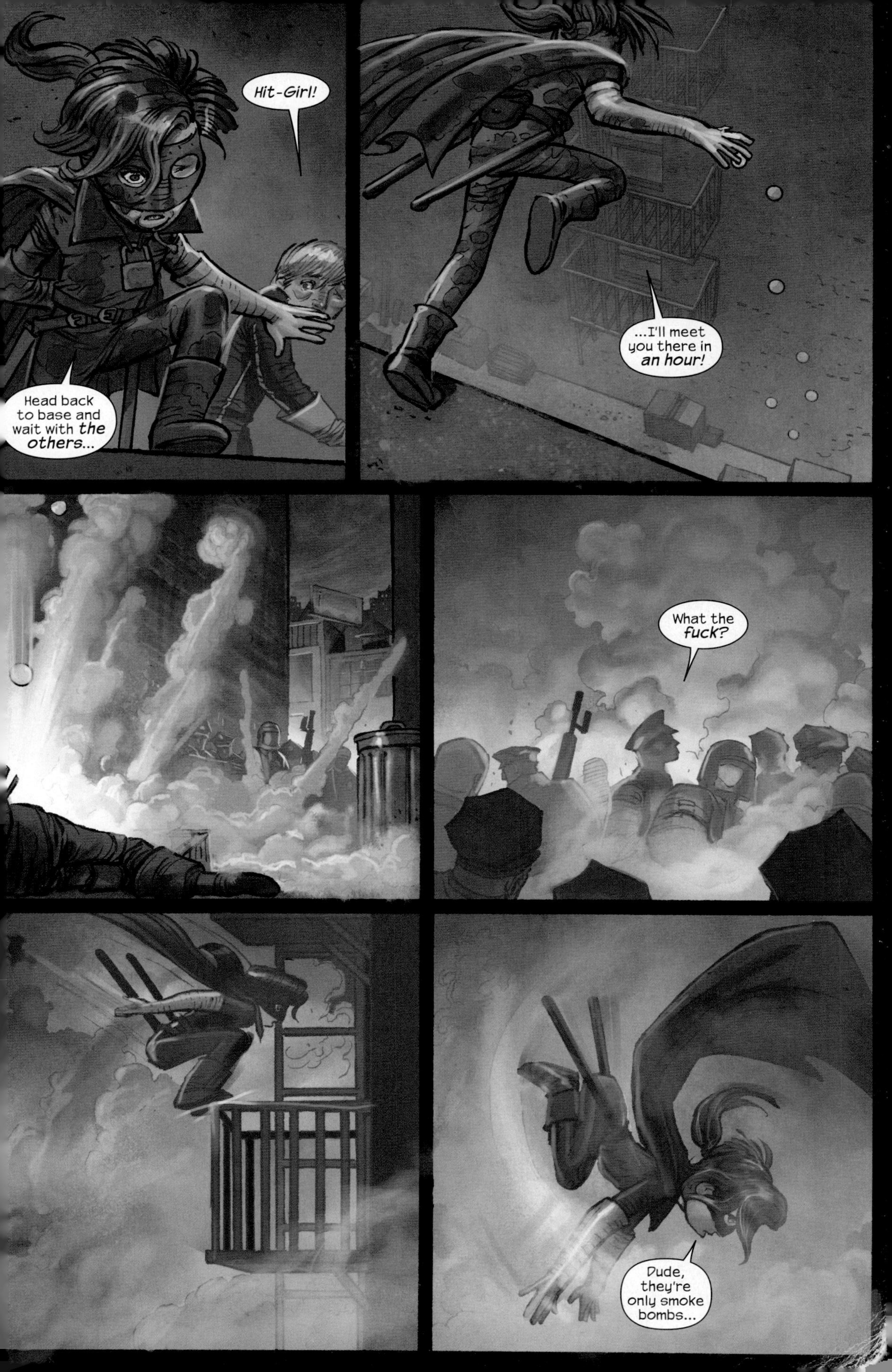
Hit-Girl!
Head back to base and wait with *the others...*
...I'll meet you there in *an hour!*
What the *fuck?*
Dude, they're only smoke bombs...

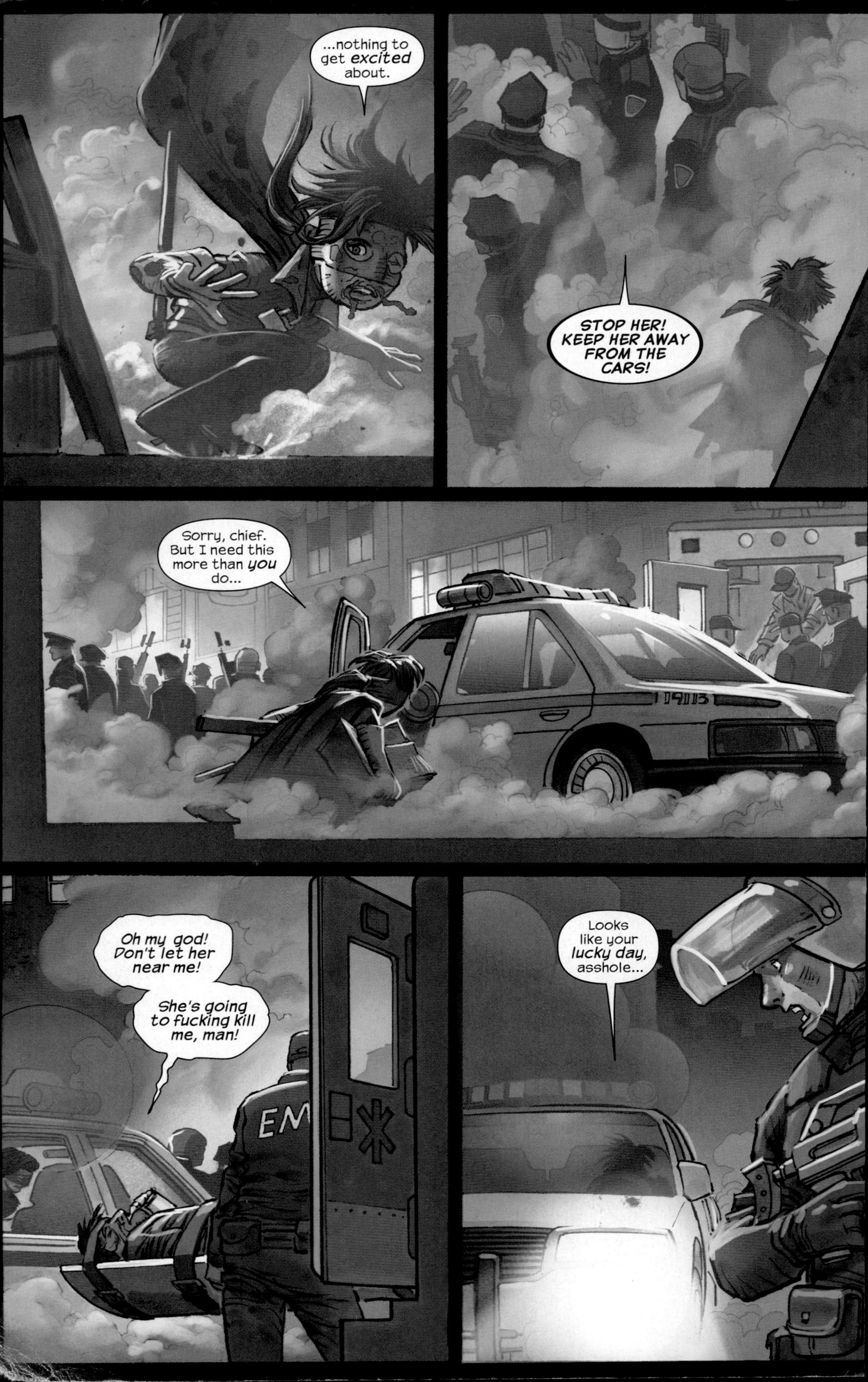
...nothing to get *excited* about.
STOP HER! KEEP HER AWAY FROM THE CARS!
Sorry, chief. But I need this more than *you* do...
Oh my god! Don't let her near me!
She's going to fucking kill me, man!
EM
Looks like your *lucky day,* asshole...

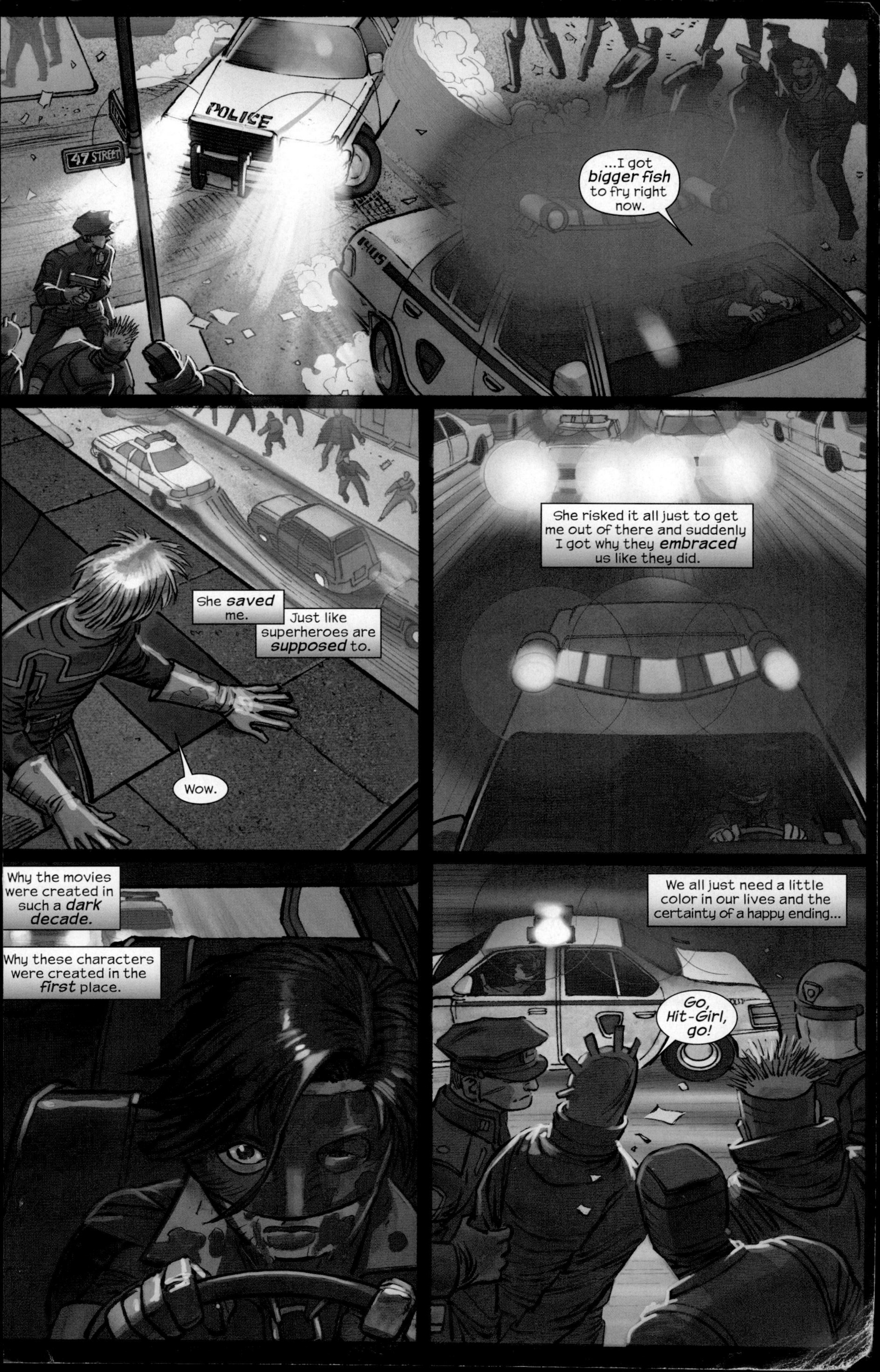
POLICE
47 STREET
...I got *bigger fish* to fry right now.
She *saved* me.
Just like superheroes are *supposed* to.
Wow.
She risked it all just to get me out of there and suddenly I got why they *embraced* us like they did.
Why the movies were created in such a *dark decade.*
Why these characters were created in the *first* place.
We all just need a little color in our lives and the certainty of a happy ending...
Go, Hit-Girl, go!

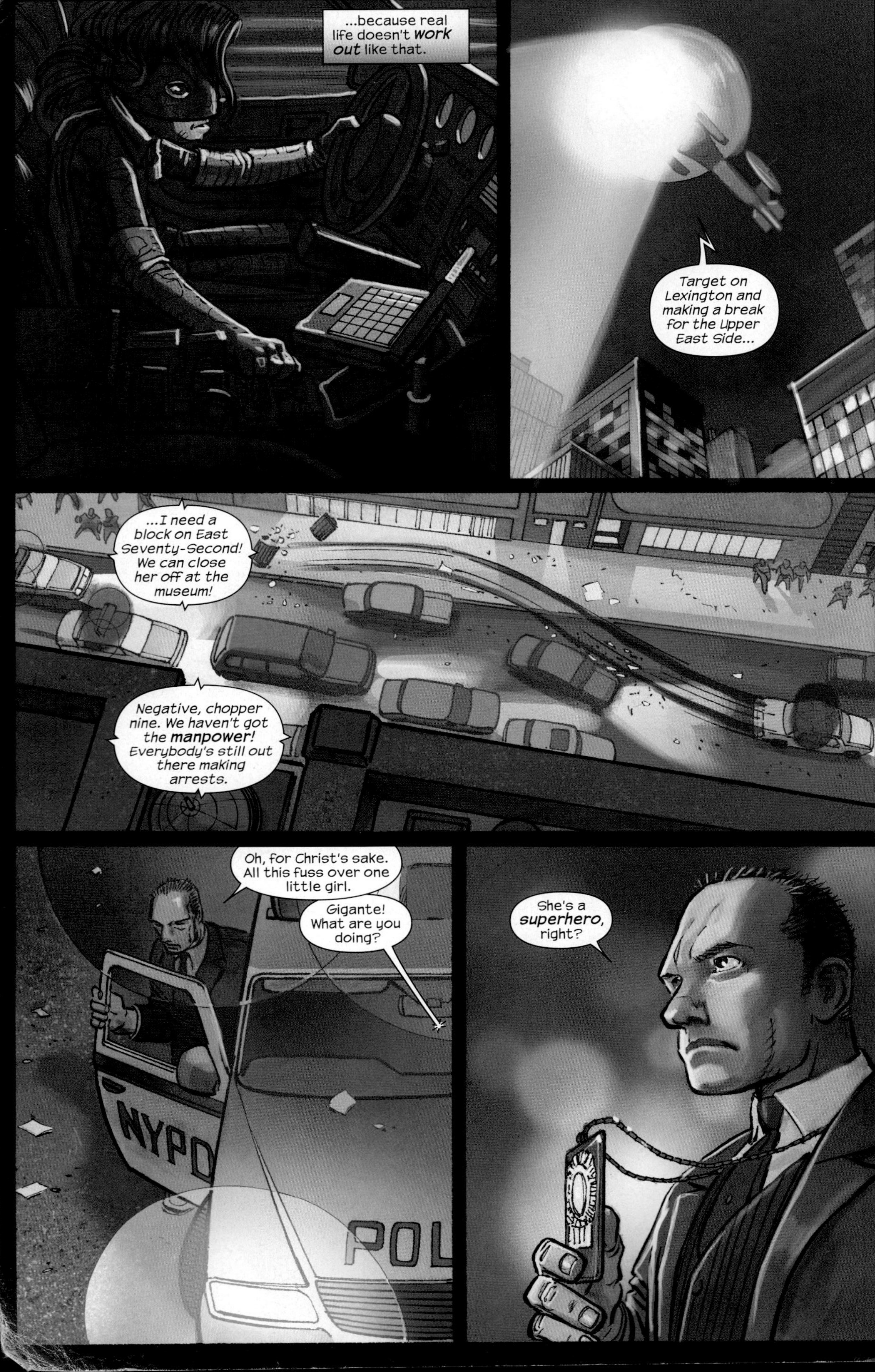
...because real life doesn't **work out** like that.
Target on Lexington and making a break for the Upper East Side...
...I need a block on East Seventy-Second! We can close her off at the museum!
Negative, chopper nine. We haven't got the **manpower!** Everybody's still out there making arrests.
Oh, for Christ's sake. All this fuss over one little girl.
Gigante! What are you doing?
NYPD
POL
She's a **superhero,** right?

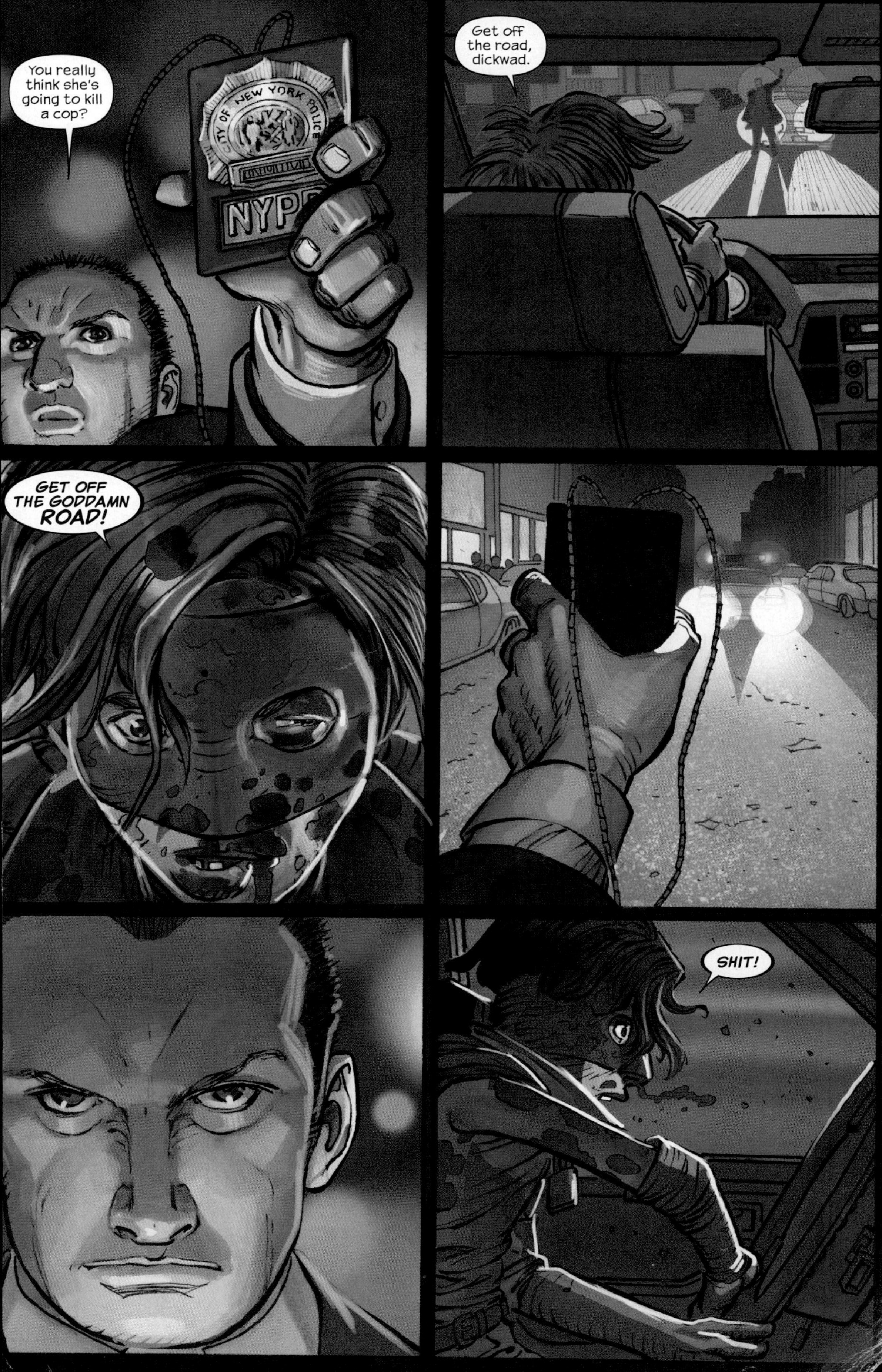
You really think she's going to kill a cop?
CITY OF NEW YORK POLICE
NYPD
Get off the road, dickwad.
GET OFF THE GODDAMN ROAD!
SHIT!

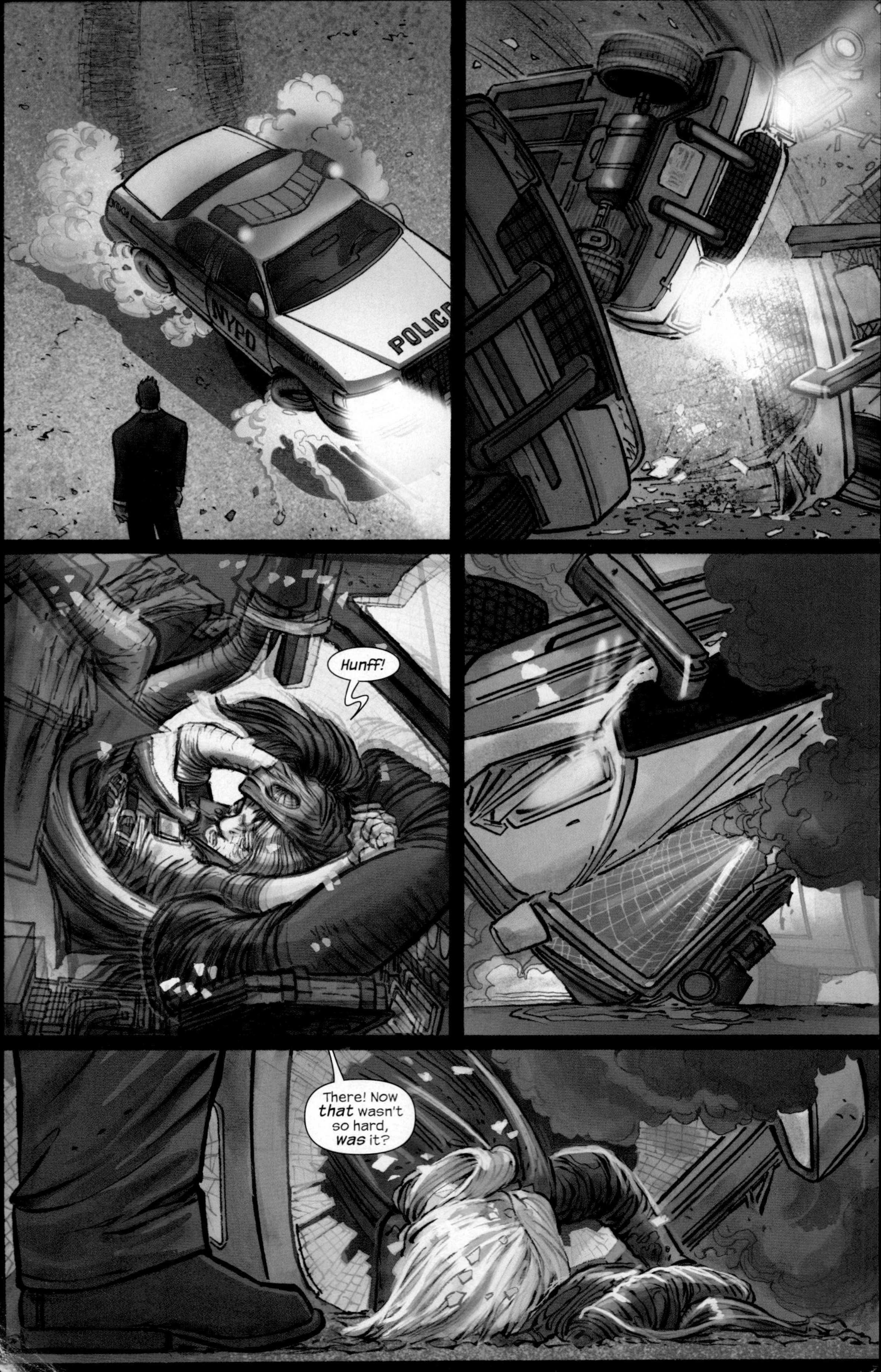
NYPO
POLICE
Hunff!
There! Now *that* wasn't so hard, *was* it?

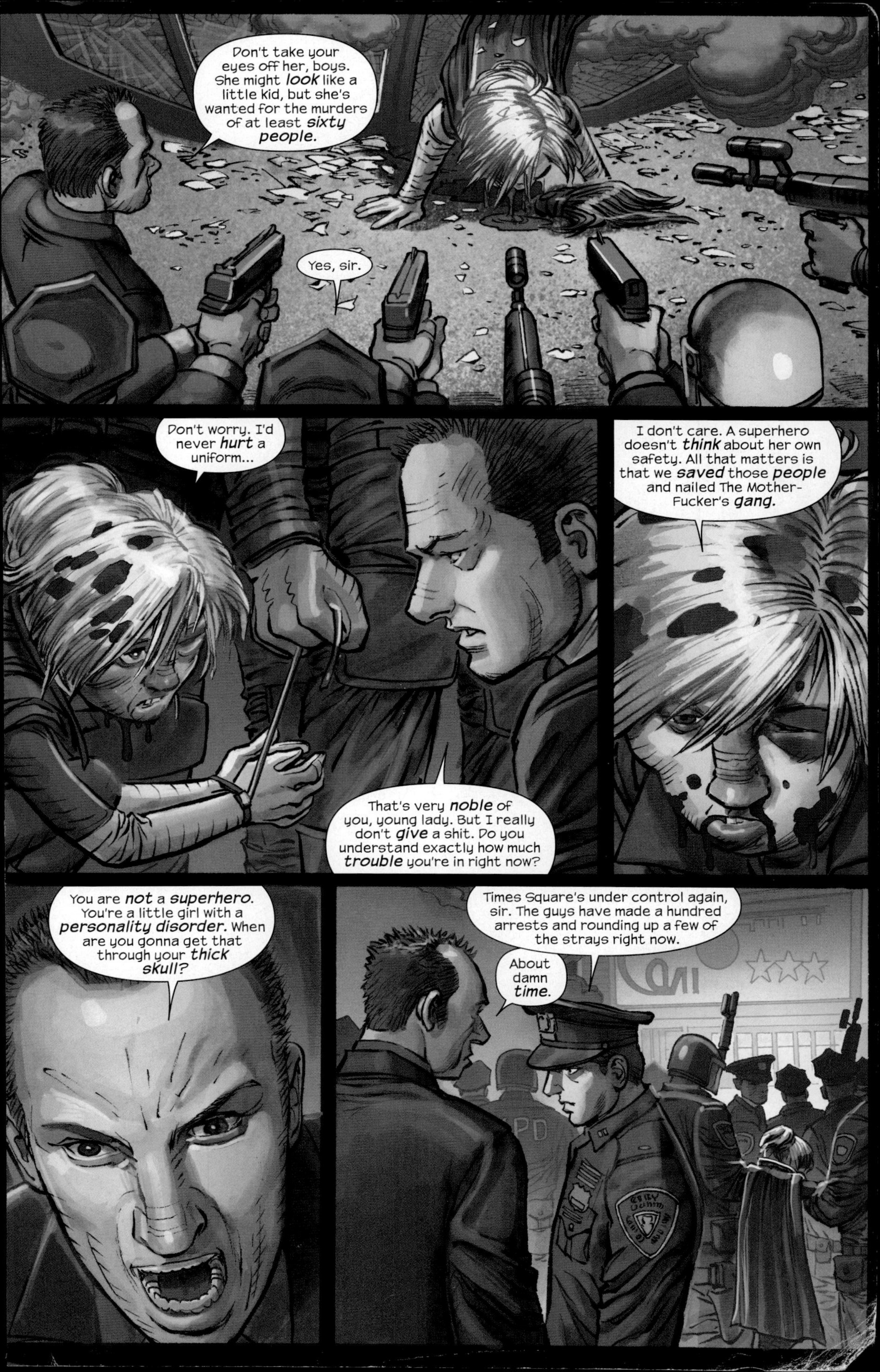
Don't take your eyes off her, boys. She might *look* like a little kid, but she's wanted for the murders of at least *sixty people.*
Yes, sir.
Don't worry. I'd never *hurt* a uniform...
That's very *noble* of you, young lady. But I really don't *give* a shit. Do you understand exactly how much *trouble* you're in right now?
I don't care. A superhero doesn't *think* about her own safety. All that matters is that we *saved* those *people* and nailed The Mother-Fucker's *gang.*
You are *not* a *superhero.* You're a little girl with a *personality disorder.* When are you gonna get that through your *thick skull?*
Times Square's under control again, sir. The guys have made a hundred arrests and rounding up a few of the strays right now.
About damn *time.*

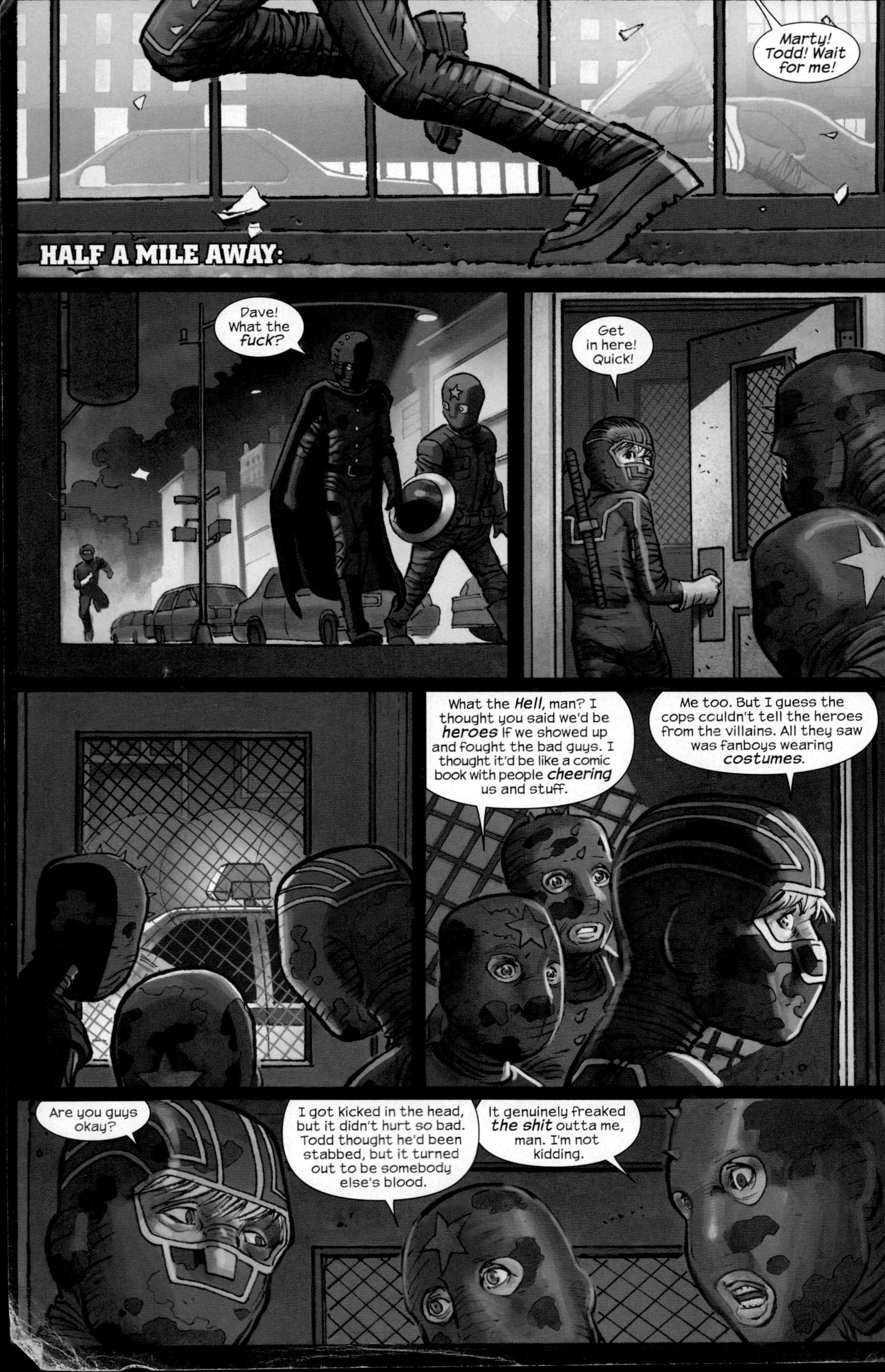
Marty! Todd! Wait for me!
HALF A MILE AWAY:
Dave! What the fuck?
Get in here! Quick!
What the Hell, man? I thought you said we'd be heroes If we showed up and fought the bad guys. I thought it'd be like a comic book with people cheering us and stuff.
Me too. But I guess the cops couldn't tell the heroes from the villains. All they saw was fanboys wearing costumes.
Are you guys okay?
I got kicked in the head, but it didn't hurt so bad. Todd thought he'd been stabbed, but it turned out to be somebody else's blood.
It genuinely freaked the shit outta me, man. I'm not kidding.

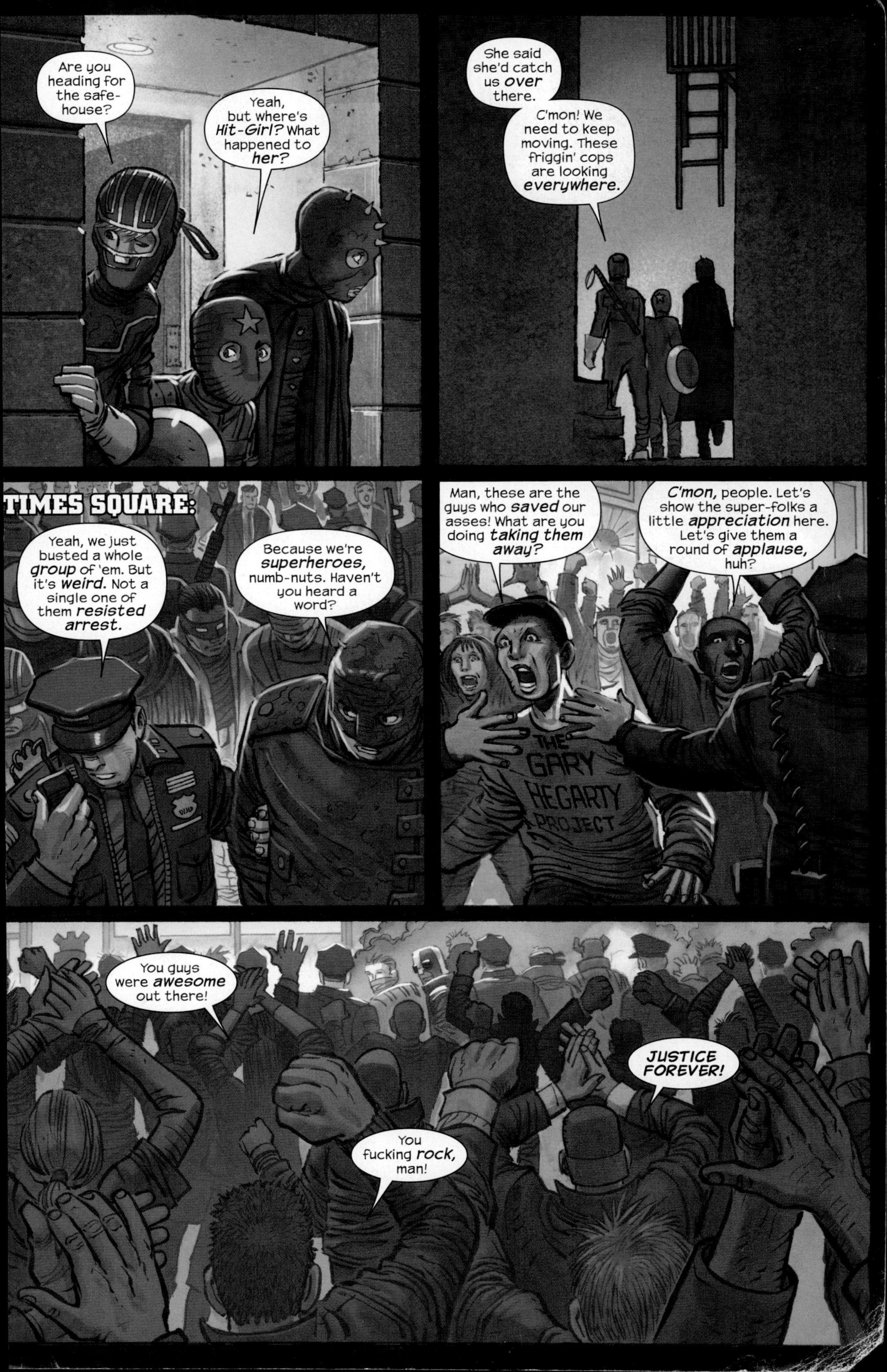
Are you heading for the safe-house?
Yeah, but where's Hit-Girl? What happened to her?
She said she'd catch us over there.
C'mon! We need to keep moving. These friggin' cops are looking everywhere.
TIMES SQUARE:
Yeah, we just busted a whole group of 'em. But it's weird. Not a single one of them resisted arrest.
Because we're superheroes, numb-nuts. Haven't you heard a word?
Man, these are the guys who saved our asses! What are you doing taking them away?
C'mon, people. Let's show the super-folks a little appreciation here. Let's give them a round of applause, huh?
THE GARY HEGARTY PROJECT
You guys were awesome out there!
JUSTICE FOREVER!
You fucking rock, man!

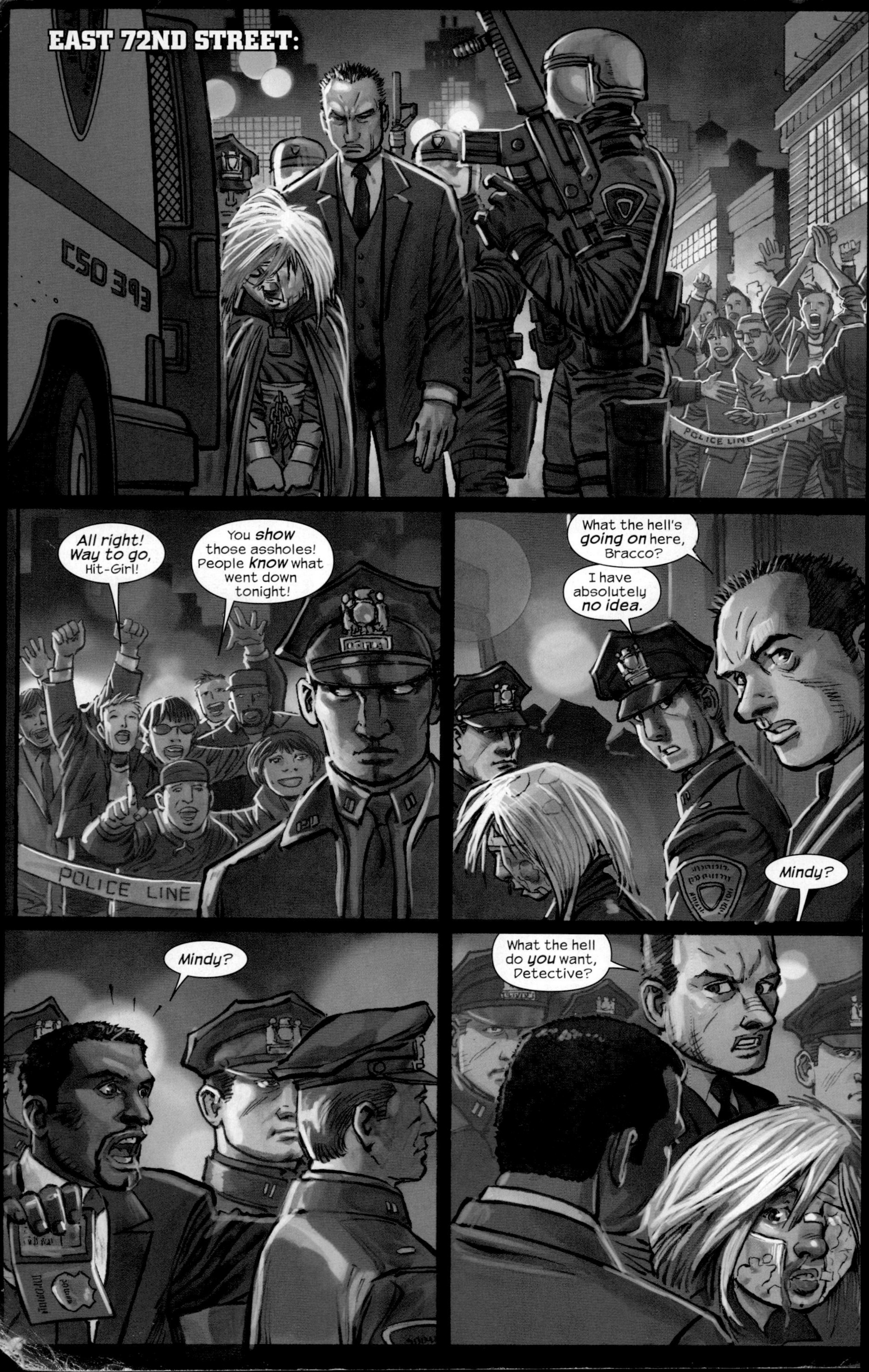

EAST 72ND STREET:
CSO 393
POLICE LINE
All right! Way to go, Hit-Girl!
You show those assholes! People know what went down tonight!
POLICE LINE
What the hell's going on here, Bracco?
I have absolutely no idea.
Mindy?
Mindy?
What the hell do you want, Detective?

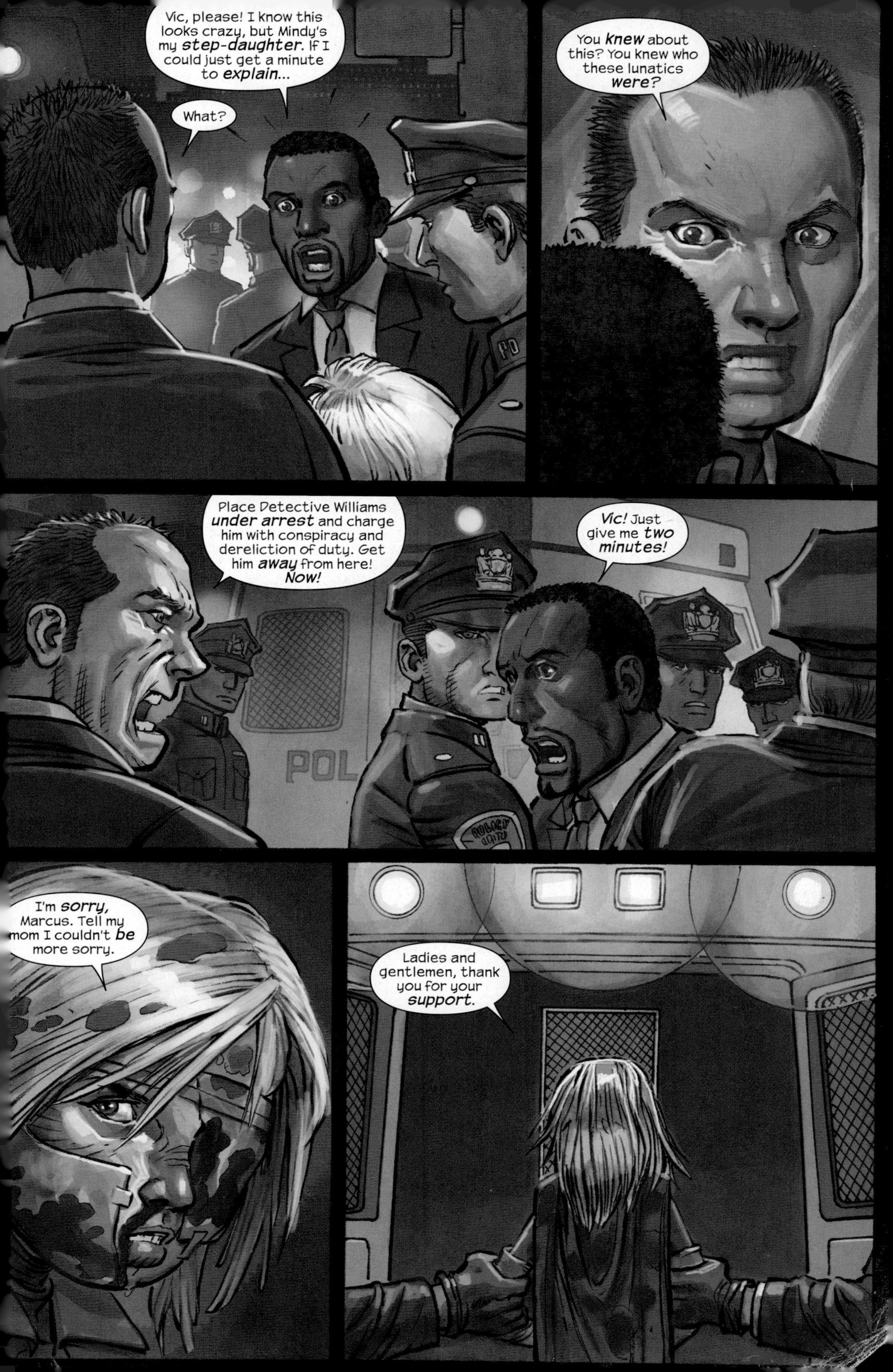
Vic, please! I know this looks crazy, but Mindy's my *step-daughter*. If I could just get a minute to *explain*...
What?
You *knew* about this? You knew who these lunatics *were*?
Place Detective Williams *under arrest* and charge him with conspiracy and dereliction of duty. Get him *away* from here! *Now!*
Vic! Just give me *two minutes!*
I'm *sorry,* Marcus. Tell my mom I couldn't *be* more sorry.
Ladies and gentlemen, thank you for your *support*.

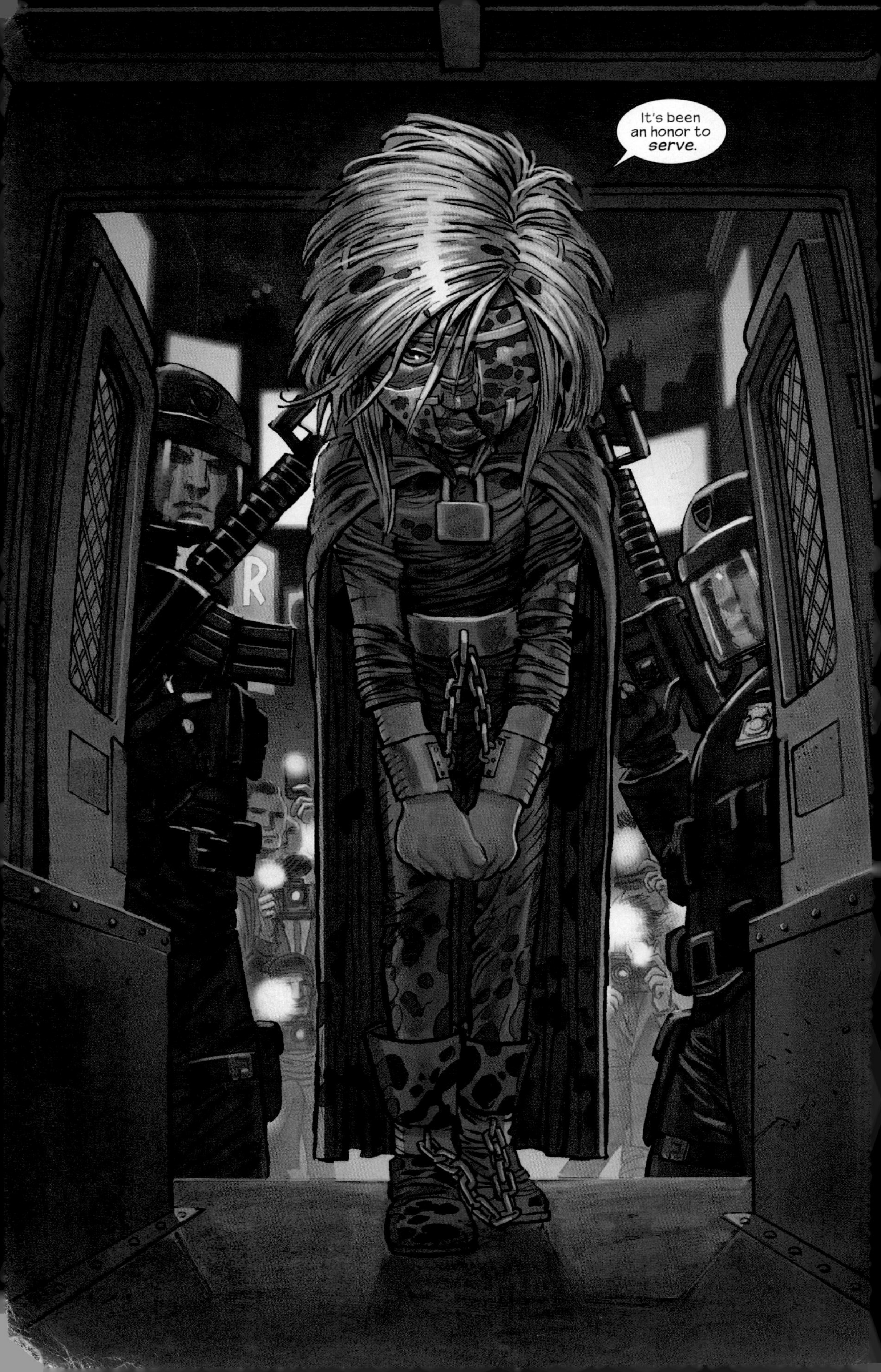
It's been an honor to serve.

END OF BOOK THREE

KICK

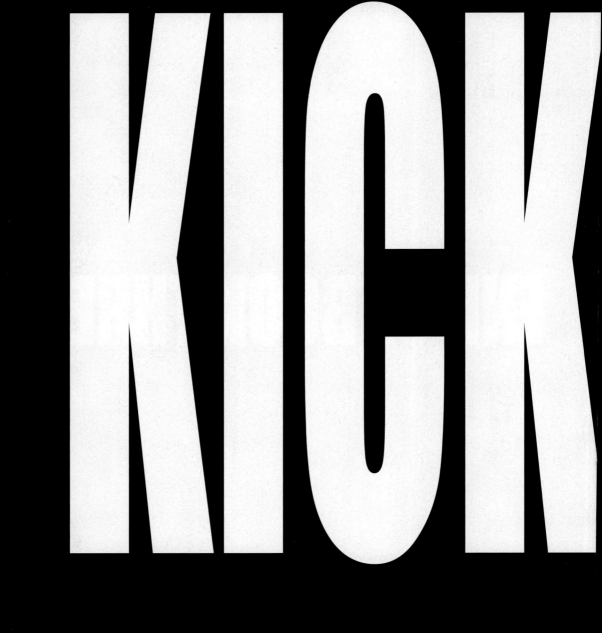

-ASS

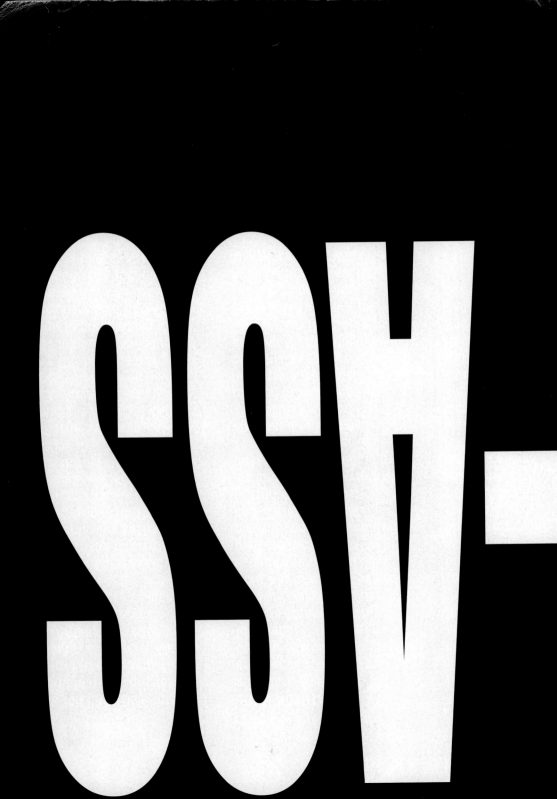

MARK MILLAR has written some of Marvel's greatest modern hits including *The Ultimates*, *Ultimate X-Men*, *Spider-Man*, *Wolverine: Old Man Logan*, and *Civil War*, the industry's biggest-selling series of the last decade. His Millarworld line boasts a roster of creator-owned smashes such as *Wanted*, turned into a blockbuster movie starring Angelina Jolie; *Kick-Ass*, which starred Nicolas Cage; and *Kick-Ass 2*, starring Jim Carrey. Millar is currently working on *Kick-Ass 3*, *Jupiter's Legacy*, and *Nemesis Returns*. In his native UK, he's the editor of *CLiNT* magazine, an advisor on film to the Scottish government, and CEO of film and TV company Millarworld Productions. He also serves as Creative Consultant on Fox's Marvel movies in Los Angeles.

JOHN ROMITA JR is a modern-day comic-art master, following in his legendary father's footsteps. Timeless runs on *Iron Man*, *Uncanny X-Men*, *Amazing Spider-Man,* and *Daredevil* helped establish him as his own man artistically, and his work on *Wolverine* and *World War Hulk* is arguably the most explosive comic art of the last decade. In addition to *Eternals* with writer Neil Gaiman, JRJR teamed with Mark Millar on the creator-owned *Kick-Ass*, later developed into a blockbuster feature film starring Nicolas Cage. Avid Spider-Man fans rejoiced at the artist's return to *Amazing Spider-Man* with the Brand New Day storylines "New Ways To Die" and "Character Assassination." He later joined writer Brian Michael Bendis on the relaunched *Avengers*. Recent titles include the blockbuster crossover *Avengers vs X-Men*, and the relaunch of *Captain America*.

TOM PALMER has worked as an illustrator in the advertising and editorial fields, but he has spent the majority of his career in comic books. His first assignment, fresh out of art school, was on *Doctor Strange*, and he has gone on to lend his inking talents to many of Marvel's top titles, including *X-Men*, *The Avengers*, *Tomb of Dracula*, and more recently *Punisher, Hulk,* and *Ghost Rider.* He lives and works in New Jersey.

AUBREY SITTERSON

began his comics career as an intern at Marvel Comics, and went on to edit fan-favorite runs on *The Irredeemable Ant-Man*, *Ghost Rider*, and more, before taking the plunge to write and edit comics freelance. Since then, he has edited *Kick-Ass*, *The Walking Dead*, and other hit books, while writing comics for Marvel, DC, Image, Oni Press, and Viz Media. Find him on the internet at aubreysitterson.com.

CHRIS ELIOPOULOS

is a multiple award-winner for his lettering, having worked on dozens of books during the twenty years he's been in the industry—including Erik Larsen's *Savage Dragon*, for which he hand-lettered the first 100 issues. Along with his success as a letterer, he also publishes his own strip *Misery Loves Sherman*, wrote and illustrated the popular *Franklin Richards: Son of a Genius* one-shots, and writes *Marvel's Lockjaw and the Pet Avengers* series.

DEAN WHITE is

one of the comic industry's best and most sought-after color artists. Well-known for his work on titles such as *The Amazing Spider-Man*, *Punisher*, *Dark Avengers*, *Captain America*, *Black Panther*, *Wolverine* and countless more, Dean's envelope-pushing rendering and color palette bring a sense of urgency and power to every page he touches.

ONE (VARIANT BY TOMMY LEE EDWARDS)

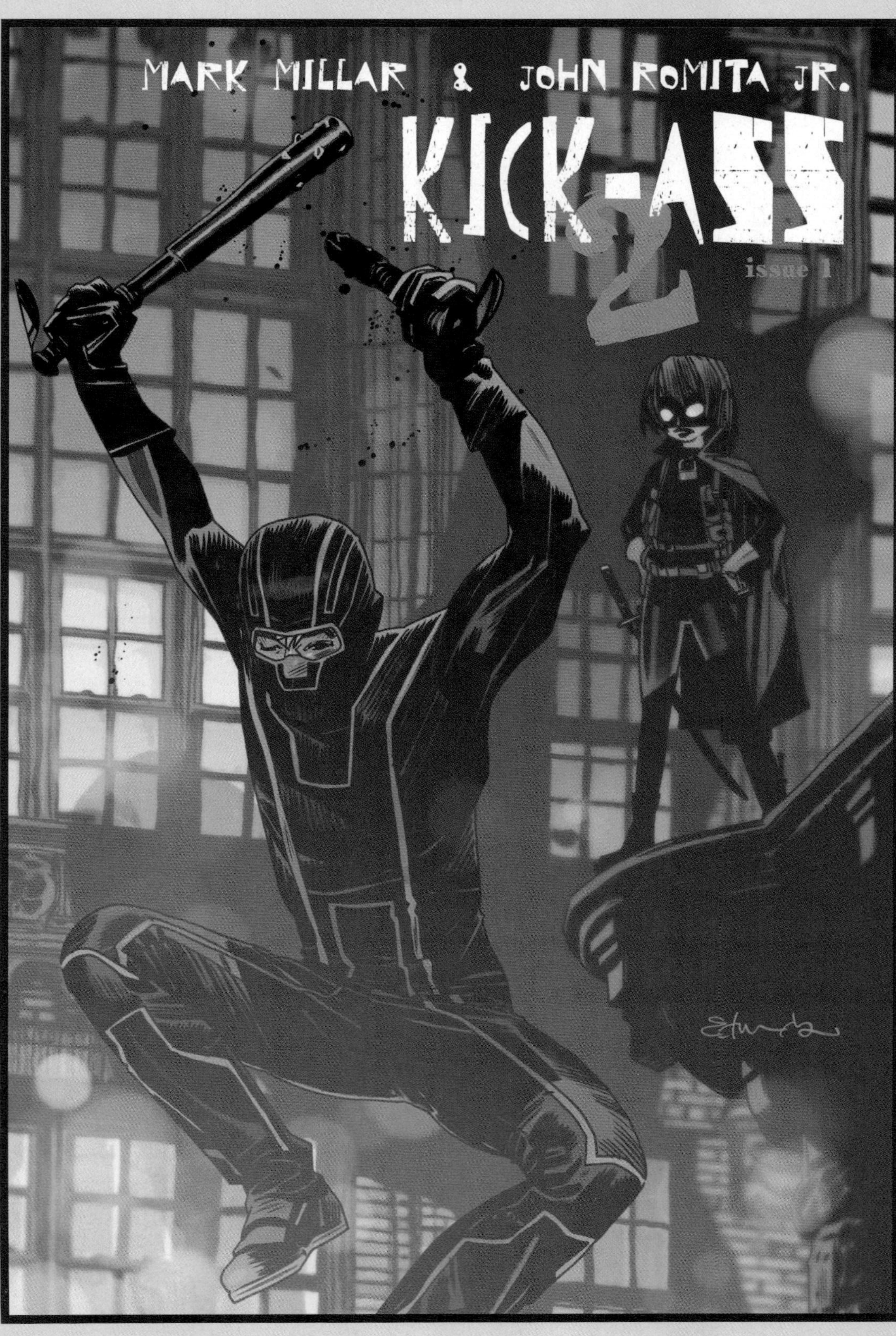

MARK MILLAR & JOHN ROMITA JR.
KICK-ASS 2
issue 1

TWO (VARIANT BY LEINIL YU)

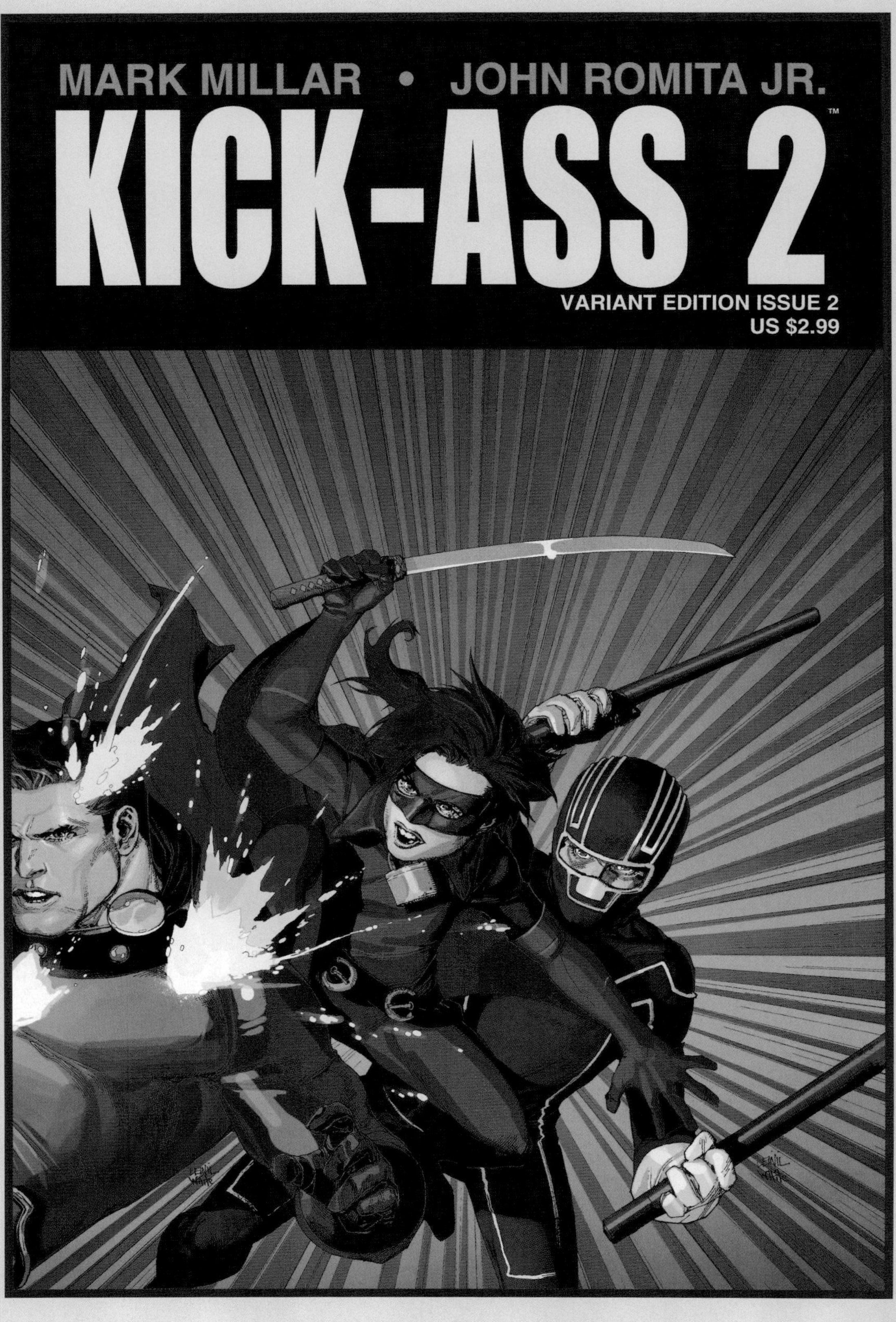
MARK MILLAR • JOHN ROMITA JR.
KICK-ASS 2™
VARIANT EDITION ISSUE 2
US $2.99

FIVE (VARIANT BY BRYAN HITCH)

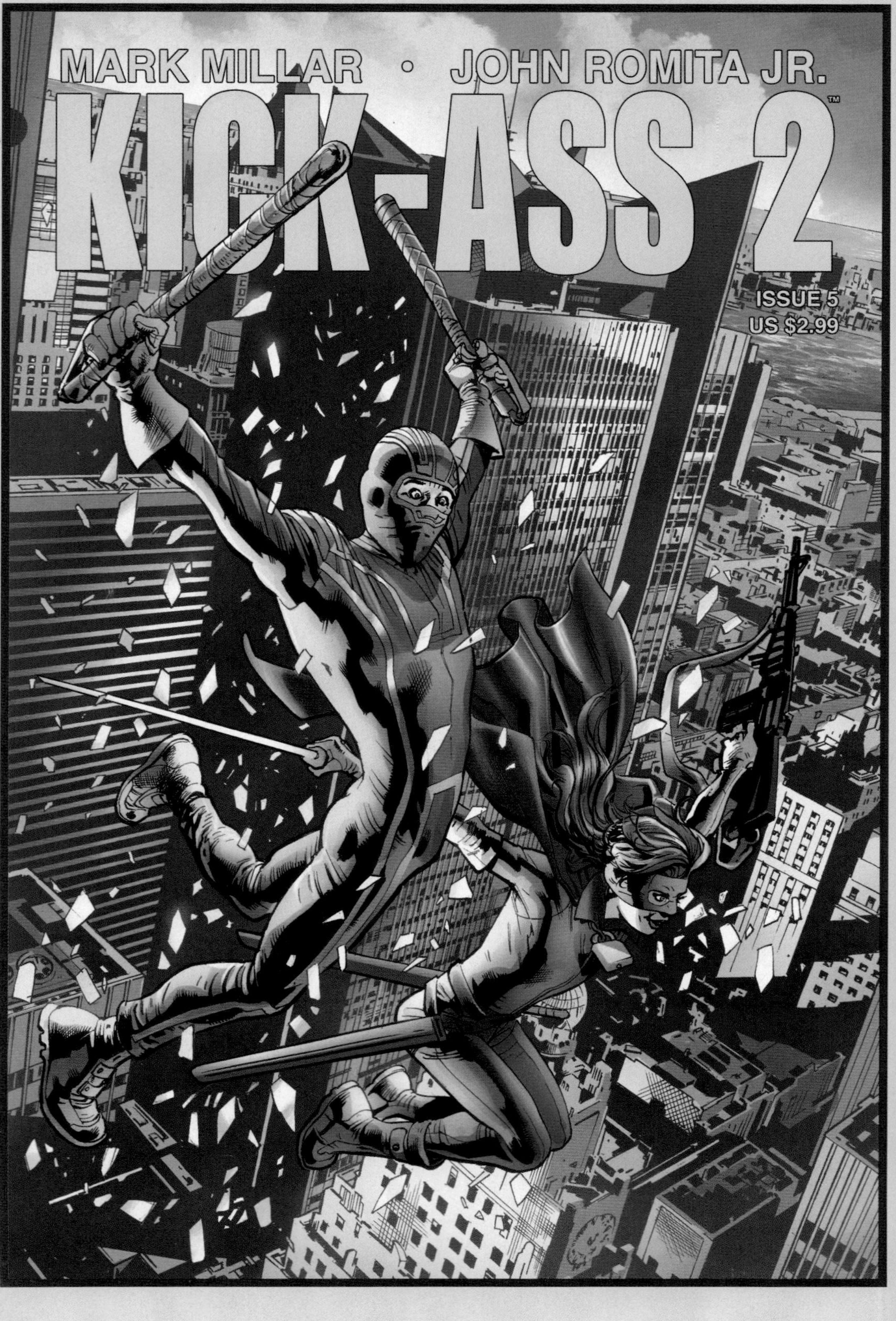
MARK MILLAR · JOHN ROMITA JR.
KICK-ASS 2™
ISSUE 5
US $2.99

FIVE (PHOTO VARIANT)

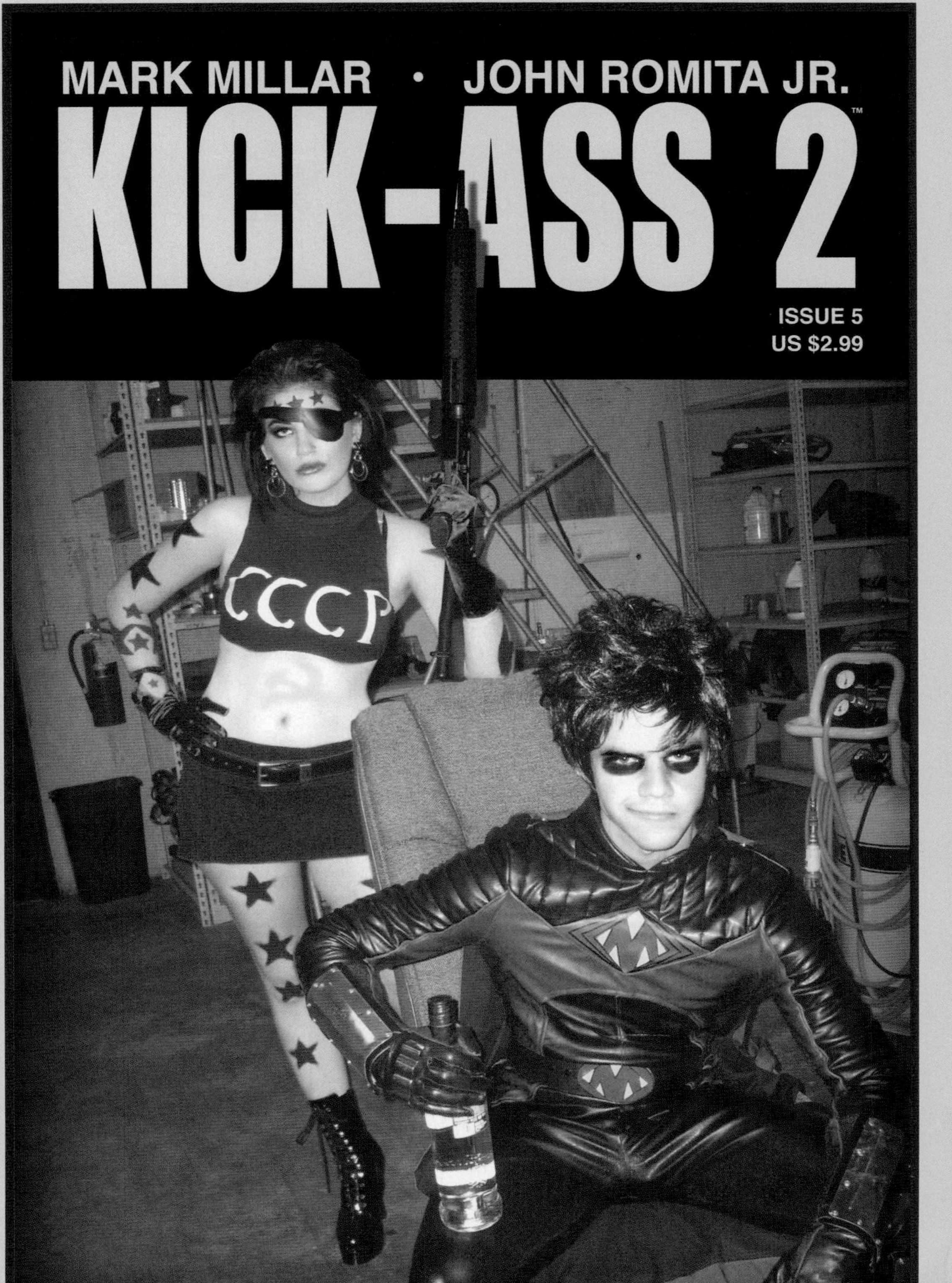
MARK MILLAR · JOHN ROMITA JR.
KICK-ASS 2™
ISSUE 5
US $2.99
CCCP

Photographer: **Wendy Nickelsen** • Mother Russia: **Destiny Nickelsen** • The Motherfucker: **Ryan Eidson**

SIX (PHOTO VARIANT)

MARK MILLAR • JOHN ROMITA JR.

KICK-ASS 2™

ISSUE 6
US $2.99

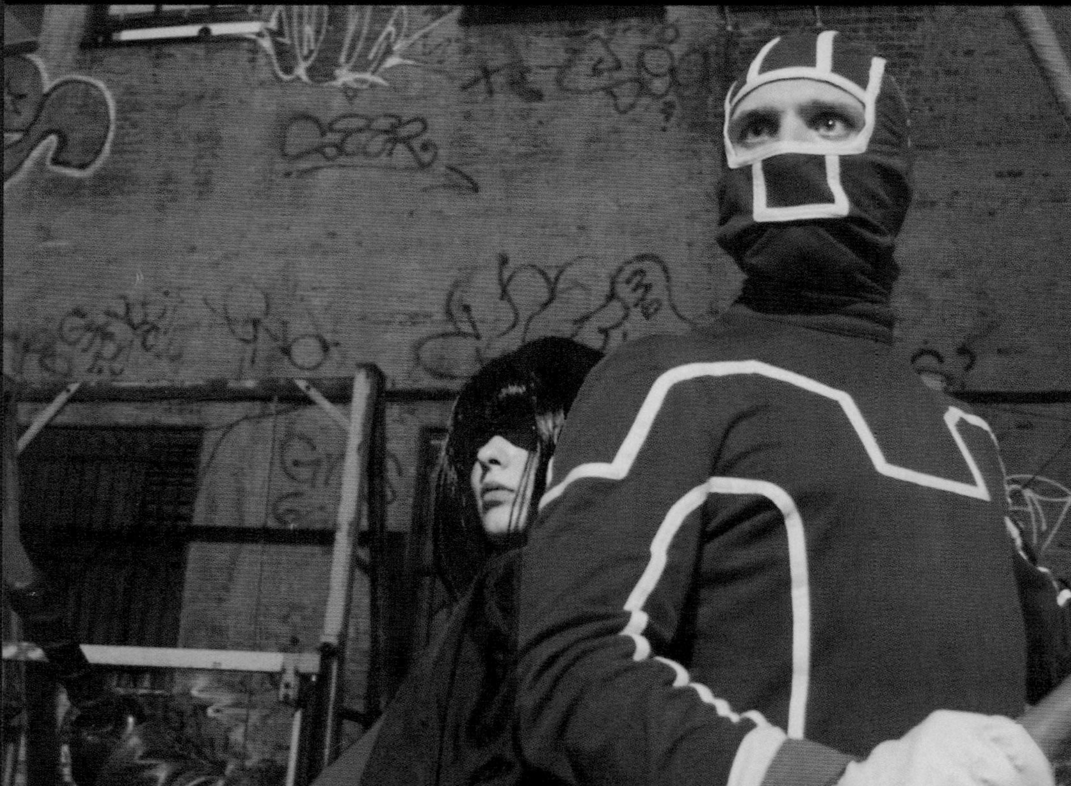

Photographer: **Destiny Nickelsen** • Hit-Girl: **Alexandra Fowler** • Kick-Ass: **Brandyn Mikel Standing-Elk Lucido**

SEVEN (PHOTO VARIANT)

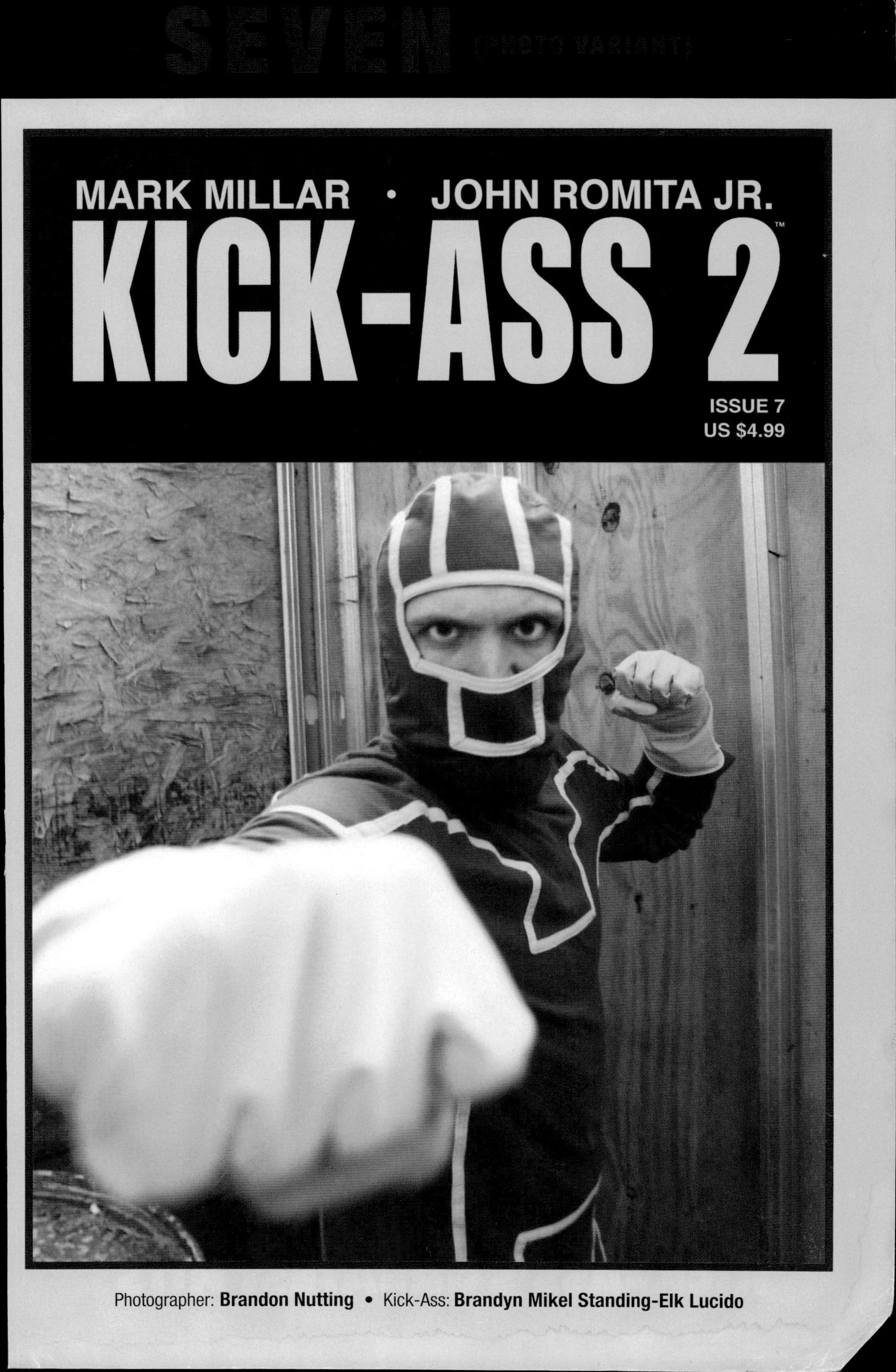
MARK MILLAR • JOHN ROMITA JR.
KICK-ASS 2™
ISSUE 7
US $4.99

Photographer: **Brandon Nutting** • Kick-Ass: **Brandyn Mikel Standing-Elk Lucido**

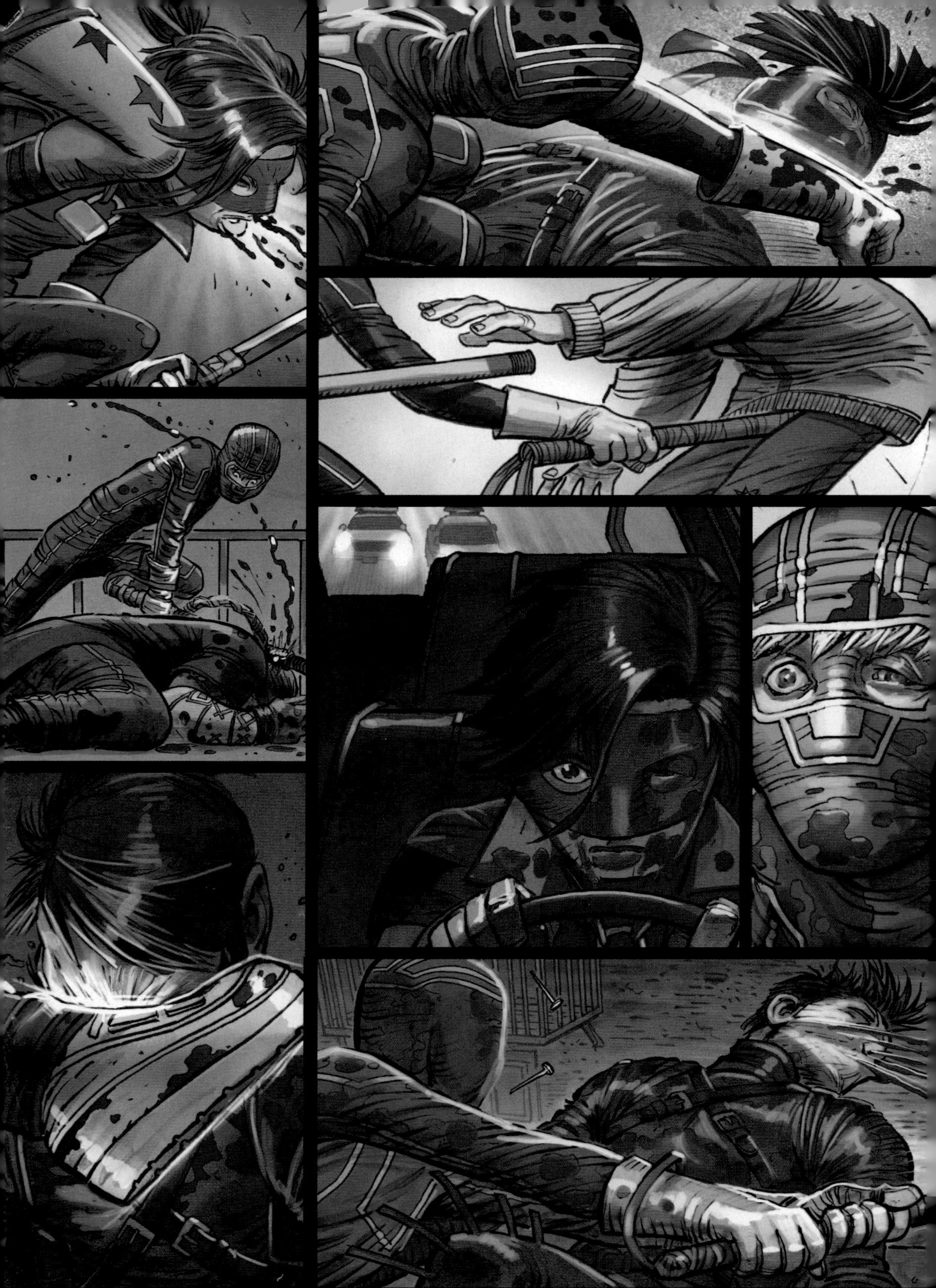

KICK-ASS'S GREATEST HITS

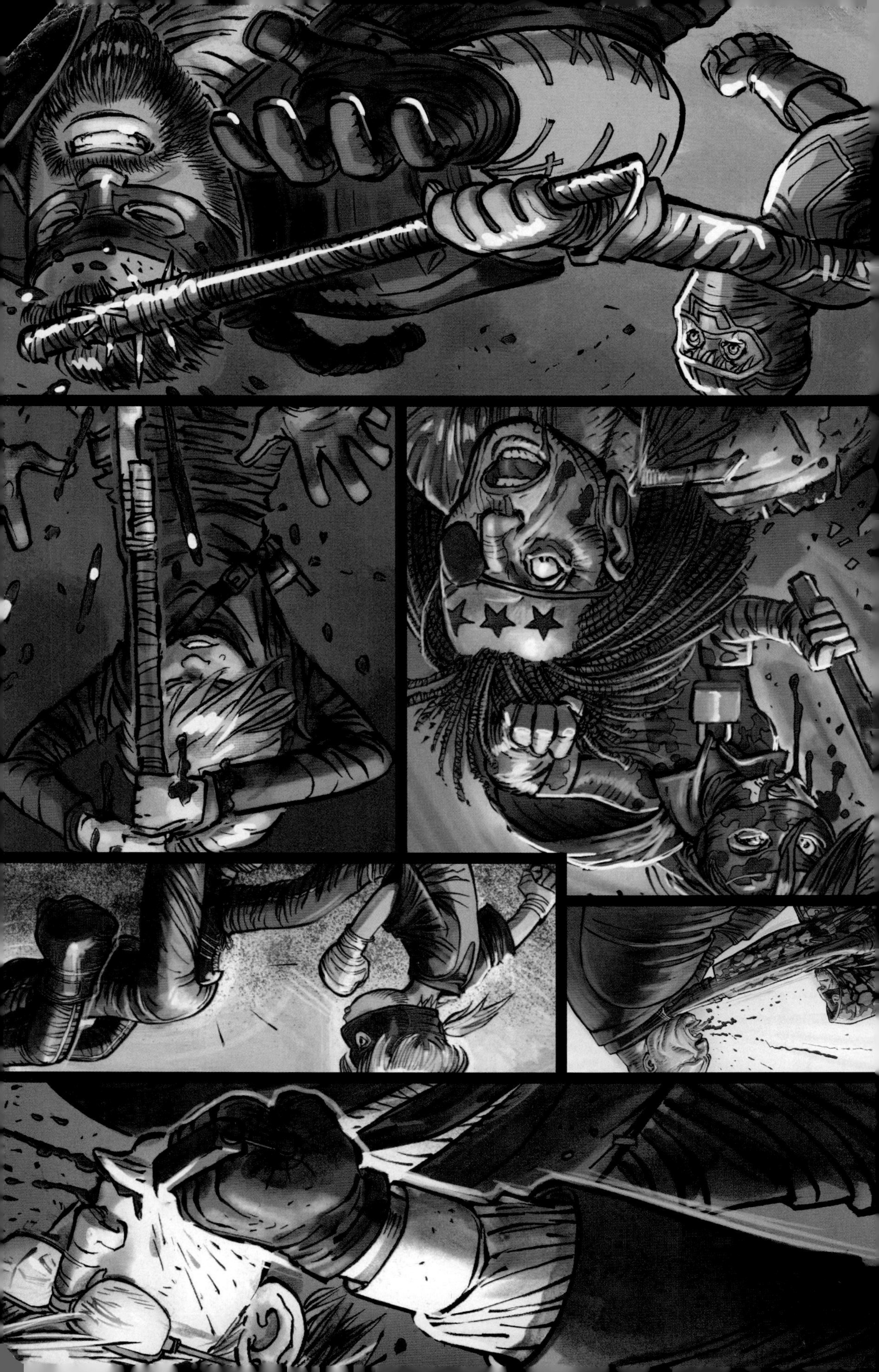

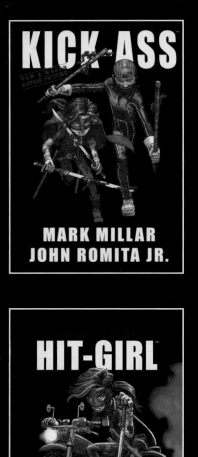

KICK-ASS

MARK MILLAR
JOHN ROMITA JR.

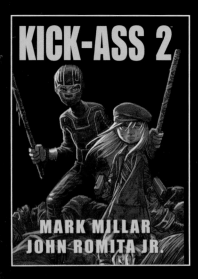

HIT-GIRL

MARK MILLAR
JOHN ROMITA JR.
TOM PALMER and DEAN WHITE

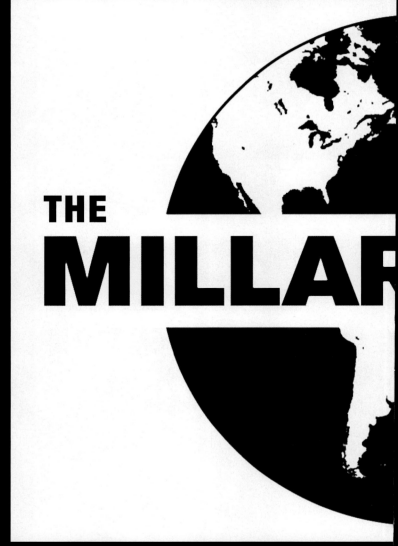

THE
MILLAR

KICK-ASS 2

MARK MILLAR
JOHN ROMITA JR.

WANTED

MARK MILLAR • JG JONES • PAUL MOUNTS
NOW A MAJOR MOTION PICTURE FROM
UNIVERSAL PICTURES
WWW.MILLARWORLD.TV

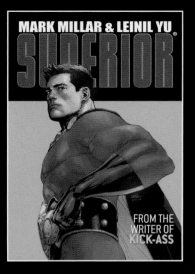

MARK MILLAR & LEINIL YU
SUPERIOR

FROM THE
WRITER OF
KICK-ASS

WORLD™

COLLECTION

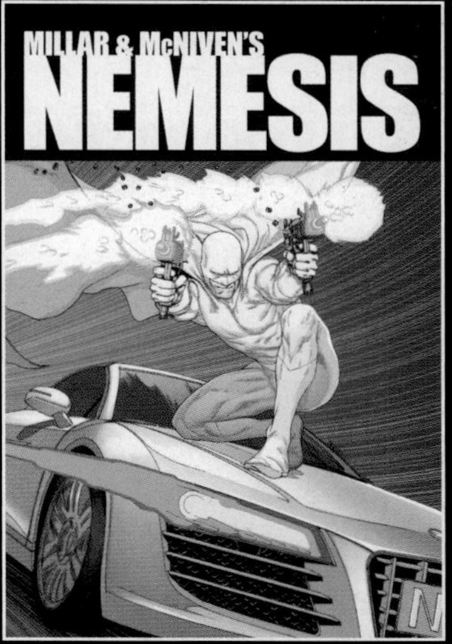

MILLAR & McNIVEN'S
NEMESIS

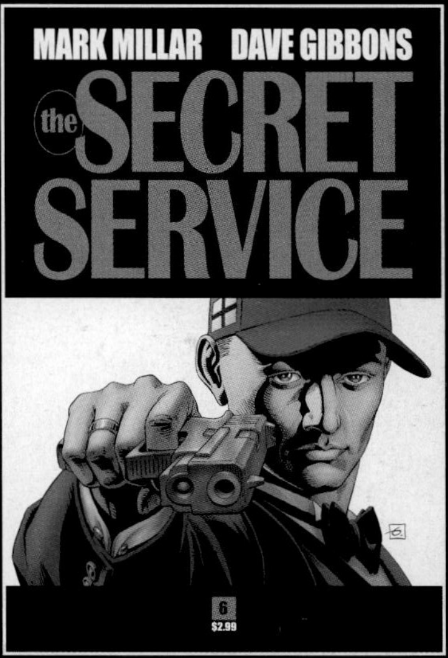

MARK MILLAR DAVE GIBBONS
the SECRET SERVICE
6
$2.99

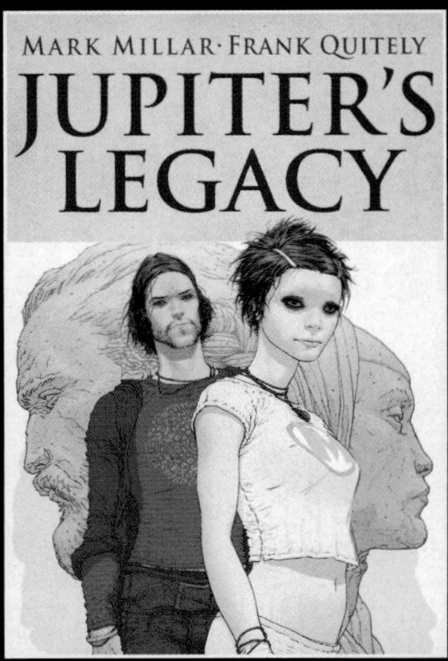

MARK MILLAR·FRANK QUITELY
JUPITER'S LEGACY

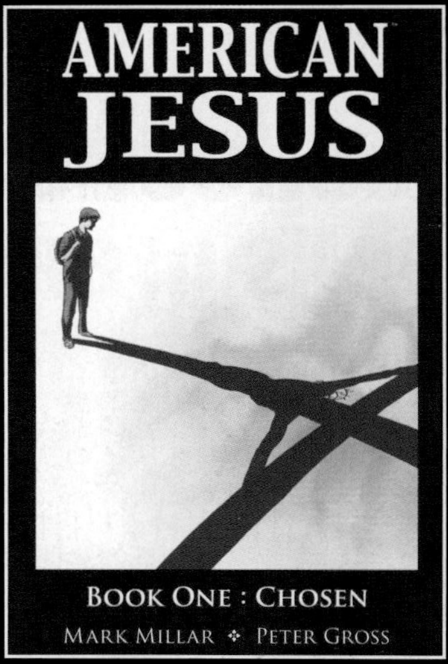

AMERICAN JESUS
BOOK ONE : CHOSEN
MARK MILLAR ❖ PETER GROSS

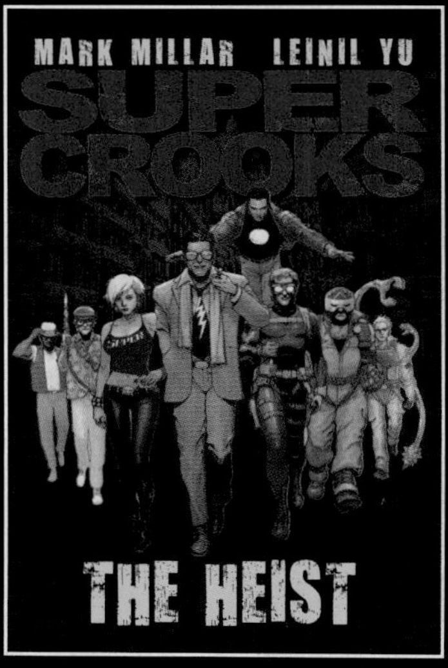

MARK MILLAR LEINIL YU
SUPER CROOKS
THE HEIST

MARVEL
GOIN' STRAIGHT!
THE MARVEL ART OF
JOHN ROMITA JR.

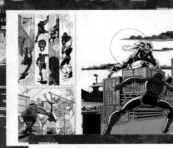

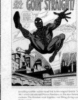

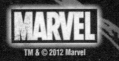

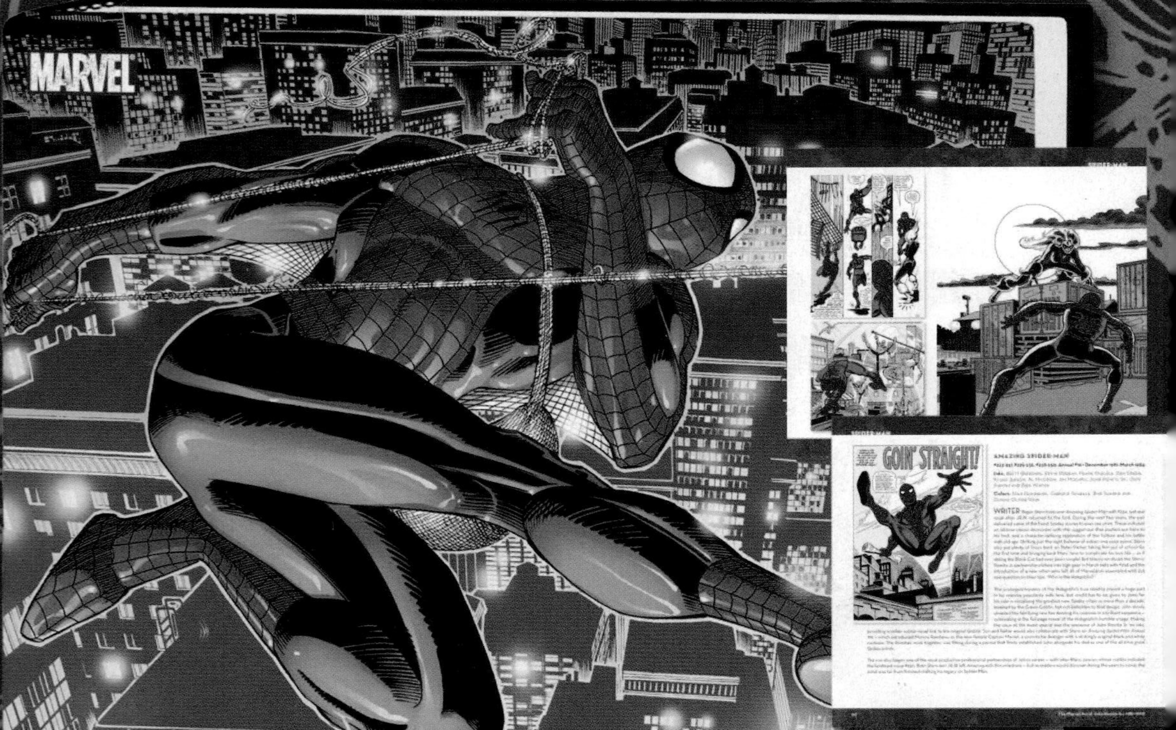

COMING SOON

JOHN ROMITA, JR.
HOWARD CHAYKIN

SHMUGGY & BIMBO

WITH A TITLE LIKE THAT, IT HAS TO BE GREAT!

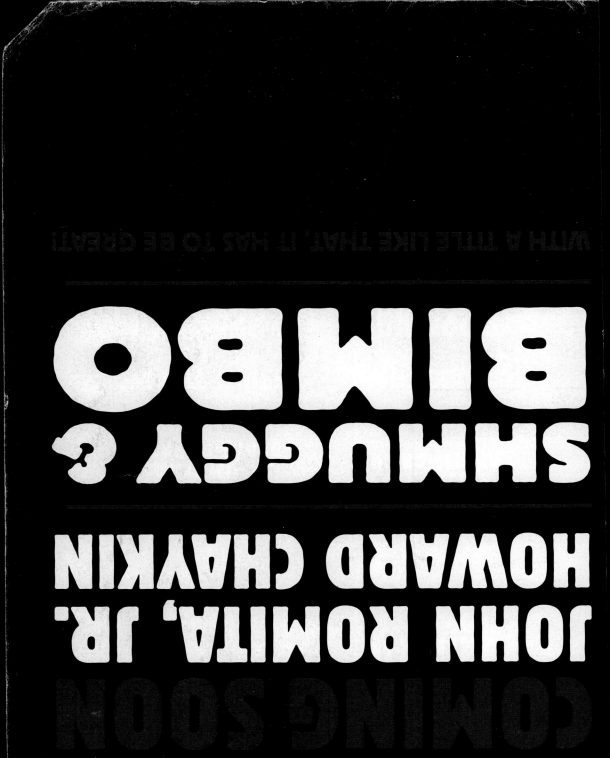

KICK-ASS READING ORDER

PART ONE

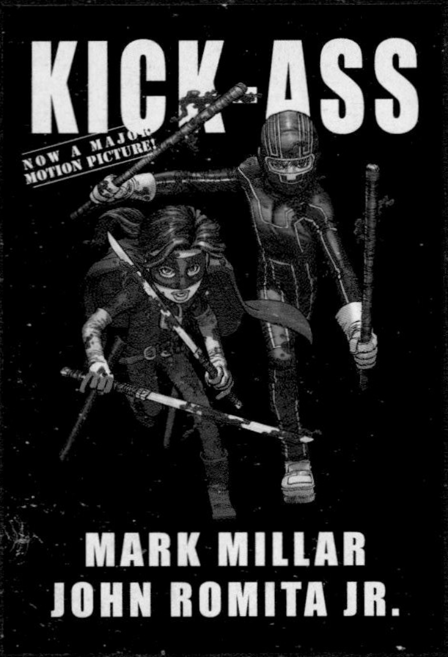
KICK-ASS
NOW A MAJOR MOTION PICTURE!
MARK MILLAR
JOHN ROMITA JR.

PART TWO

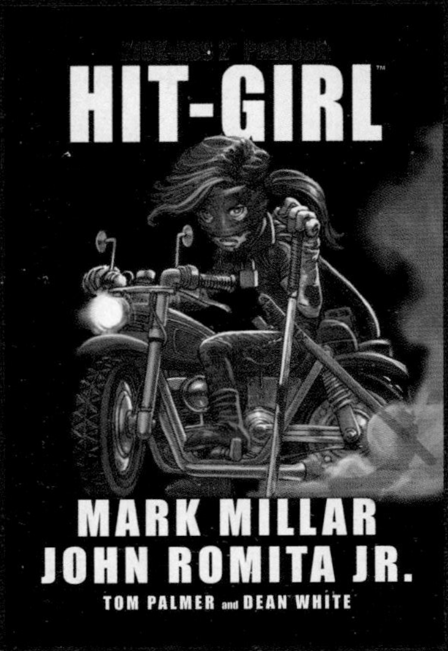
HIT-GIRL
MARK MILLAR
JOHN ROMITA JR.
TOM PALMER and DEAN WHITE

PART THREE

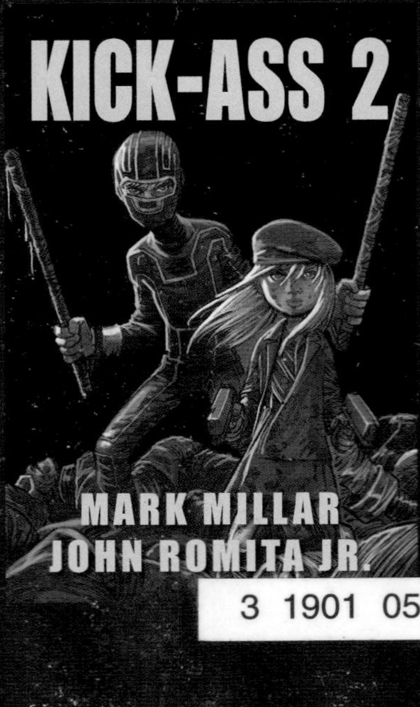
KICK-ASS 2
MARK MILLAR
JOHN ROMITA JR.

PART FOUR

KICK-ASS 3

THE GRAND FINALE

MAY 2013